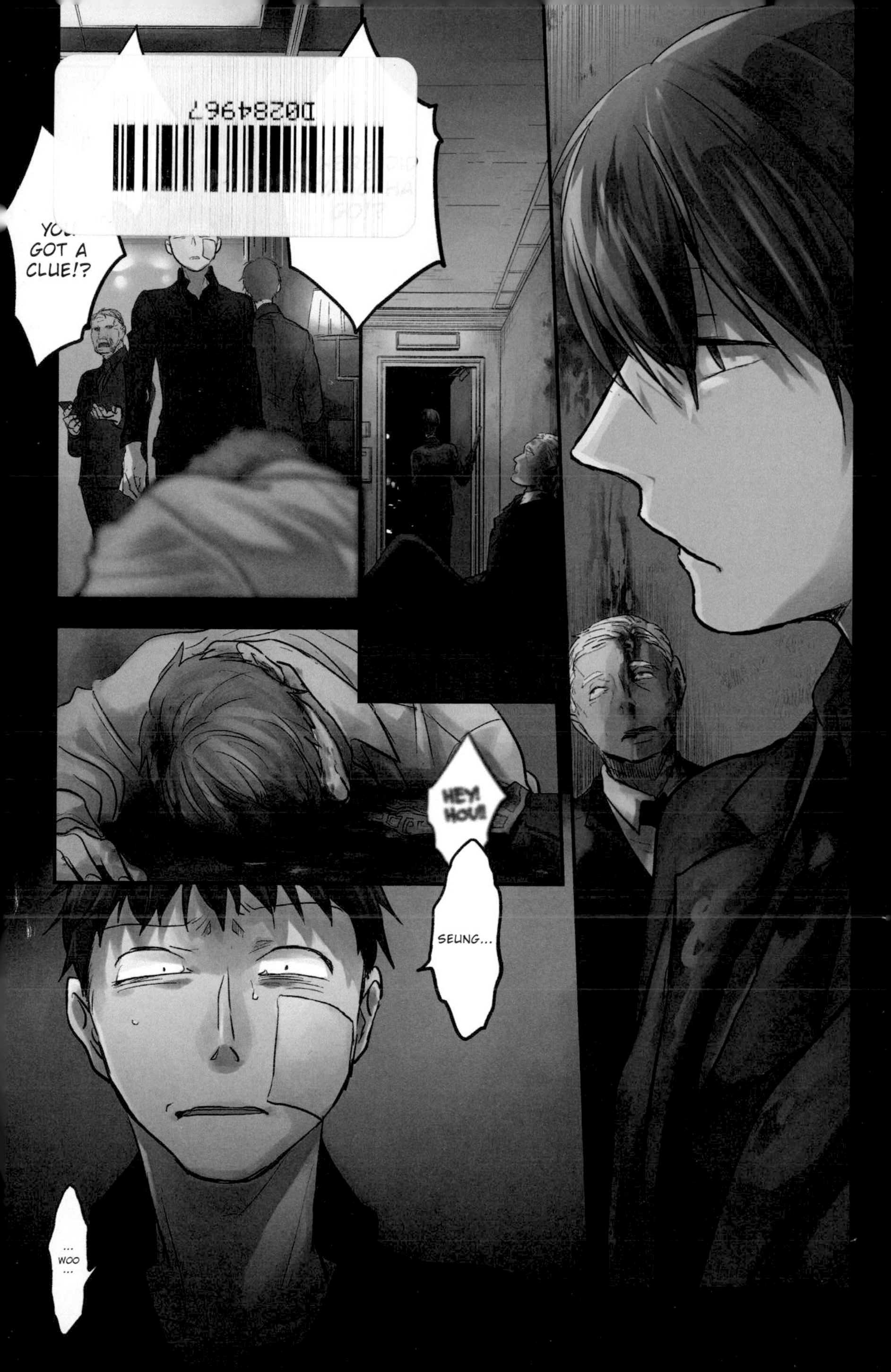
YOU GOT A CLUE!?
HEY! HOU!!
SEUNG...
...WOO...

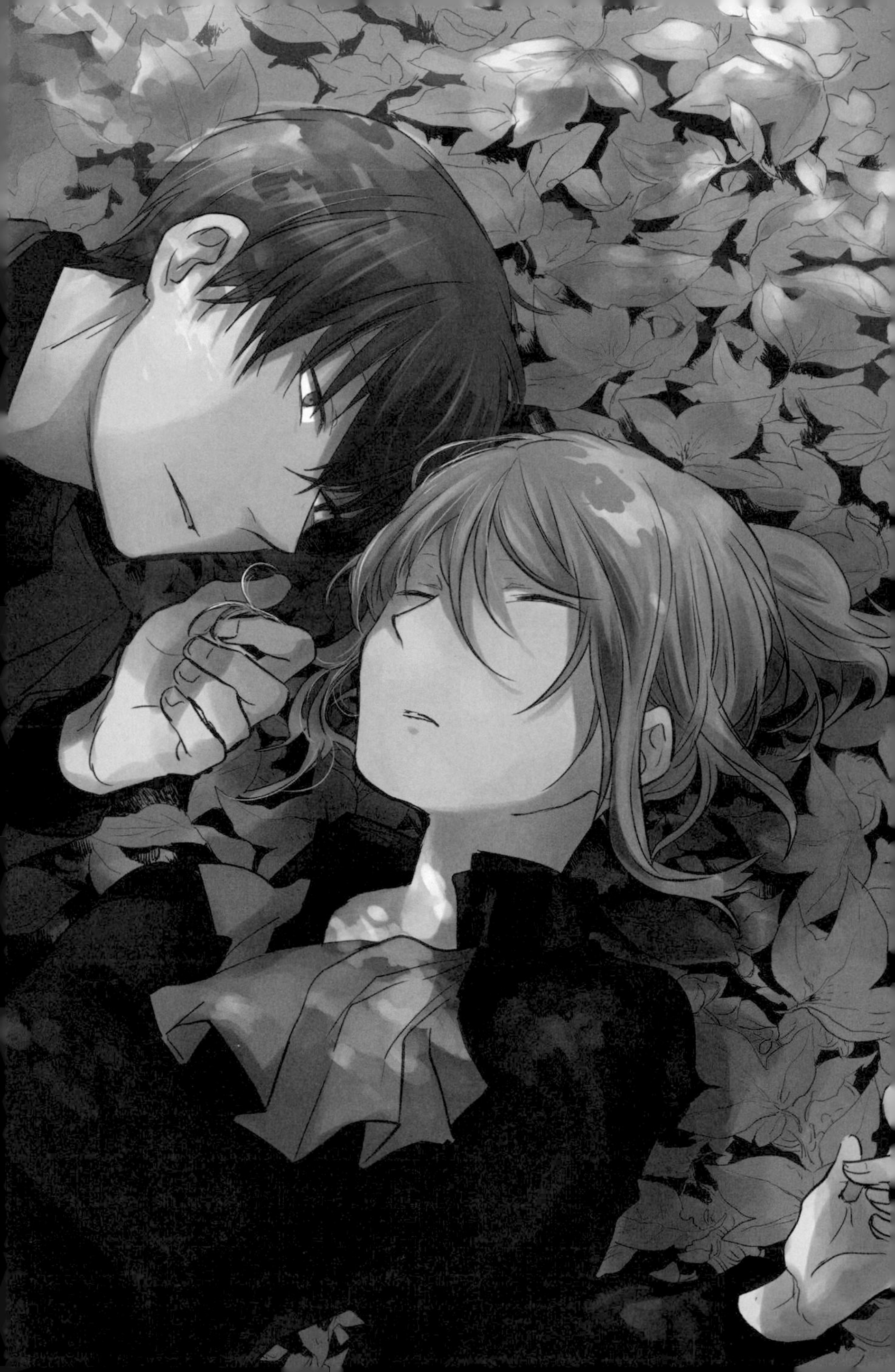

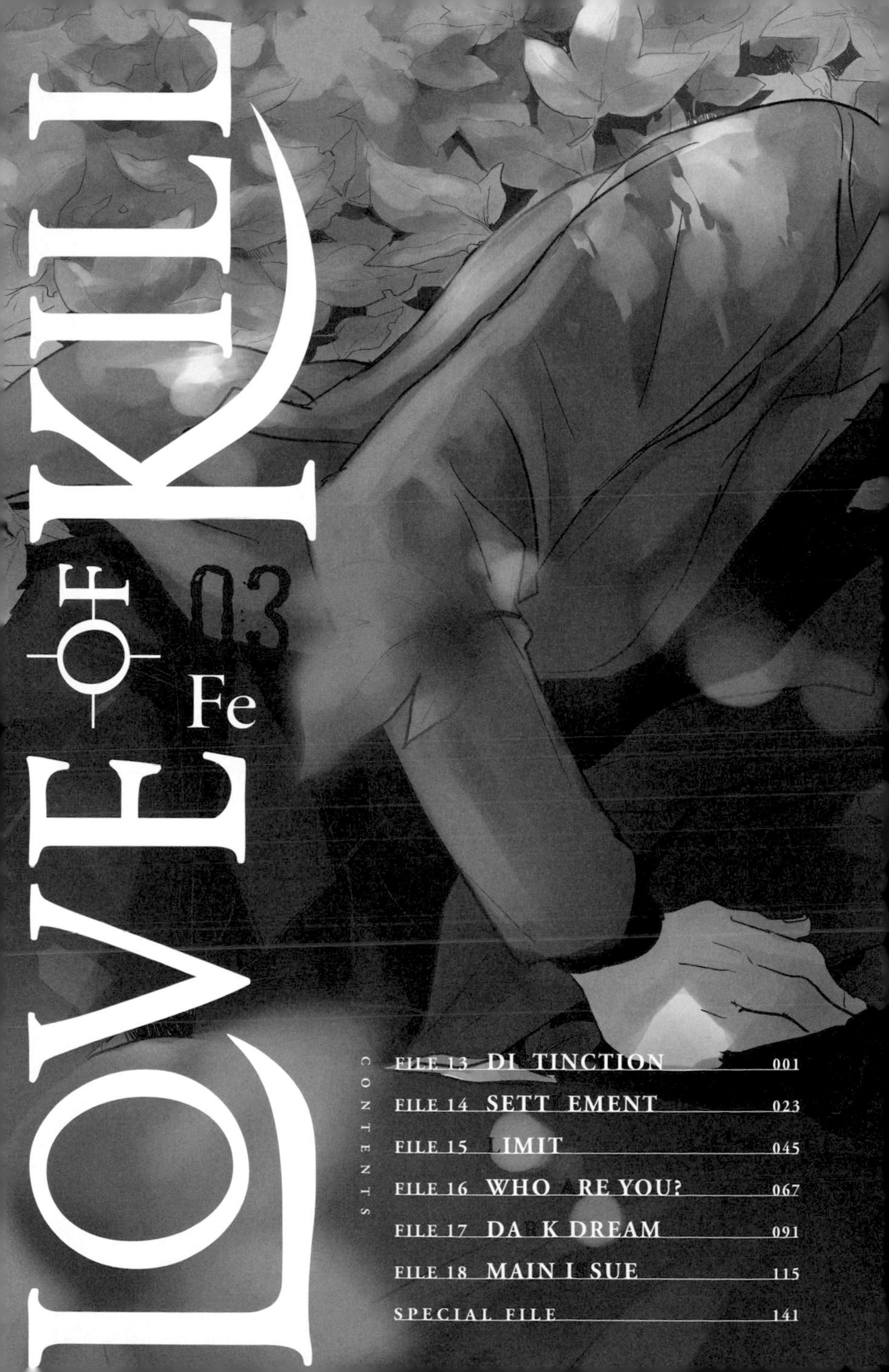

LOVE OF KILL

03

Fe

CONTENTS

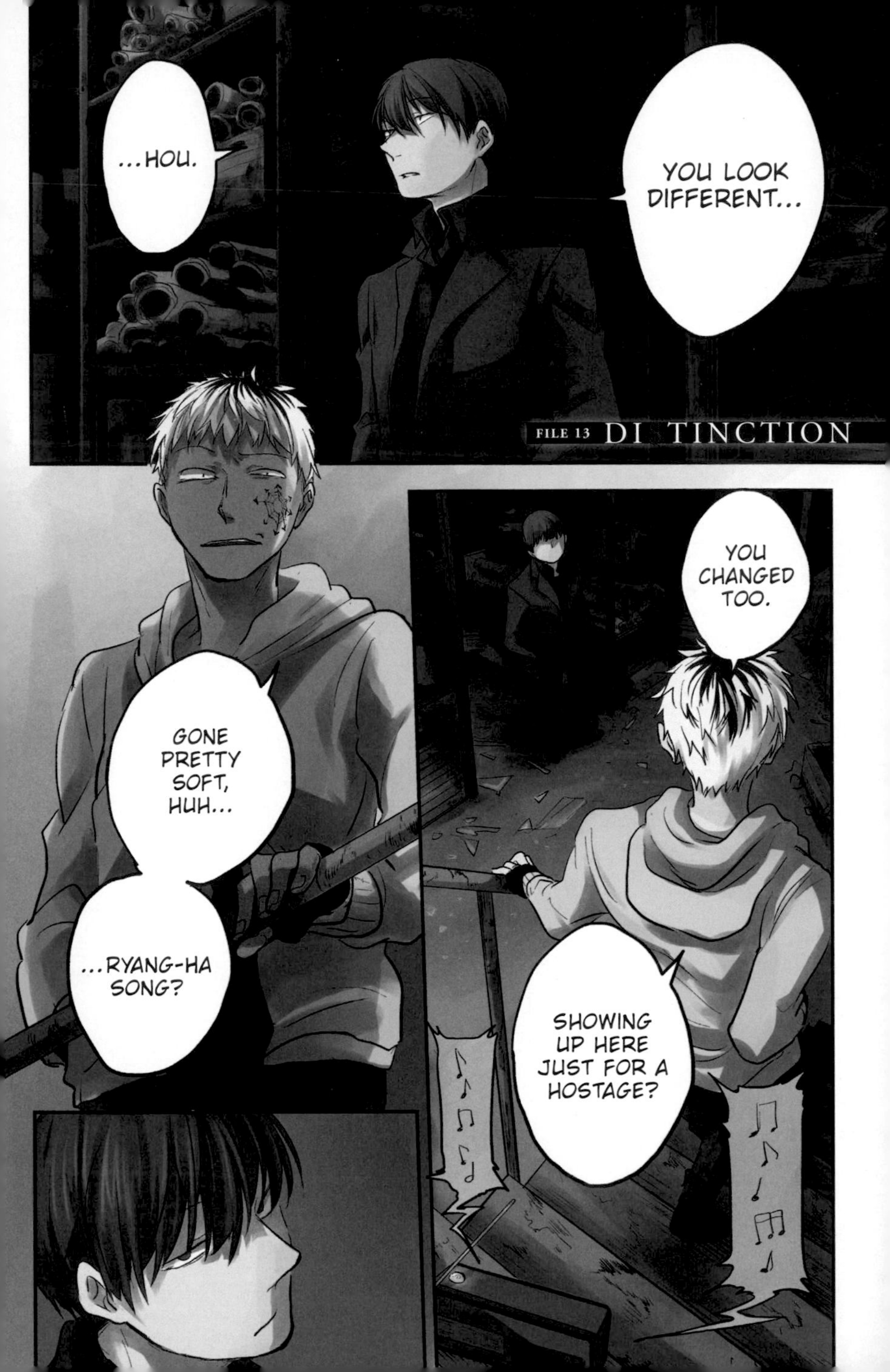
YOU LOOK DIFFERENT...
...HOU.
FILE 13 DI TINCTION
YOU CHANGED TOO.
SHOWING UP HERE JUST FOR A HOSTAGE?
GONE PRETTY SOFT, HUH...
...RYANG-HA SONG?

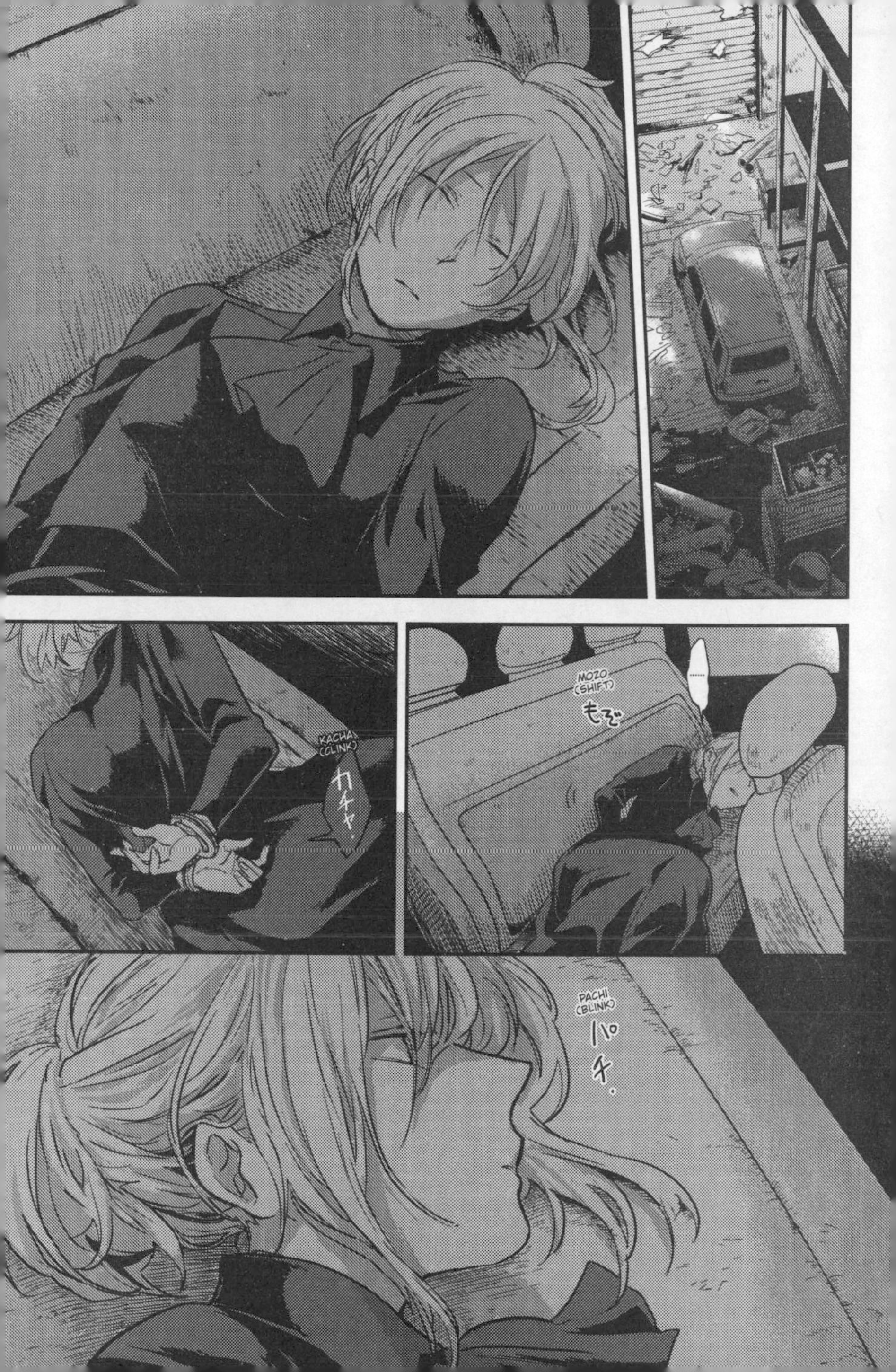
……
MOZO (SHIFT)
もぞ
KACHA (CLINK)
カチャ
PACHI (BLINK)
パチ.

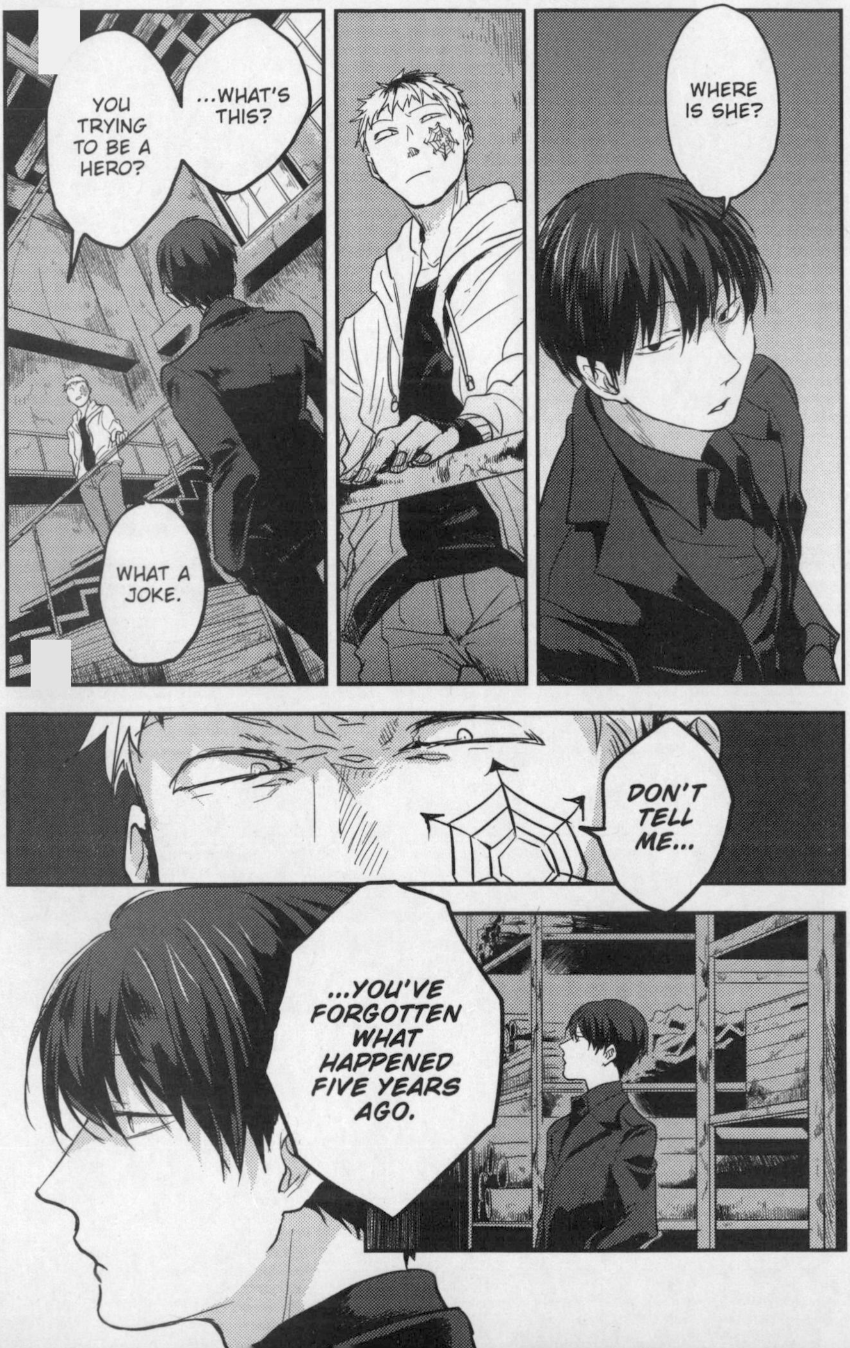
WHERE IS SHE?
...WHAT'S THIS?
YOU TRYING TO BE A HERO?
WHAT A JOKE.
DON'T TELL ME...
...YOU'VE FORGOTTEN WHAT HAPPENED FIVE YEARS AGO.

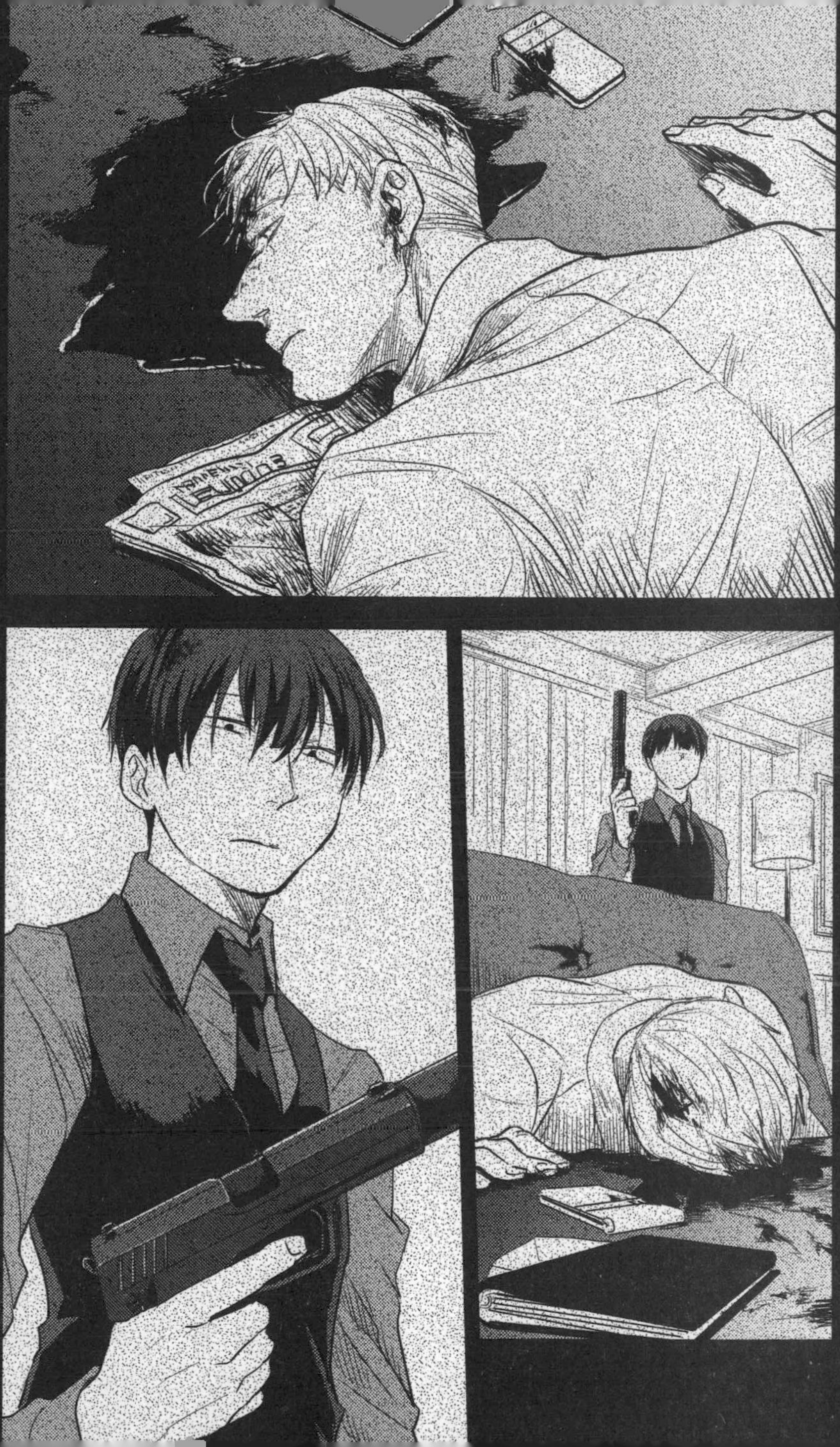

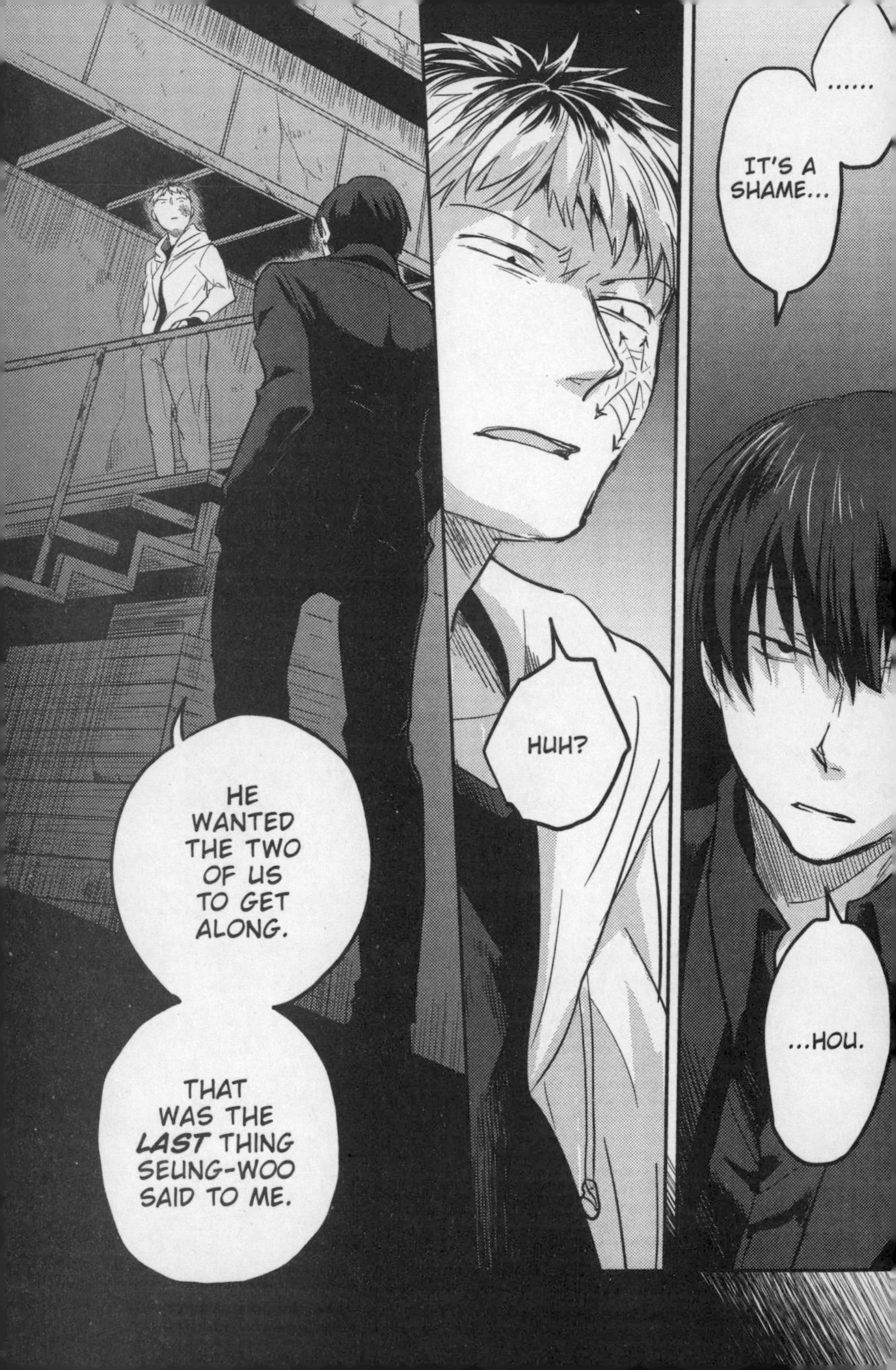
......
IT'S A SHAME...
...HOU.
HUH?
HE WANTED THE TWO OF US TO GET ALONG.
THAT WAS THE *LAST* THING SEUNG-WOO SAID TO ME.

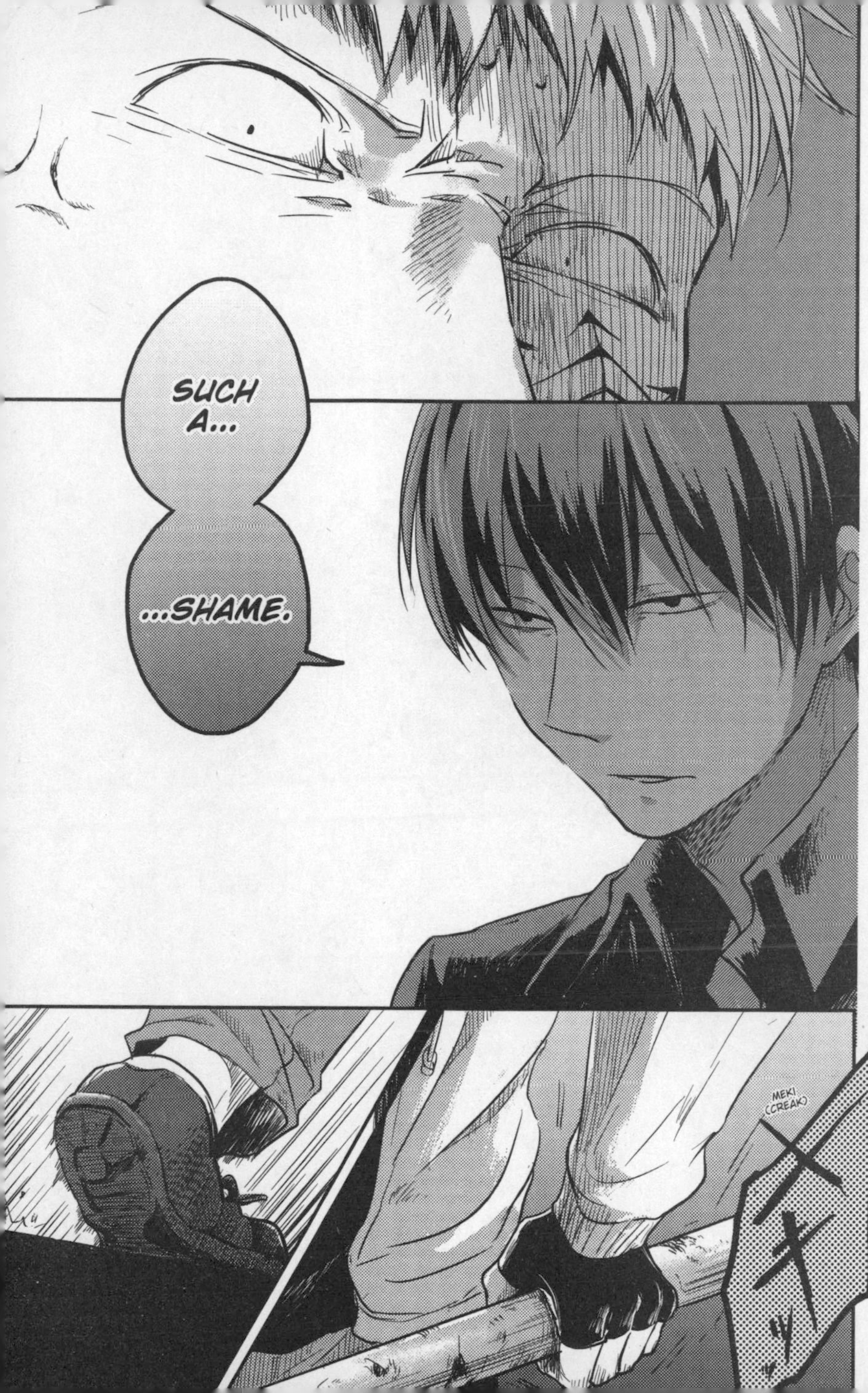
SUCH A...
...SHAME.
MEKI (CREAK)

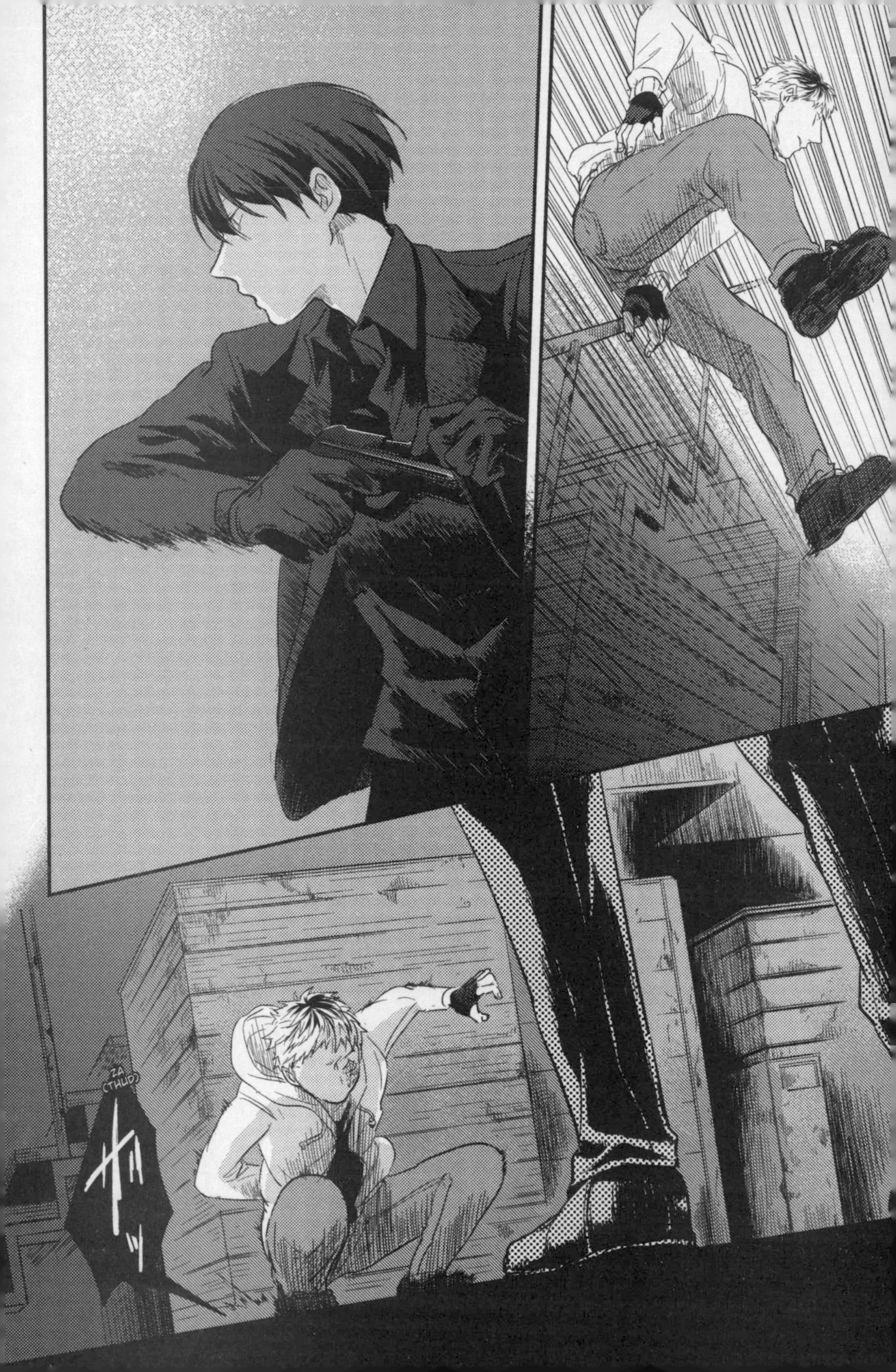
ZA
(THUD)

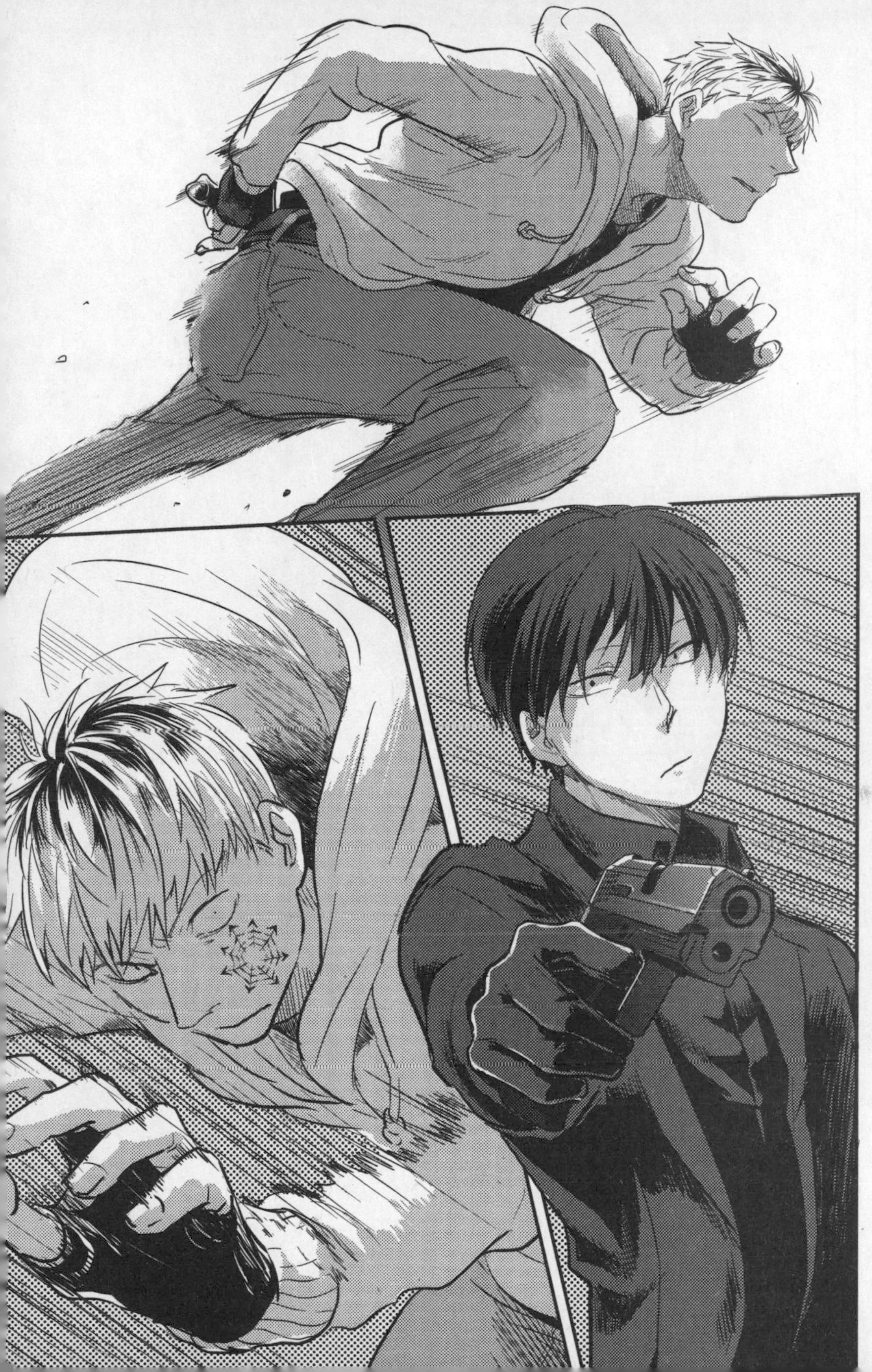

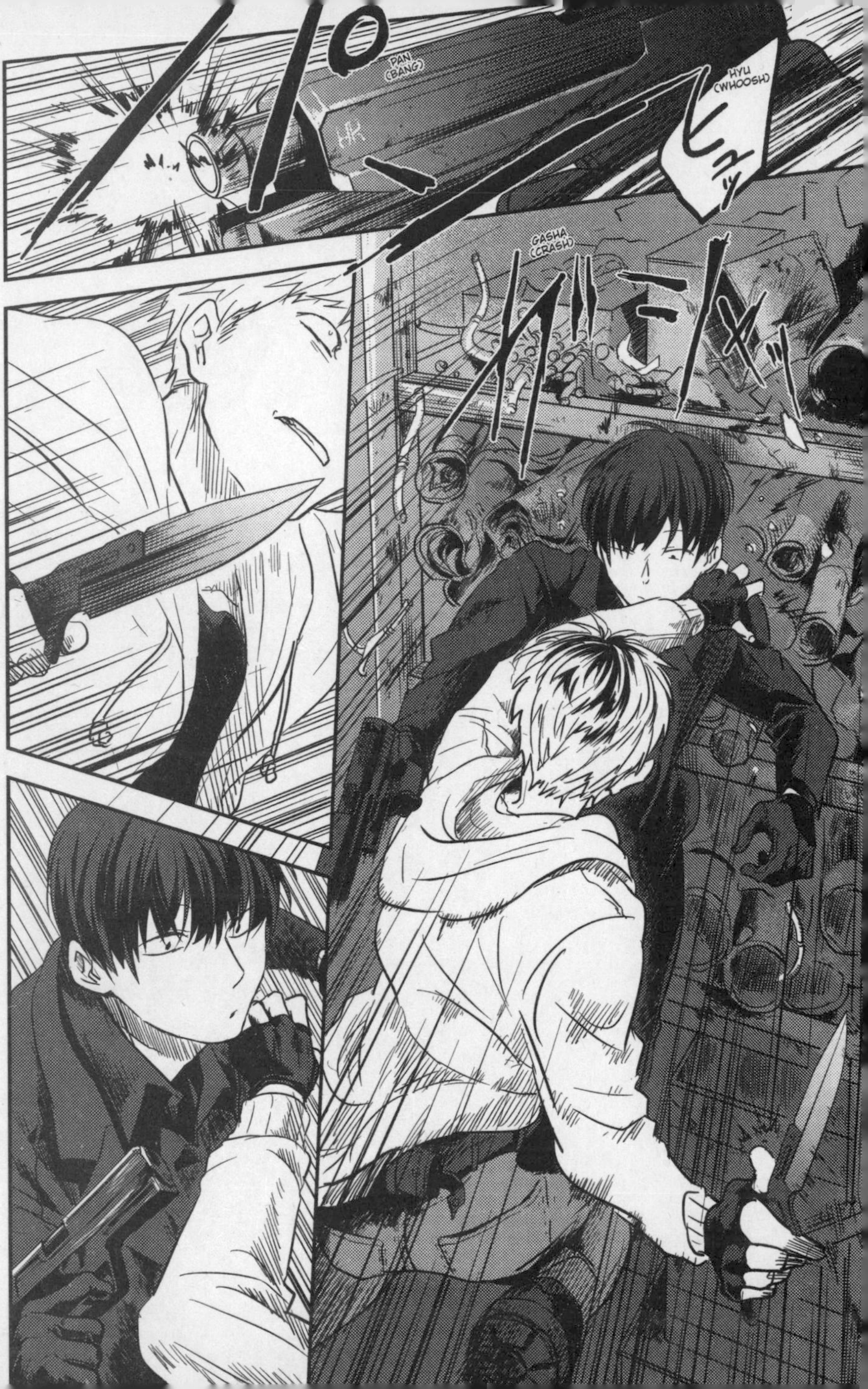
HYU (WHOOSH)
PAN (BANG)
HK
GASHA (CRASH)

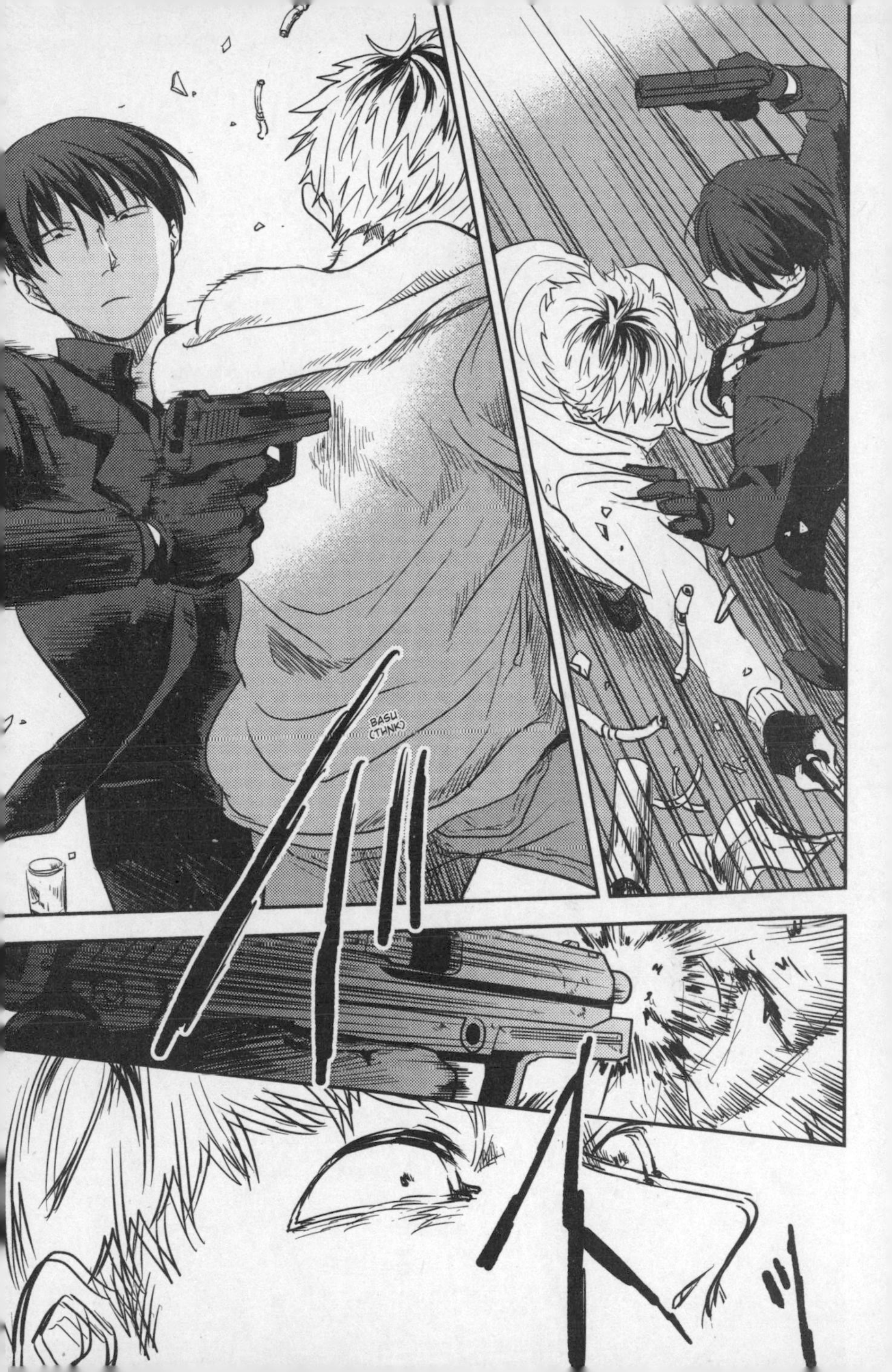
BASU
(THNK)

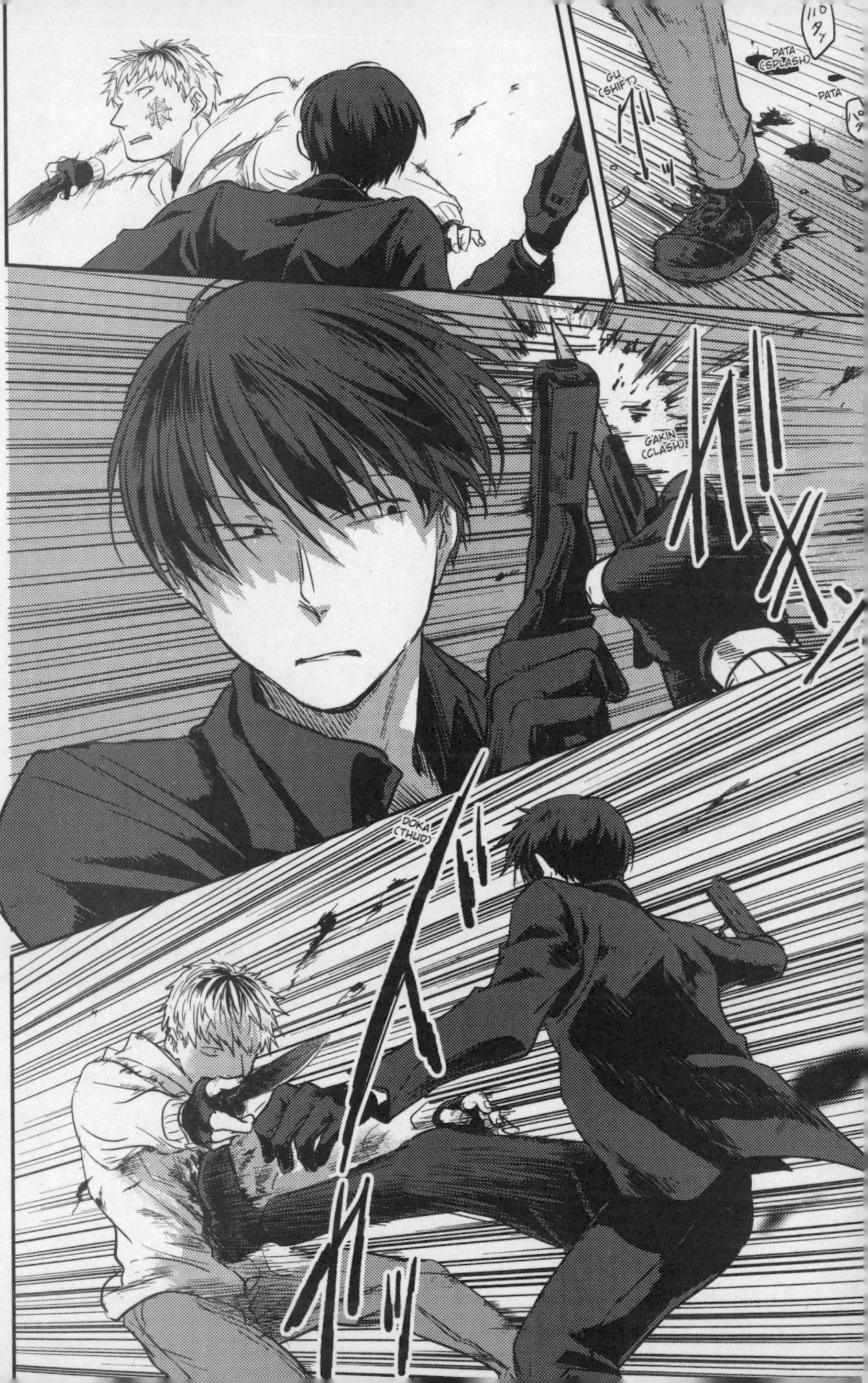
PATA (SPLASH)
PATA
GU (SHIFT)
GAKIN (CLASH)
DOKA (THUD)

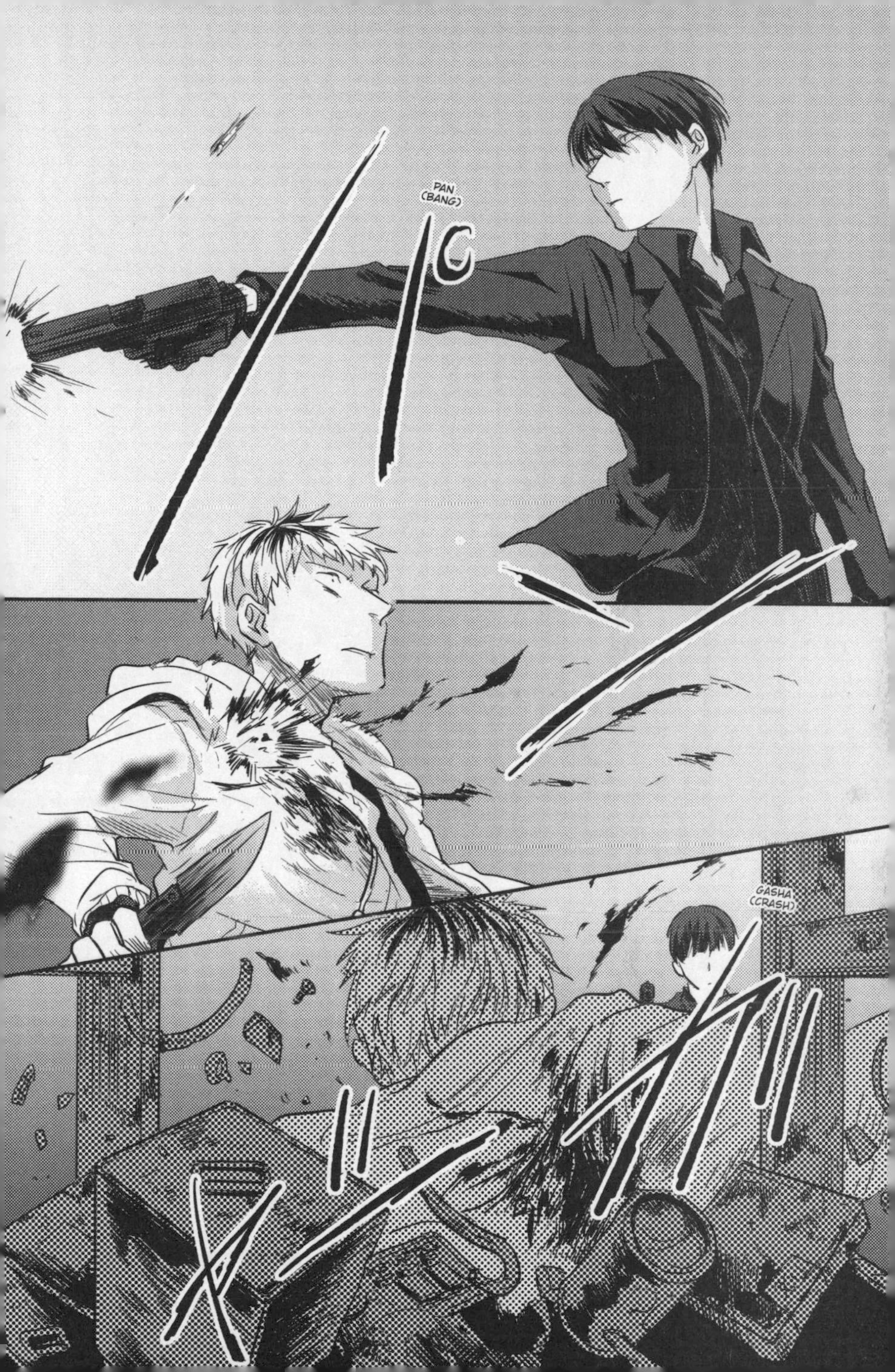
PAN
(BANG)
GASHA
(CRASH)

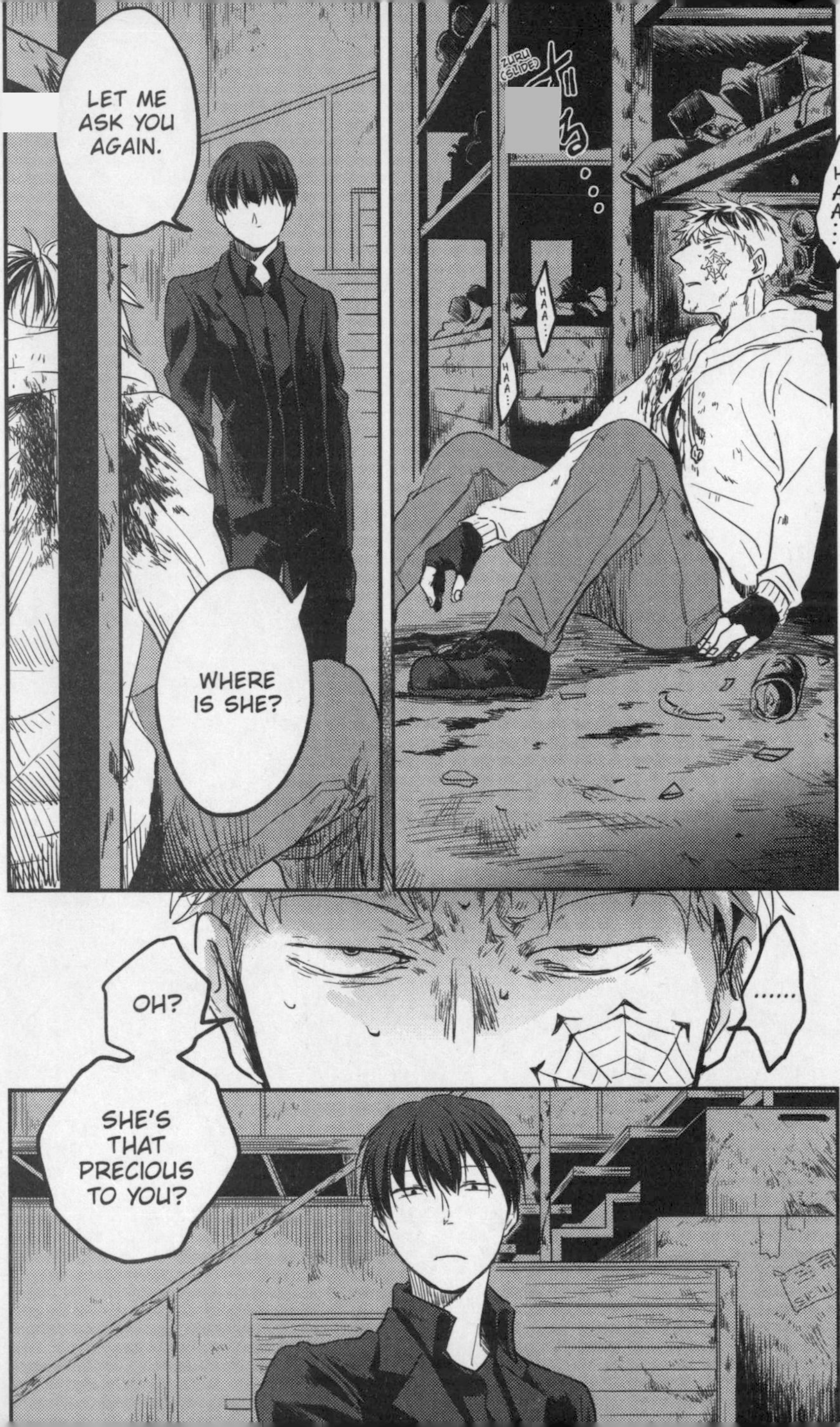

ZURU (SLIDE)
HAA...
HAA...
HAA...
LET ME ASK YOU AGAIN.
WHERE IS SHE?
......
OH?
SHE'S THAT PRECIOUS TO YOU?

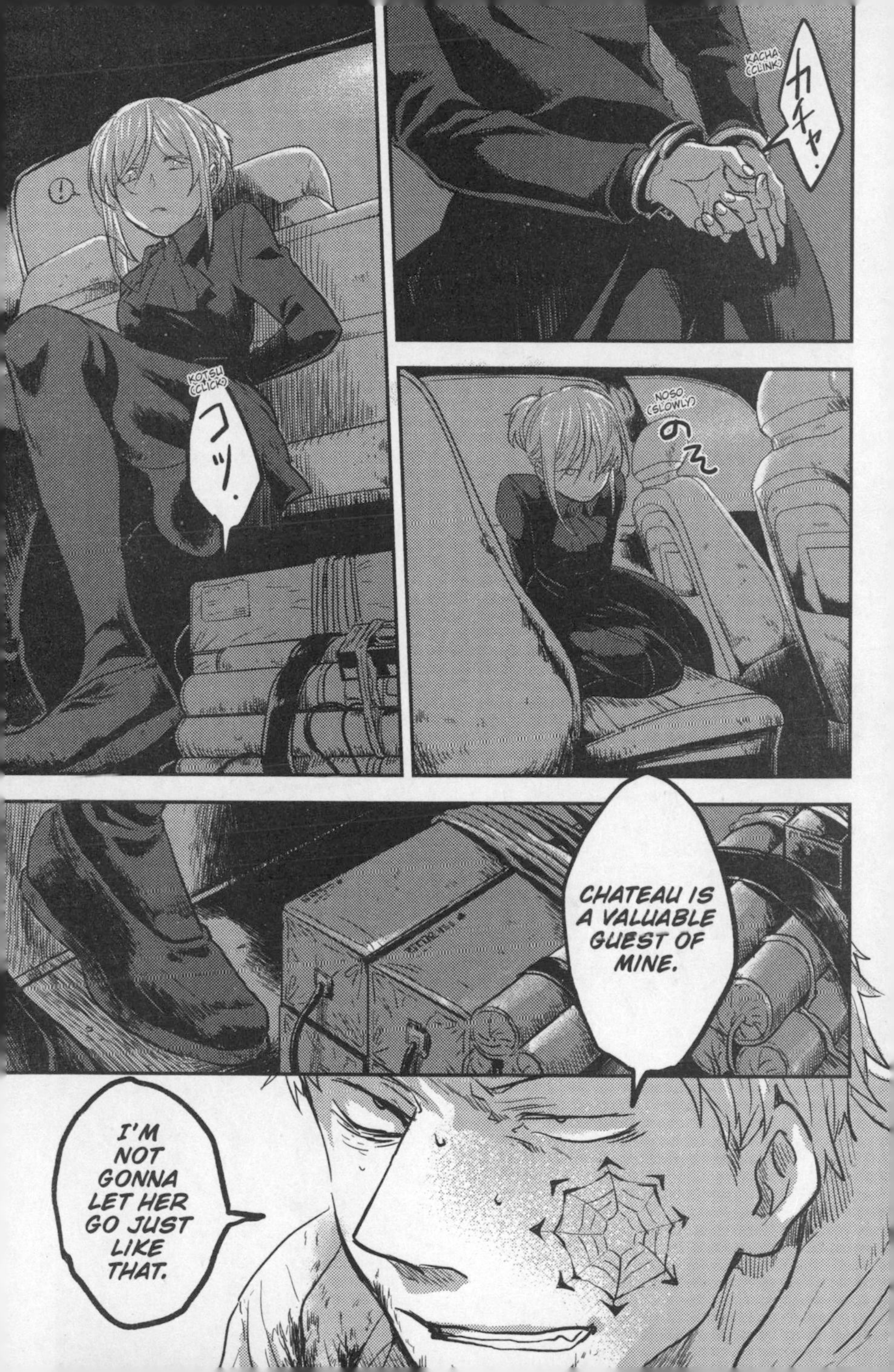
カチャ.
KACHA (CLINK)
のそ
NOSO (SLOWLY)
コツ.
KOTSU (CLICK)
CHATEAU IS A VALUABLE GUEST OF MINE.
I'M NOT GONNA LET HER GO JUST LIKE THAT.

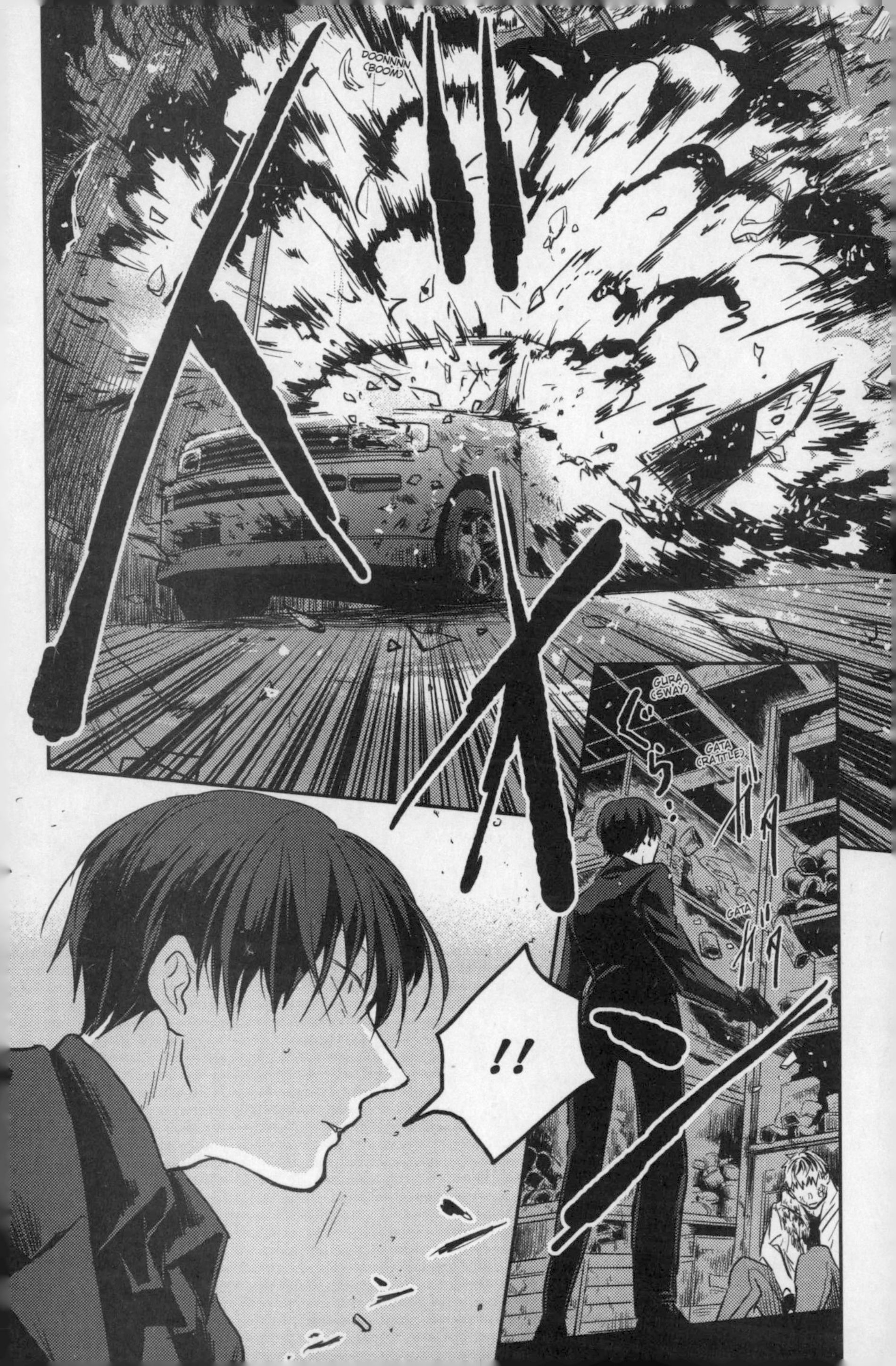
DOONNNN (BOOM)
GURA (SWAY)
GATA (RATTLE)
GATA
!!

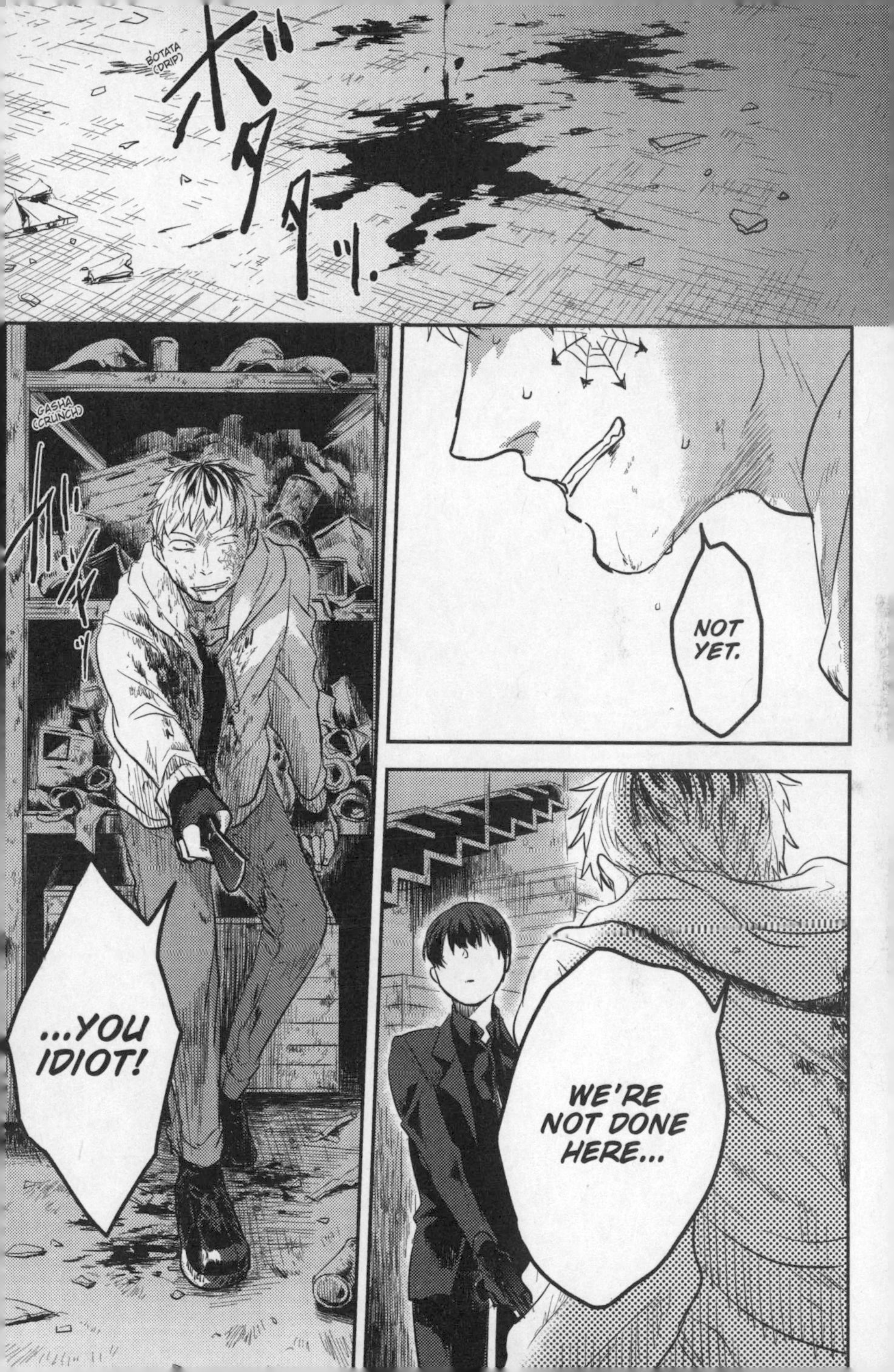
BOTATA (DRIP)
NOT YET.
WE'RE NOT DONE HERE...
GASHA (CRUNCH)
...YOU IDIOT!

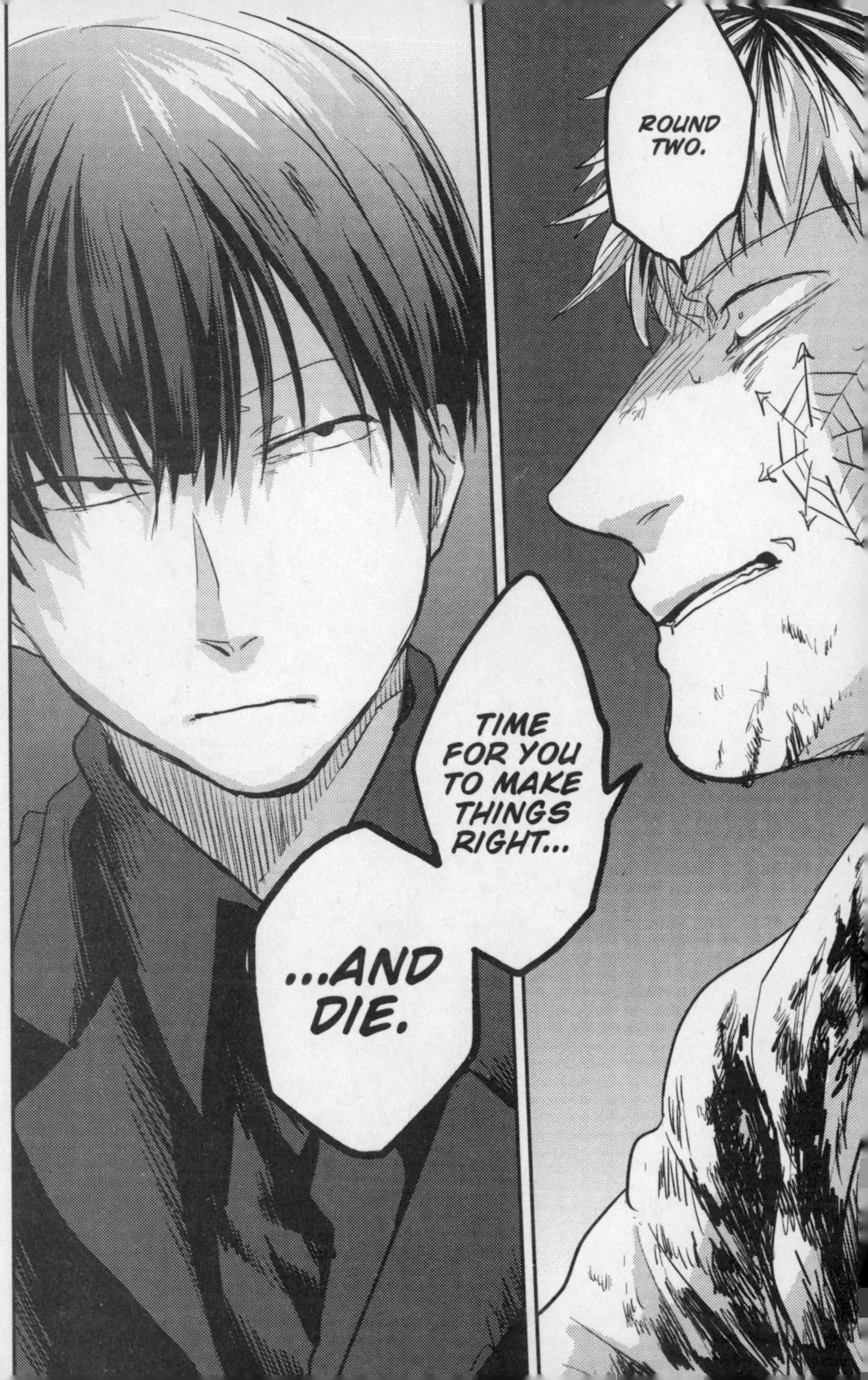
ROUND TWO.
TIME FOR YOU TO MAKE THINGS RIGHT...
...AND DIE.

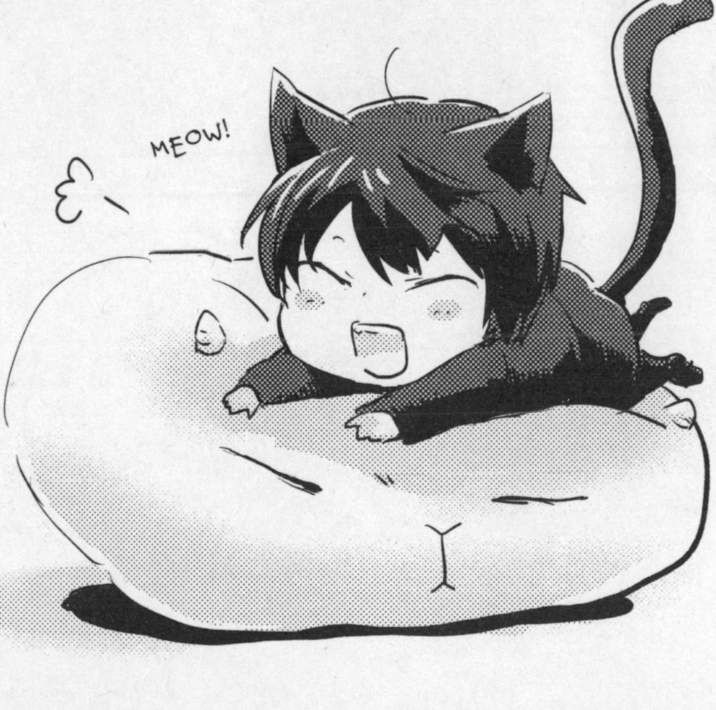
MEOW!

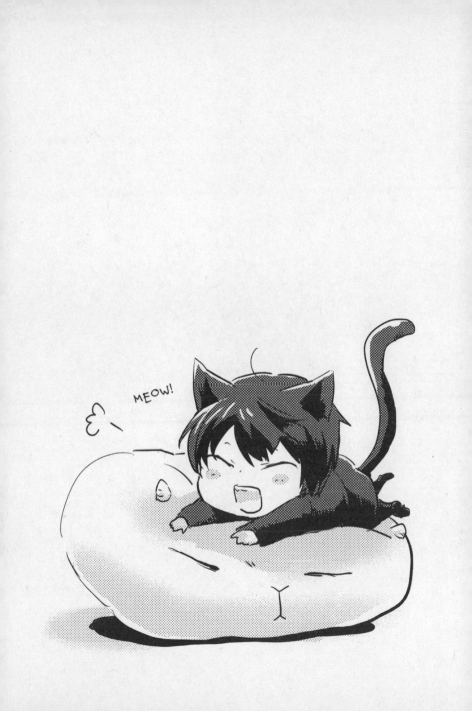

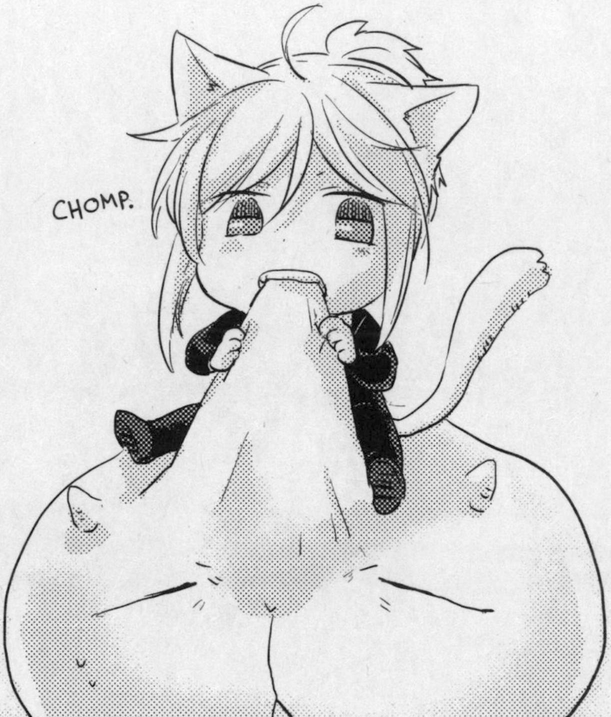
CHOMP.

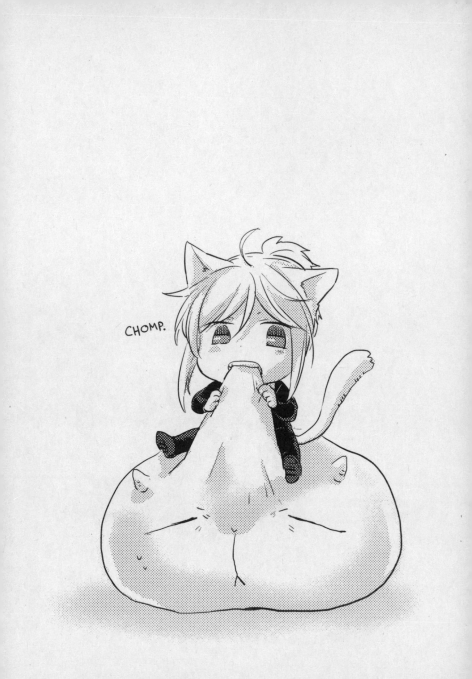

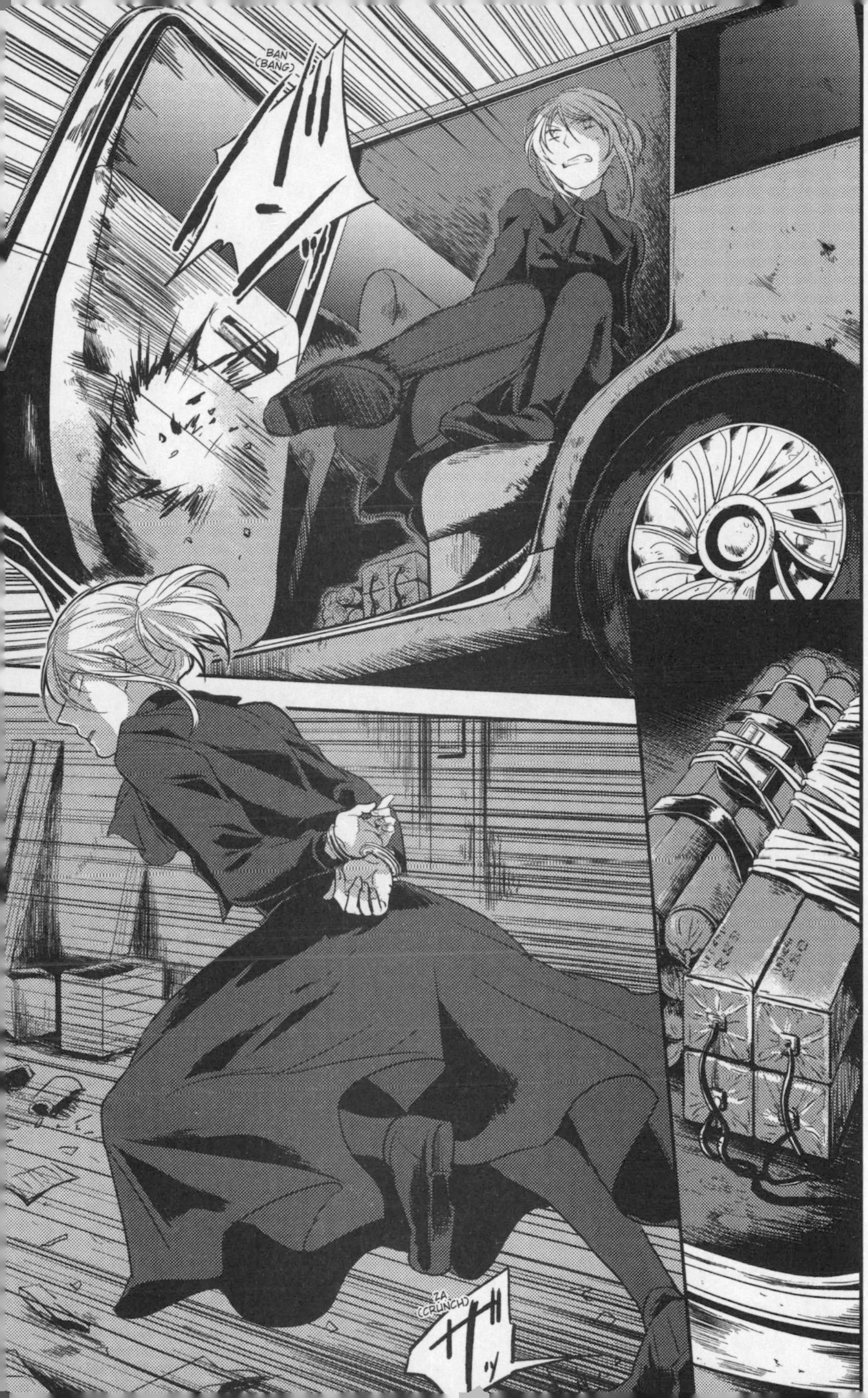
BAN
(BANG)
ZA
(CRUNCH)

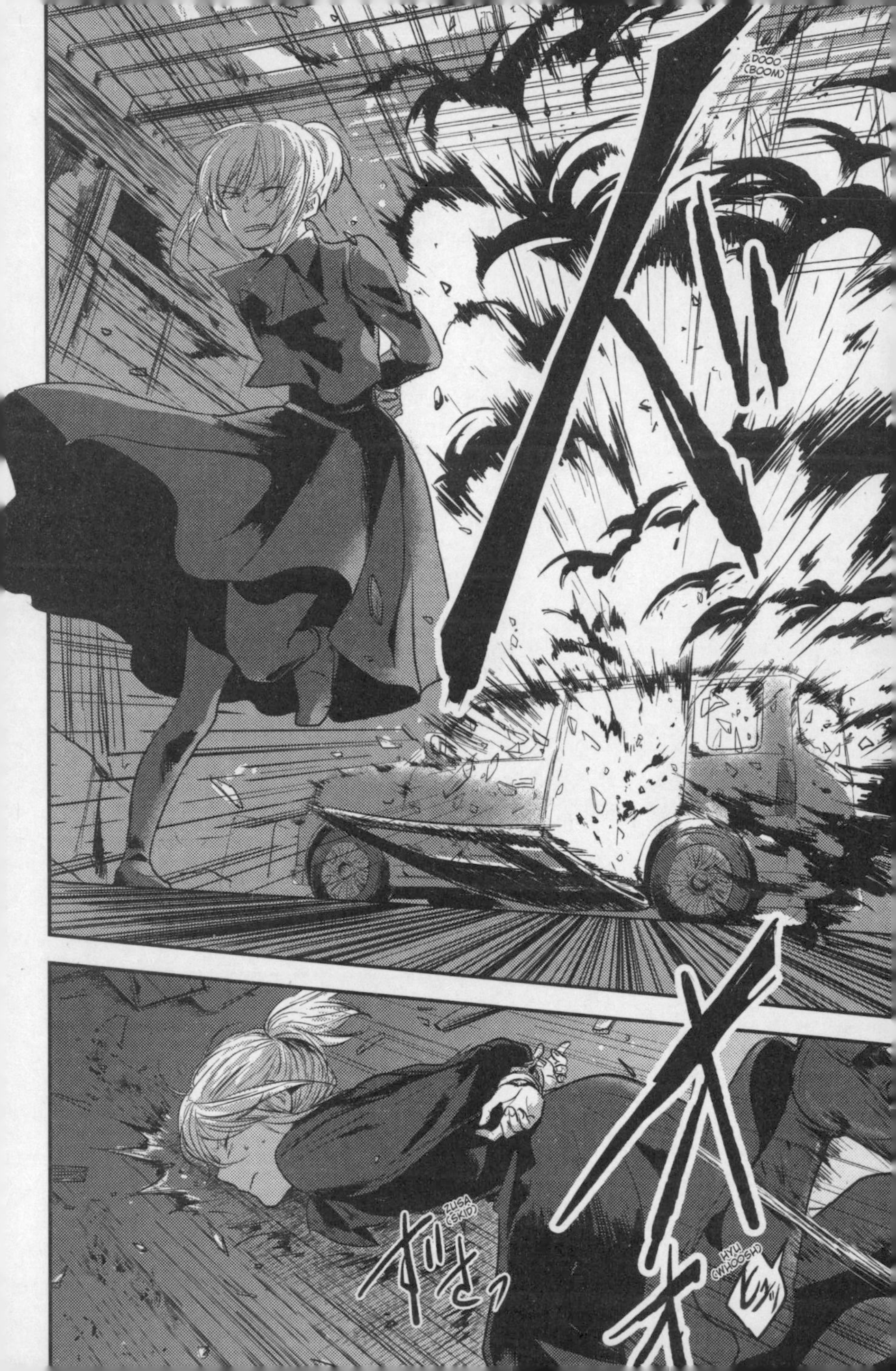
DOOO
(BOOM)
ZUSA
(SKID)
HYU
(WHOOSH)

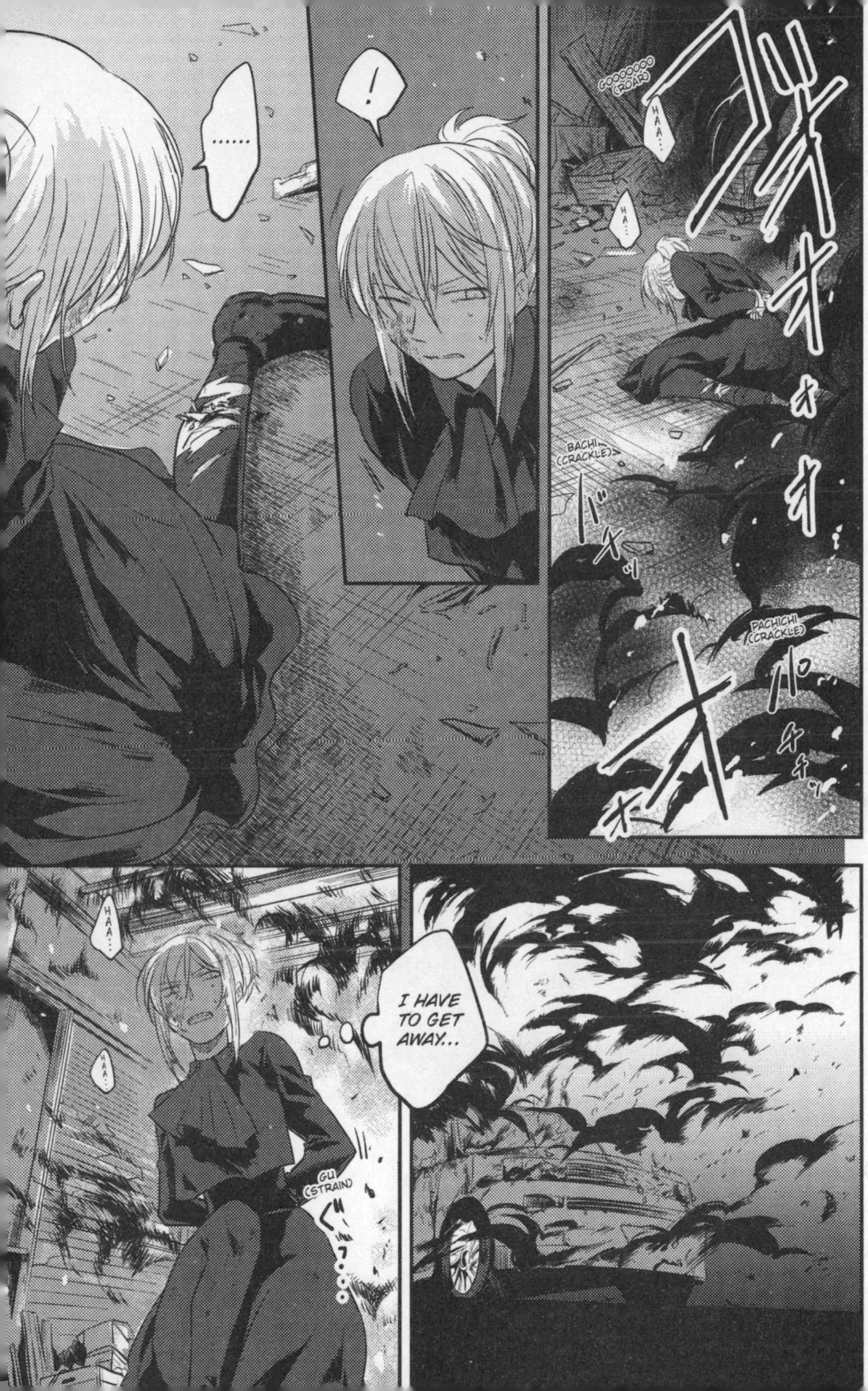

GOOOOOOO (ROAR)
HAA...
HA...
BACHI (CRACKLE)
PACHICHI (CRACKLE)
!
......
HAA...
I HAVE TO GET AWAY...
HAA...
GU (STRAIN)

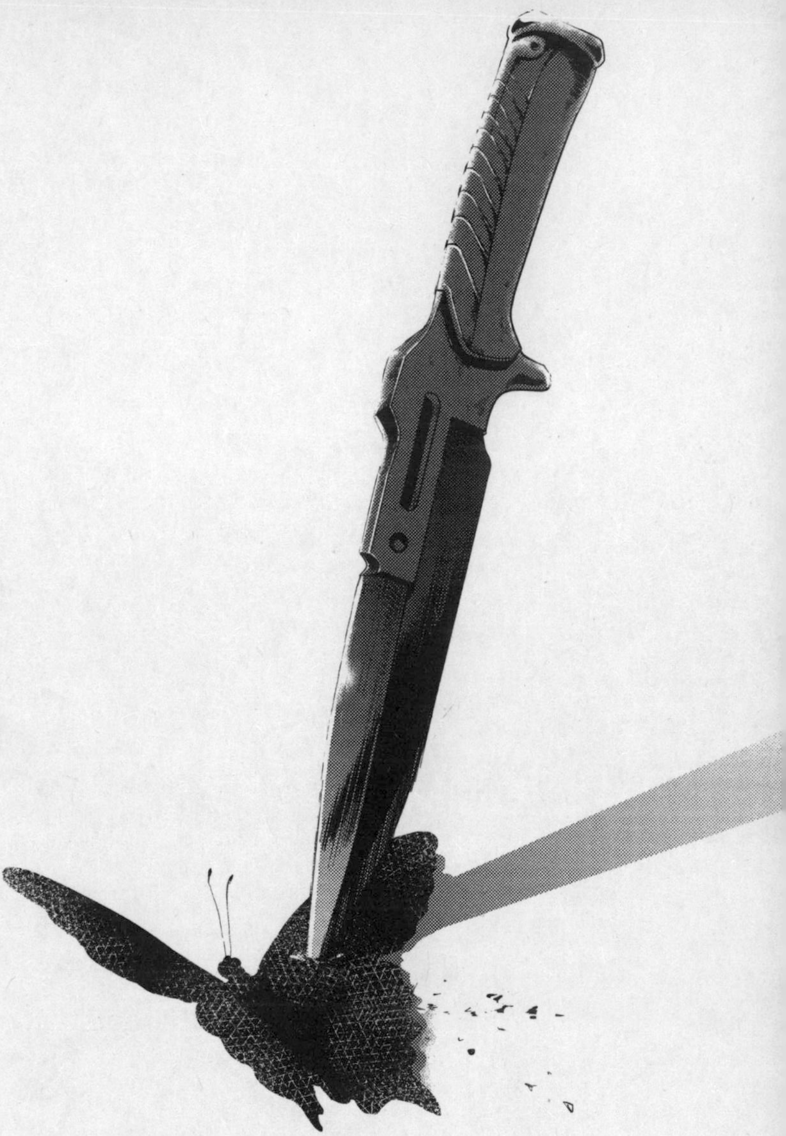

FILE 14 SETTLEMENT

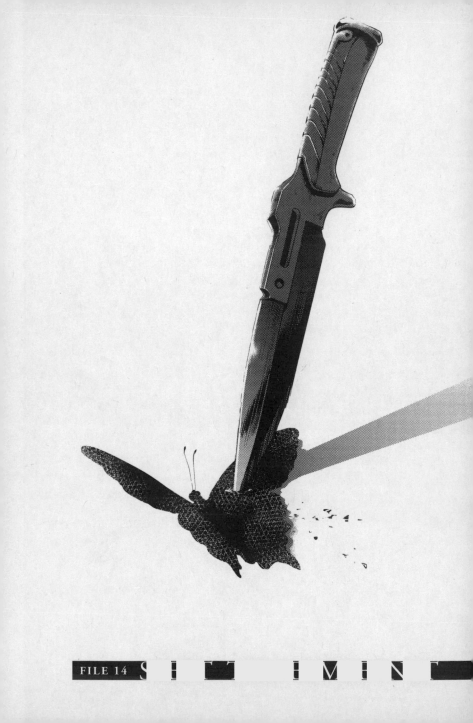

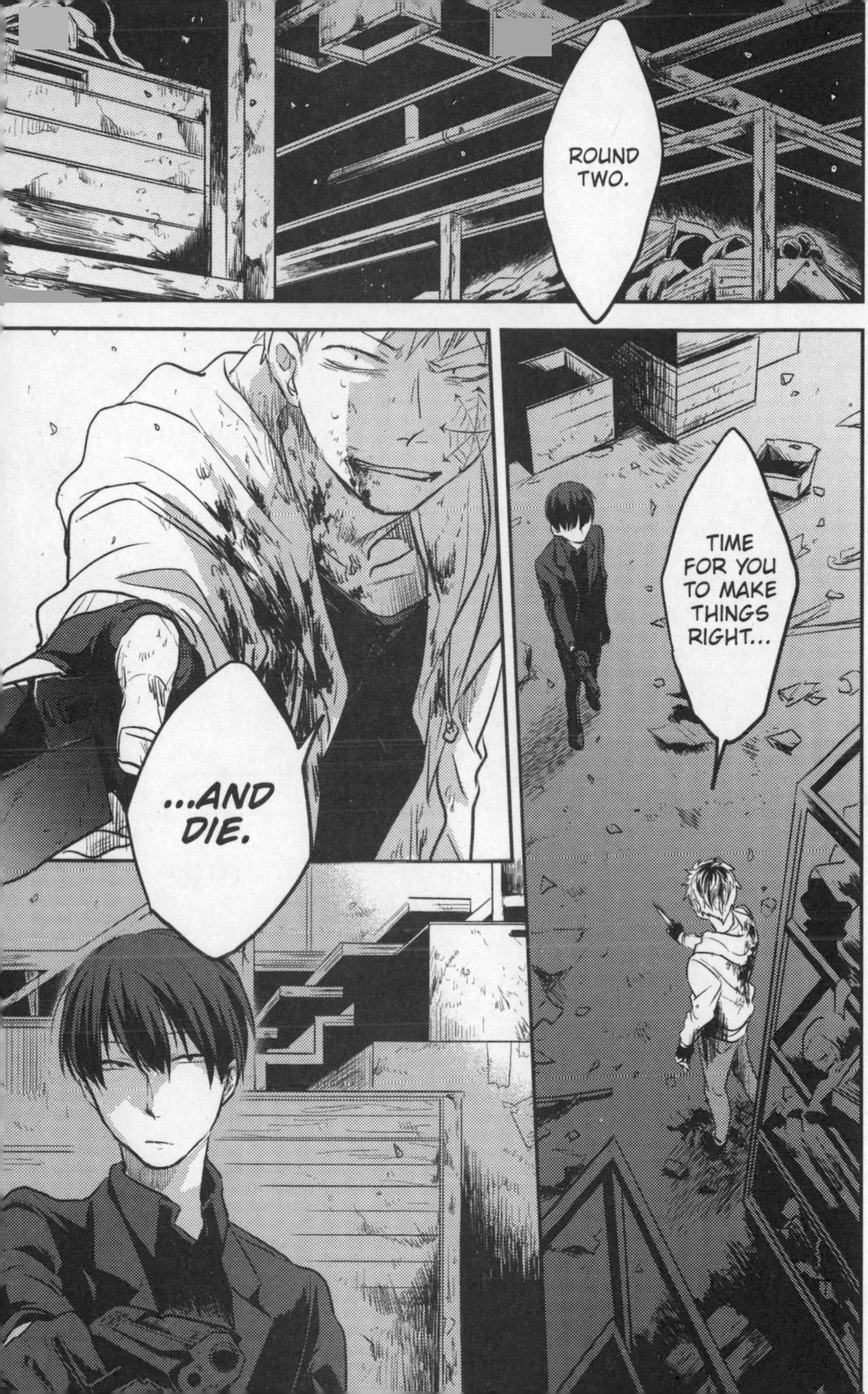
ROUND TWO.
TIME FOR YOU TO MAKE THINGS RIGHT...
...AND DIE.

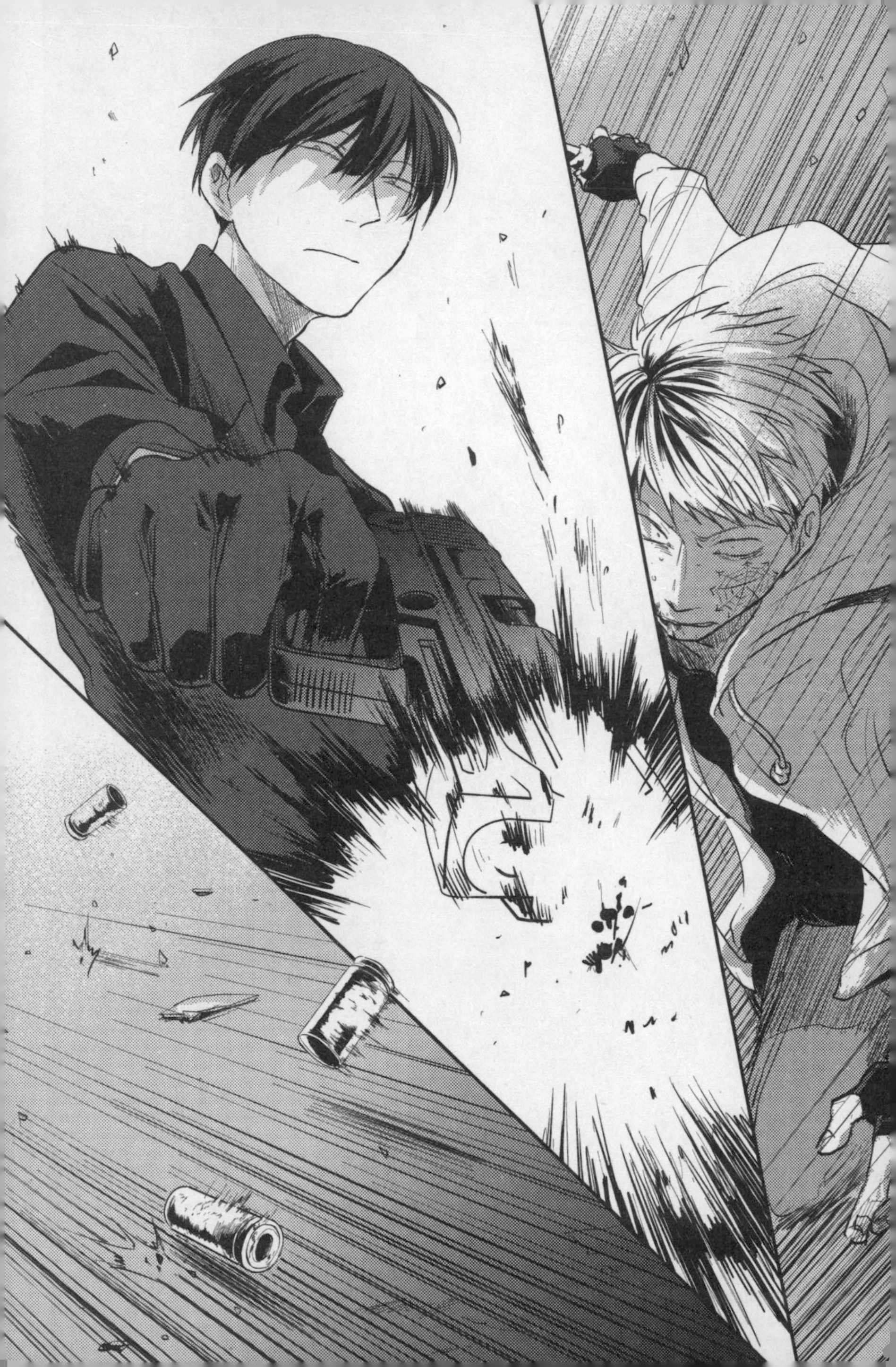

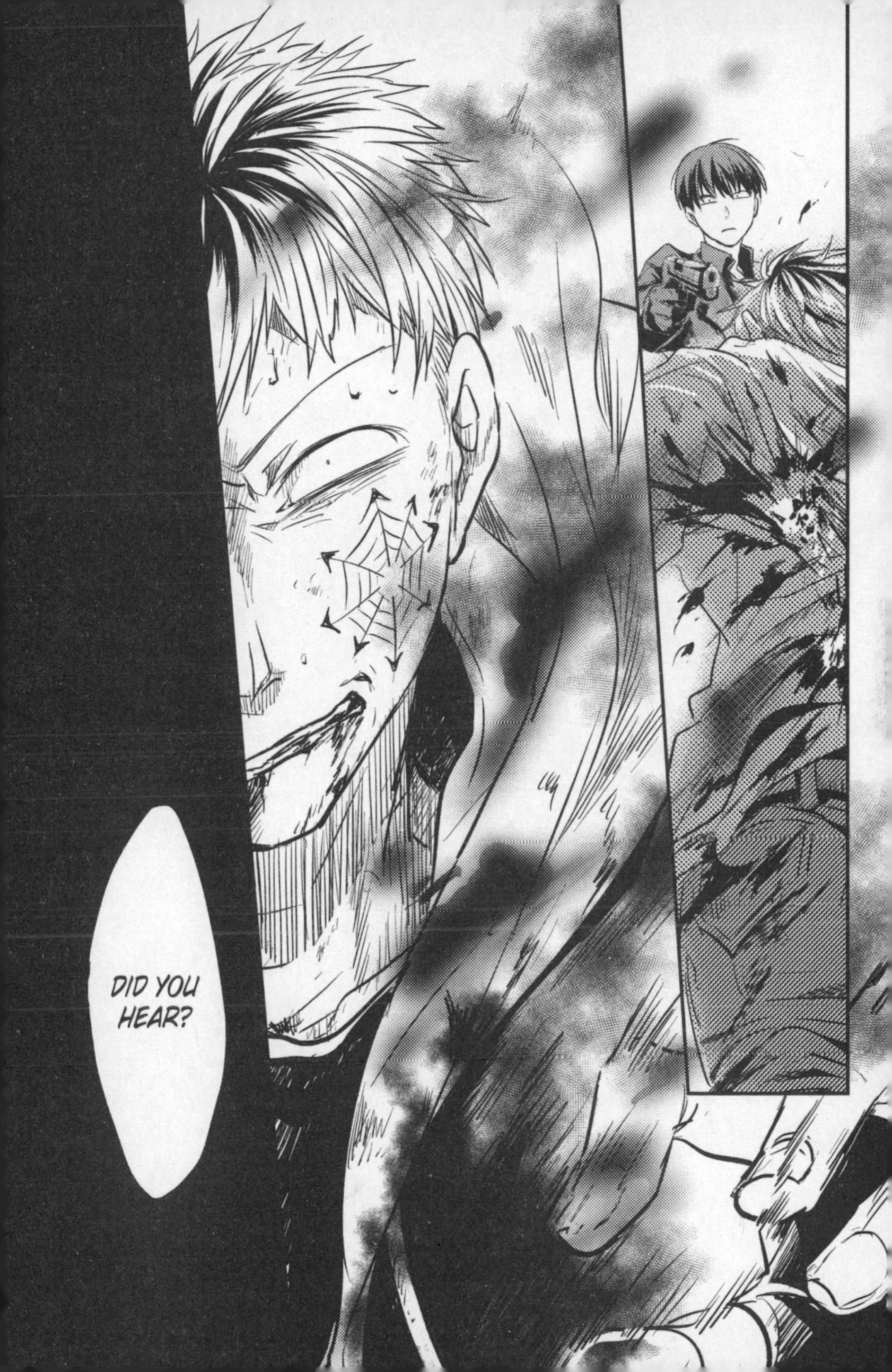
DID YOU HEAR?

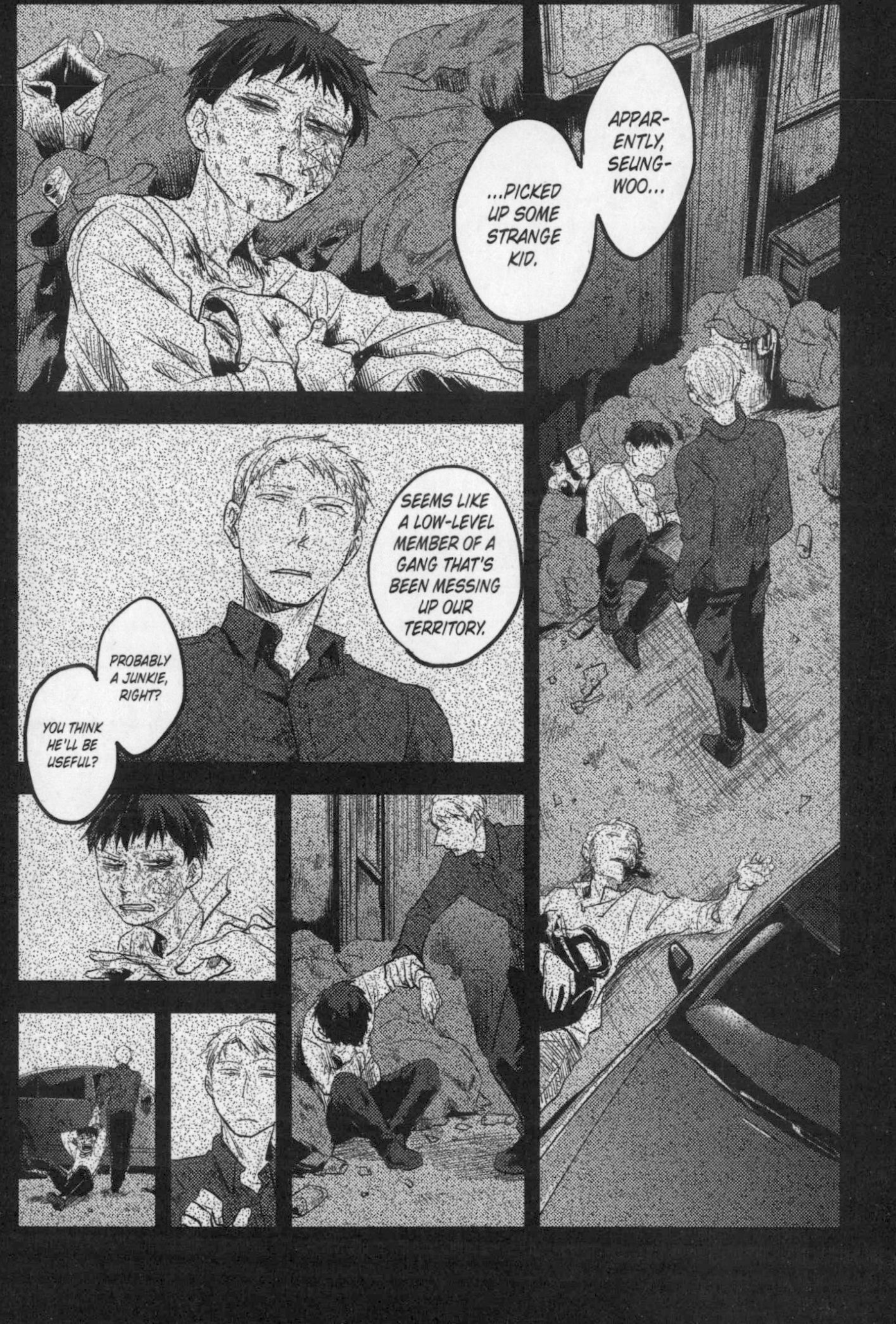
APPAR-ENTLY, SEUNG-WOO...
...PICKED UP SOME STRANGE KID.
SEEMS LIKE A LOW-LEVEL MEMBER OF A GANG THAT'S BEEN MESSING UP OUR TERRITORY.
PROBABLY A JUNKIE, RIGHT?
YOU THINK HE'LL BE USEFUL?

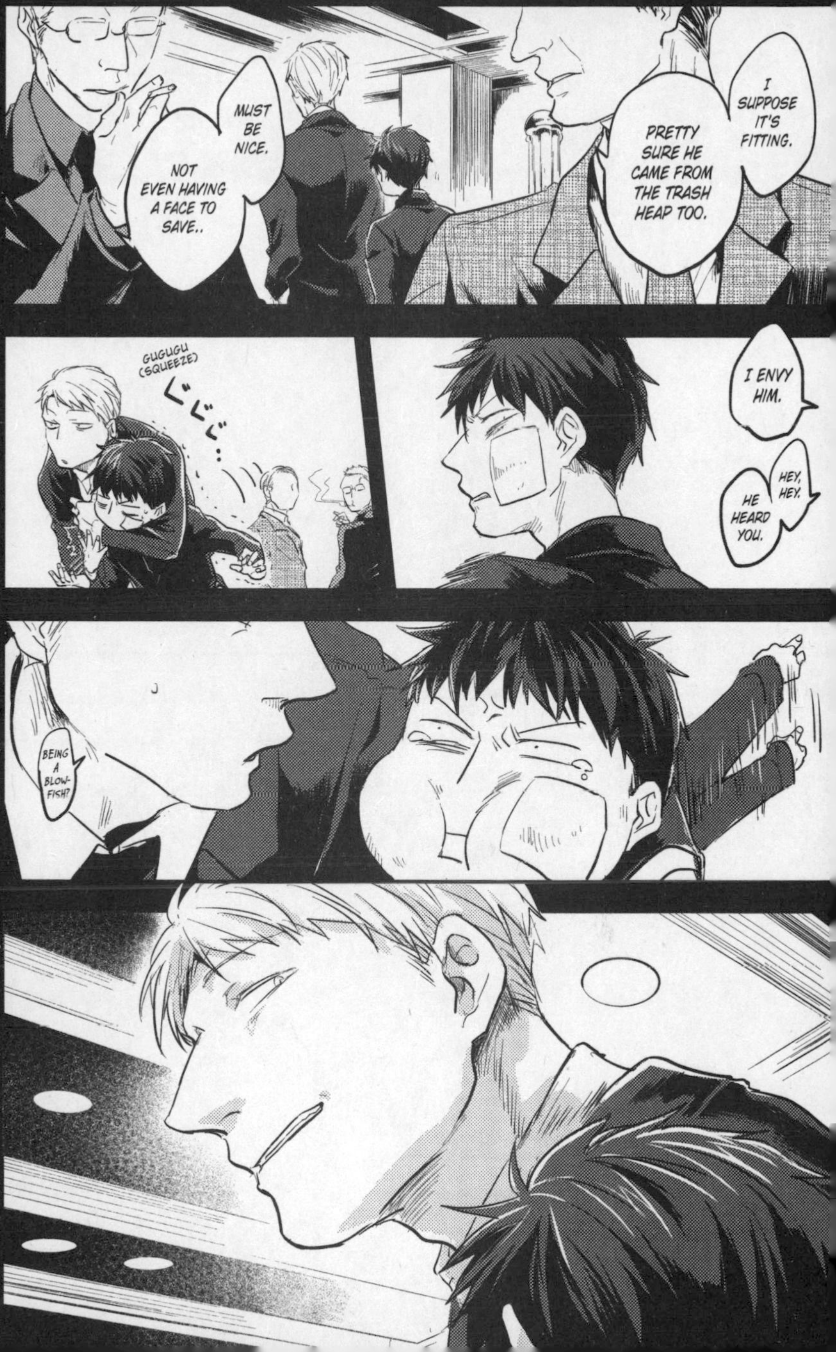
I SUPPOSE IT'S FITTING.
PRETTY SURE HE CAME FROM THE TRASH HEAP TOO.
MUST BE NICE.
NOT EVEN HAVING A FACE TO SAVE..
I ENVY HIM.
HEY, HEY.
HE HEARD YOU.
GUGUGU (SQUEEZE)
ぐぐぐ..
BEING A BLOW-FISH?

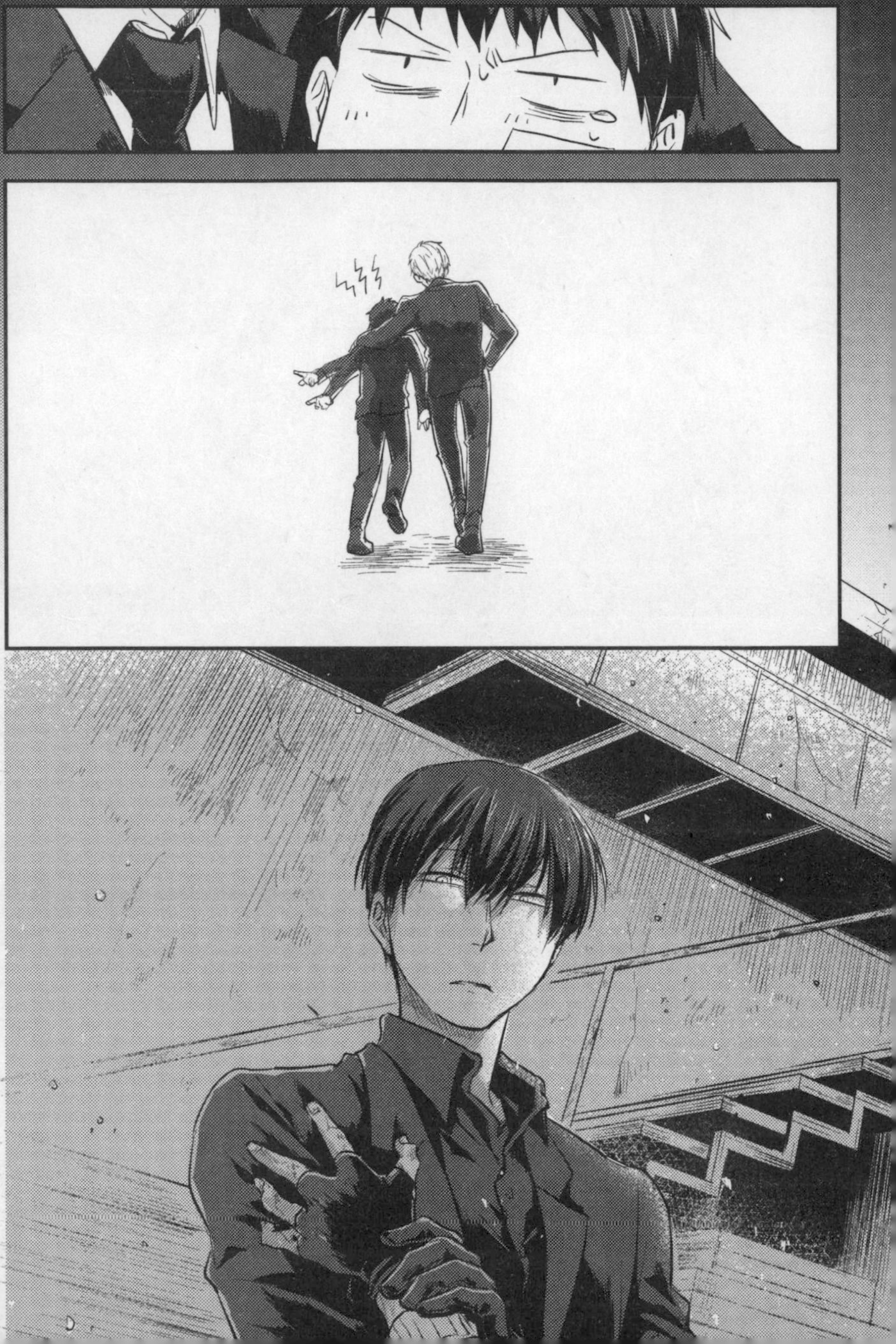

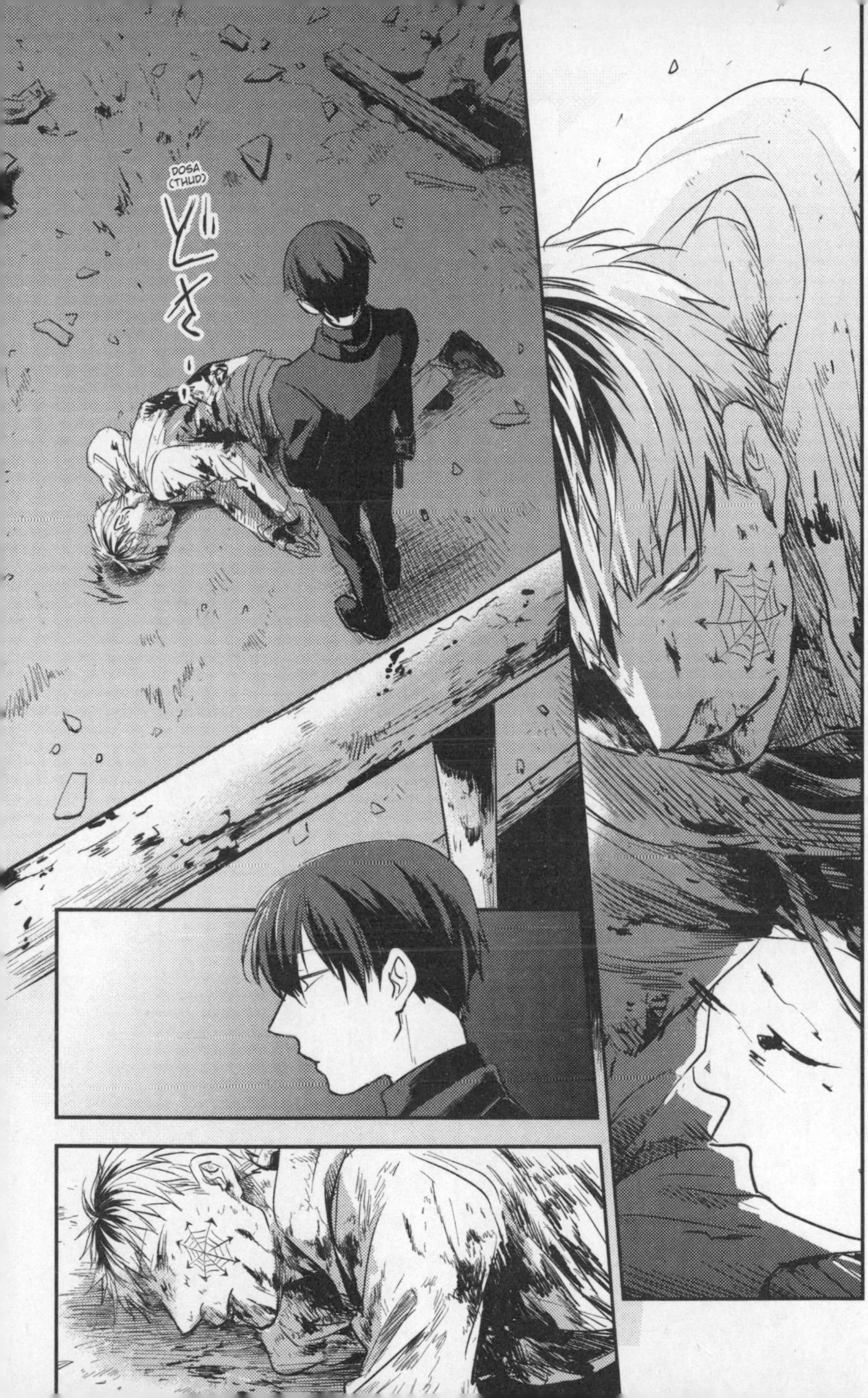
DOSA
(THUD)
どさ…

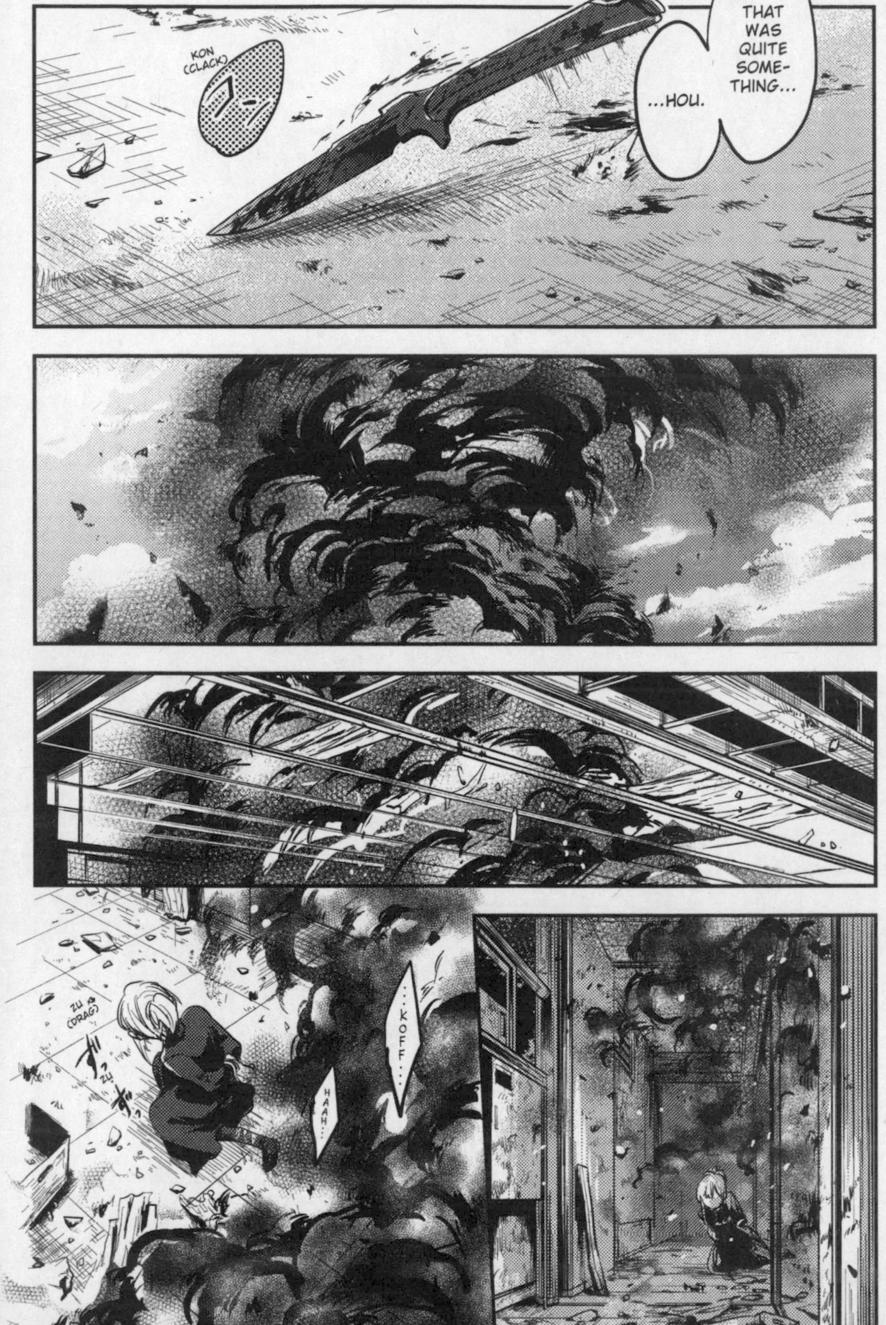
THAT WAS QUITE SOMETHING...
...HOU.
KON (CLACK)
...KOFF...
HAAH...
ZU (DRAG)

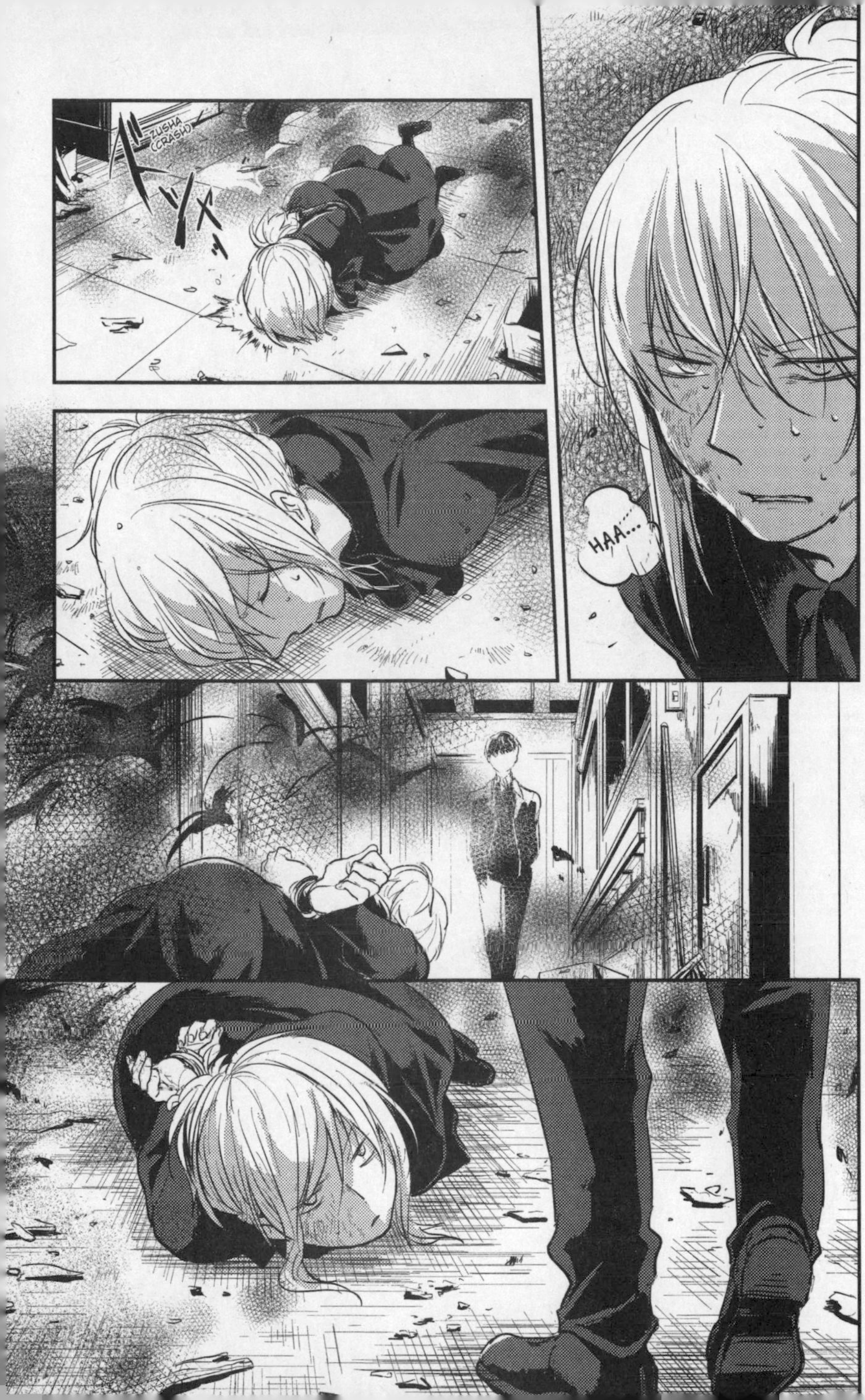
HAA...
ZUSHA (CRASH)

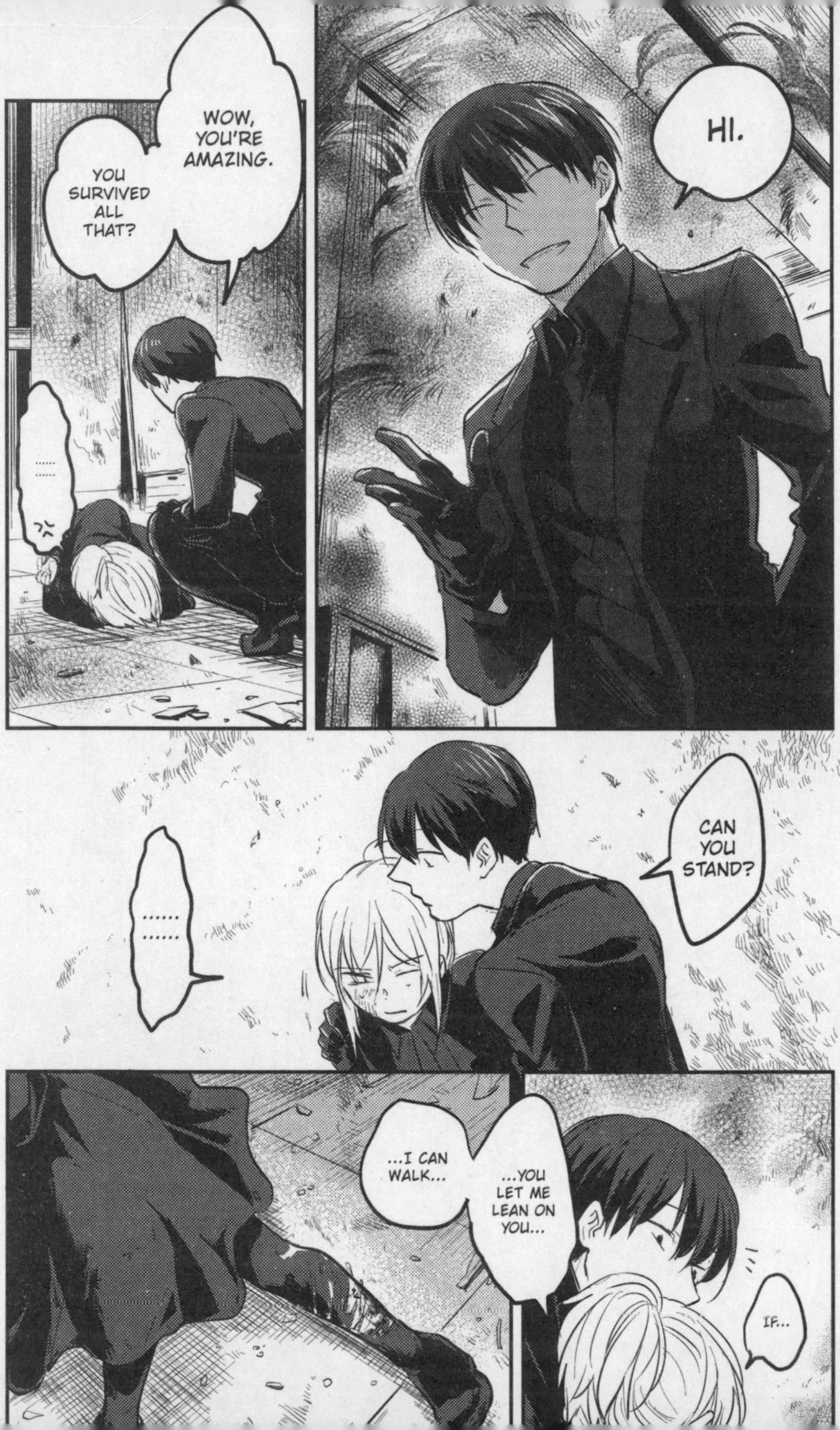
HI.
WOW, YOU'RE AMAZING.
YOU SURVIVED ALL THAT?
......
......
CAN YOU STAND?
......
......
...YOU LET ME LEAN ON YOU...
...I CAN WALK...
IF...

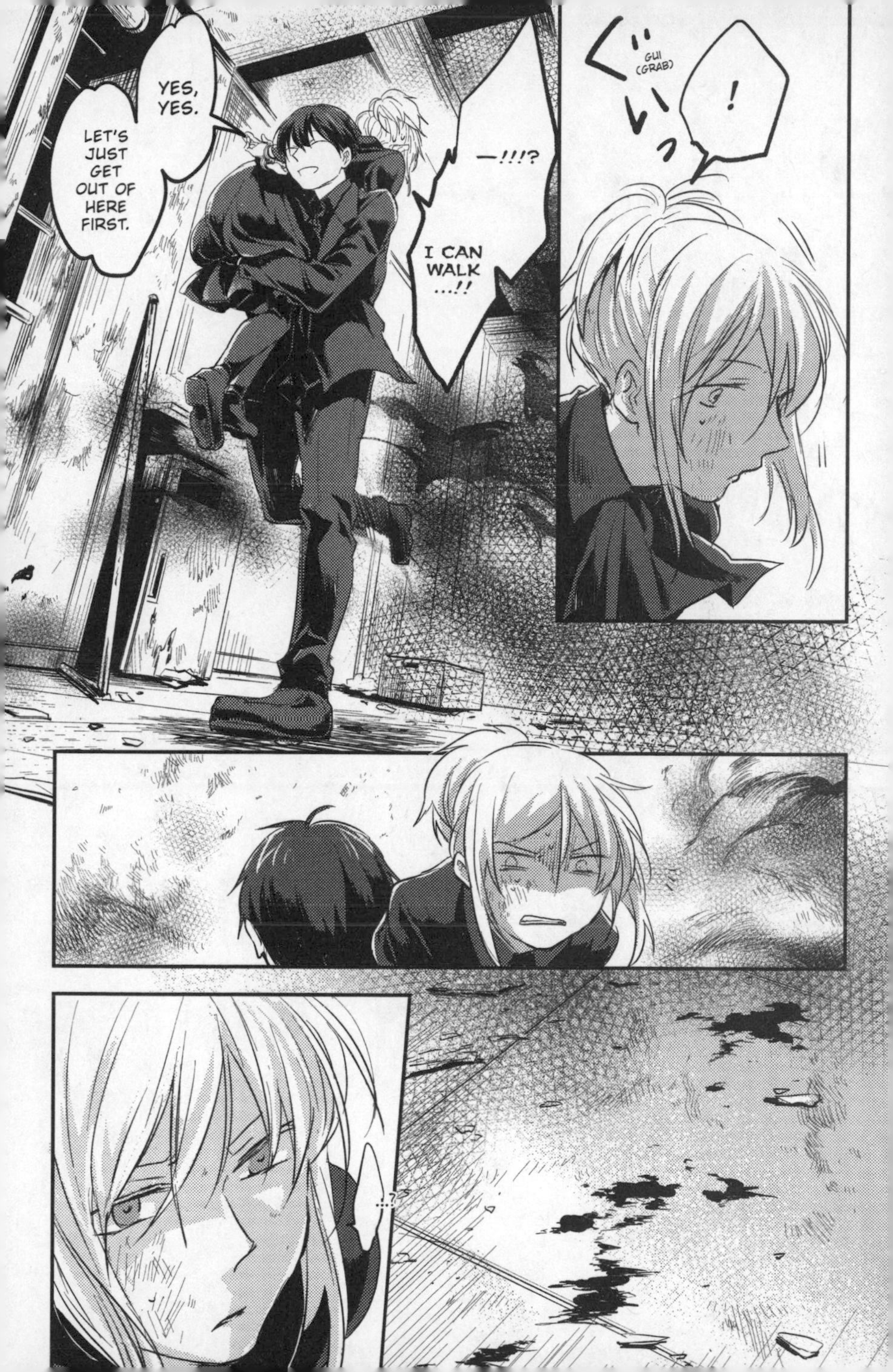
ぐいっ
GUI (GRAB)
!
—!!!?
I CAN WALK ...!!
YES, YES.
LET'S JUST GET OUT OF HERE FIRST.
...?

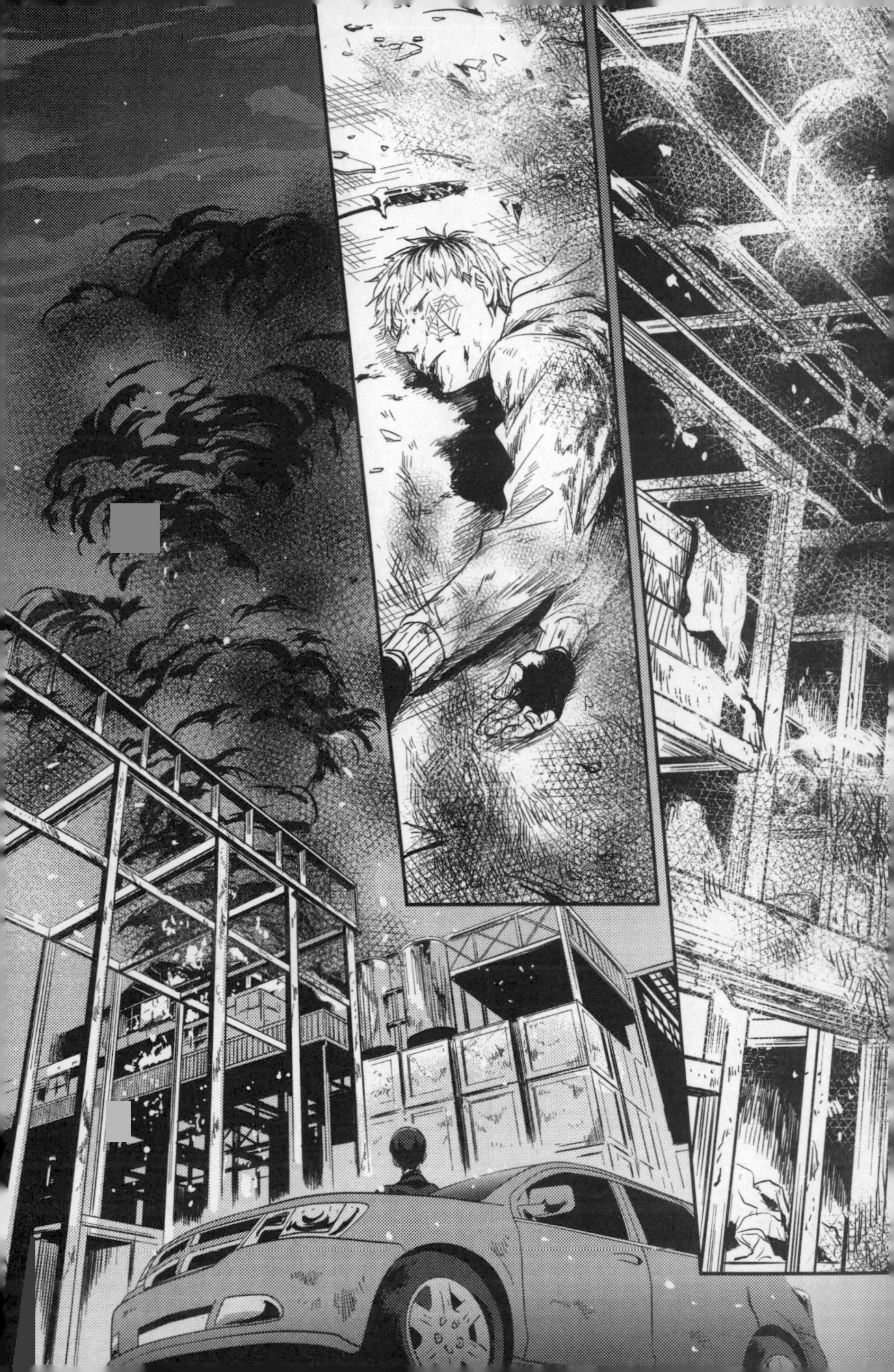

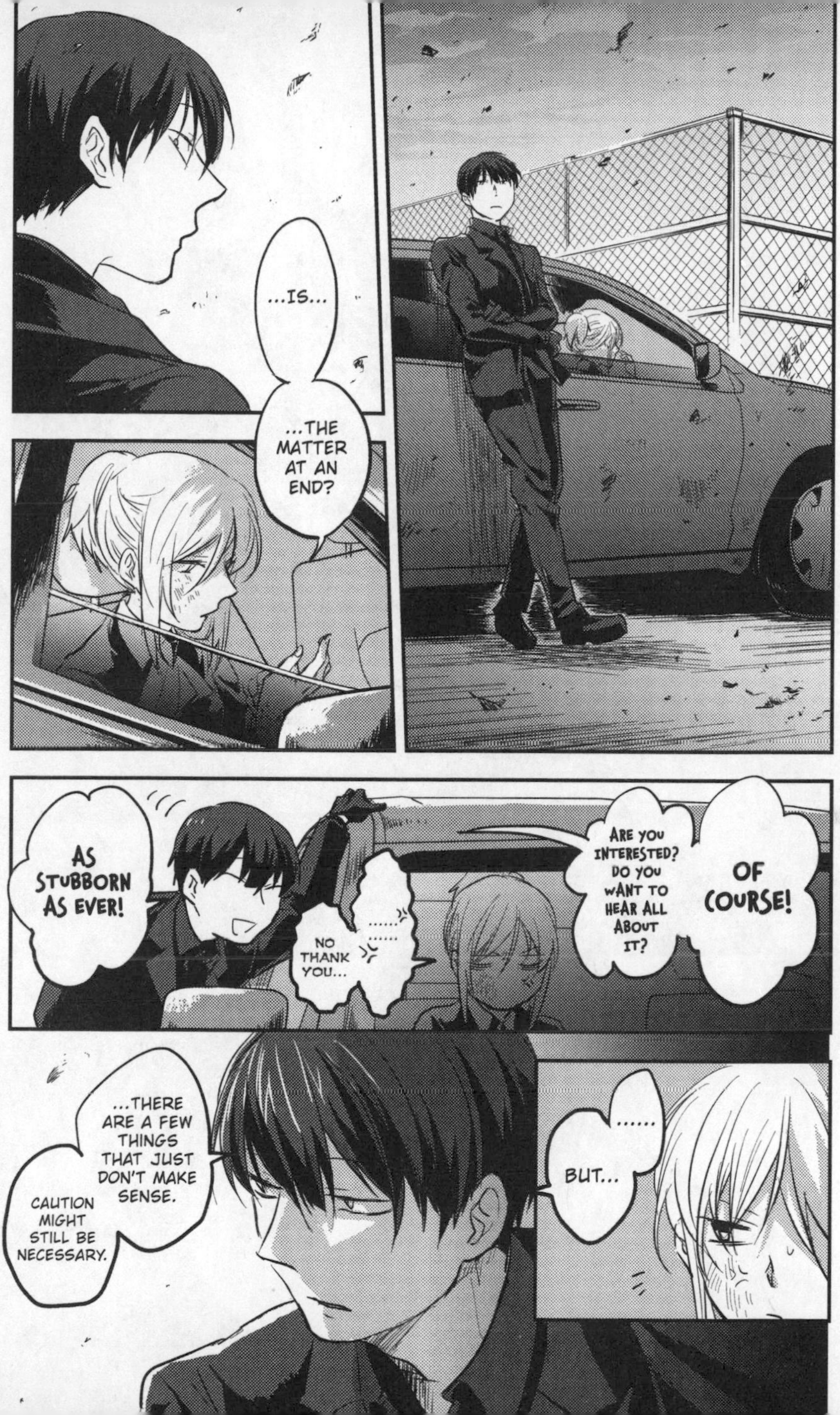
...IS...
...THE MATTER AT AN END?
OF COURSE!
ARE YOU INTERESTED? DO YOU WANT TO HEAR ALL ABOUT IT?
.... NO THANK YOU...
AS STUBBORN AS EVER!
......
BUT...
...THERE ARE A FEW THINGS THAT JUST DON'T MAKE SENSE.
CAUTION MIGHT STILL BE NECESSARY.

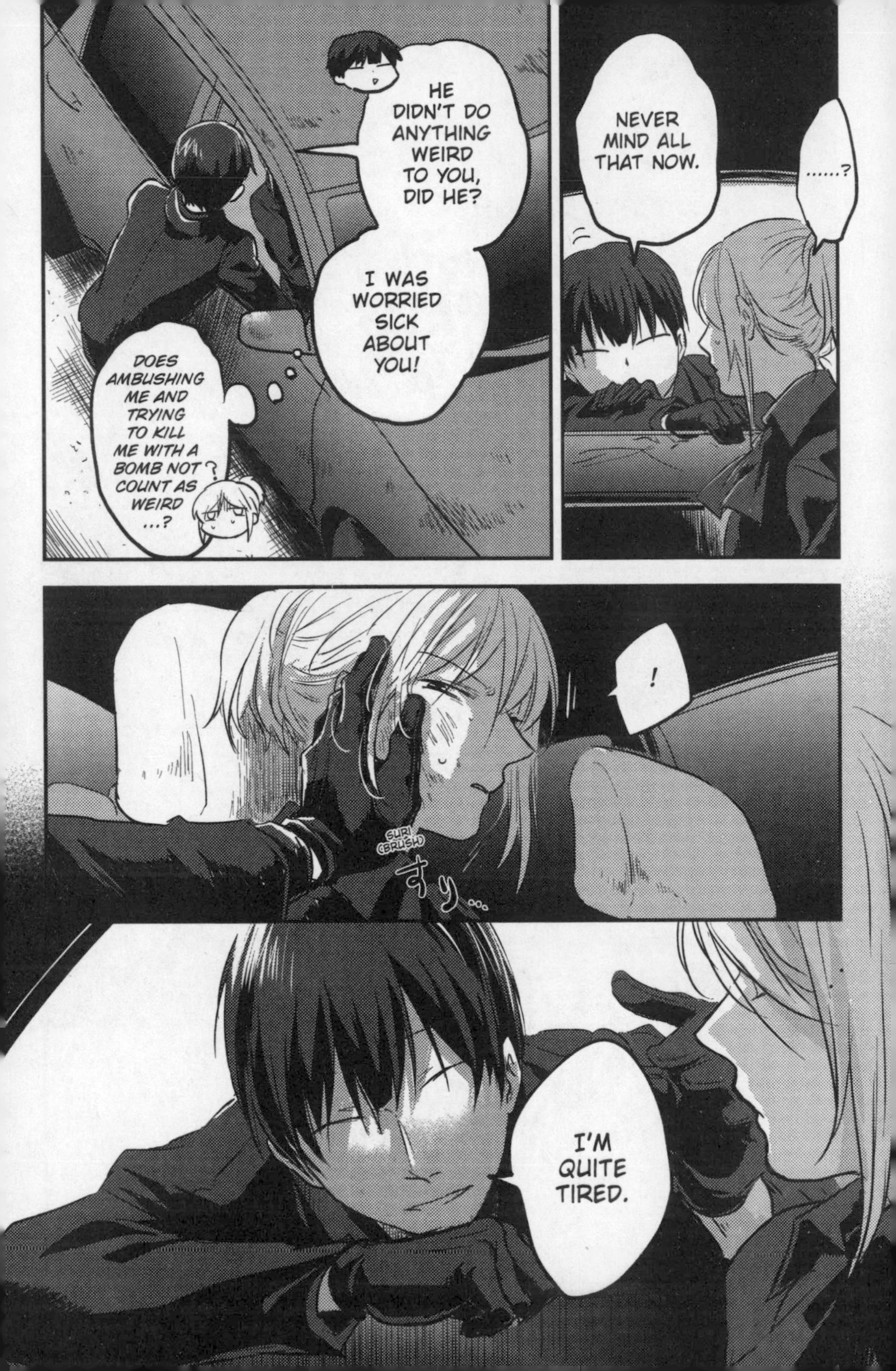
......?
NEVER MIND ALL THAT NOW.
HE DIDN'T DO ANYTHING WEIRD TO YOU, DID HE?
I WAS WORRIED SICK ABOUT YOU!
DOES AMBUSHING ME AND TRYING TO KILL ME WITH A BOMB NOT COUNT AS WEIRD ...?
!
SURI (BRUSH)
すり…
I'M QUITE TIRED.

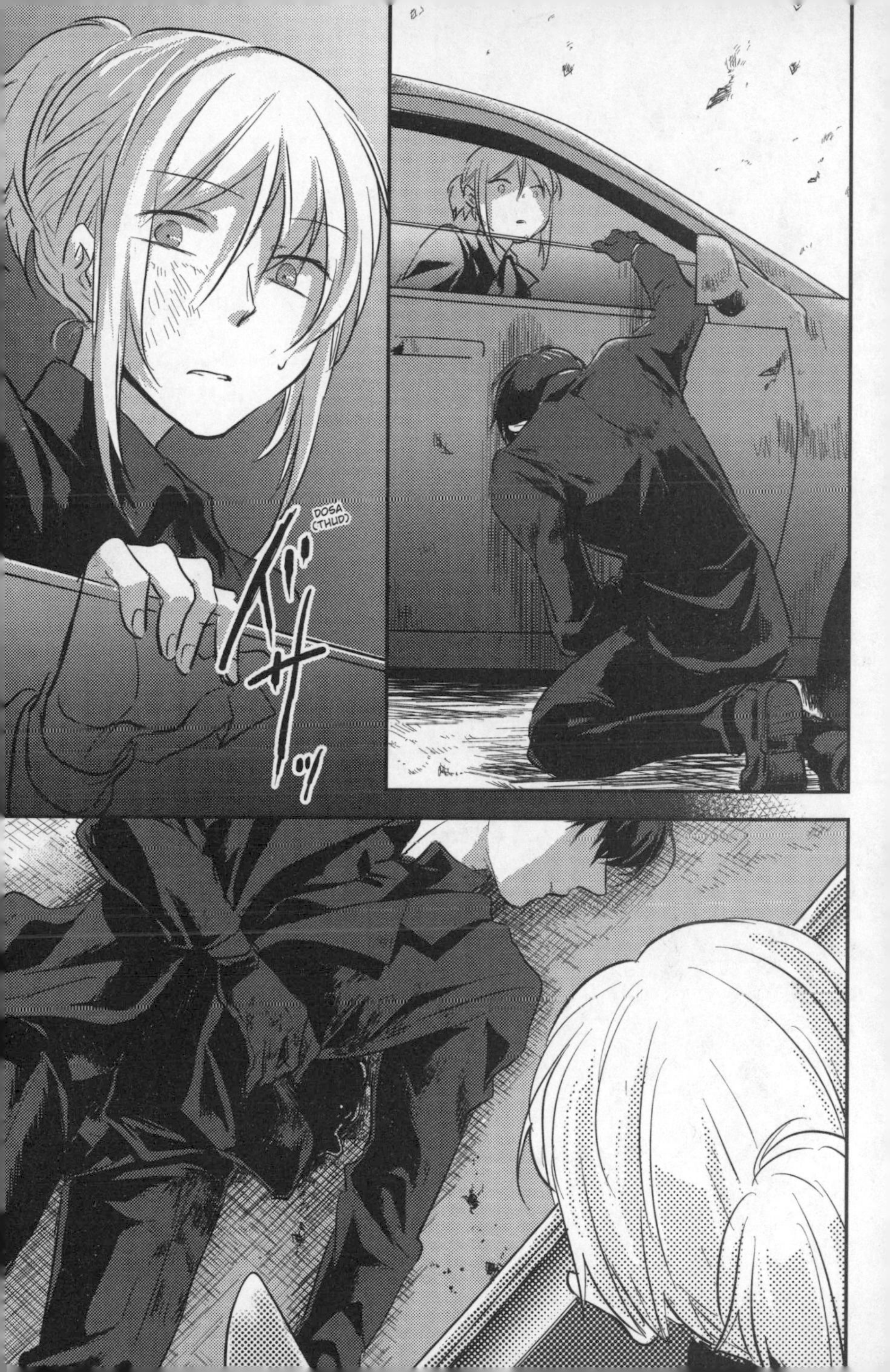
DOSA (THUD)

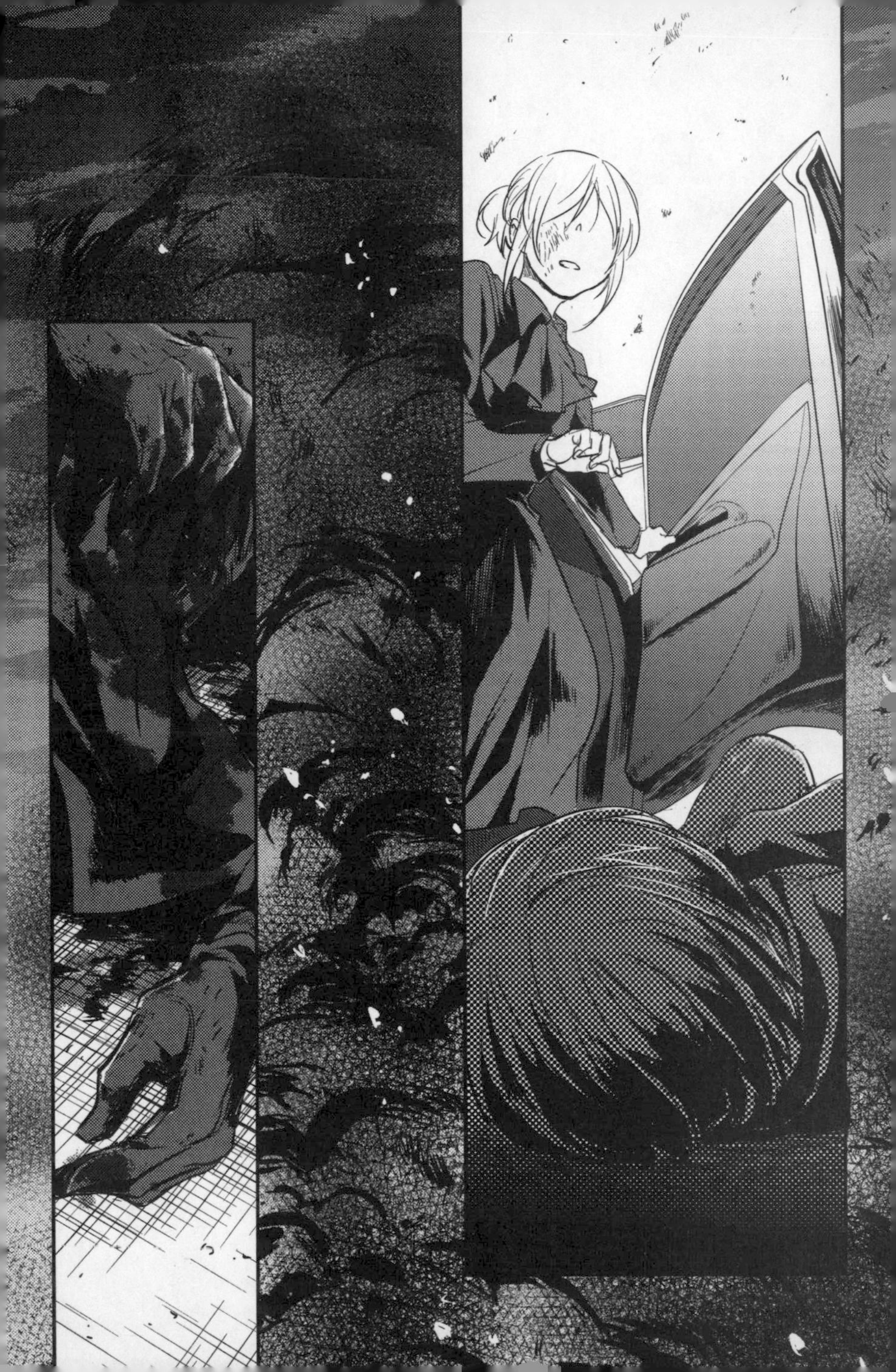

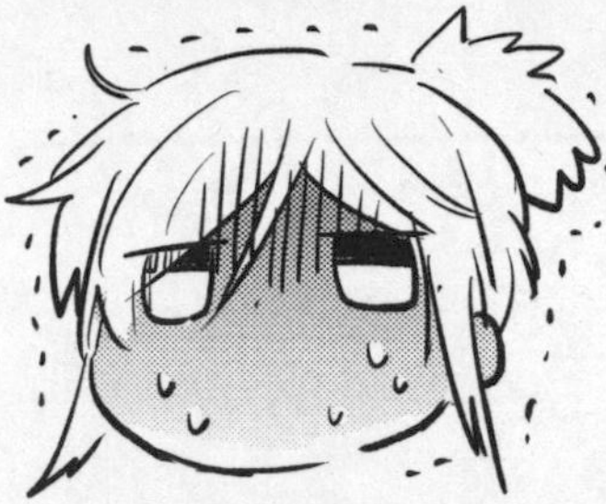

THE SECOND

TAGLINE RANKING

HOW PALE DO THEY MAKE CHATEAU-SAN'S FACE TURN?

NOTE: TAGLINES ARE THE SENTENCES INCLUDED ON TITLE PAGES AND SUCH WHEN A MANGA IS PUBLISHED IN A MAGAZINE. I THINK MY EDITOR COMES UP WITH THEM. THE MORE CRINGEWORTHY THEY ARE, THE HIGHER THEIR SCORE. THIS WAS POPULAR WITH SOME PEOPLE, SO I WILL COVER SLIGHTLY MORE OF THEM THIS TIME.

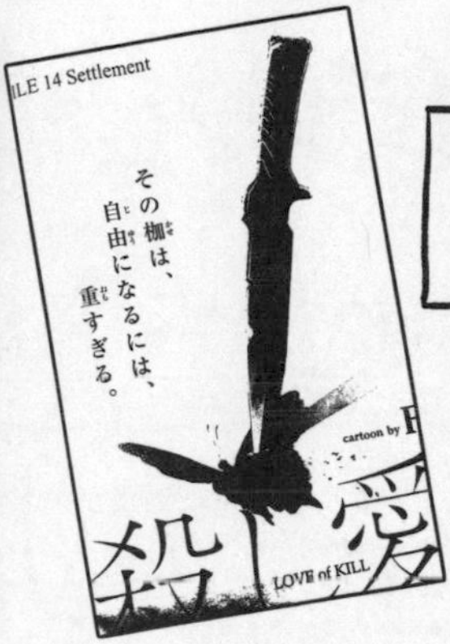
ILE 14 Settlement
その枷は、自由になるには、重すぎる。
cartoon by F
殺し愛
LOVE of KILL

5TH

THESE SHACKLES ARE FAR TOO HEAVY TO BREAK FREE OF.
(CHAPTER 14, TITLE PAGE)

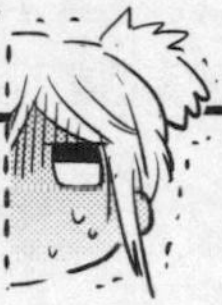

PALLOR LEVEL: 0.5

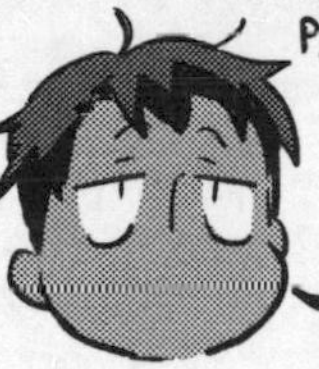

THESE WORDS ARE NOT DIRECTED TOWARD CHATEAU, SO HER PALLOR LEVEL IS LOW. THEY MAKE A VERY COOL IMPRESSION.

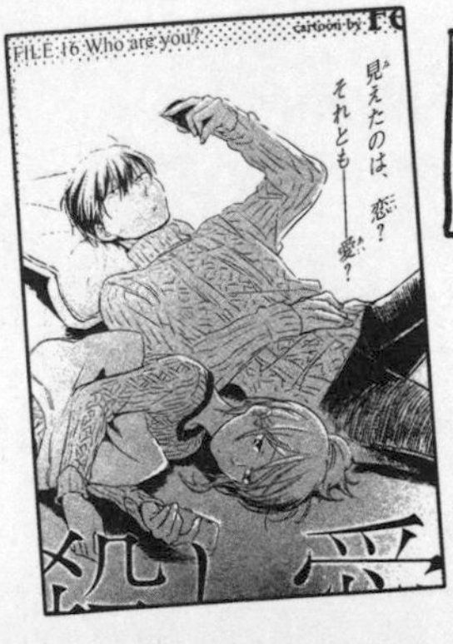
FILE 16 Who are you?
cartoon by F
見えたのは、恋？
それとも——愛？

4TH

WAS THAT A SIGN OF A CRUSH? OR WAS IT...LOVE?
(CHAPTER 16, TITLE PAGE)

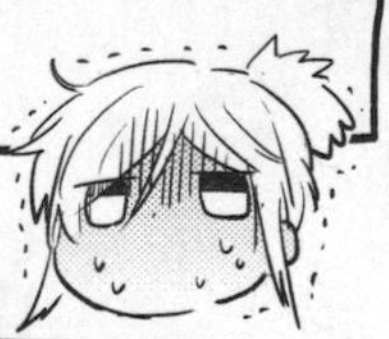

PALLOR LEVEL: 1

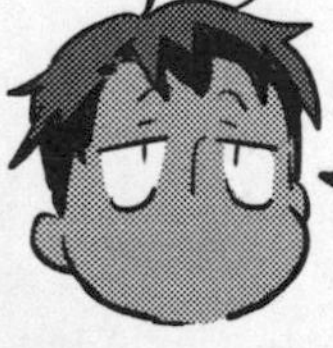

TALKING ABOUT CRUSHES AND LOVE IS IMPERTINENT.

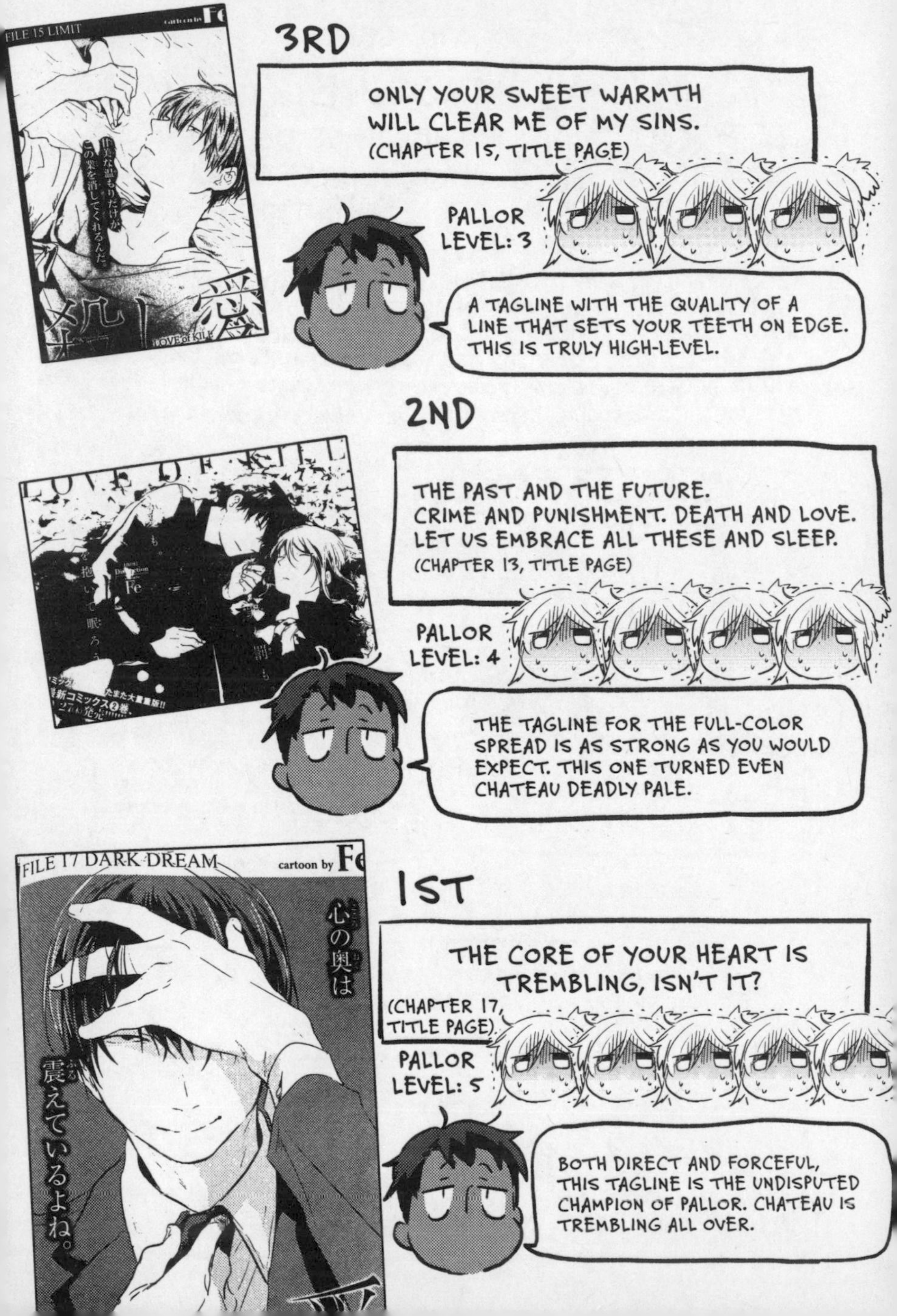
3RD
FILE 15 LIMIT
cartoon by Fe
甘美な温もりだけが この業を消してくれるんだ。
LOVE of KILL
ONLY YOUR SWEET WARMTH WILL CLEAR ME OF MY SINS.
(CHAPTER 15, TITLE PAGE)
PALLOR LEVEL: 3
A TAGLINE WITH THE QUALITY OF A LINE THAT SETS YOUR TEETH ON EDGE. THIS IS TRULY HIGH-LEVEL.
2ND
Fe
THE PAST AND THE FUTURE. CRIME AND PUNISHMENT. DEATH AND LOVE. LET US EMBRACE ALL THESE AND SLEEP.
(CHAPTER 13, TITLE PAGE)
PALLOR LEVEL: 4
THE TAGLINE FOR THE FULL-COLOR SPREAD IS AS STRONG AS YOU WOULD EXPECT. THIS ONE TURNED EVEN CHATEAU DEADLY PALE.
1ST
FILE 17 DARK DREAM
cartoon by Fe
心の奥は 震えているよね。
THE CORE OF YOUR HEART IS TREMBLING, ISN'T IT?
(CHAPTER 17, TITLE PAGE)
PALLOR LEVEL: 5
BOTH DIRECT AND FORCEFUL, THIS TAGLINE IS THE UNDISPUTED CHAMPION OF PALLOR. CHATEAU IS TREMBLING ALL OVER.

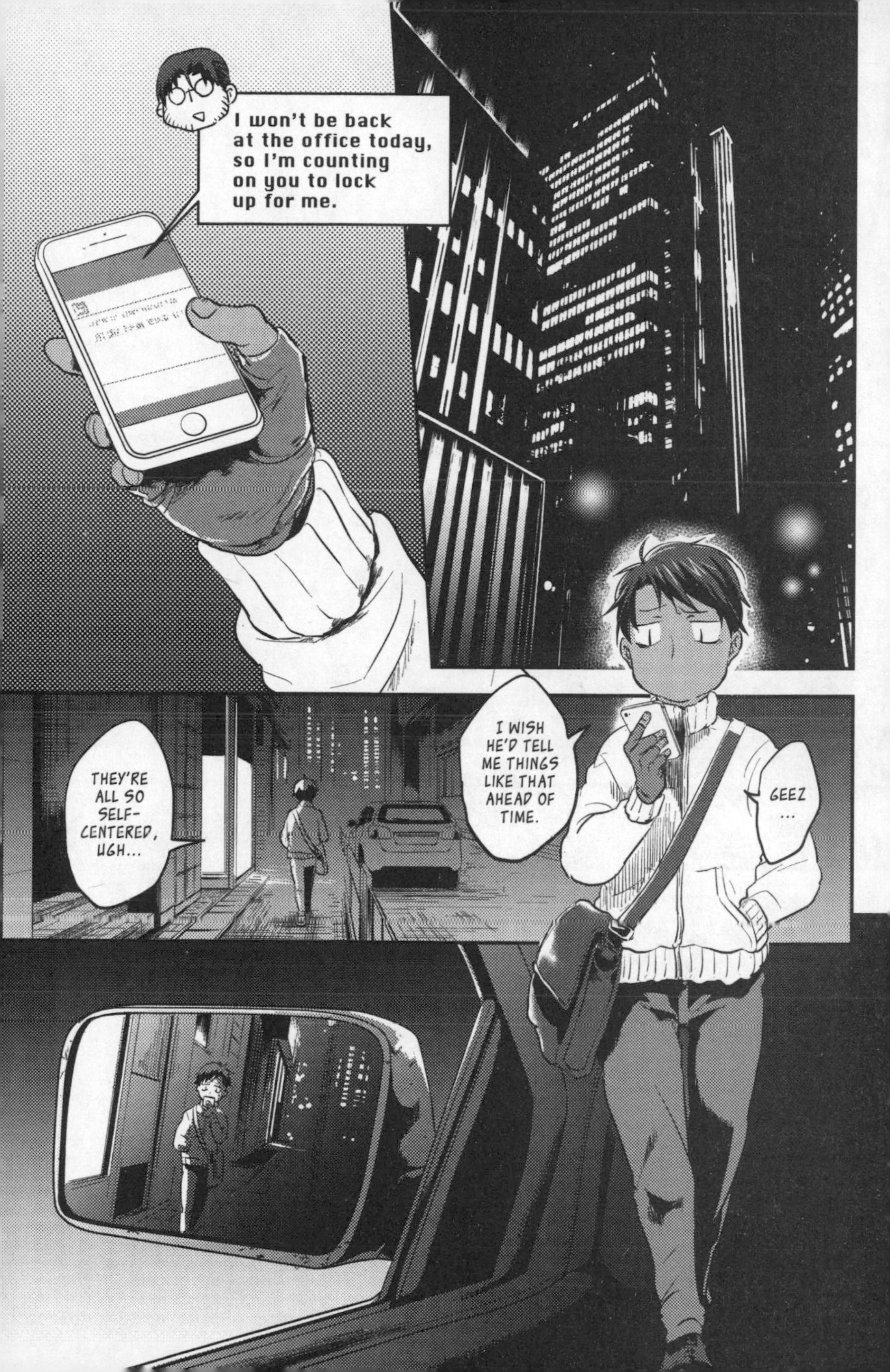
I won't be back at the office today, so I'm counting on you to lock up for me.
GEEZ...
I WISH HE'D TELL ME THINGS LIKE THAT AHEAD OF TIME.
THEY'RE ALL SO SELF-CENTERED, UGH...

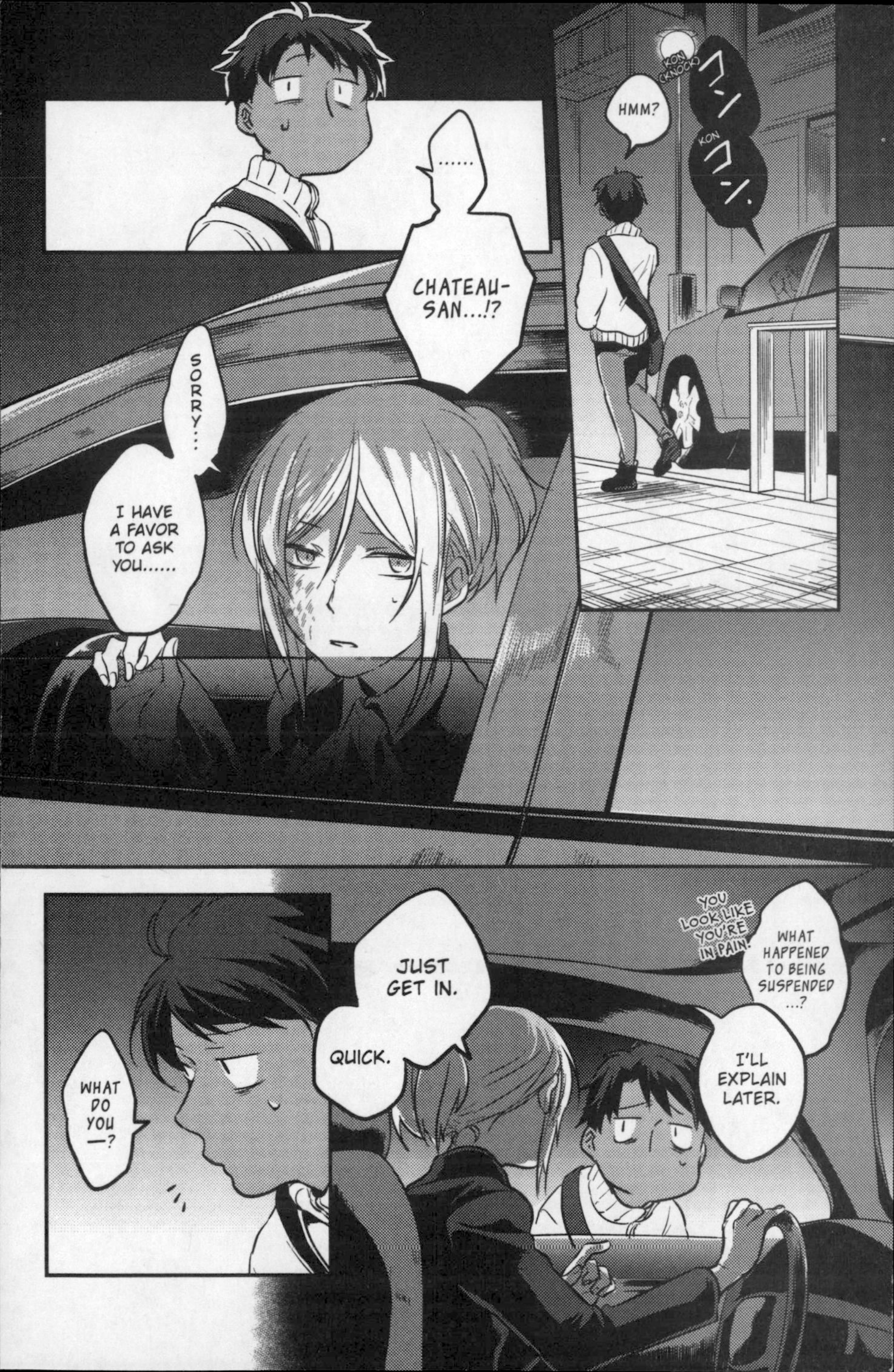

KON (KNOCK)
KON
HMM?
......
CHATEAU-SAN...!?
SORRY...
I HAVE A FAVOR TO ASK YOU......
YOU LOOK LIKE YOU'RE IN PAIN.
WHAT HAPPENED TO BEING SUSPENDED...?
I'LL EXPLAIN LATER.
JUST GET IN.
QUICK.
WHAT DO YOU—?

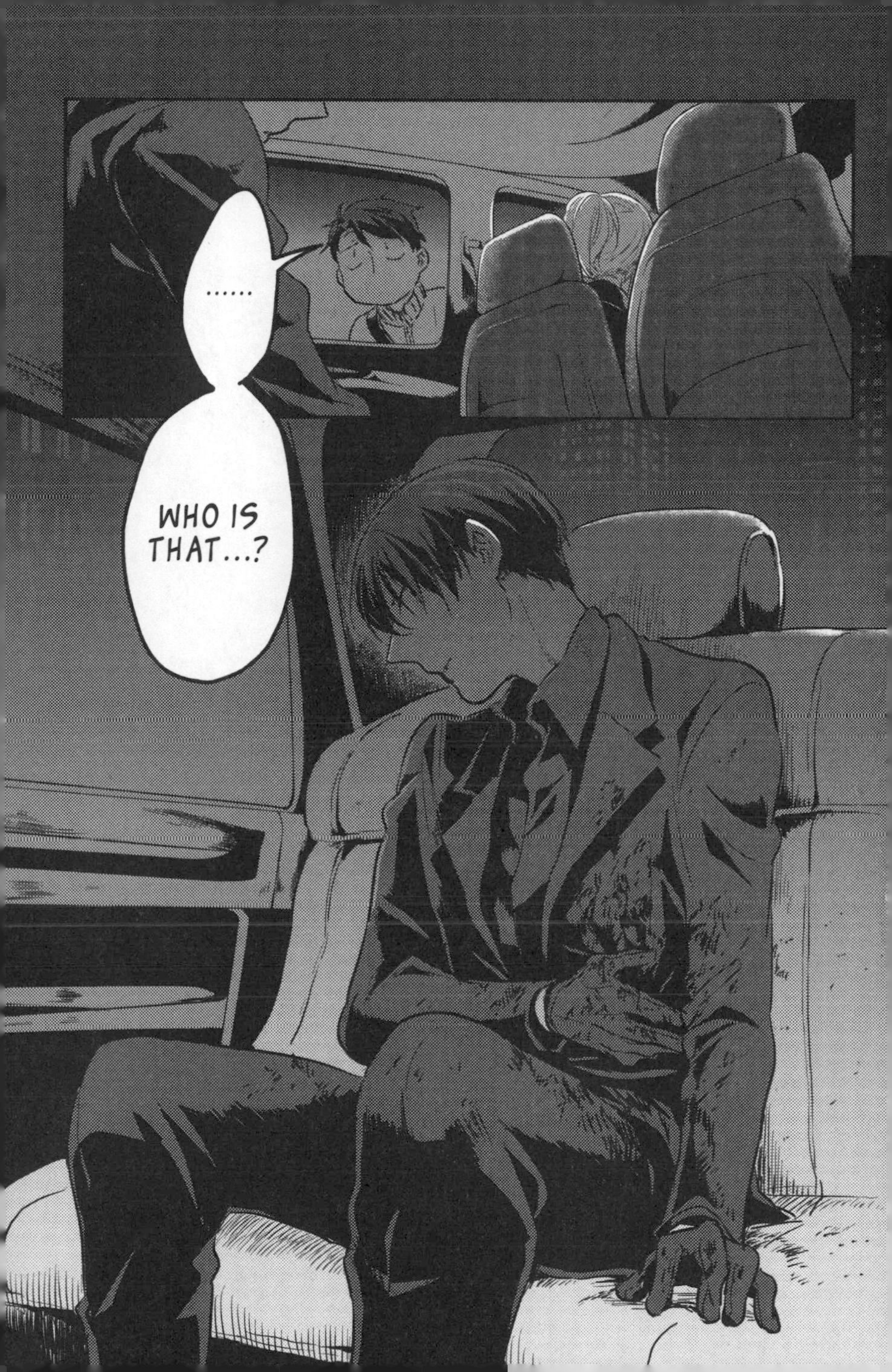

......
WHO IS THAT...?

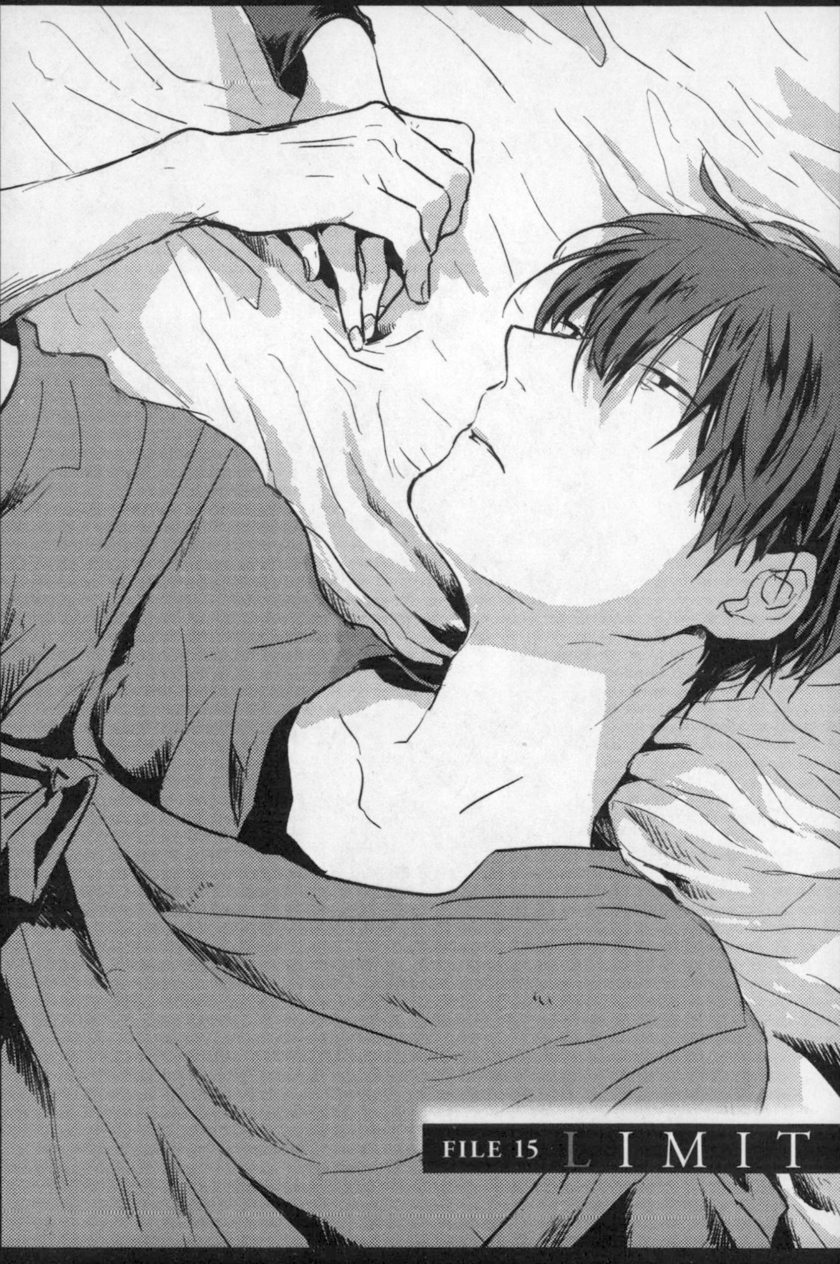
FILE 15 LIMIT

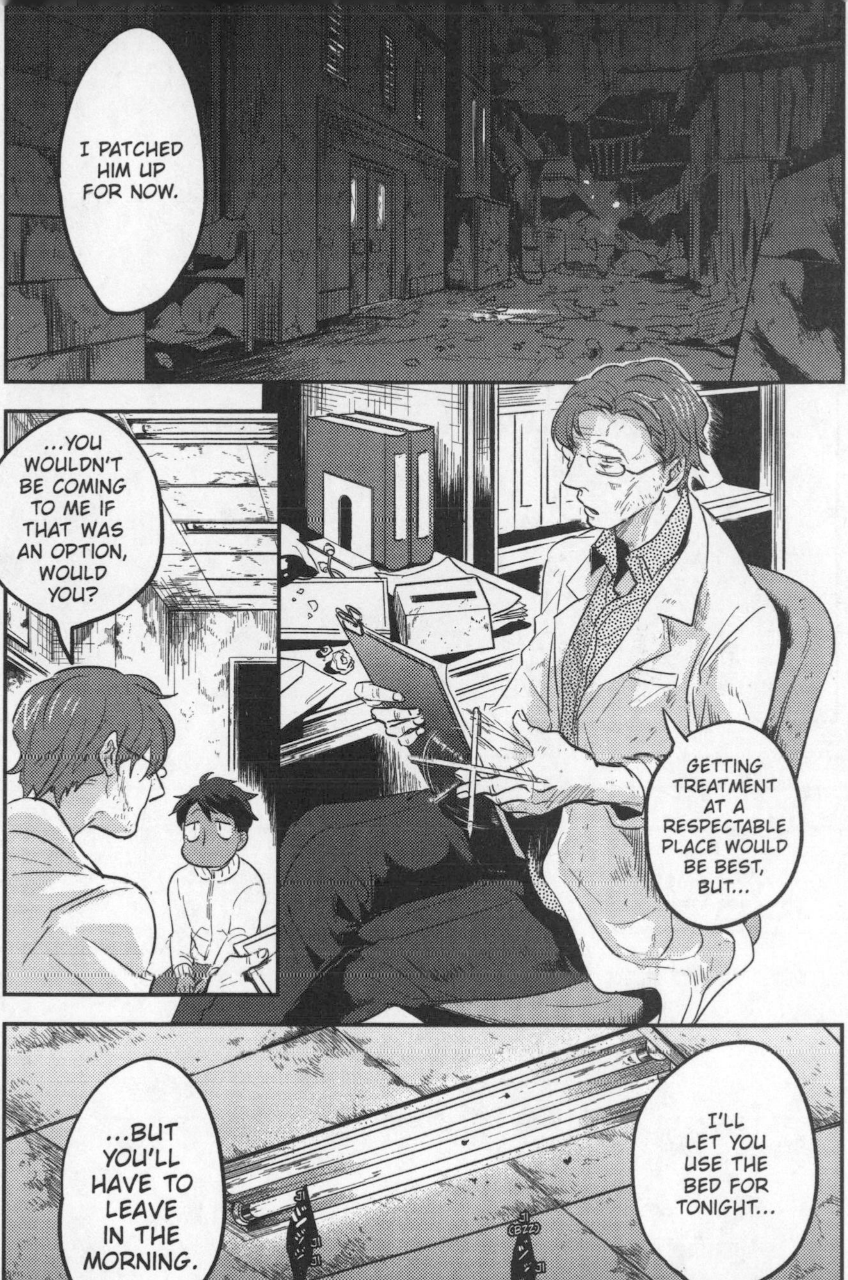
I PATCHED HIM UP FOR NOW.
GETTING TREATMENT AT A RESPECTABLE PLACE WOULD BE BEST, BUT...
...YOU WOULDN'T BE COMING TO ME IF THAT WAS AN OPTION, WOULD YOU?
I'LL LET YOU USE THE BED FOR TONIGHT...
(BZZ)
...BUT YOU'LL HAVE TO LEAVE IN THE MORNING.

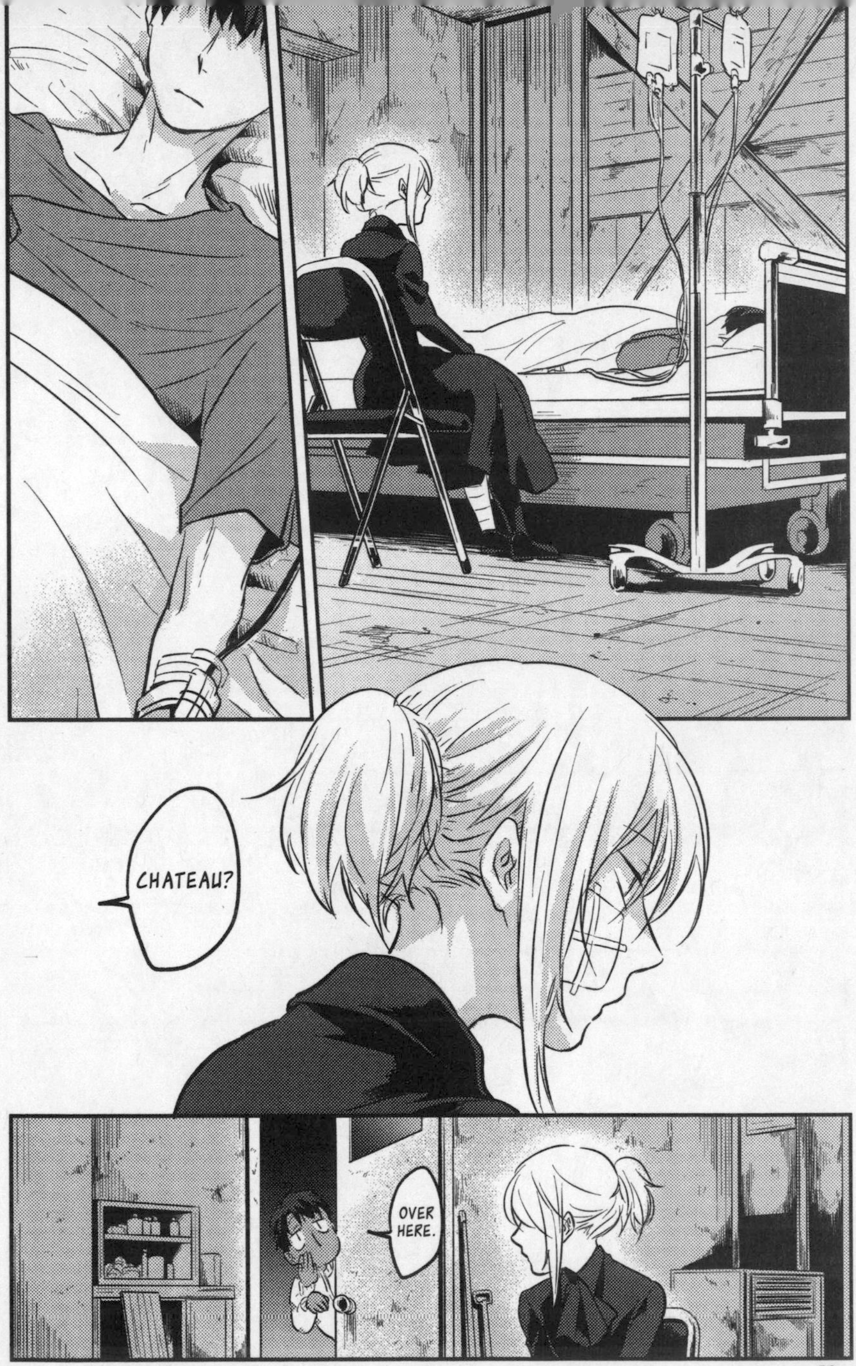
CHATEAU?
OVER HERE.

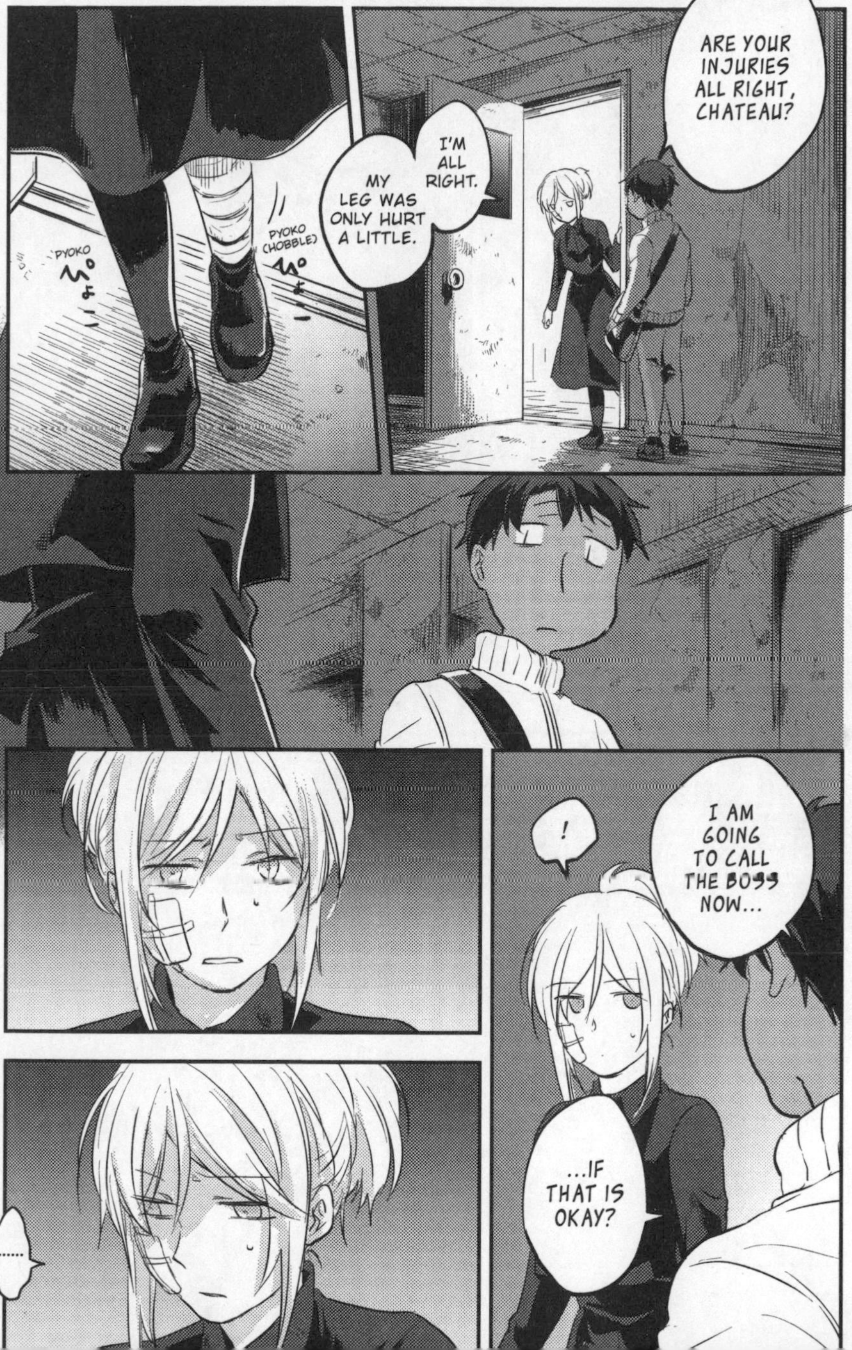
ARE YOUR INJURIES ALL RIGHT, CHATEAU?
I'M ALL RIGHT.
MY LEG WAS ONLY HURT A LITTLE.
PYOKO (HOBBLE)
ぴょこ
PYOKO
ぴょこ
!
I AM GOING TO CALL THE BOSS NOW...
...IF THAT IS OKAY?
......

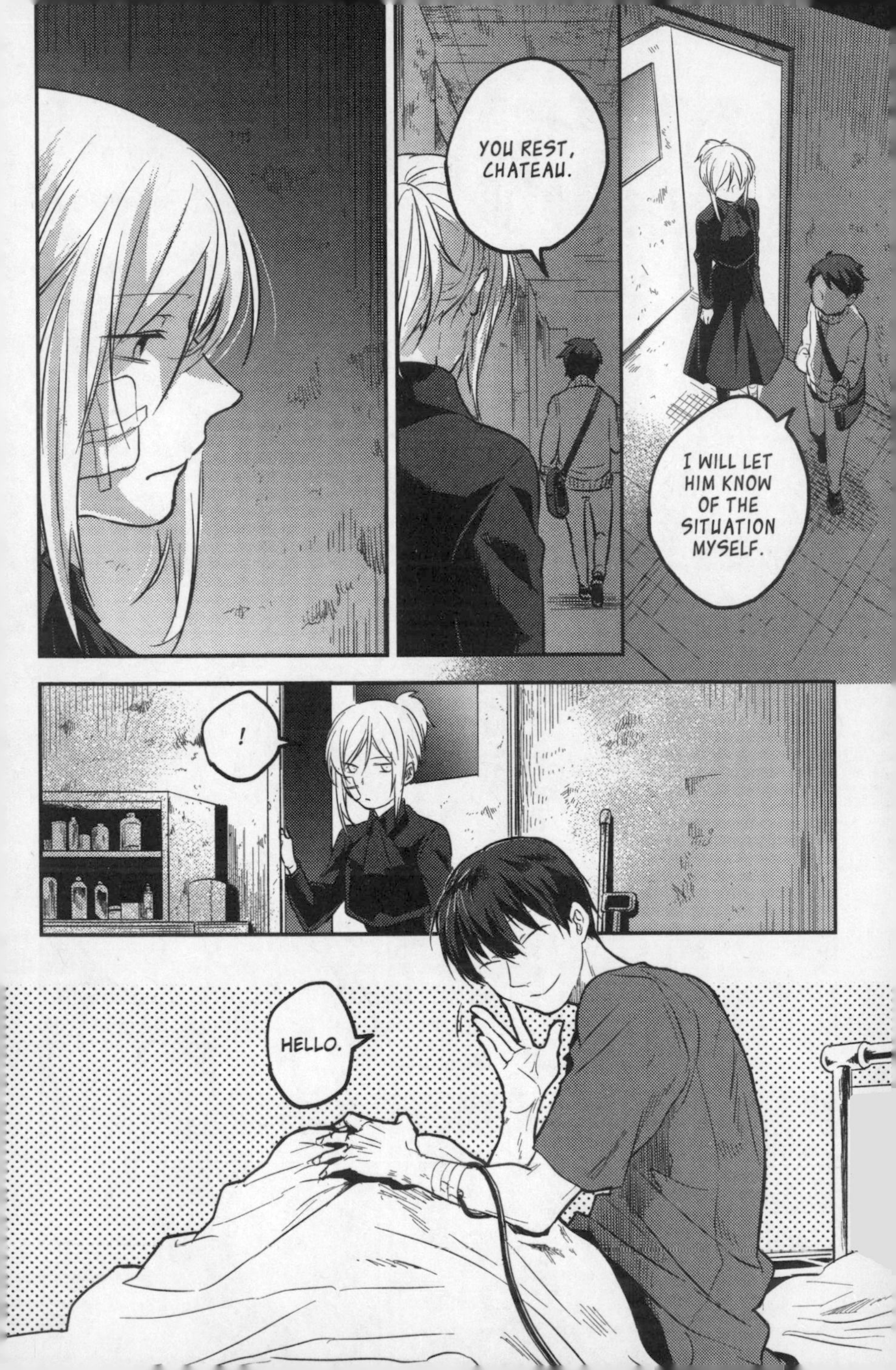
I WILL LET HIM KNOW OF THE SITUATION MYSELF.
YOU REST, CHATEAU.
!
HELLO.

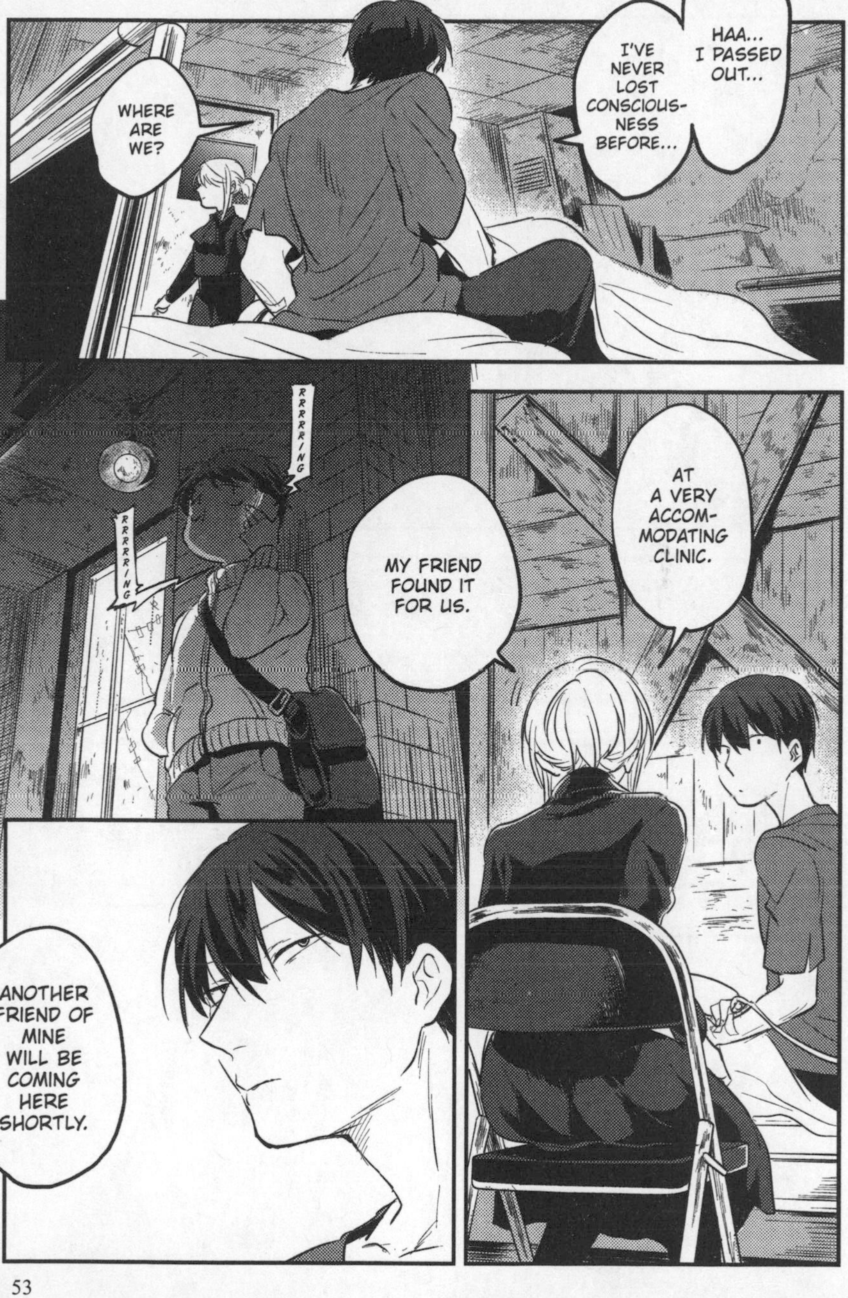
HAA... I PASSED OUT...
I'VE NEVER LOST CONSCIOUS-NESS BEFORE...
WHERE ARE WE?
AT A VERY ACCOM-MODATING CLINIC.
MY FRIEND FOUND IT FOR US.
RRRRRING
RRRRRING
ANOTHER FRIEND OF MINE WILL BE COMING HERE SHORTLY.

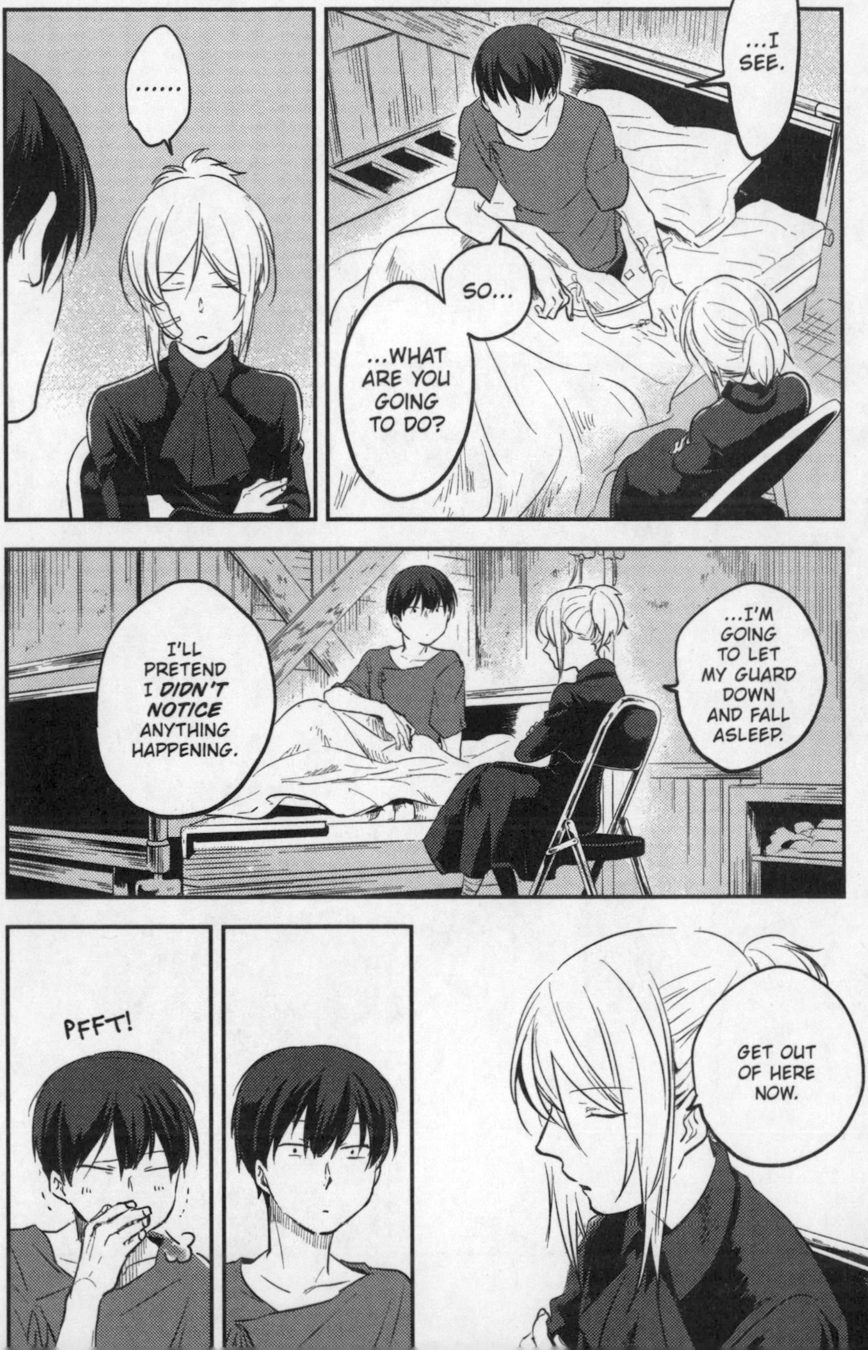
...I SEE.
SO...
...WHAT ARE YOU GOING TO DO?
....
...I'M GOING TO LET MY GUARD DOWN AND FALL ASLEEP.
I'LL PRETEND I *DIDN'T NOTICE* ANYTHING HAPPENING.
GET OUT OF HERE NOW.
PFFT!

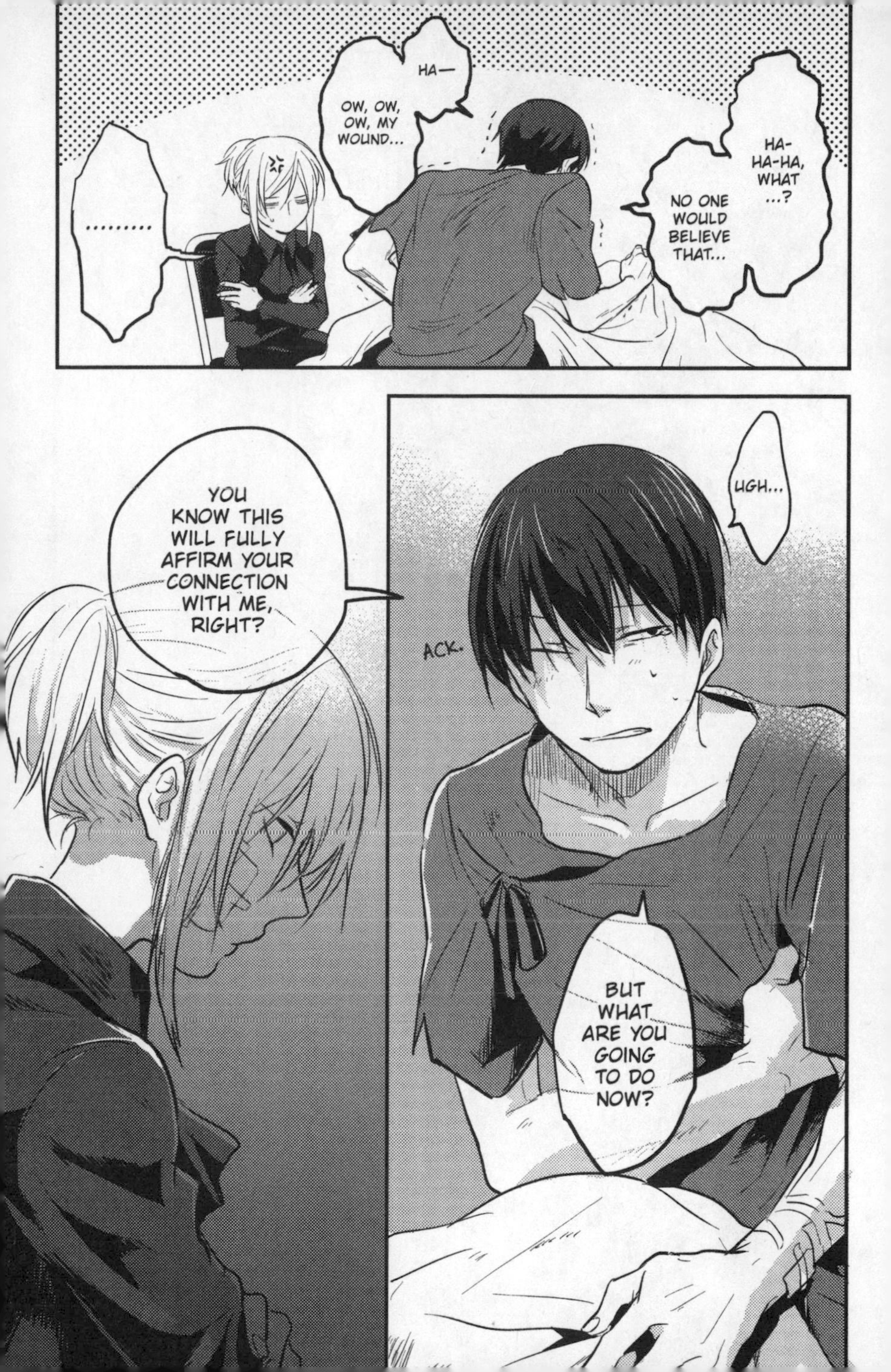
HA-HA-HA, WHAT ...?
NO ONE WOULD BELIEVE THAT...
HA—
OW, OW, OW, MY WOUND...
....
UGH...
ACK.
BUT WHAT ARE YOU GOING TO DO NOW?
YOU KNOW THIS WILL FULLY AFFIRM YOUR CONNECTION WITH ME, RIGHT?

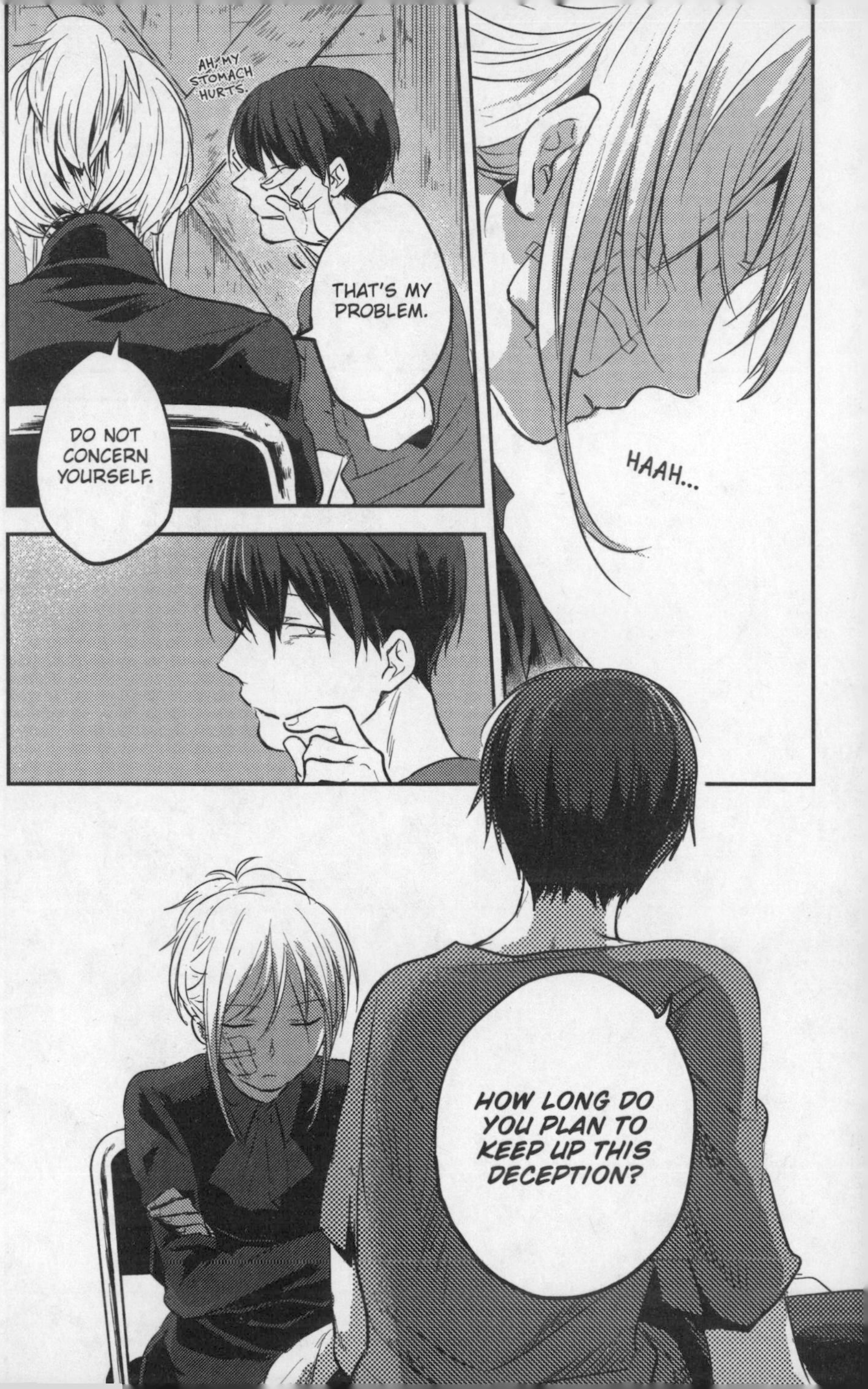
HAAH...
AH, MY STOMACH HURTS.
THAT'S MY PROBLEM.
DO NOT CONCERN YOURSELF.
HOW LONG DO YOU PLAN TO KEEP UP THIS DECEPTION?

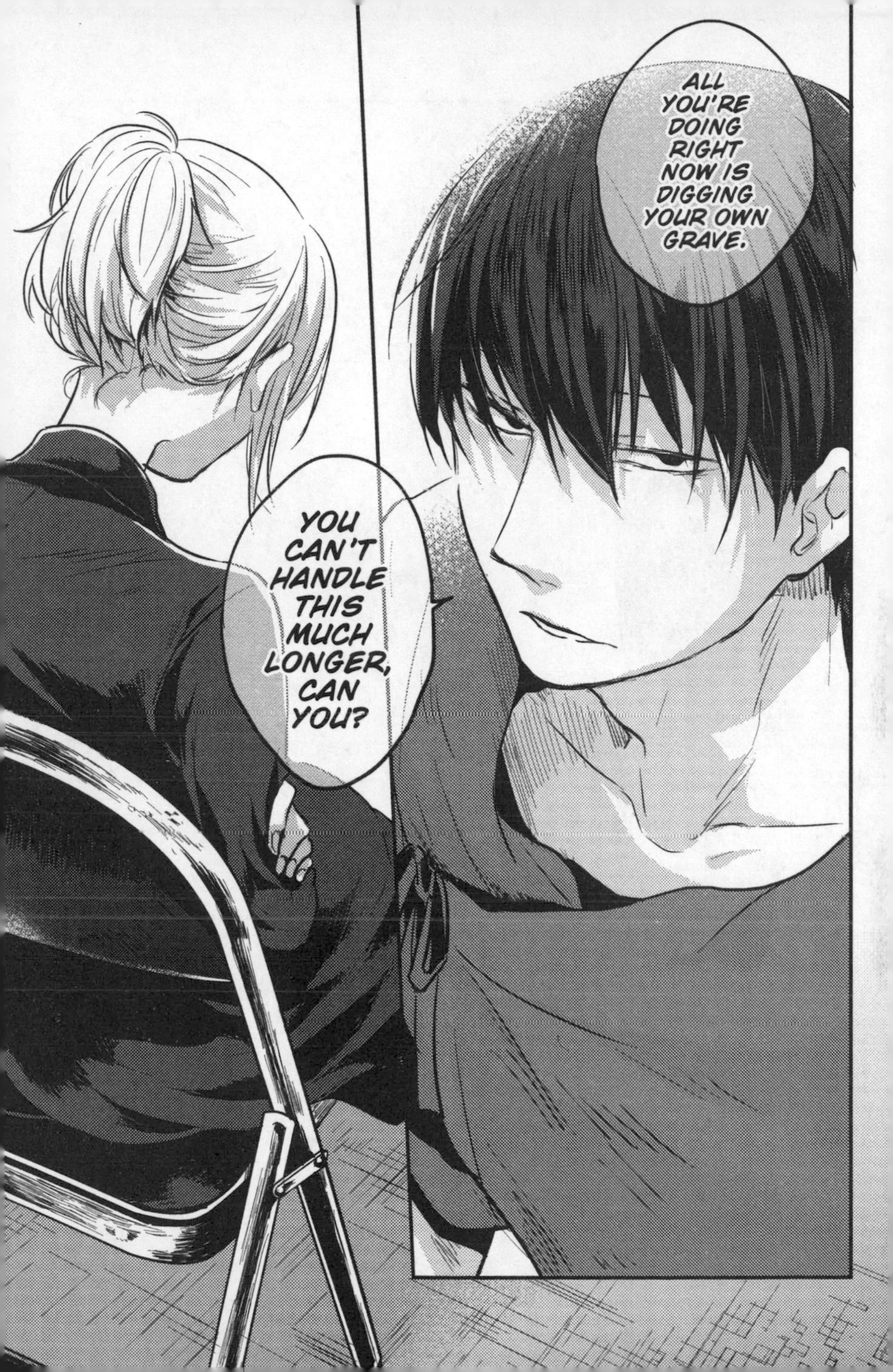
ALL YOU'RE DOING RIGHT NOW IS DIGGING YOUR OWN GRAVE.
YOU CAN'T HANDLE THIS MUCH LONGER, CAN YOU?

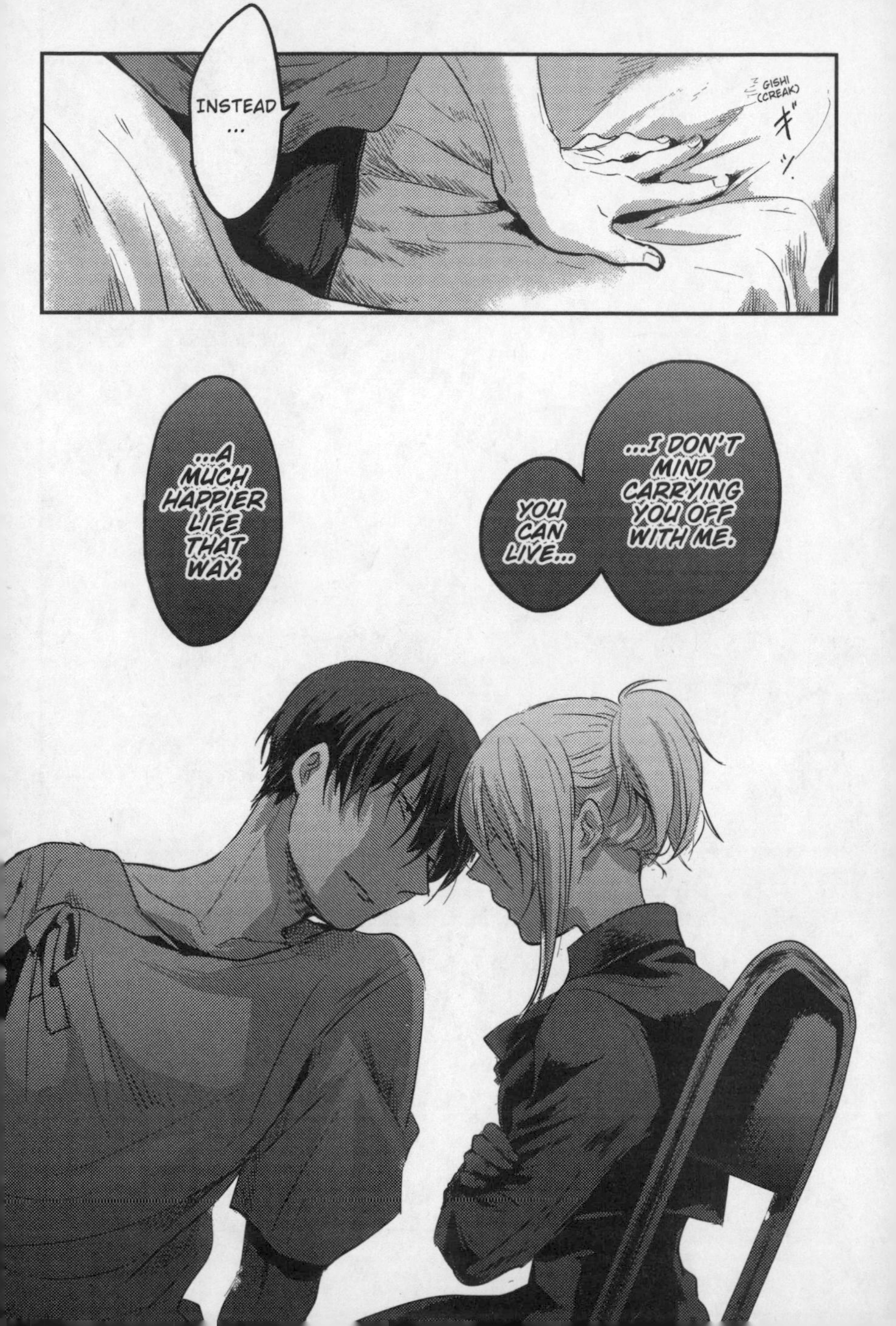
GISHI (CREAK)
INSTEAD ...
...I DON'T MIND CARRYING YOU OFF WITH ME.
YOU CAN LIVE...
...A MUCH HAPPIER LIFE THAT WAY.

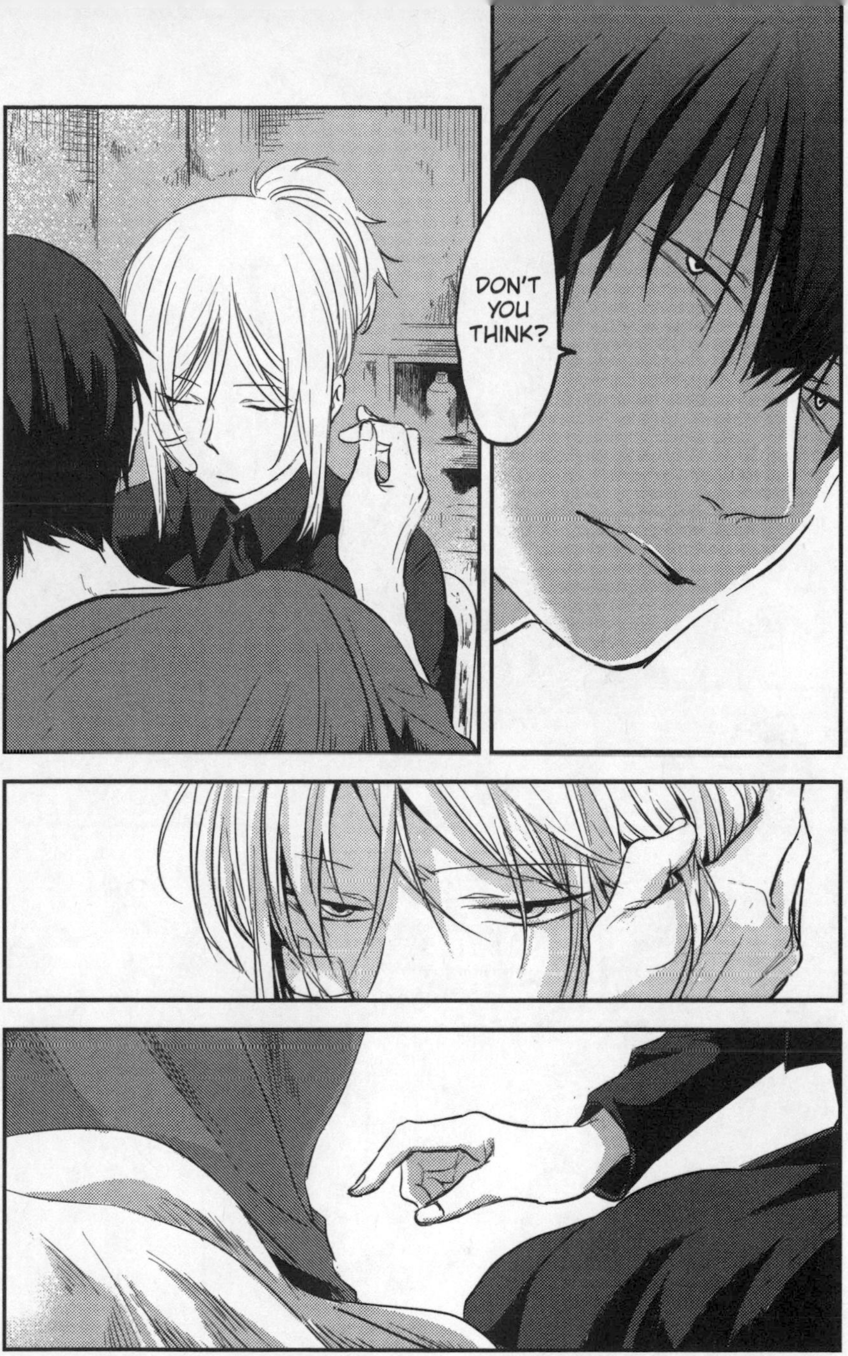
DON'T YOU THINK?

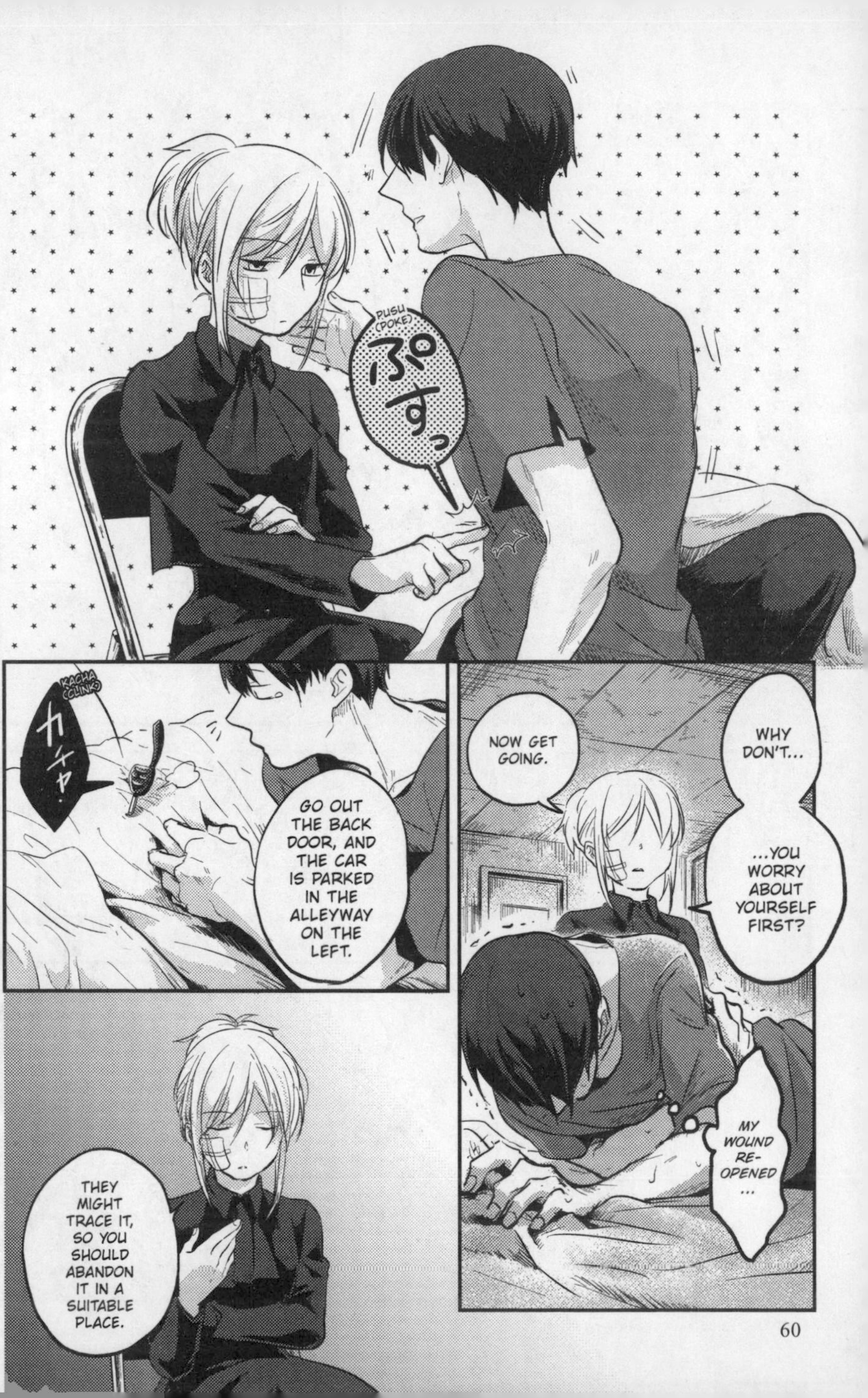
PUSU (POKE)
ぷすっ
WHY DON'T...
...YOU WORRY ABOUT YOURSELF FIRST?
NOW GET GOING.
MY WOUND RE-OPENED...
GO OUT THE BACK DOOR, AND THE CAR IS PARKED IN THE ALLEYWAY ON THE LEFT.
KACHA (CLINK)
カチャ
THEY MIGHT TRACE IT, SO YOU SHOULD ABANDON IT IN A SUITABLE PLACE.

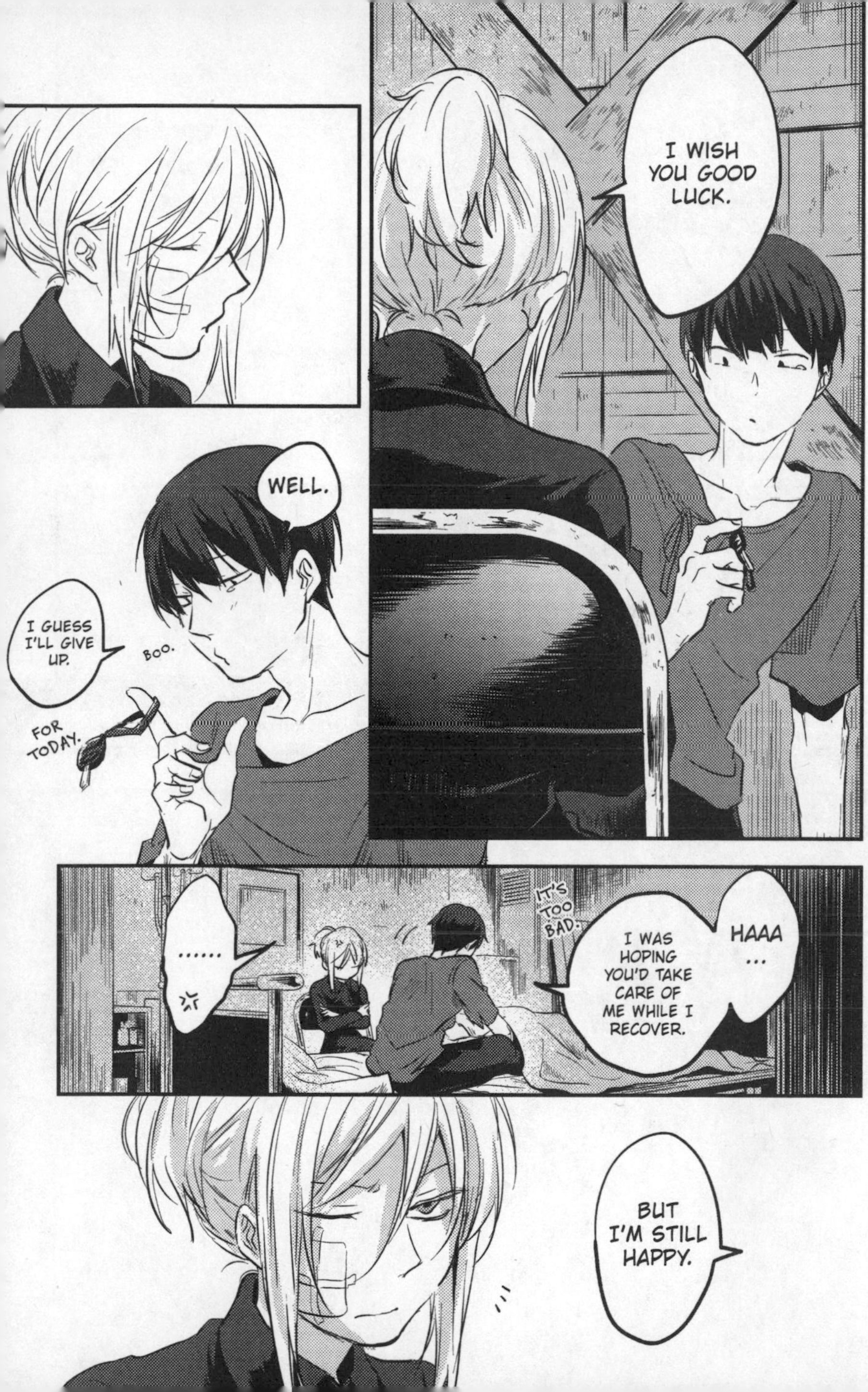
I WISH YOU GOOD LUCK.
WELL.
I GUESS I'LL GIVE UP.
BOO.
FOR TODAY.
HAAA ...
I WAS HOPING YOU'D TAKE CARE OF ME WHILE I RECOVER.
IT'S TOO BAD.
......
BUT I'M STILL HAPPY.

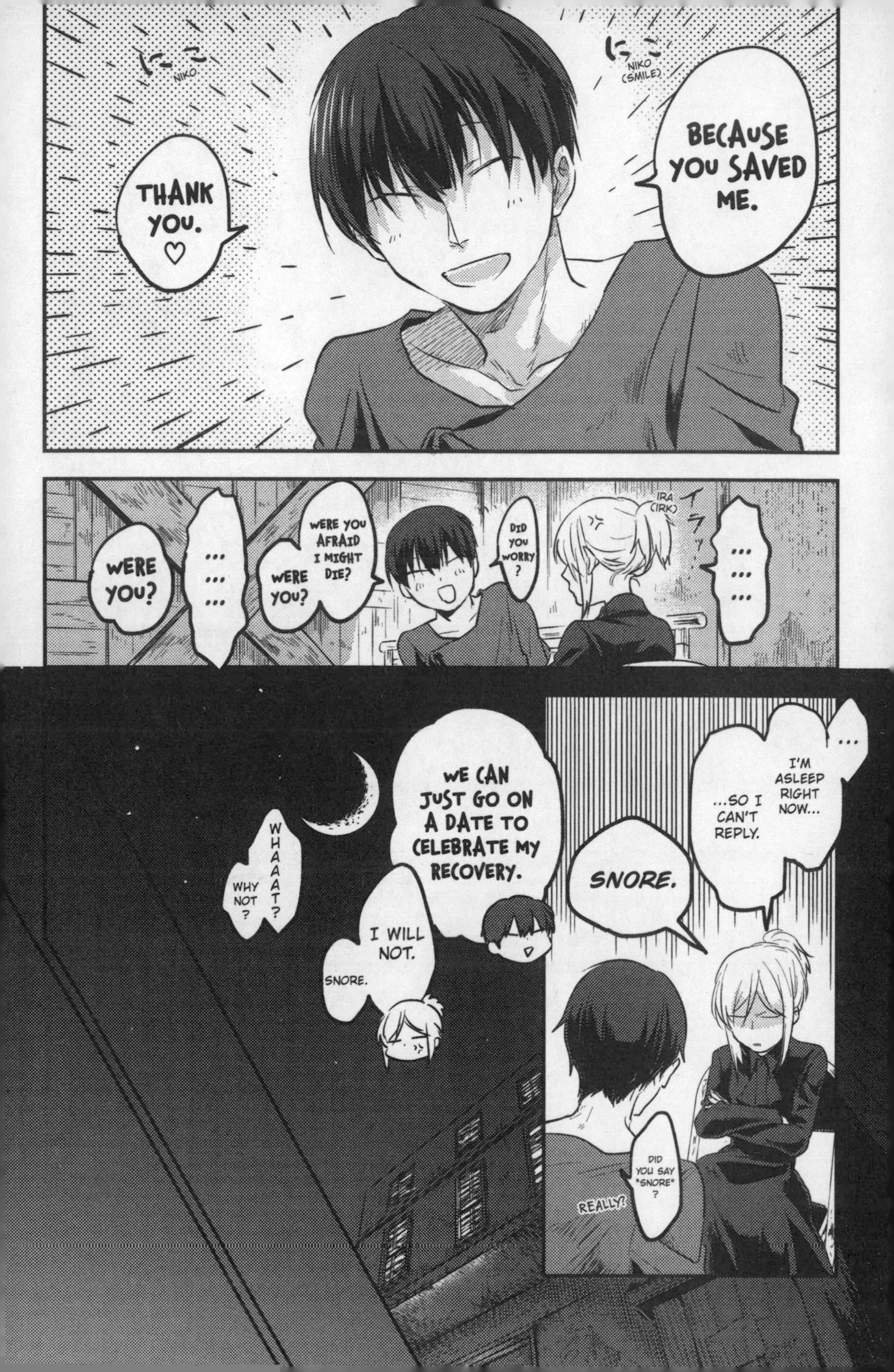
にこ NIKO (SMILE)
BECAUSE YOU SAVED ME.
にこ NIKO
THANK YOU. ♡
イラッ IRA (IRK)
... ...
DID YOU WORRY?
WERE YOU AFRAID I MIGHT DIE?
WERE YOU?
... ...
WERE YOU?
...
I'M ASLEEP RIGHT NOW...
...SO I CAN'T REPLY.
SNORE.
DID YOU SAY "SNORE"?
REALLY?
WE CAN JUST GO ON A DATE TO CELEBRATE MY RECOVERY.
I WILL NOT.
SNORE.
WHAAAAT?
WHY NOT?

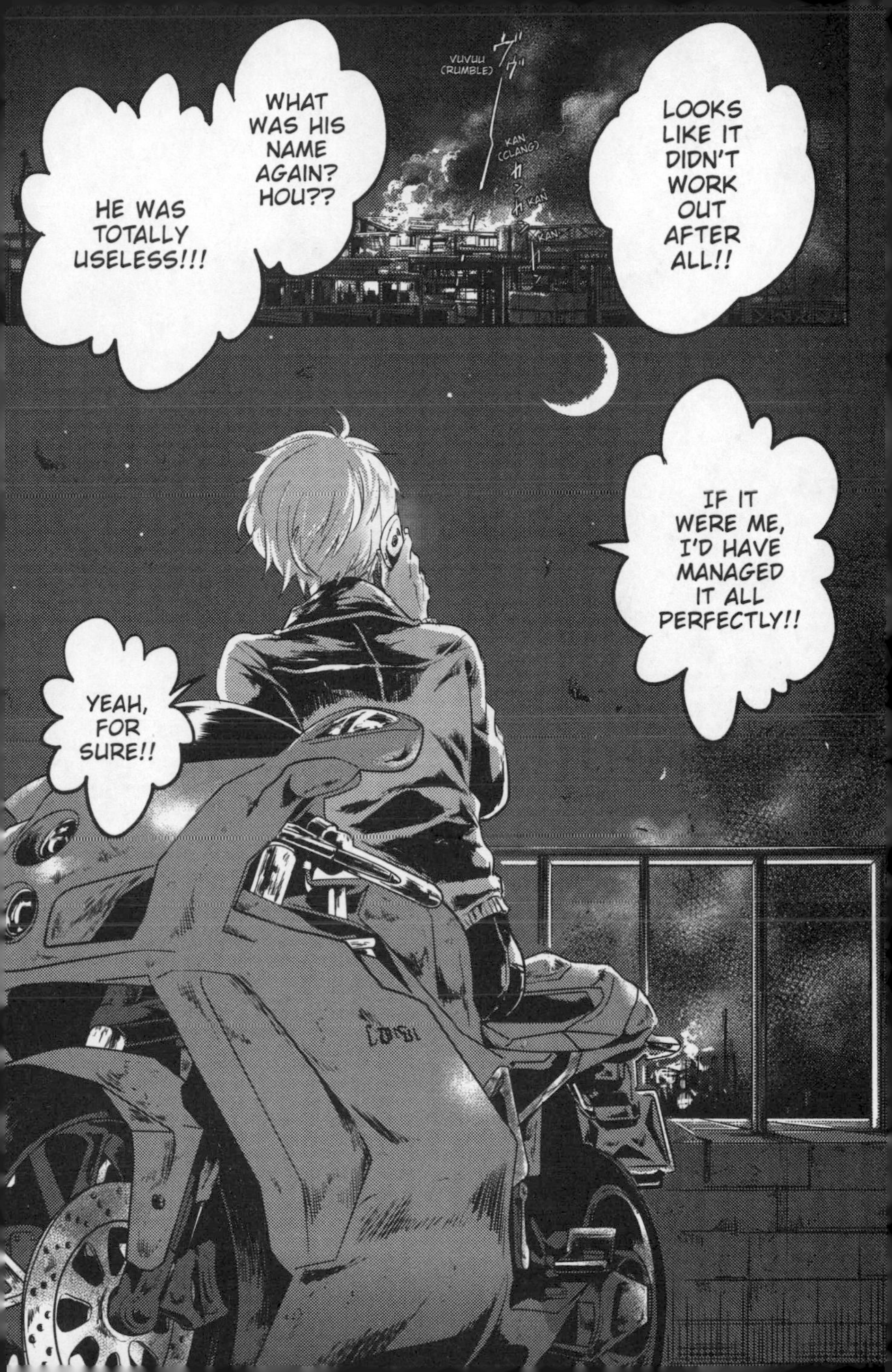
LOOKS LIKE IT DIDN'T WORK OUT AFTER ALL!!
VUVUU (RUMBLE)
KAN (CLANG)
KAN
KAN
WHAT WAS HIS NAME AGAIN? HOU??
HE WAS TOTALLY USELESS!!!
IF IT WERE ME, I'D HAVE MANAGED IT ALL PERFECTLY!!
YEAH, FOR SURE!!

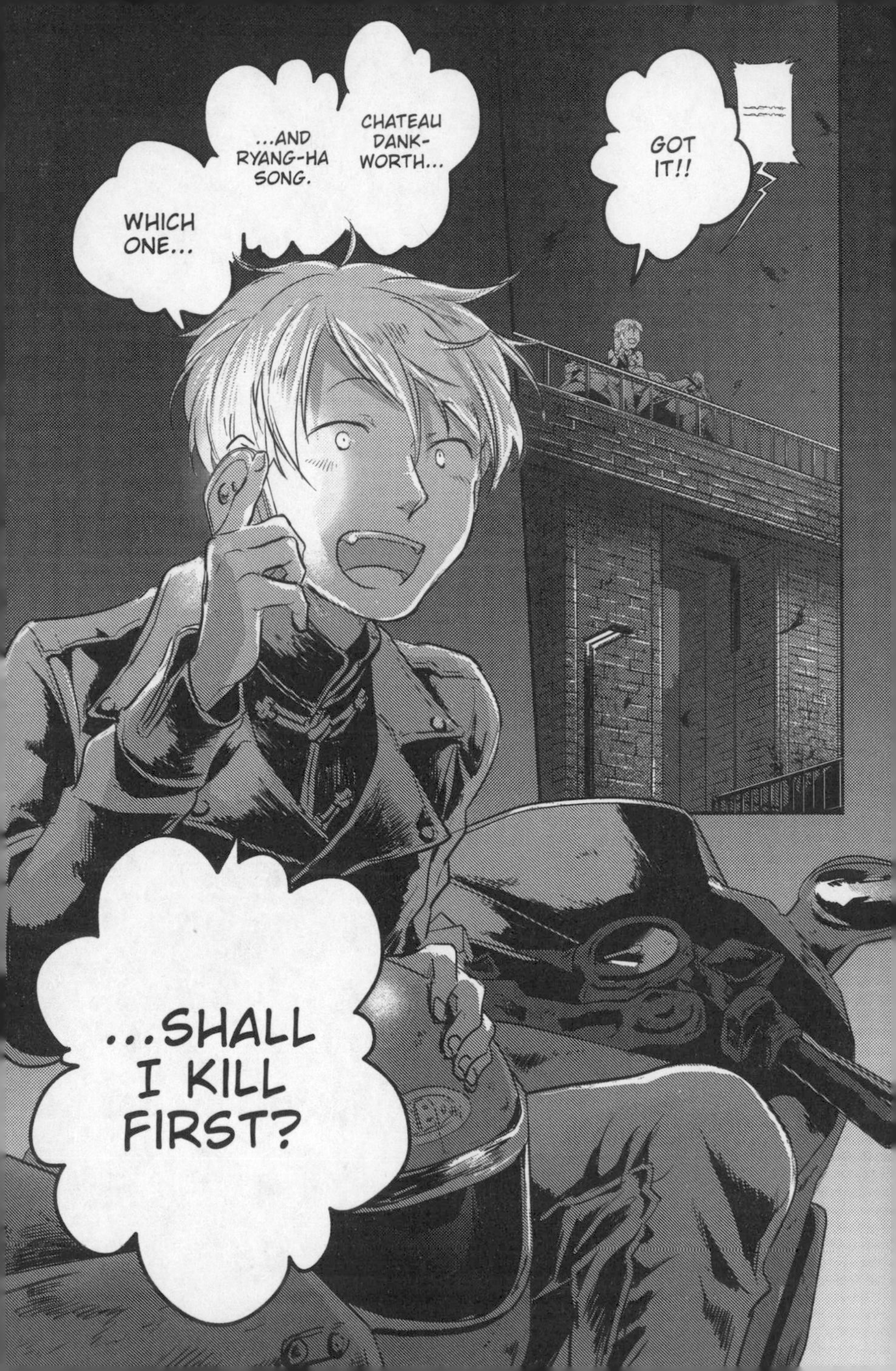
GOT IT!!
CHATEAU DANK-WORTH...
...AND RYANG-HA SONG.
WHICH ONE...
...SHALL I KILL FIRST?

FILE 13: DISTINCTION

THESE WERE ACTUALLY THE LEAD COLOR PAGES IN THE MAGAZINE. HOU SPOUTS WONDERFULLY CHEESY LINES LIKE "YOU TRYING TO BE A HERO?" AND "ROUND TWO." I'M QUITE FOND OF THAT KIND OF THING, LOL, SO I FOUND HOU AN EASY CHARACTER TO WRITE DIALOGUE FOR.

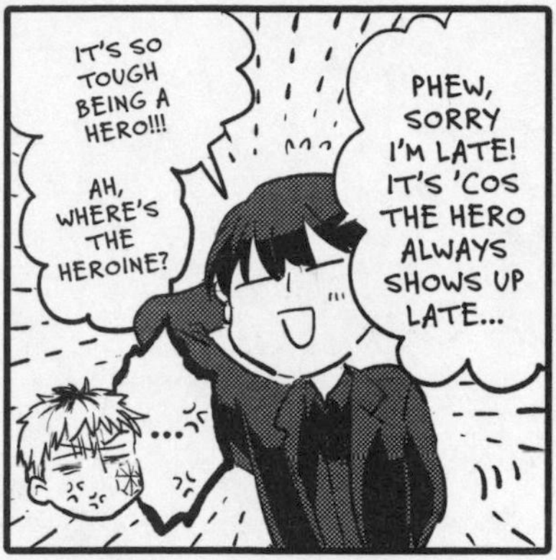
PHEW, SORRY I'M LATE! IT'S 'COS THE HERO ALWAYS SHOWS UP LATE...
IT'S SO TOUGH BEING A HERO!!!
AH, WHERE'S THE HEROINE?
...

FILE 14: SETTLEMENT

IN THIS CHAPTER, CHATEAU BREAKS HER OWN RECORD FOR NEVER DYING. SEEING AS IT'S THIS MANGA, SHE SURVIVED, BUT IF THIS WAS *ANO**ER*, SHE WOULD'VE DIED IN CHAPTER 10... ON REFLECTION, I DO WISH I HAD DEVELOPED THE SHOWDOWN WITH HOU A LITTLE MORE...IT'S OVER TOO QUICKLY...

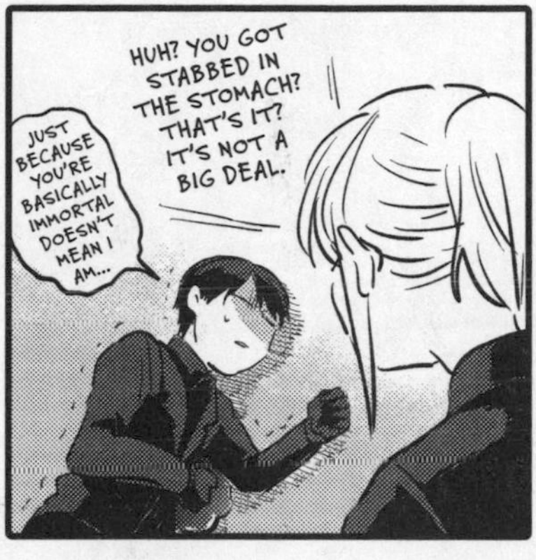
HUH? YOU GOT STABBED IN THE STOMACH? THAT'S IT? IT'S NOT A BIG DEAL.
JUST BECAUSE YOU'RE BASICALLY IMMORTAL DOESN'T MEAN I AM...

FILE 15: LIMIT

A BREATHER CHAPTER.
I INTENDED TO LET INDIAN GUY SHOW OFF HIS ABILITY, BUT THAT FAILED SOMEWHAT, LOL...
A NEW CHARACTER ALSO APPEARED, BUT IT TURNED INTO ANOTHER CASE OF AN ENEMY CHARACTER WHOSE NAME DOESN'T CROP UP FOR SEVERAL CHAPTERS AFTER THEIR FIRST APPEARANCE...
IT'S HOU ALL OVER AGAIN...

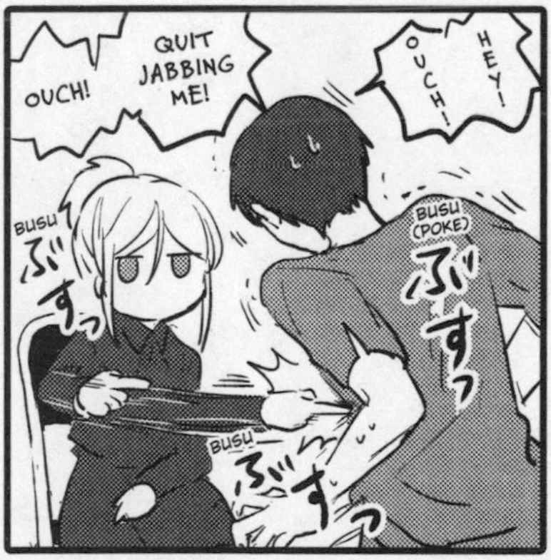
HEY!
OUCH!
QUIT JABBING ME!
OUCH!
BUSU (POKE)
ぶすっ
BUSU
ぶすっ
BUSU
ぶすっ

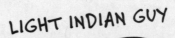

LIGHT INDIAN GUY

- LIGHT SKIN
- BLOND HAIR AND BLUE EYES
- ANGELIC CURLS

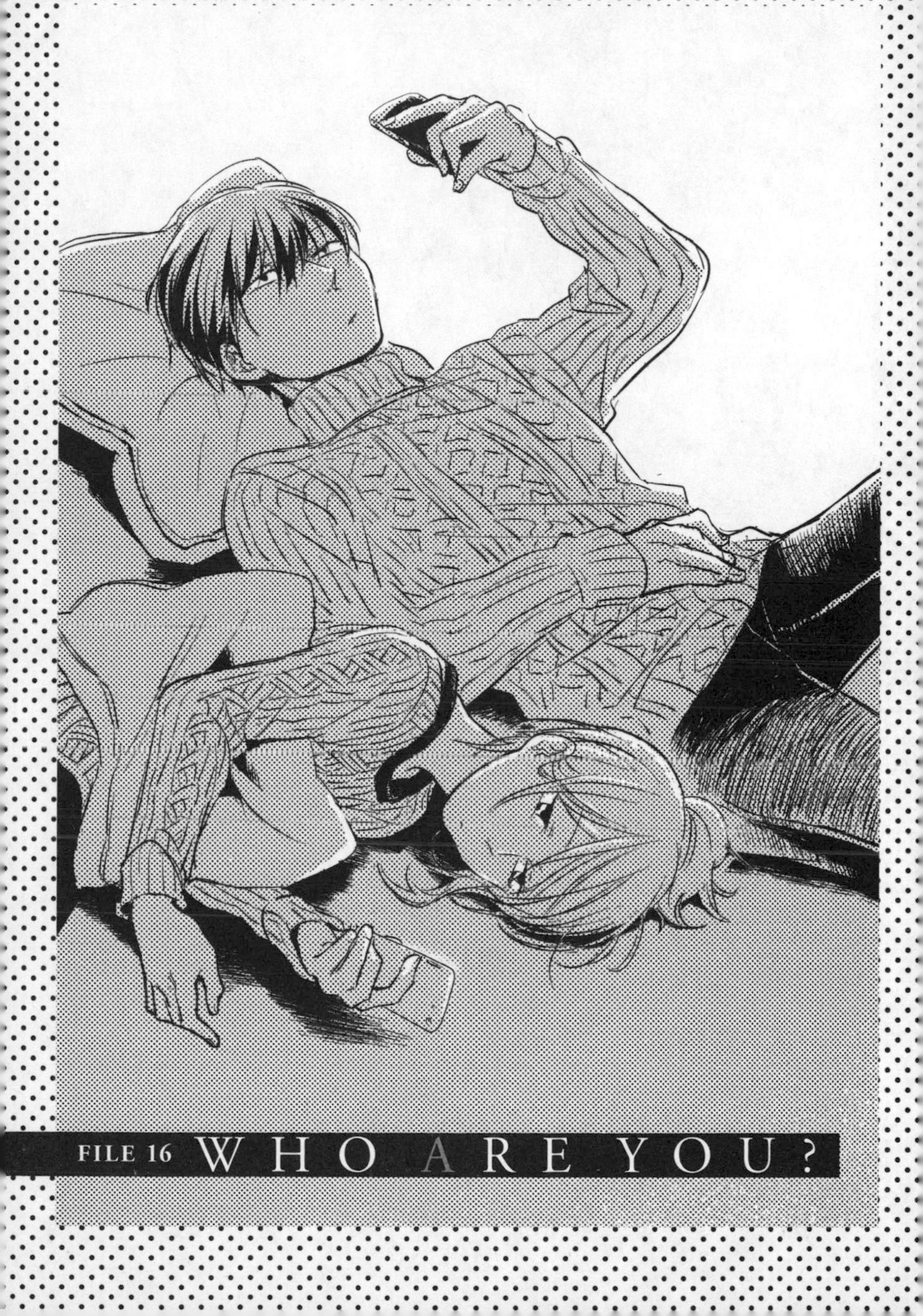

FILE 16 WHO ARE YOU?

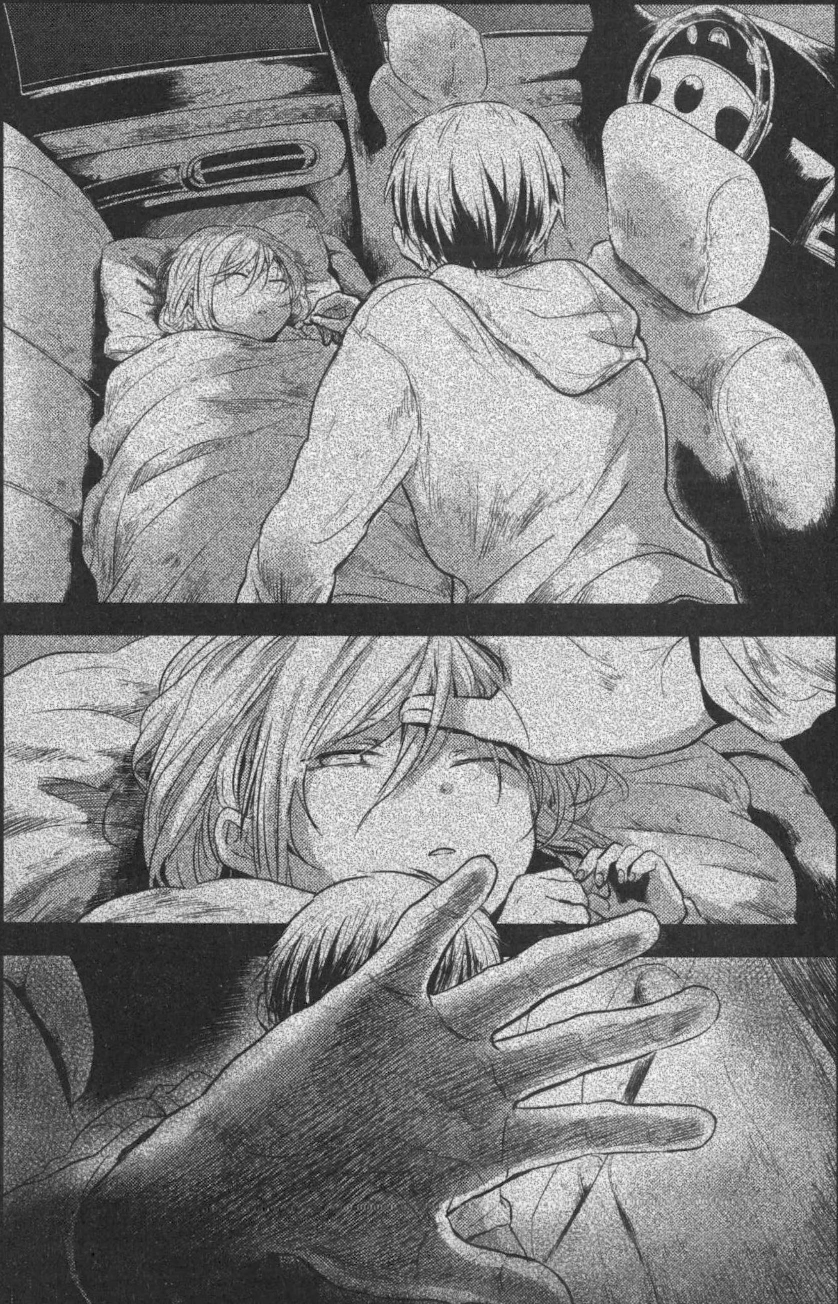

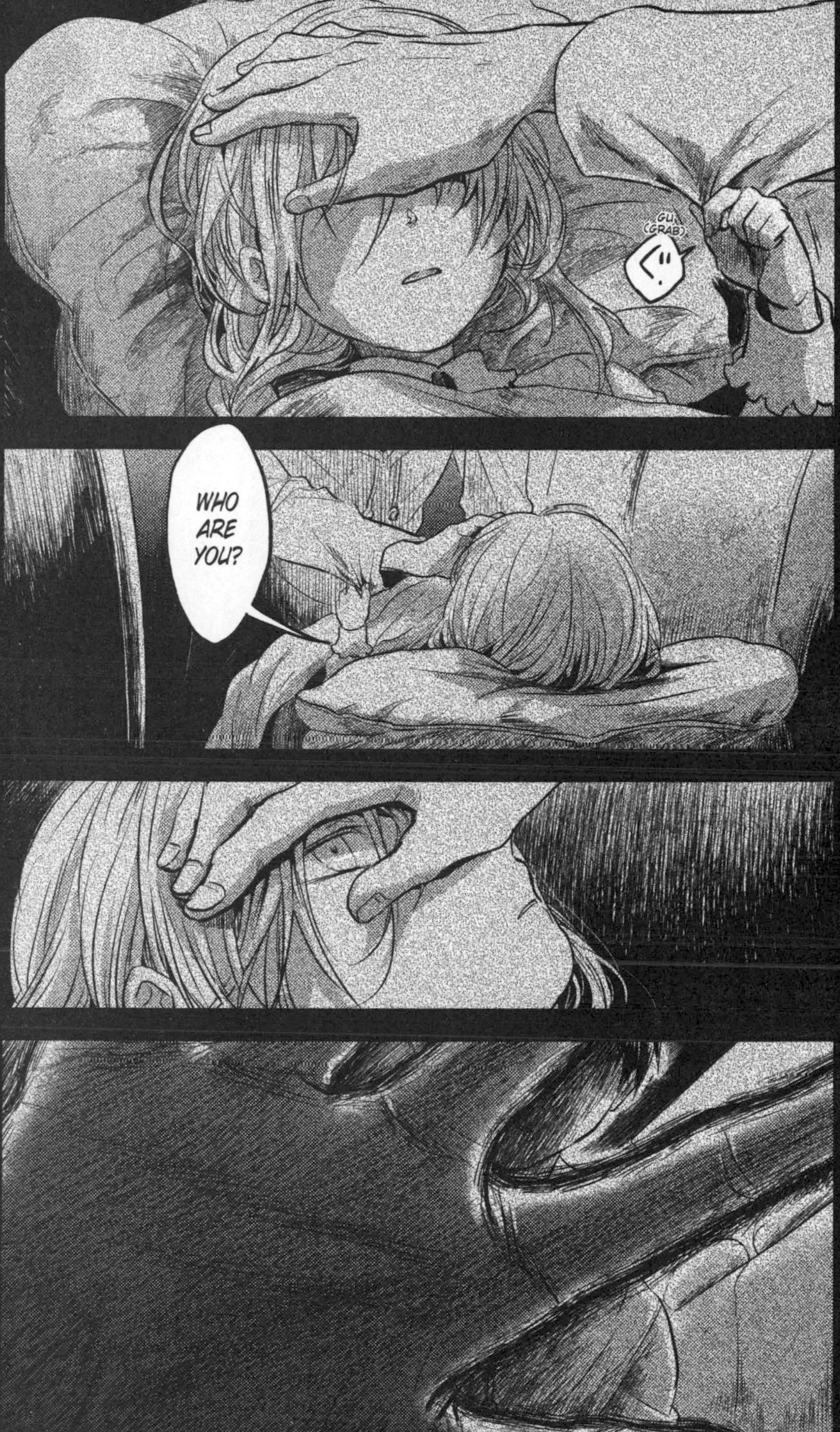
GU (GRAB)
WHO ARE YOU?

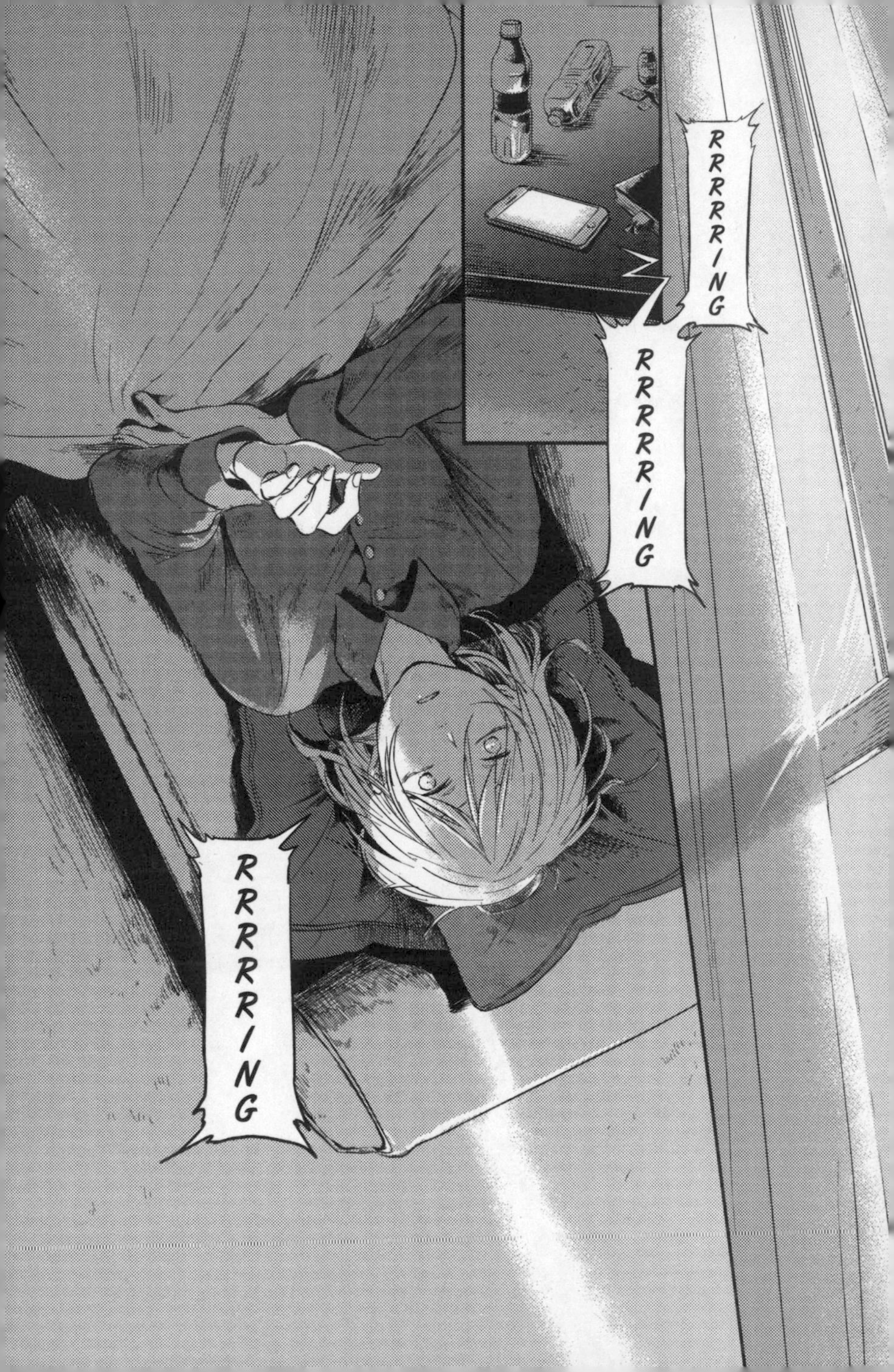
RRRRRING
RRRRRING
RRRRRING

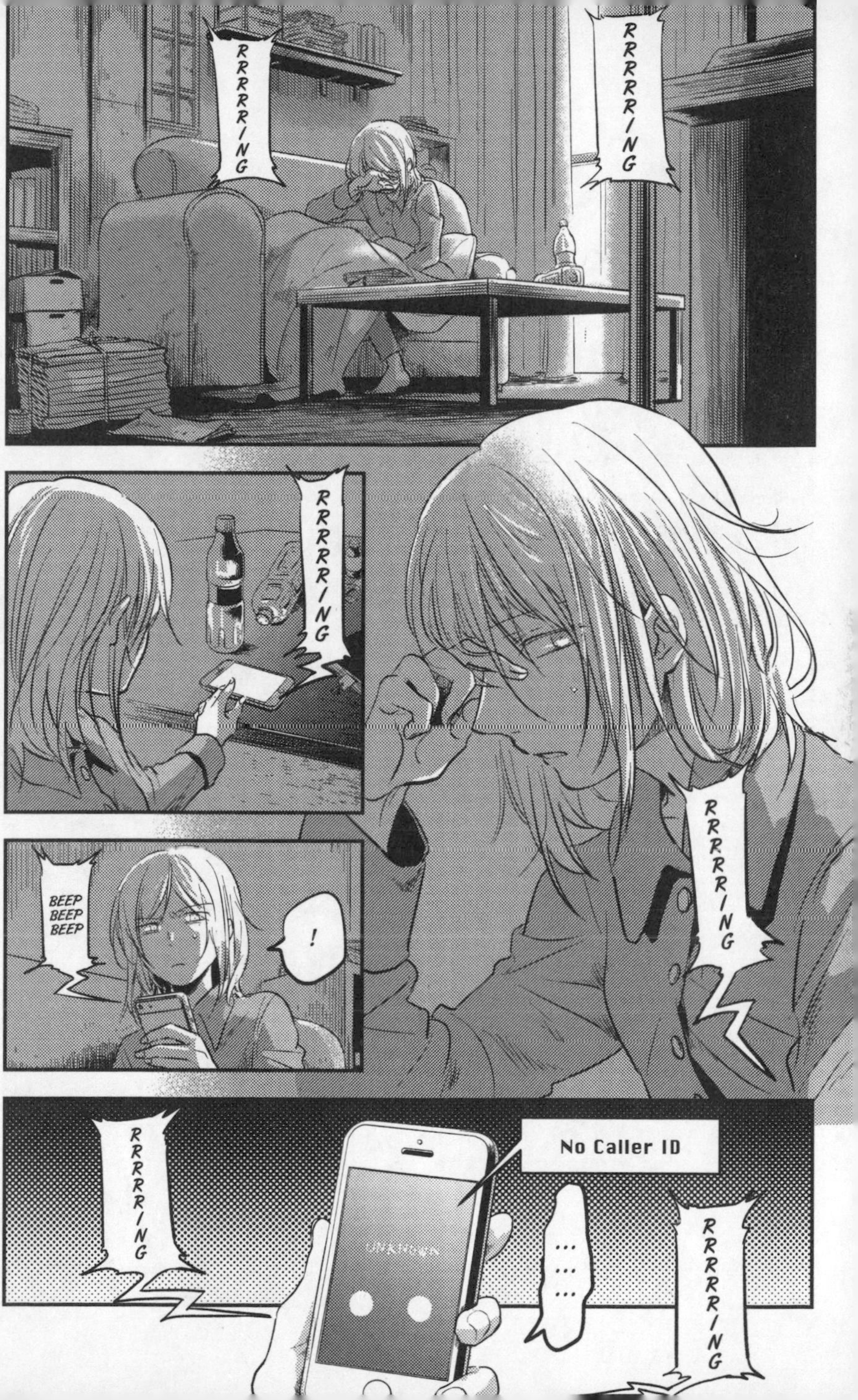

RRRRRING
RRRRRING
RRRRRING
RRRRRING
BEEP BEEP BEEP
!
No Caller ID
RRRRRING
...
...
...
RRRRRING

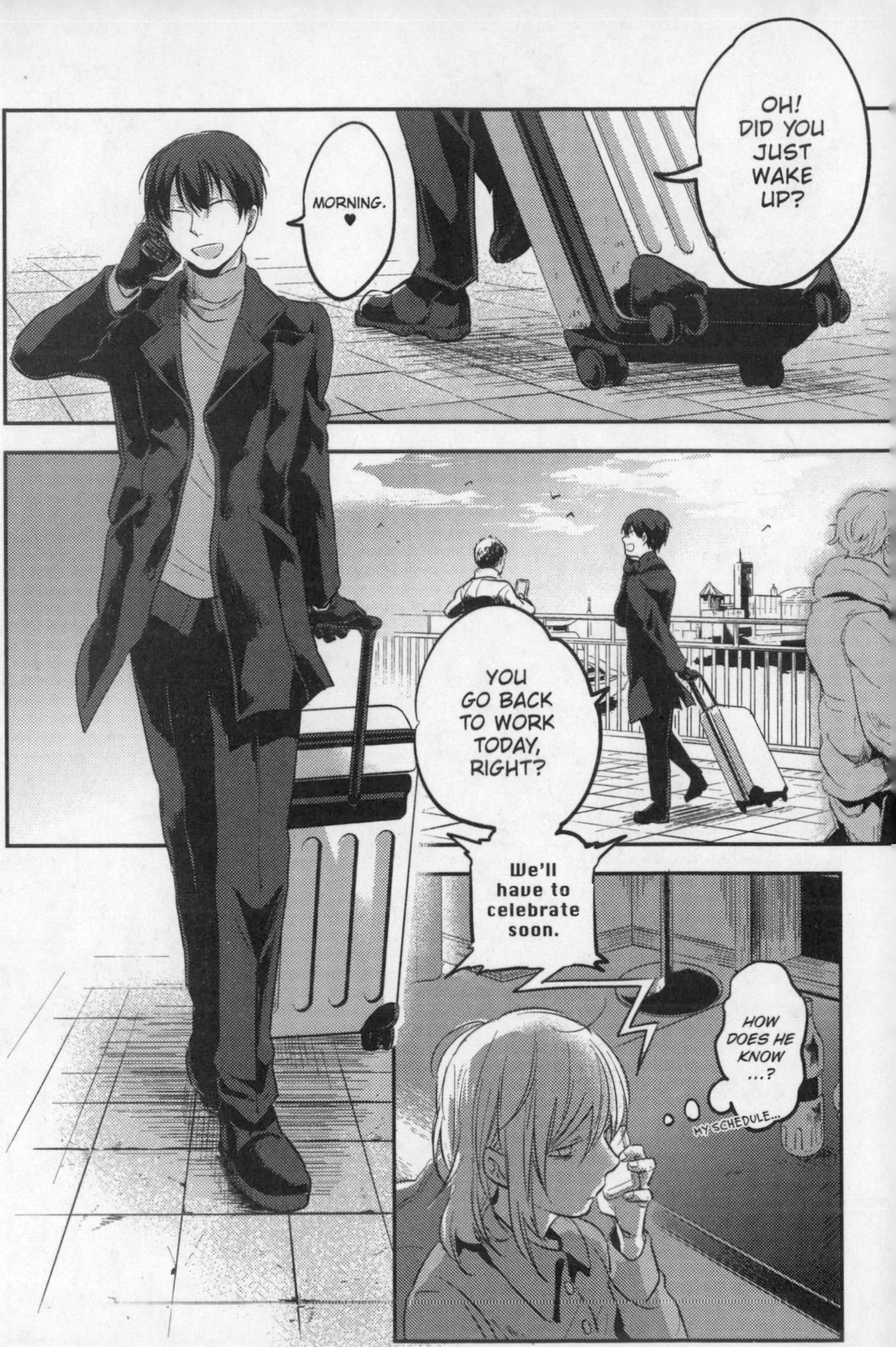
OH! DID YOU JUST WAKE UP?
YOU GO BACK TO WORK TODAY, RIGHT?
We'll have to celebrate soon.
HOW DOES HE KNOW ...?
MY SCHEDULE...
MORNING. ♥

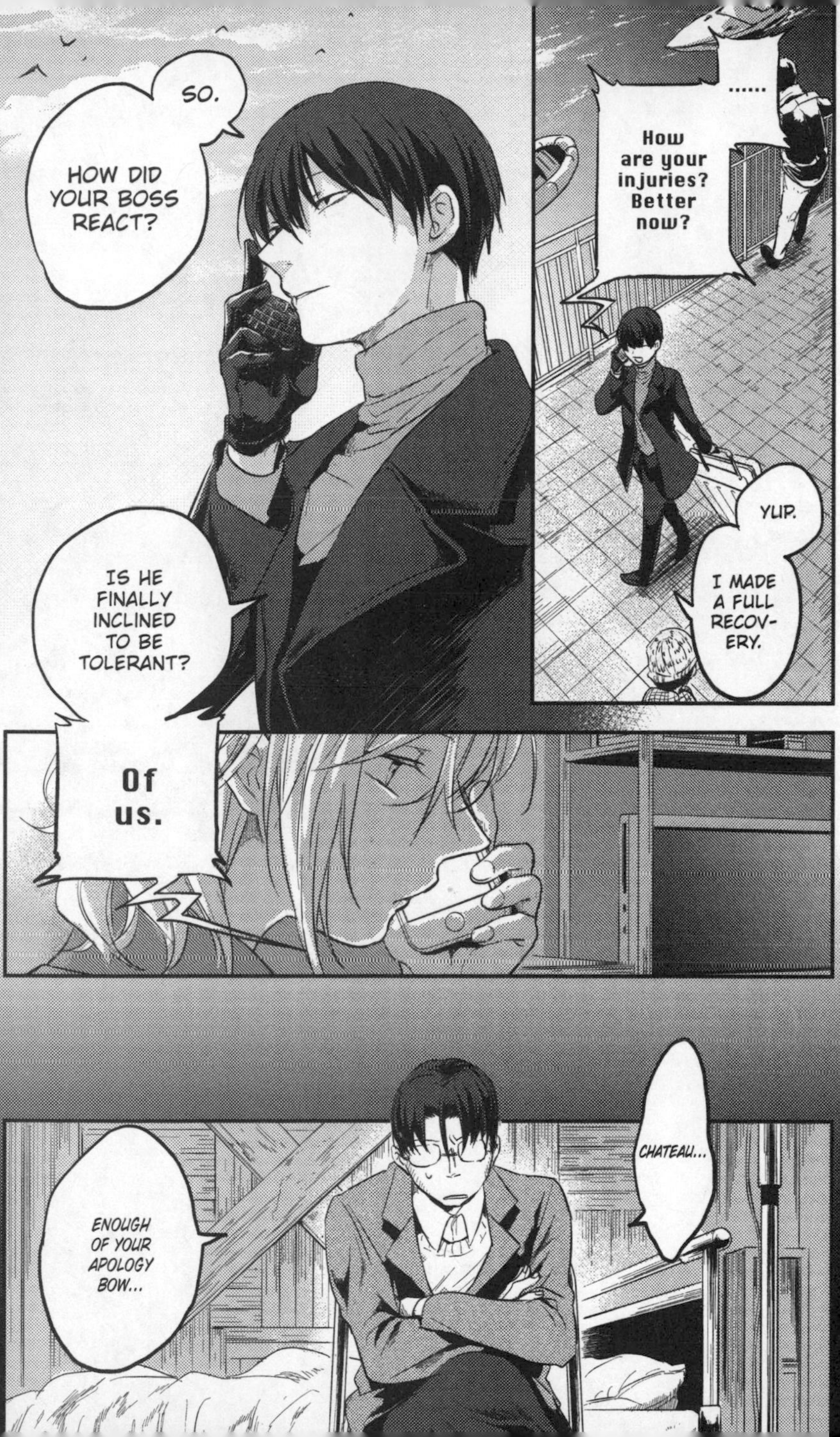
......
How are your injuries? Better now?
YUP.
I MADE A FULL RECOVERY.
SO.
HOW DID YOUR BOSS REACT?
IS HE FINALLY INCLINED TO BE TOLERANT?
Of us.
CHATEAU...
ENOUGH OF YOUR APOLOGY BOW...

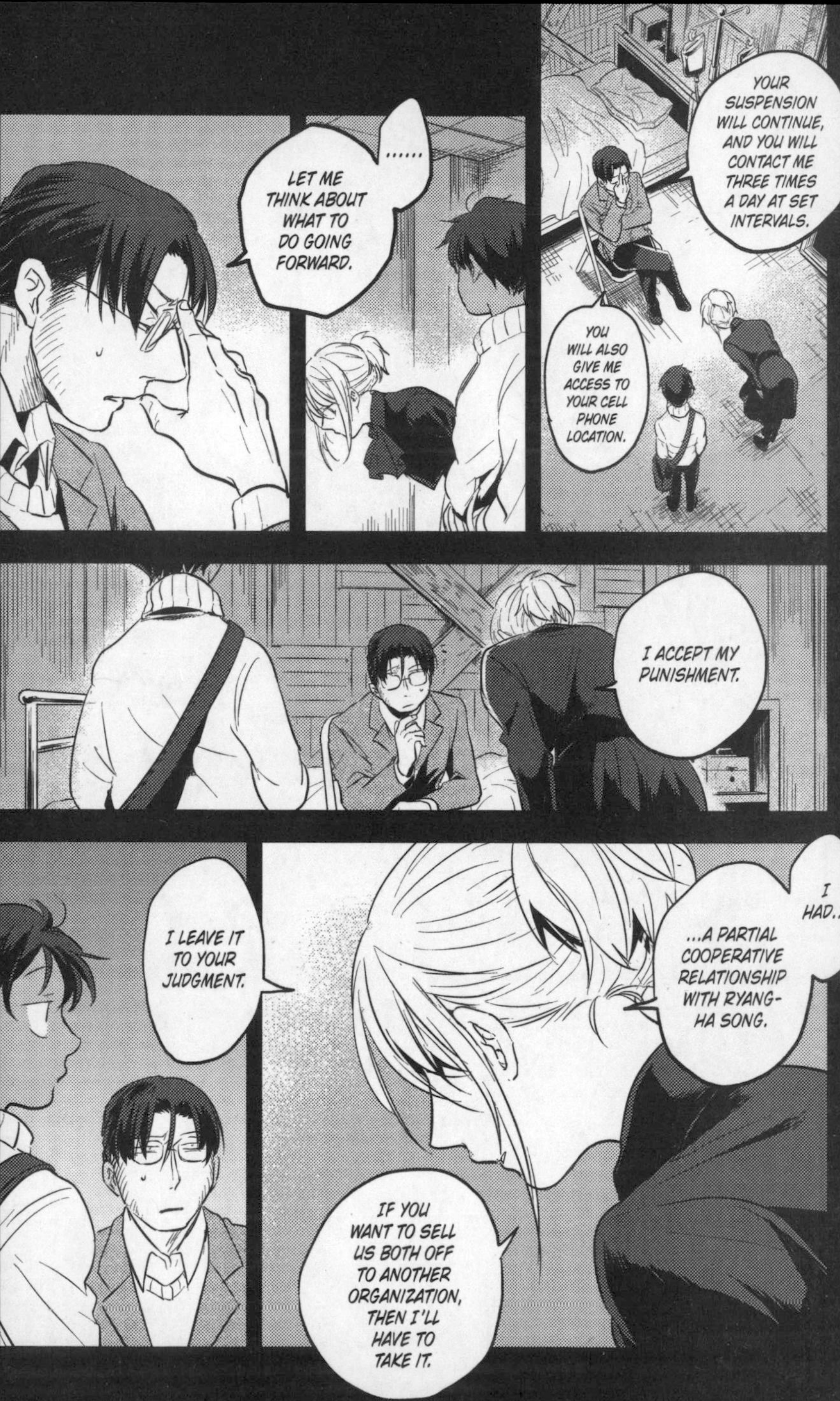
YOUR SUSPENSION WILL CONTINUE, AND YOU WILL CONTACT ME THREE TIMES A DAY AT SET INTERVALS.
YOU WILL ALSO GIVE ME ACCESS TO YOUR CELL PHONE LOCATION.
......
LET ME THINK ABOUT WHAT TO DO GOING FORWARD.
I ACCEPT MY PUNISHMENT.
I HAD...
...A PARTIAL COOPERATIVE RELATIONSHIP WITH RYANG-HA SONG.
IF YOU WANT TO SELL US BOTH OFF TO ANOTHER ORGANIZATION, THEN I'LL HAVE TO TAKE IT.
I LEAVE IT TO YOUR JUDGMENT.

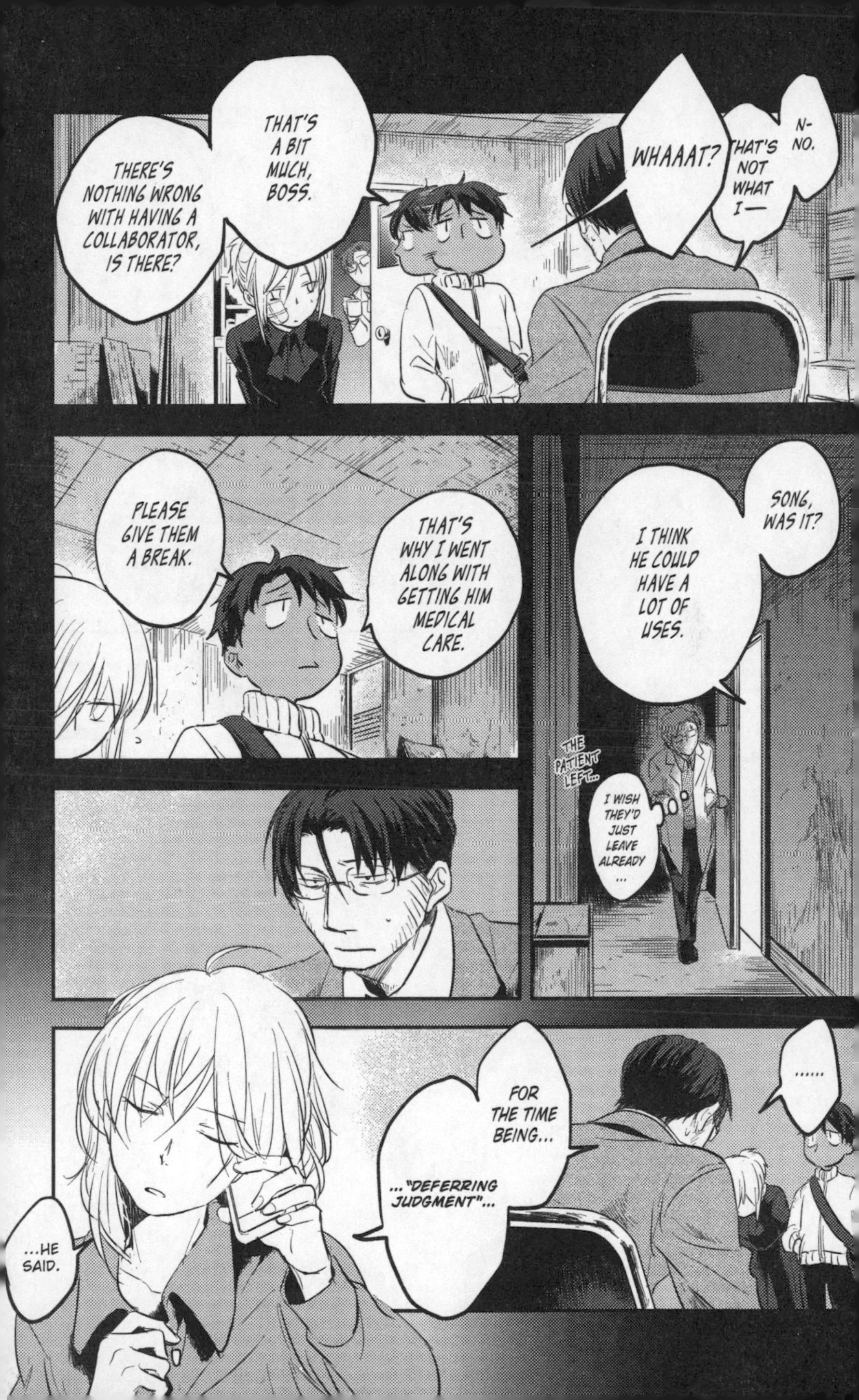
N-NO.
THAT'S NOT WHAT I—
WHAAAT?
THAT'S A BIT MUCH, BOSS.
THERE'S NOTHING WRONG WITH HAVING A COLLABORATOR, IS THERE?
SONG, WAS IT?
I THINK HE COULD HAVE A LOT OF USES.
THE PATIENT LEFT...
I WISH THEY'D JUST LEAVE ALREADY...
THAT'S WHY I WENT ALONG WITH GETTING HIM MEDICAL CARE.
PLEASE GIVE THEM A BREAK.
......
FOR THE TIME BEING...
..."DEFERRING JUDGMENT"...
...HE SAID.

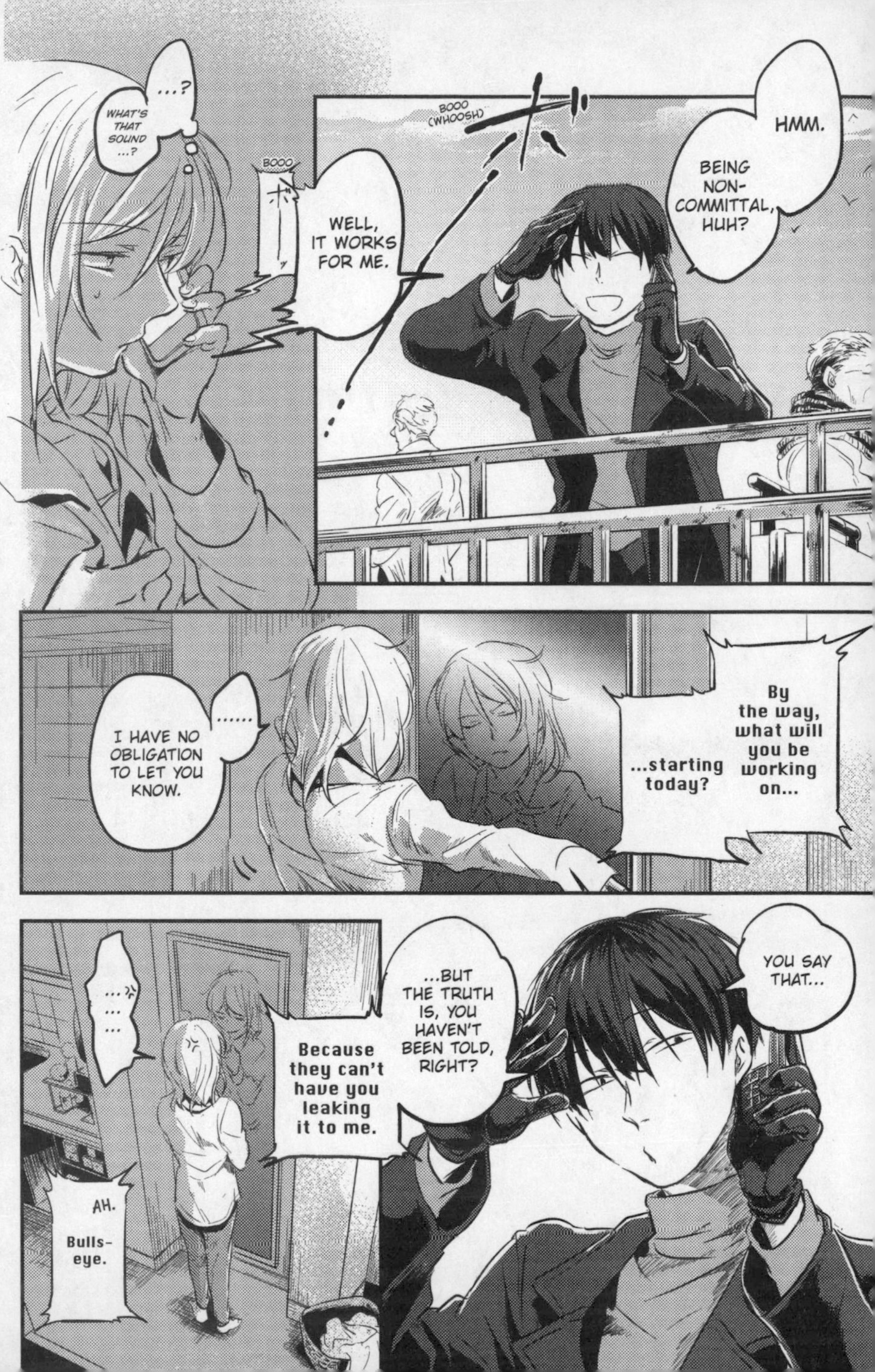
HMM.
BEING NON-COMMITTAL, HUH?
BOOO (WHOOSH)
WELL, IT WORKS FOR ME.
BOOO
...?
WHAT'S THAT SOUND ...?
By the way, what will you be working on...
...starting today?
......
I HAVE NO OBLIGATION TO LET YOU KNOW.
YOU SAY THAT...
...BUT THE TRUTH IS, YOU HAVEN'T BEEN TOLD, RIGHT?
Because they can't have you leaking it to me.
... ...
AH.
Bulls-eye.

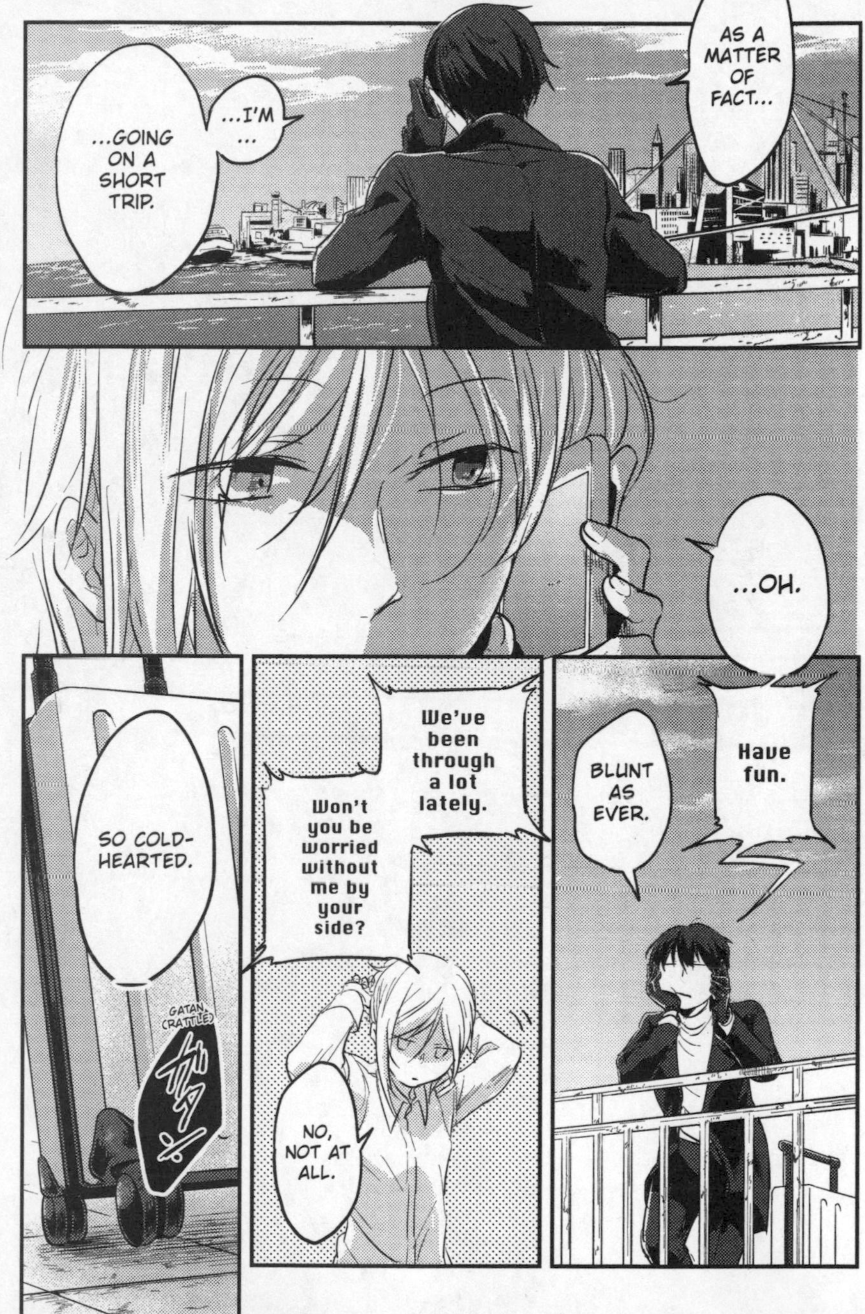

AS A MATTER OF FACT...
...I'M ...
...GOING ON A SHORT TRIP.
...OH.
Have fun.
BLUNT AS EVER.
We've been through a lot lately.
Won't you be worried without me by your side?
NO, NOT AT ALL.
SO COLD-HEARTED.
GATAN (RATTLE)

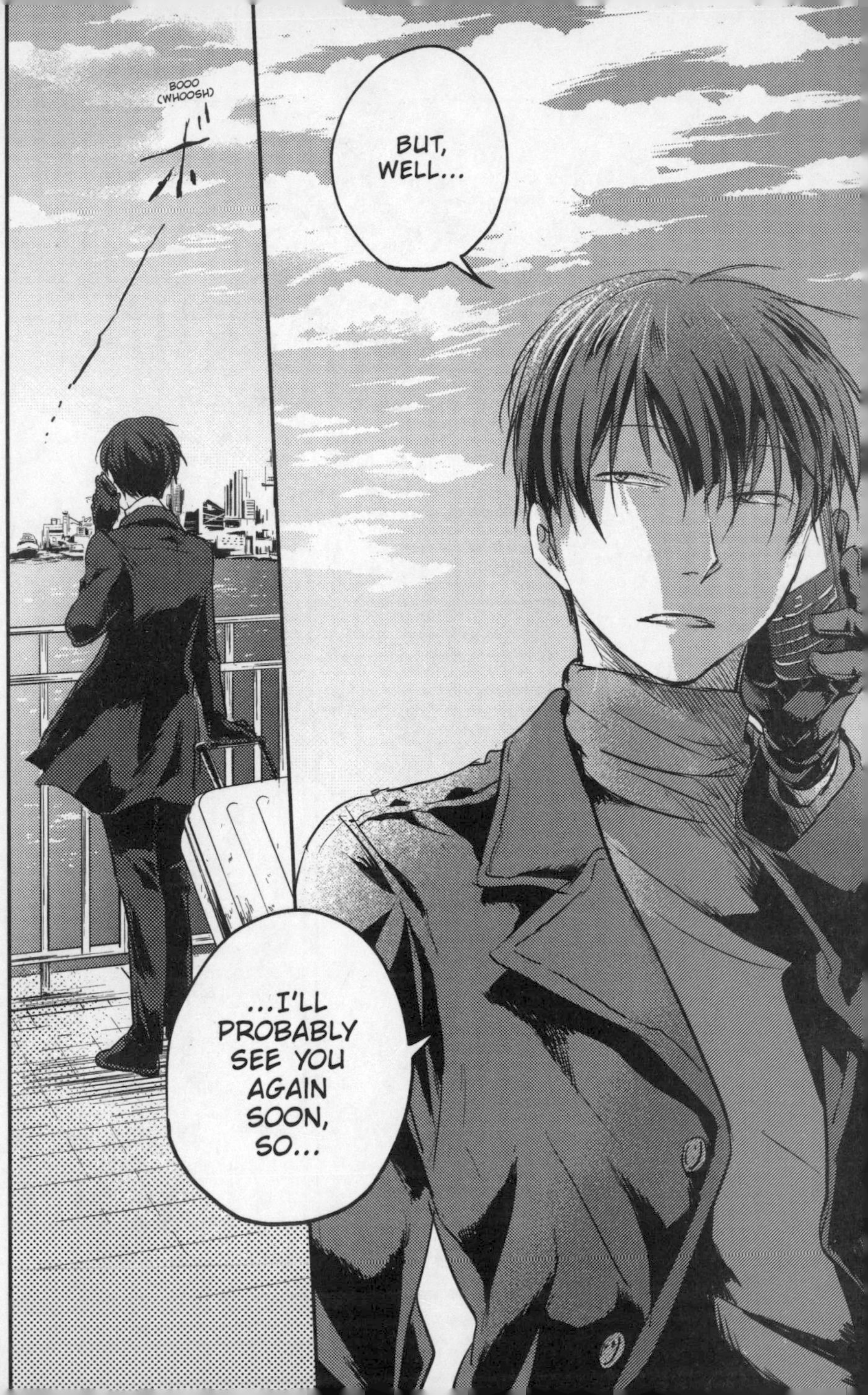
BUT, WELL...
...I'LL PROBABLY SEE YOU AGAIN SOON, SO...
BOOO (WHOOSH)

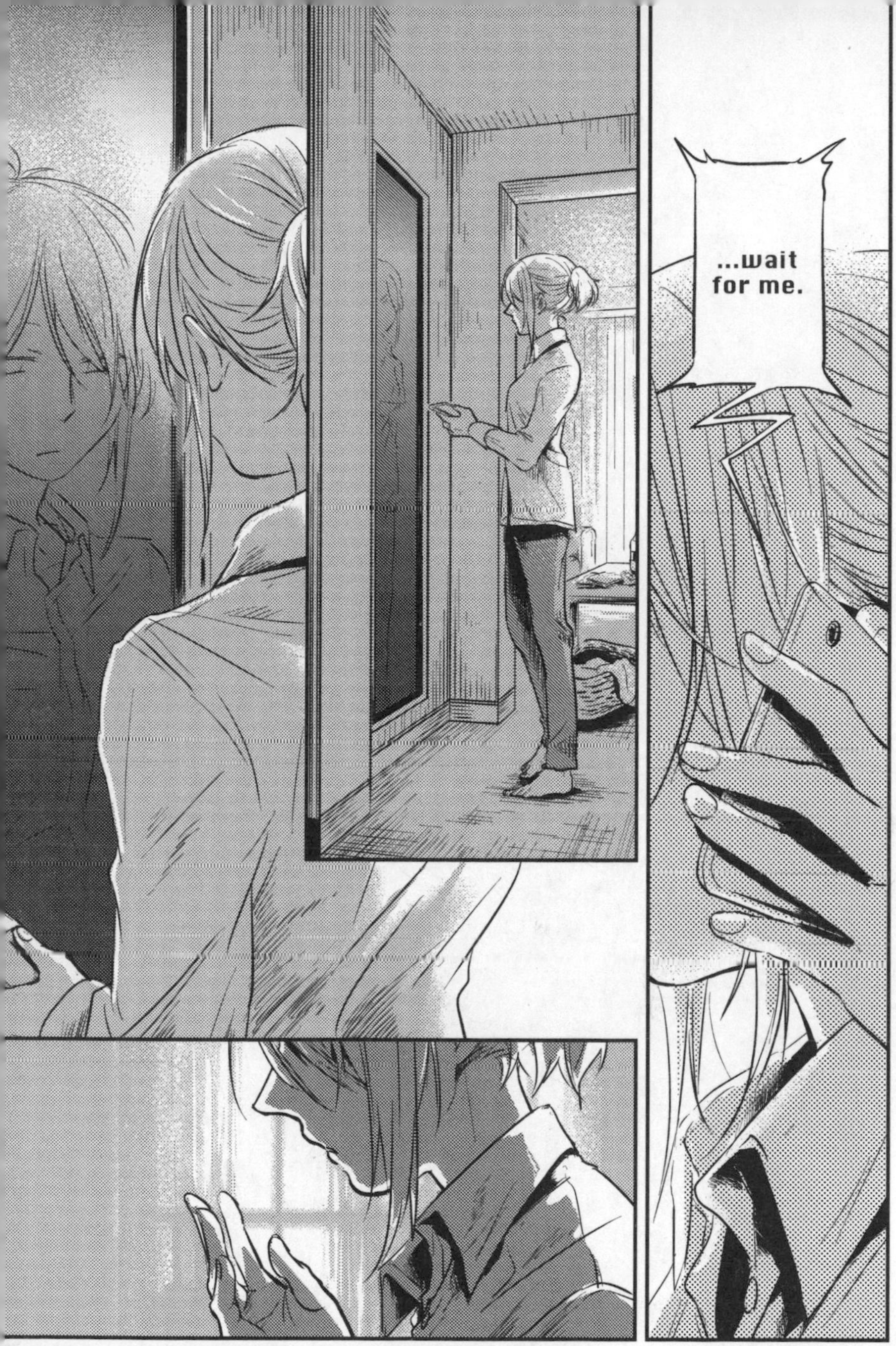
...wait for me.

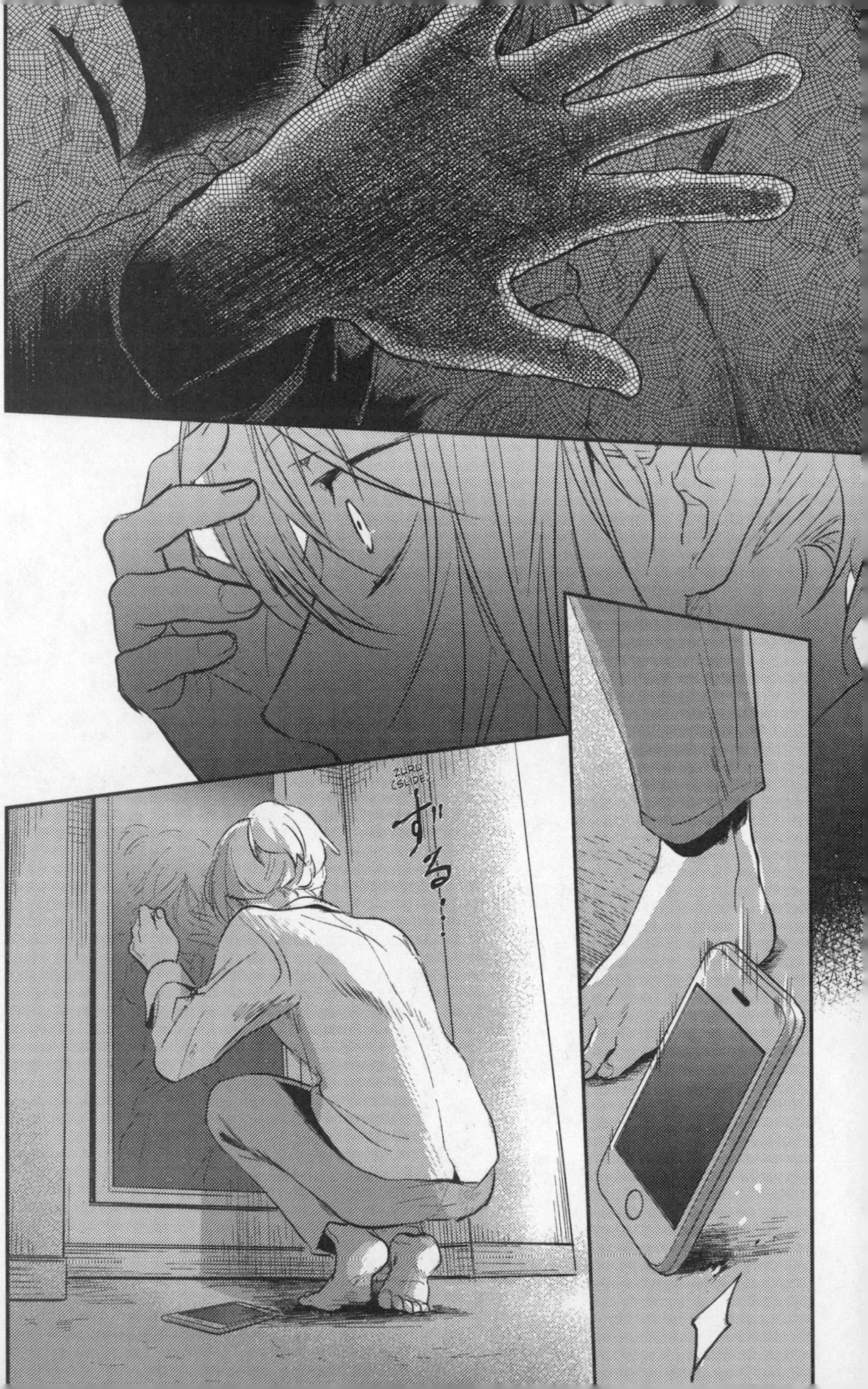
ZURU (SLIDE)
ずる……

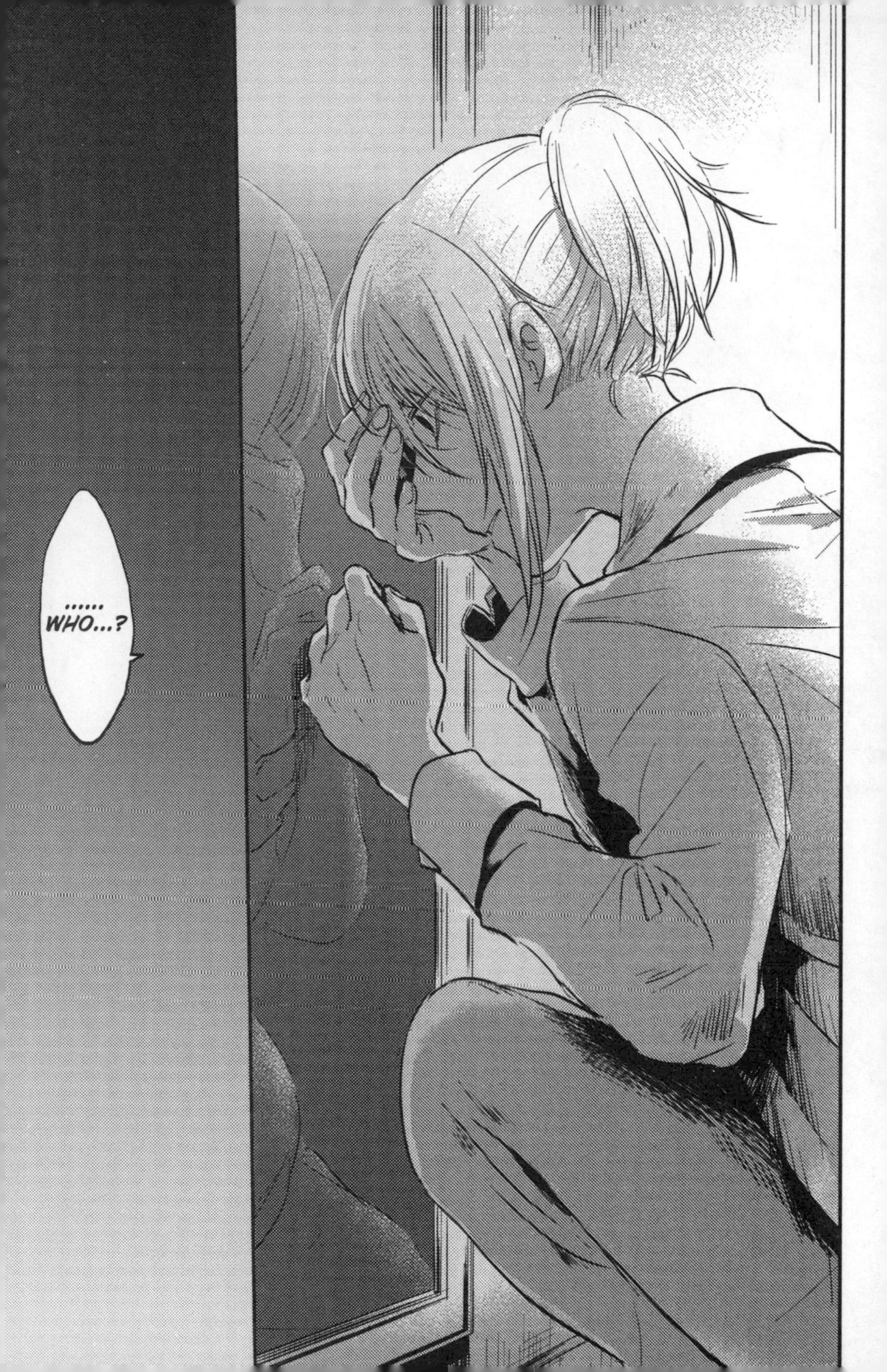
......
WHO...?

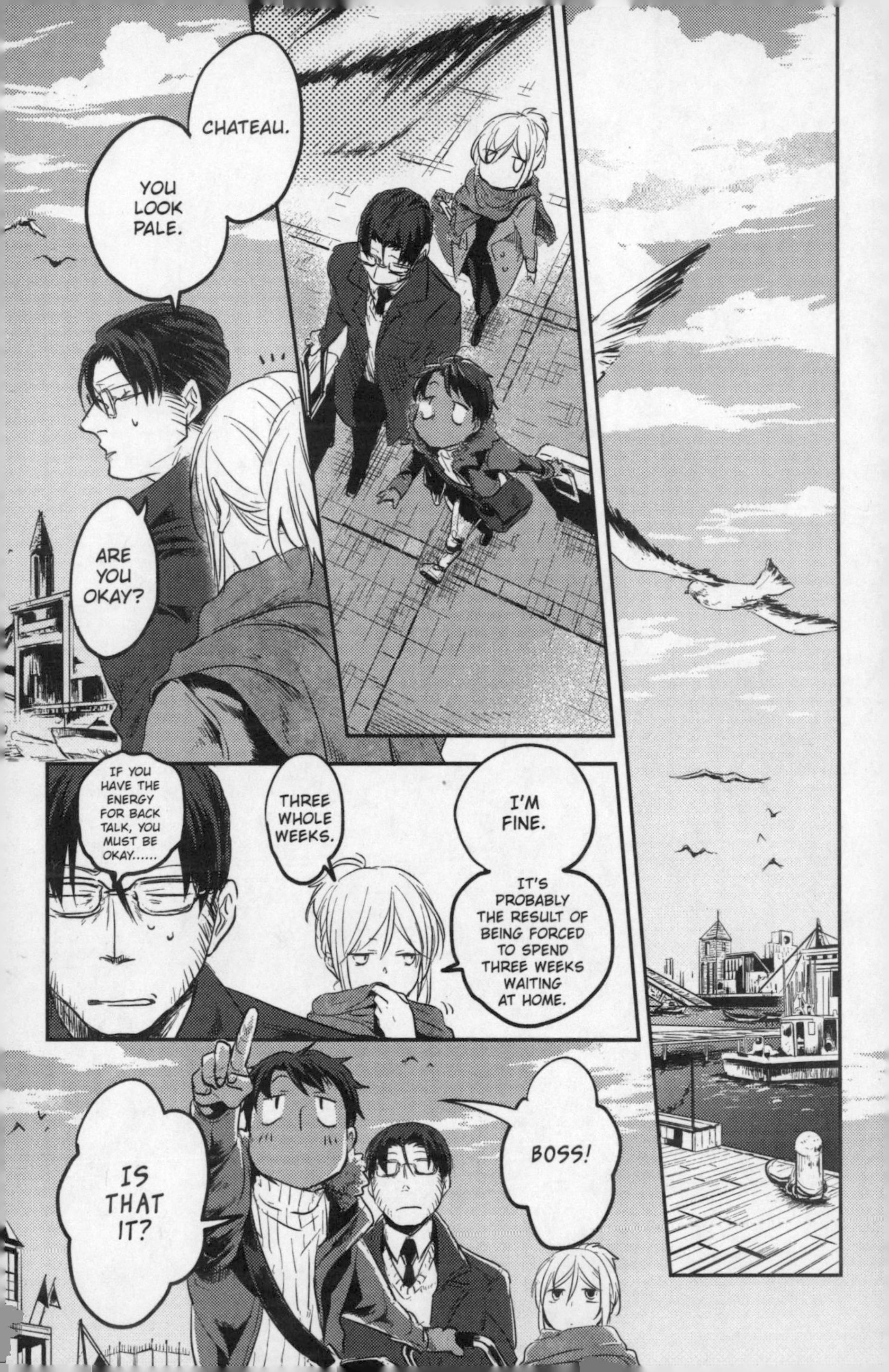
CHATEAU.
YOU LOOK PALE.
ARE YOU OKAY?
I'M FINE.
IT'S PROBABLY THE RESULT OF BEING FORCED TO SPEND THREE WEEKS WAITING AT HOME.
THREE WHOLE WEEKS.
IF YOU HAVE THE ENERGY FOR BACK TALK, YOU MUST BE OKAY......
BOSS!
IS THAT IT?

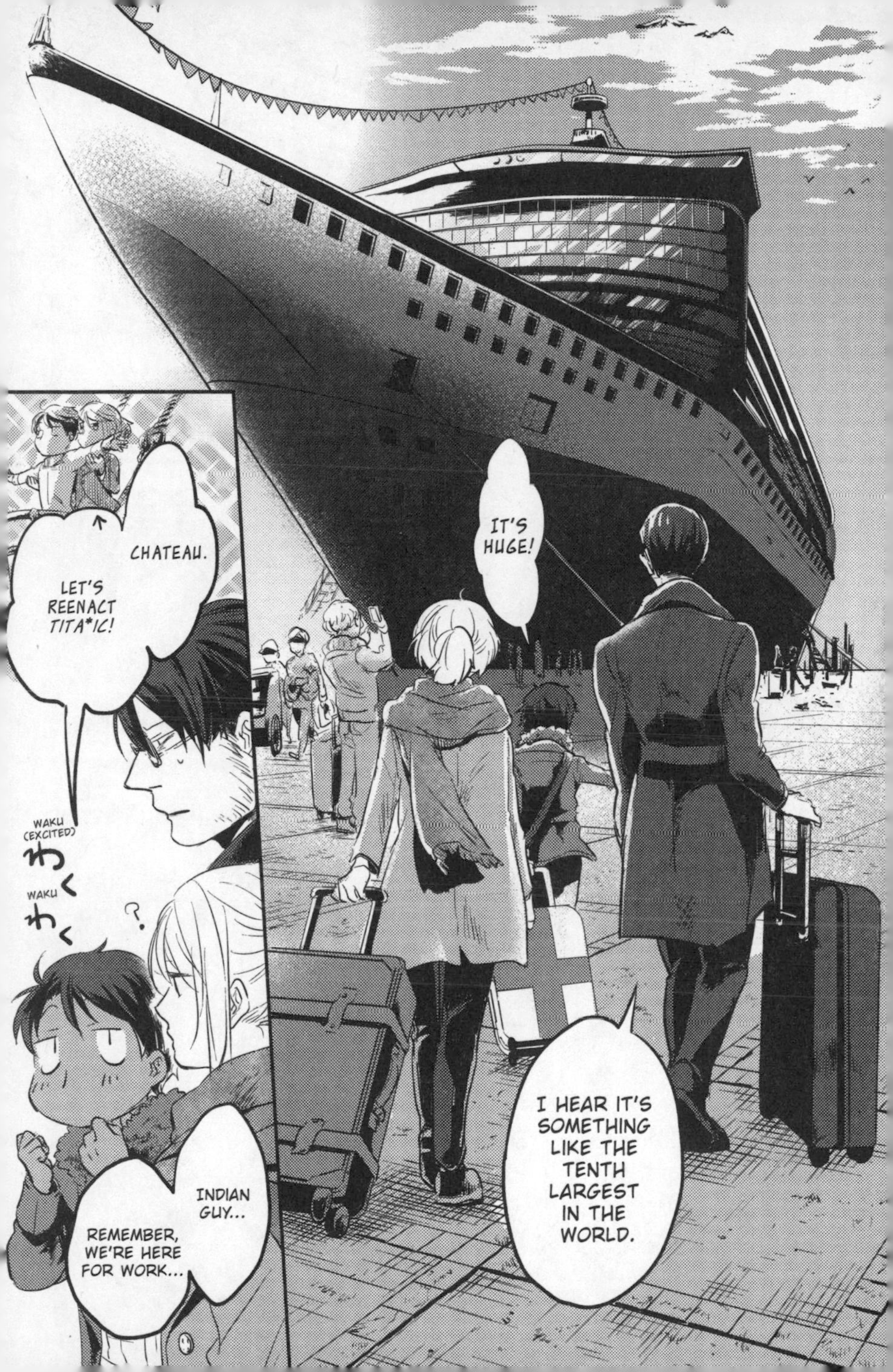
IT'S HUGE!
I HEAR IT'S SOMETHING LIKE THE TENTH LARGEST IN THE WORLD.
CHATEAU. LET'S REENACT TITA*IC!
WAKU (EXCITED) わく WAKU わく
?
INDIAN GUY... REMEMBER, WE'RE HERE FOR WORK...

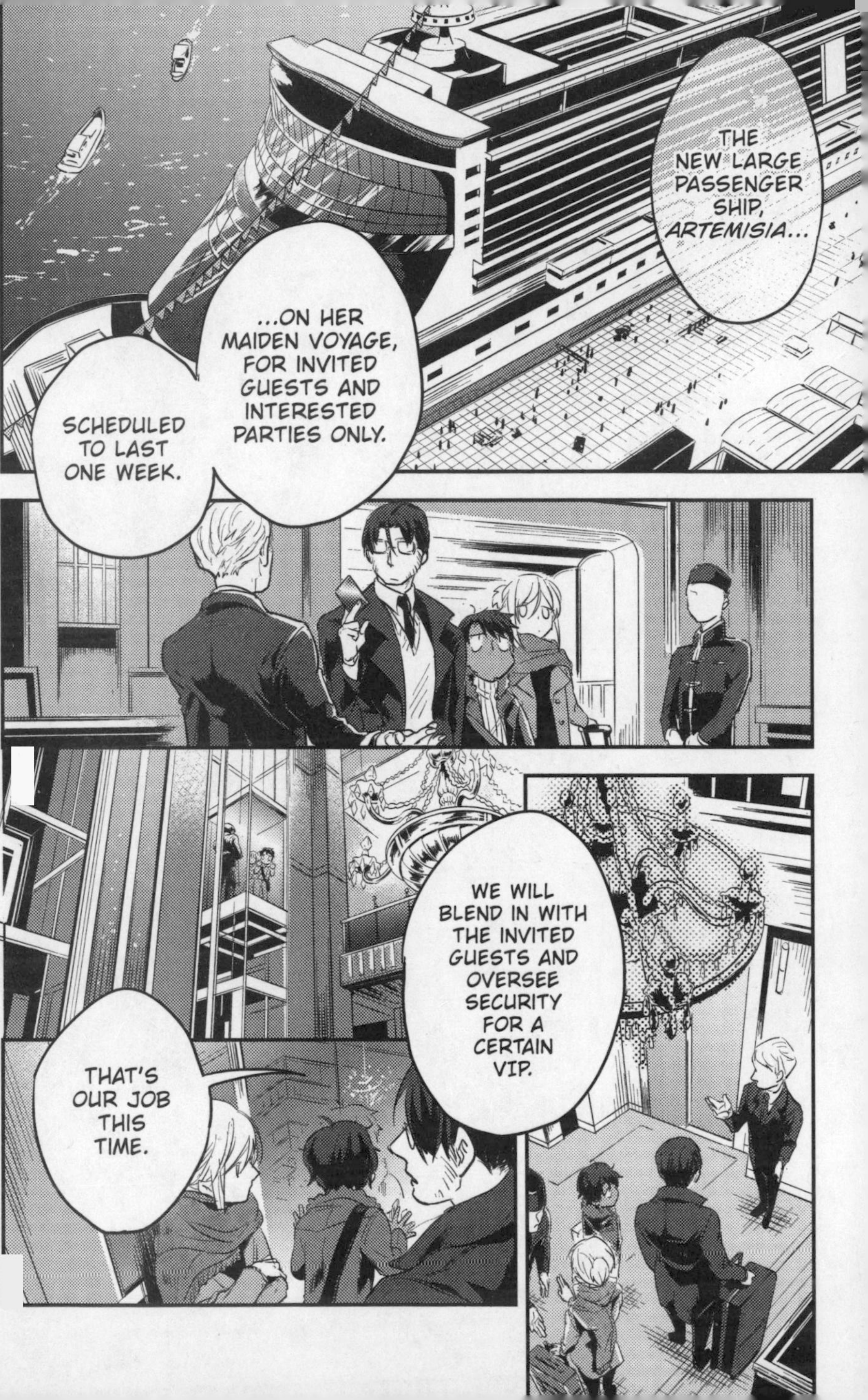
THE NEW LARGE PASSENGER SHIP, ARTEMISIA...
...ON HER MAIDEN VOYAGE, FOR INVITED GUESTS AND INTERESTED PARTIES ONLY.
SCHEDULED TO LAST ONE WEEK.
WE WILL BLEND IN WITH THE INVITED GUESTS AND OVERSEE SECURITY FOR A CERTAIN VIP.
THAT'S OUR JOB THIS TIME.

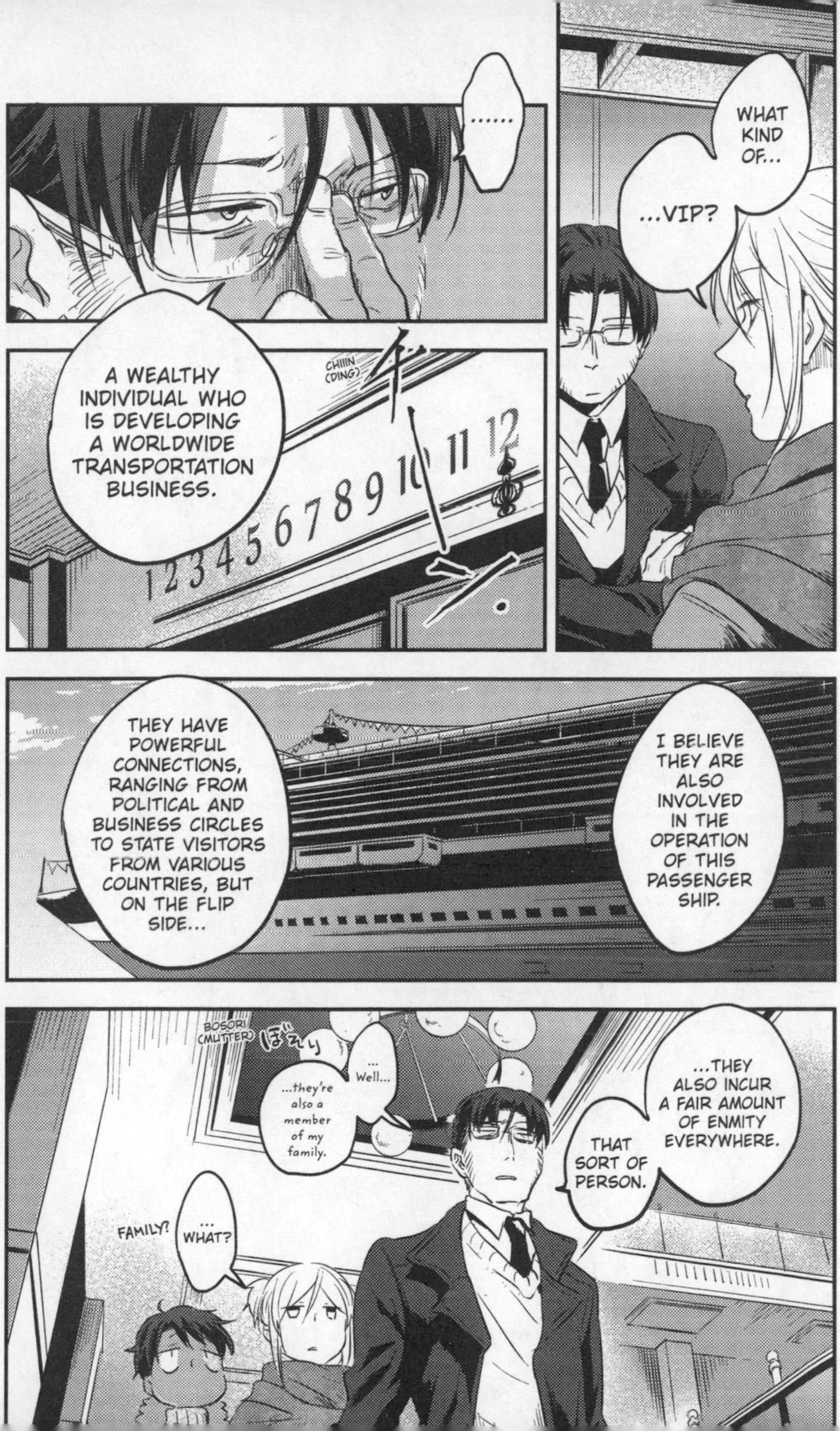
WHAT KIND OF...
...VIP?
......
A WEALTHY INDIVIDUAL WHO IS DEVELOPING A WORLDWIDE TRANSPORTATION BUSINESS.
CHIIIN (DING)
I BELIEVE THEY ARE ALSO INVOLVED IN THE OPERATION OF THIS PASSENGER SHIP.
THEY HAVE POWERFUL CONNECTIONS, RANGING FROM POLITICAL AND BUSINESS CIRCLES TO STATE VISITORS FROM VARIOUS COUNTRIES, BUT ON THE FLIP SIDE...
...THEY ALSO INCUR A FAIR AMOUNT OF ENMITY EVERYWHERE.
THAT SORT OF PERSON.
BOSORI (MUTTER)
... Well...
...they're also a member of my family.
... WHAT?
FAMILY?

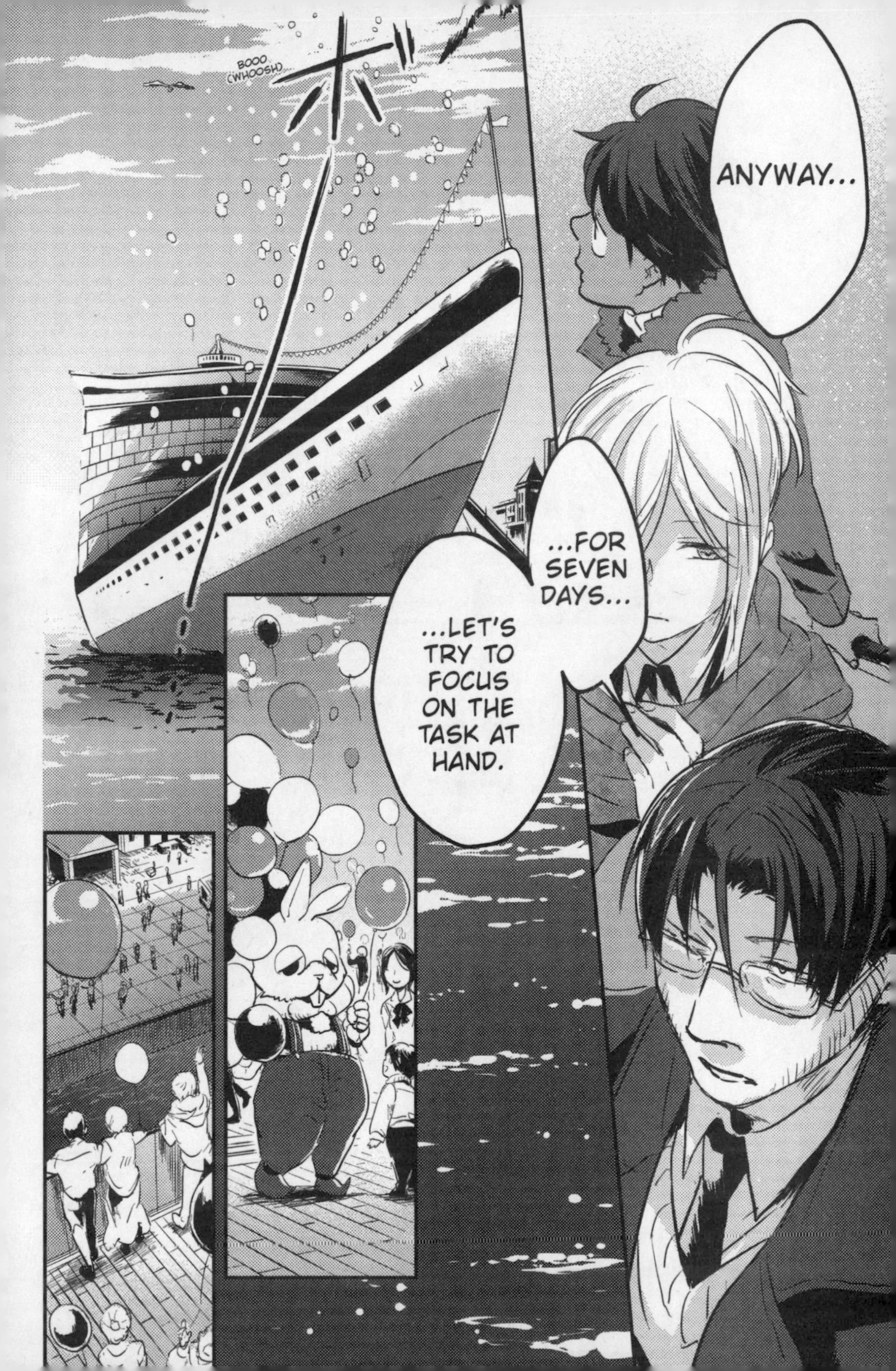
ANYWAY...
...FOR SEVEN DAYS...
...LET'S TRY TO FOCUS ON THE TASK AT HAND.
BOOO (WHOOSH)

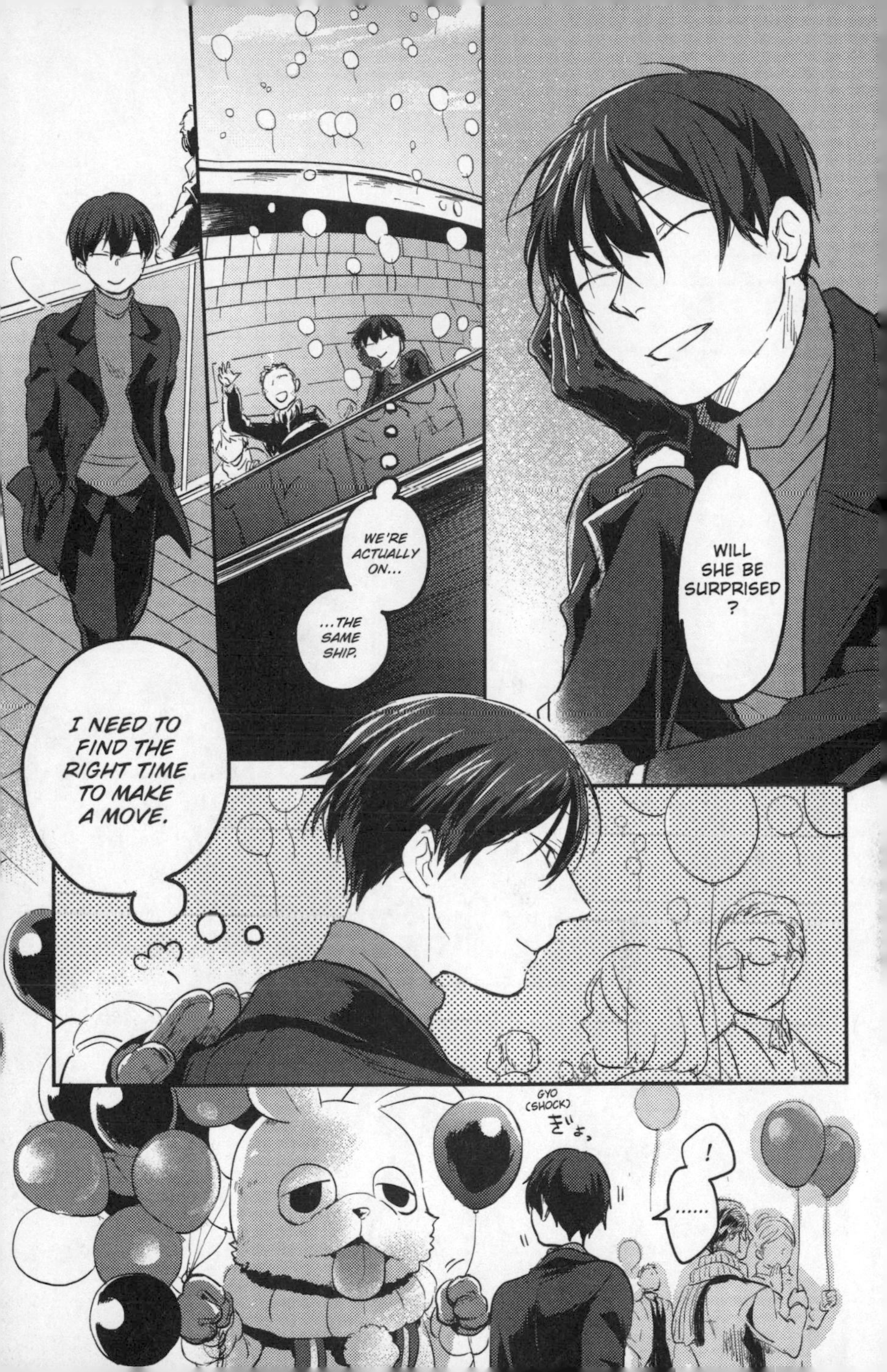
WILL SHE BE SURPRISED ?
WE'RE ACTUALLY ON...
...THE SAME SHIP.
I NEED TO FIND THE RIGHT TIME TO MAKE A MOVE.
GYO (SHOCK)
ぎょっ
!
......

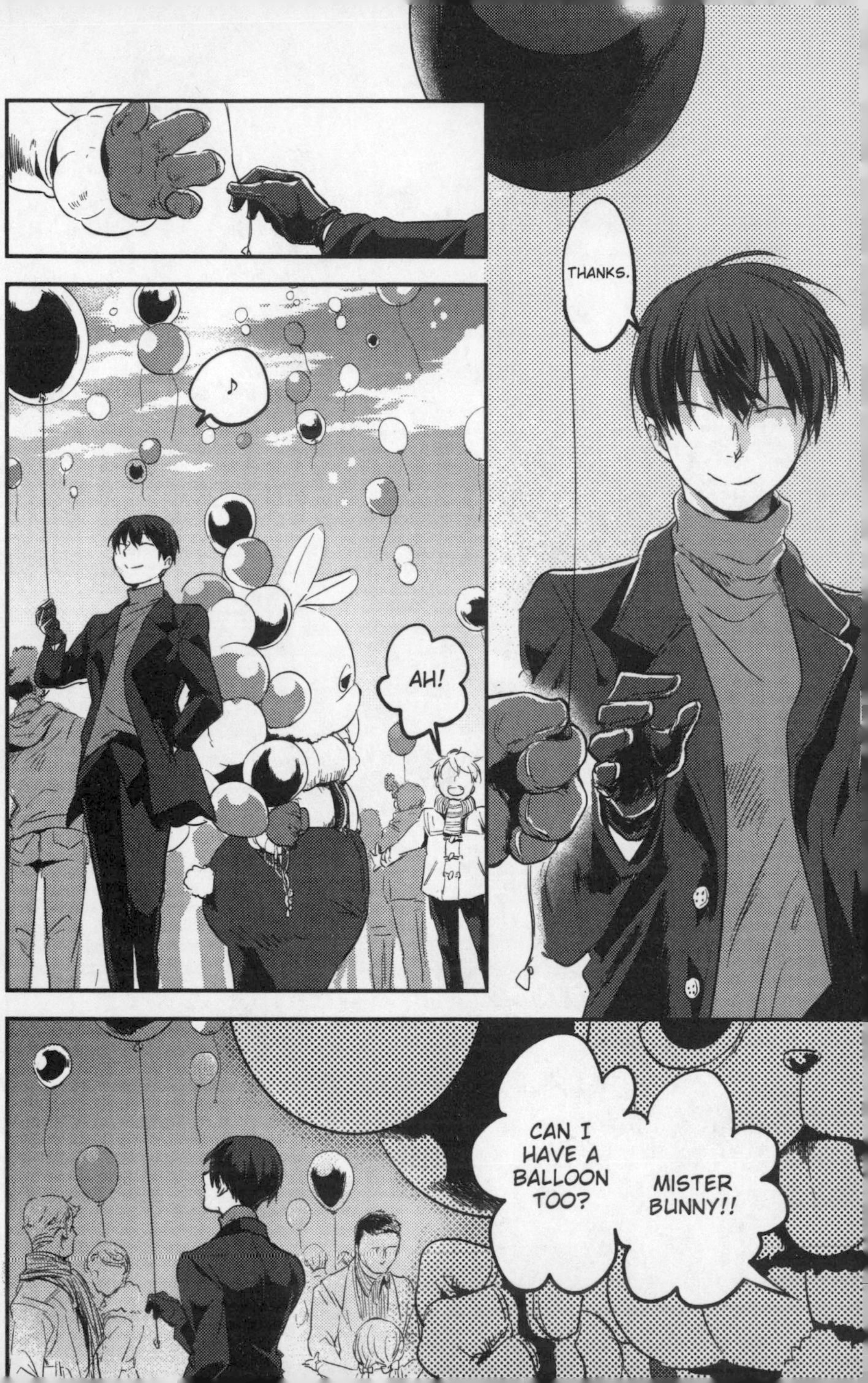
THANKS.
♪
AH!
MISTER BUNNY!! CAN I HAVE A BALLOON TOO?

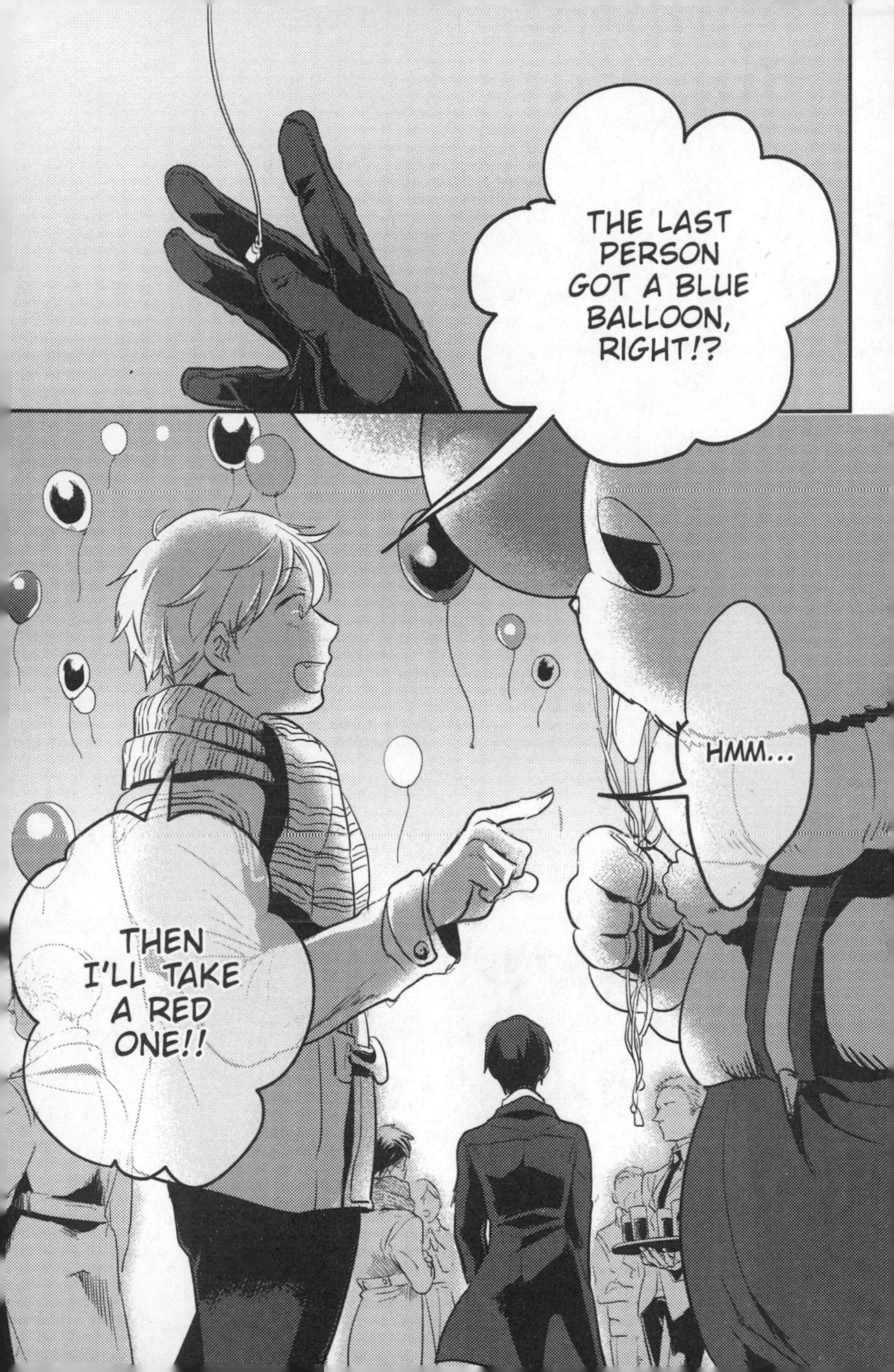
THE LAST PERSON GOT A BLUE BALLOON, RIGHT!?
HMM...
THEN I'LL TAKE A RED ONE!!

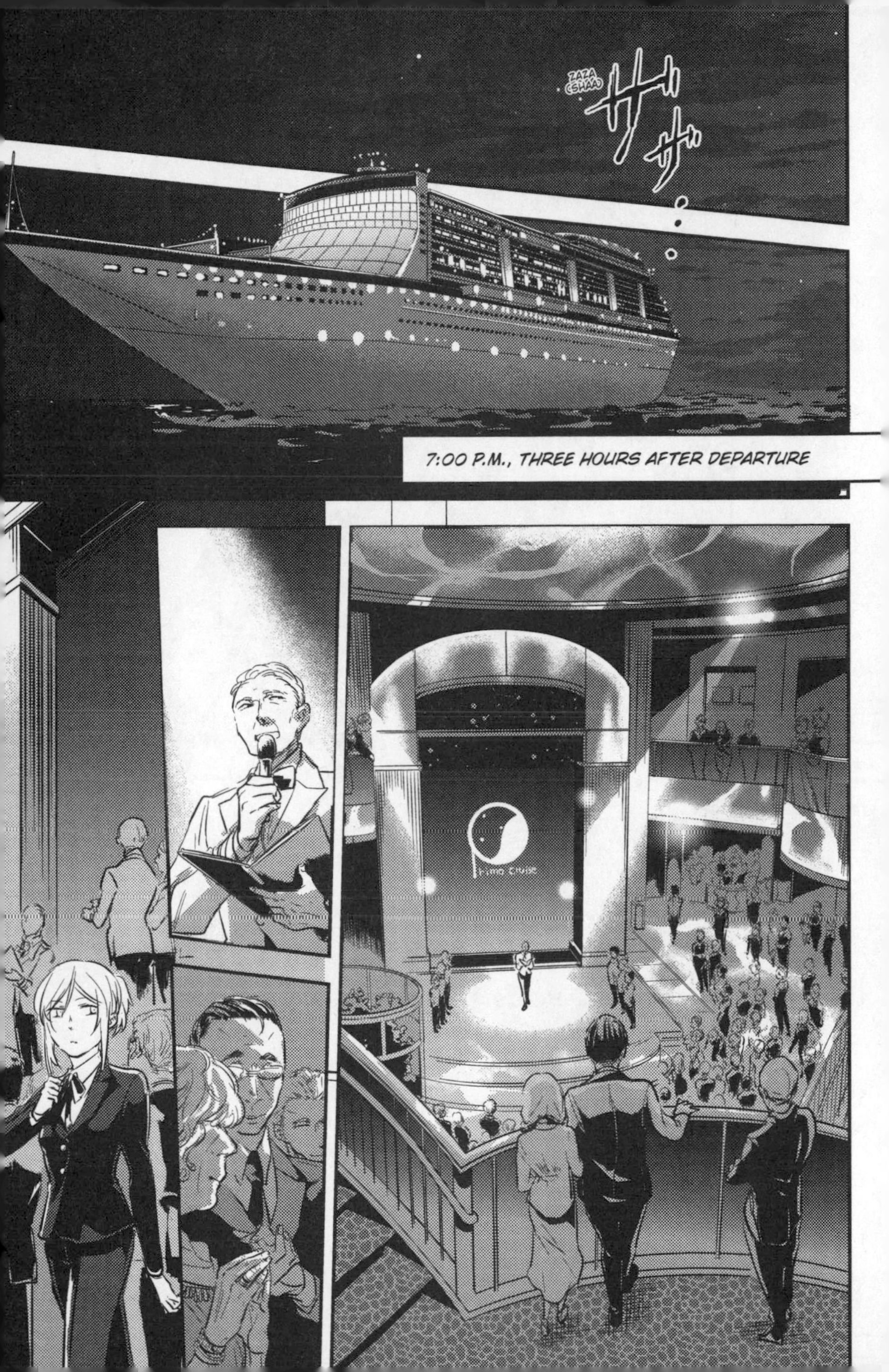
ZAZA (SHAA)
ザザ…
7:00 P.M., THREE HOURS AFTER DEPARTURE
Primo Cruise

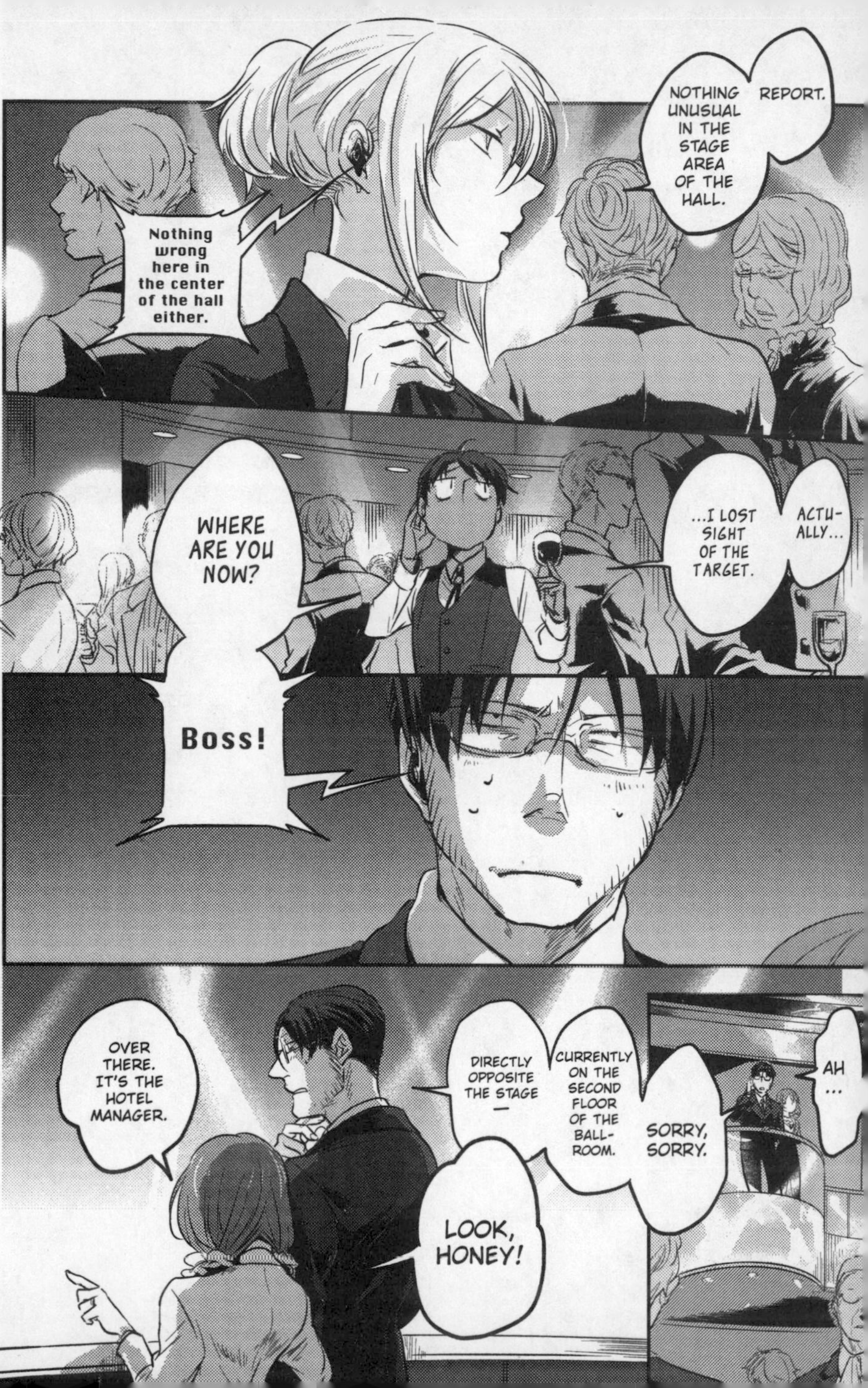
REPORT.
NOTHING UNUSUAL IN THE STAGE AREA OF THE HALL.
Nothing wrong here in the center of the hall either.
ACTU-ALLY...
...I LOST SIGHT OF THE TARGET.
WHERE ARE YOU NOW?
Boss!
AH ...
SORRY, SORRY.
CURRENTLY ON THE SECOND FLOOR OF THE BALL-ROOM.
DIRECTLY OPPOSITE THE STAGE —
LOOK, HONEY!
OVER THERE. IT'S THE HOTEL MANAGER.

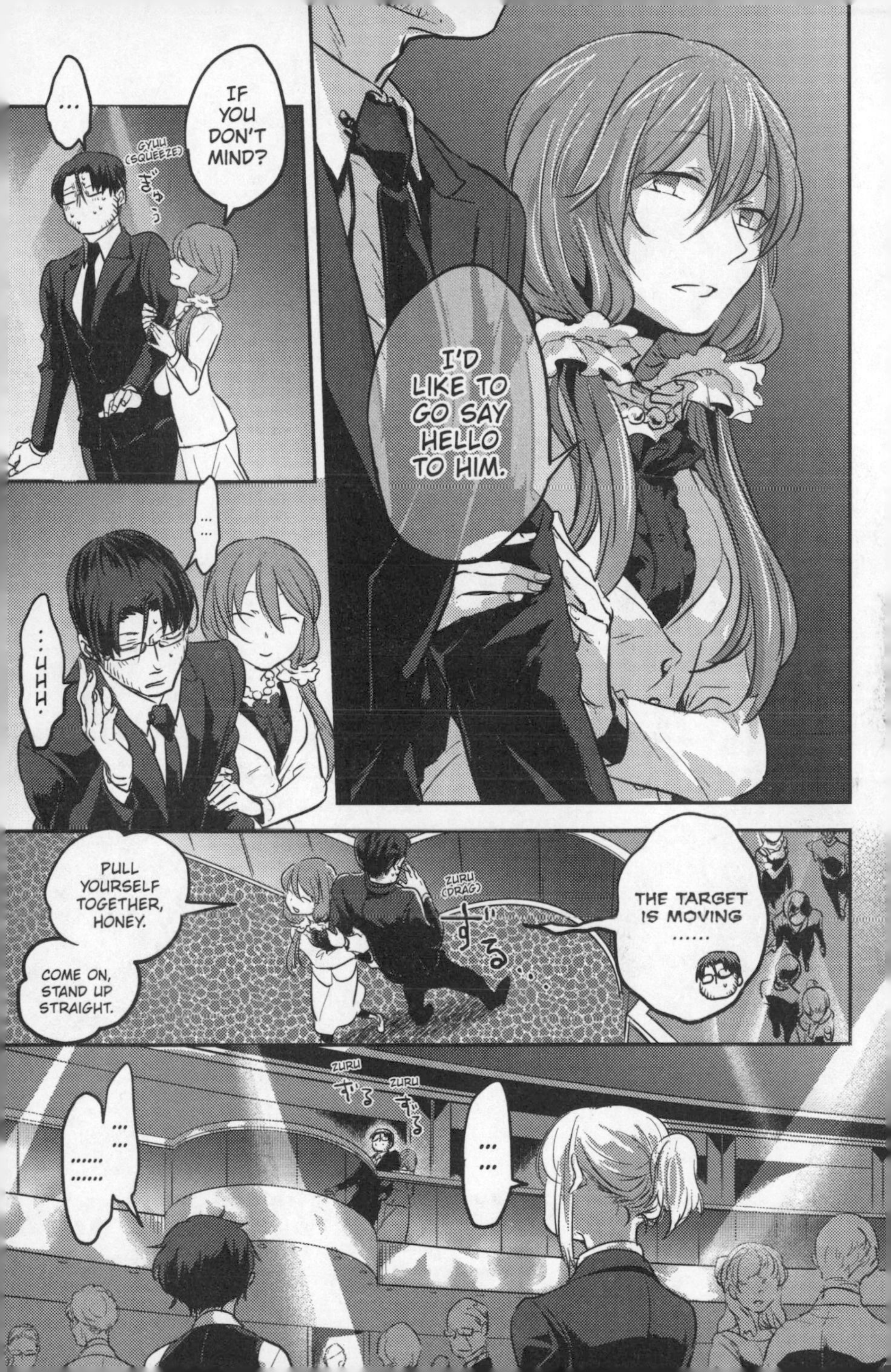
I'D LIKE TO GO SAY HELLO TO HIM.
IF YOU DON'T MIND?
GYUU (SQUEEZE)
ぎゅう
...
......
...UHH.
THE TARGET IS MOVING ......
ZURU (DRAG)
ずる
PULL YOURSELF TOGETHER, HONEY.
COME ON, STAND UP STRAIGHT.
ZURU ZURU
ずる ずる
... ...
... ...

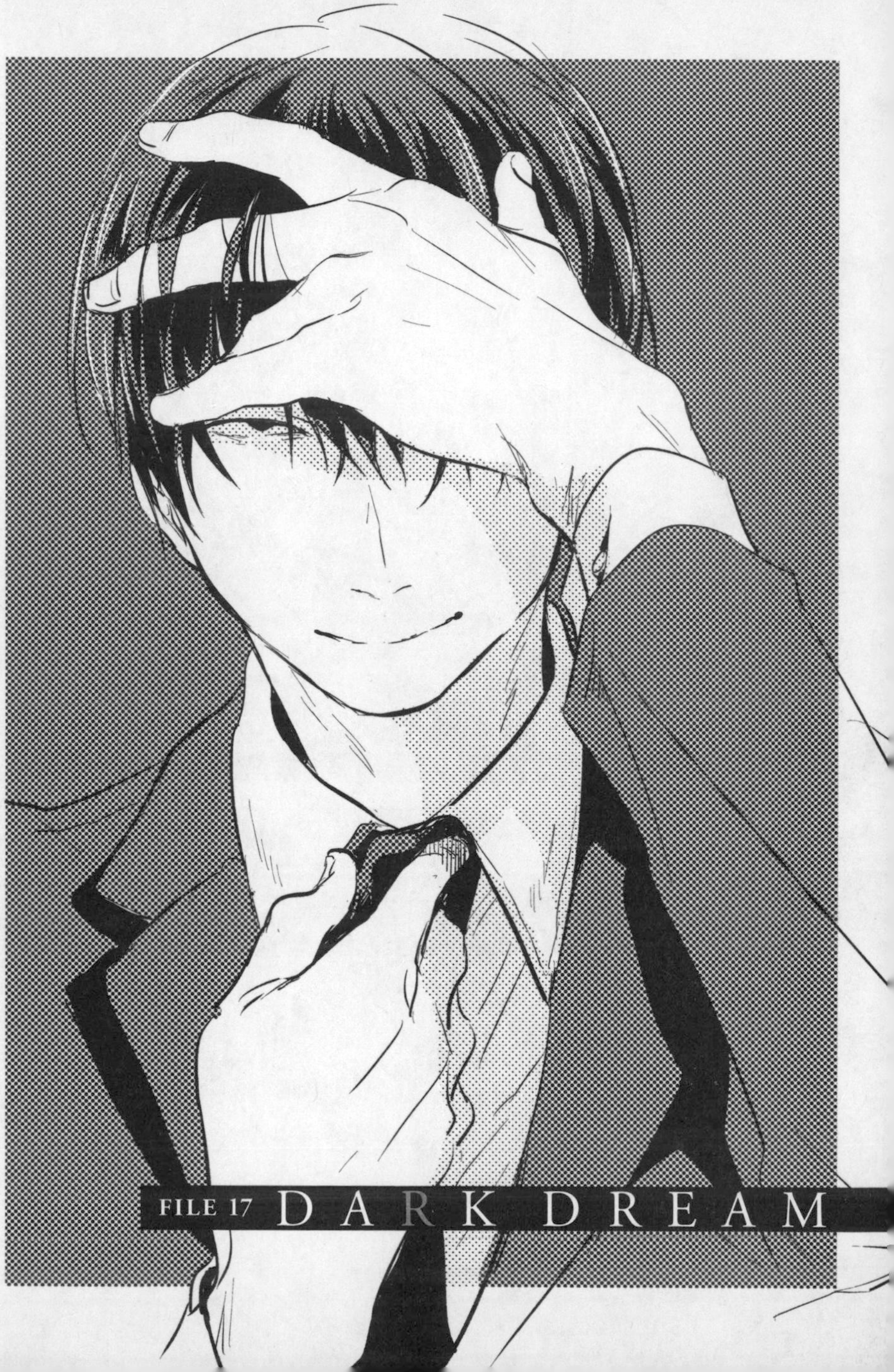

FILE 17 DARK DREAM

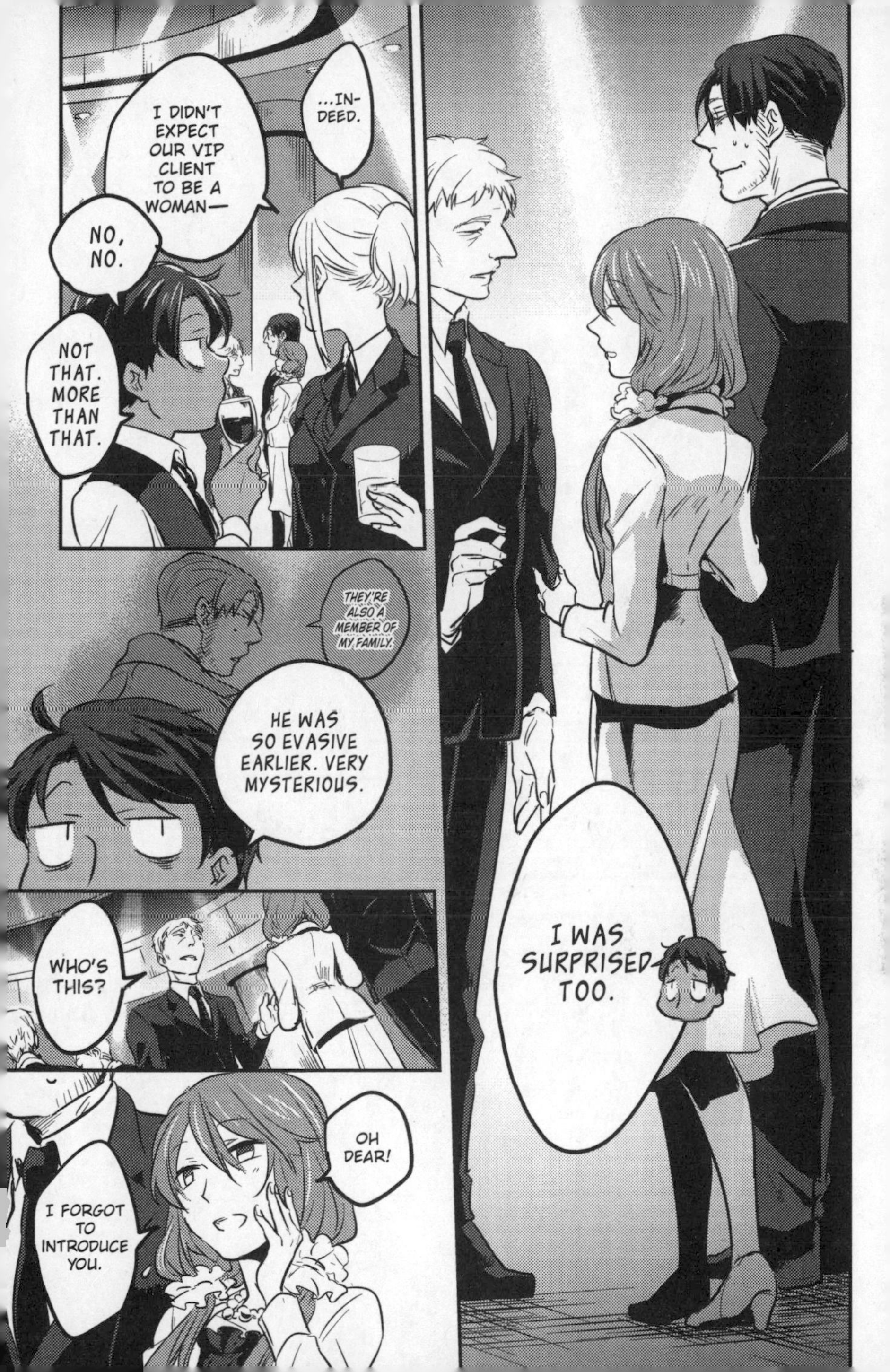
I WAS SURPRISED TOO.
...IN-DEED.
I DIDN'T EXPECT OUR VIP CLIENT TO BE A WOMAN—
NO, NO.
NOT THAT. MORE THAN THAT.
THEY'RE ALSO A MEMBER OF MY FAMILY.
HE WAS SO EVASIVE EARLIER. VERY MYSTERIOUS.
WHO'S THIS?
OH DEAR!
I FORGOT TO INTRODUCE YOU.

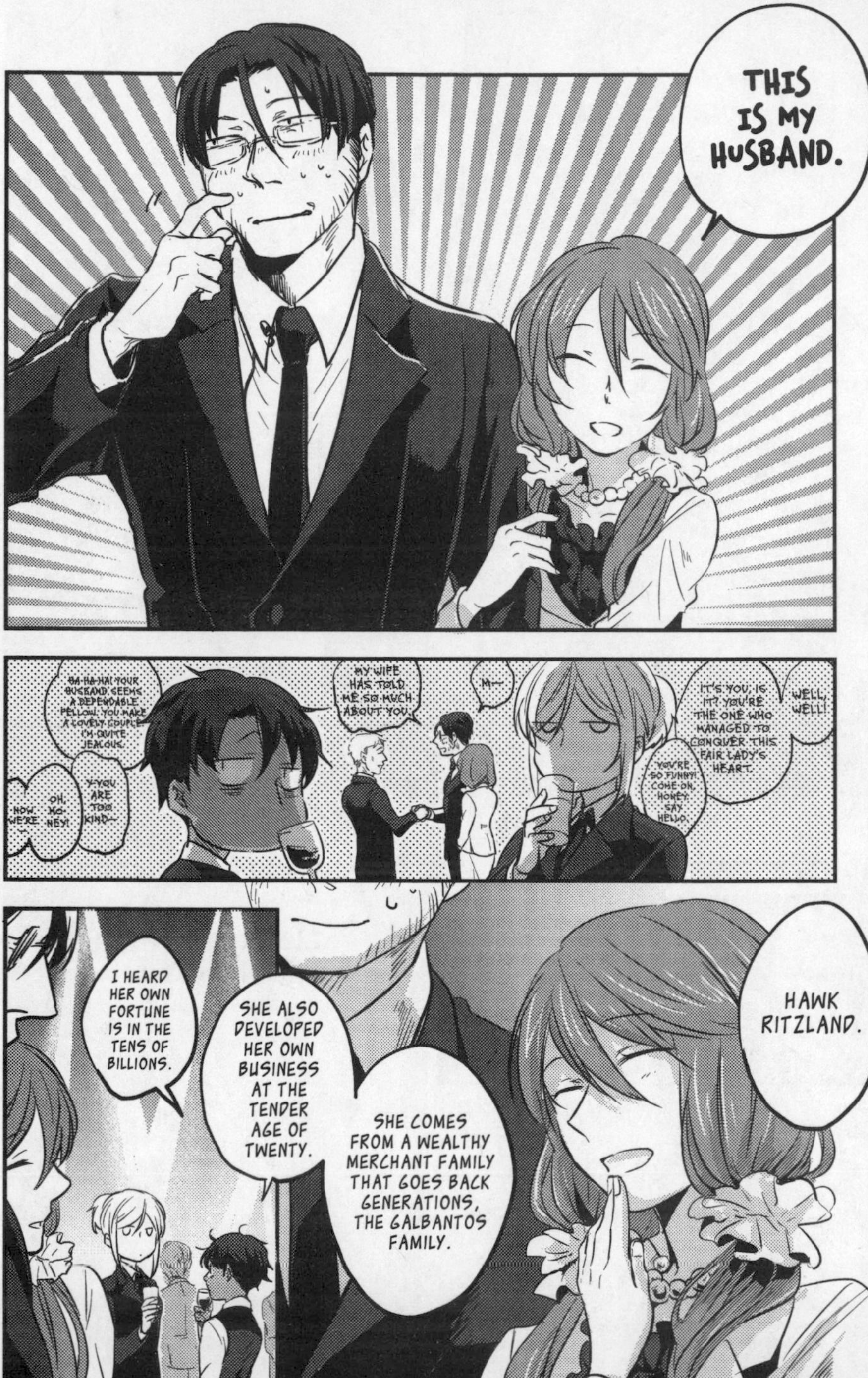
THIS IS MY HUSBAND.
WELL, WELL!
IT'S YOU, IS IT? YOU'RE THE ONE WHO MANAGED TO CONQUER THIS FAIR LADY'S HEART.
YOU'RE SO FUNNY! COME ON, HONEY. SAY HELLO.
M—
MY WIFE HAS TOLD ME SO MUCH ABOUT YOU.
HA-HA-HA! YOUR HUSBAND SEEMS A DEPENDABLE FELLOW. YOU MAKE A LOVELY COUPLE. I'M QUITE JEALOUS.
Y-YOU ARE TOO KIND—
OH, HO-NEY!
NOW, WE'RE—
HAWK RITZLAND.
SHE COMES FROM A WEALTHY MERCHANT FAMILY THAT GOES BACK GENERATIONS, THE GALBANTOS FAMILY.
SHE ALSO DEVELOPED HER OWN BUSINESS AT THE TENDER AGE OF TWENTY.
I HEARD HER OWN FORTUNE IS IN THE TENS OF BILLIONS.

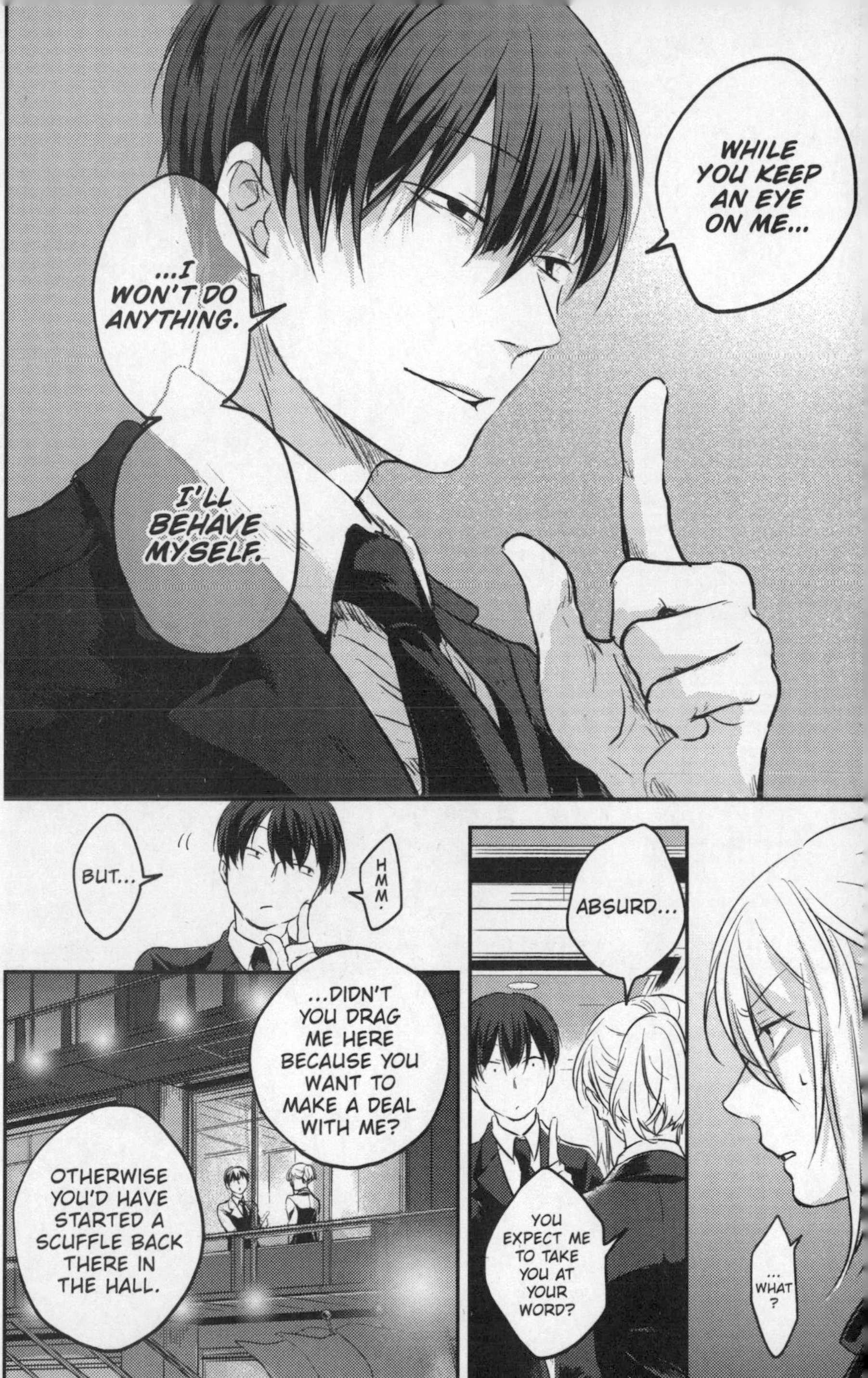
WHILE YOU KEEP AN EYE ON ME...
...I WON'T DO ANYTHING.
I'LL BEHAVE MYSELF.
...WHAT?
ABSURD...
YOU EXPECT ME TO TAKE YOU AT YOUR WORD?
HMM.
BUT...
...DIDN'T YOU DRAG ME HERE BECAUSE YOU WANT TO MAKE A DEAL WITH ME?
OTHERWISE YOU'D HAVE STARTED A SCUFFLE BACK THERE IN THE HALL.

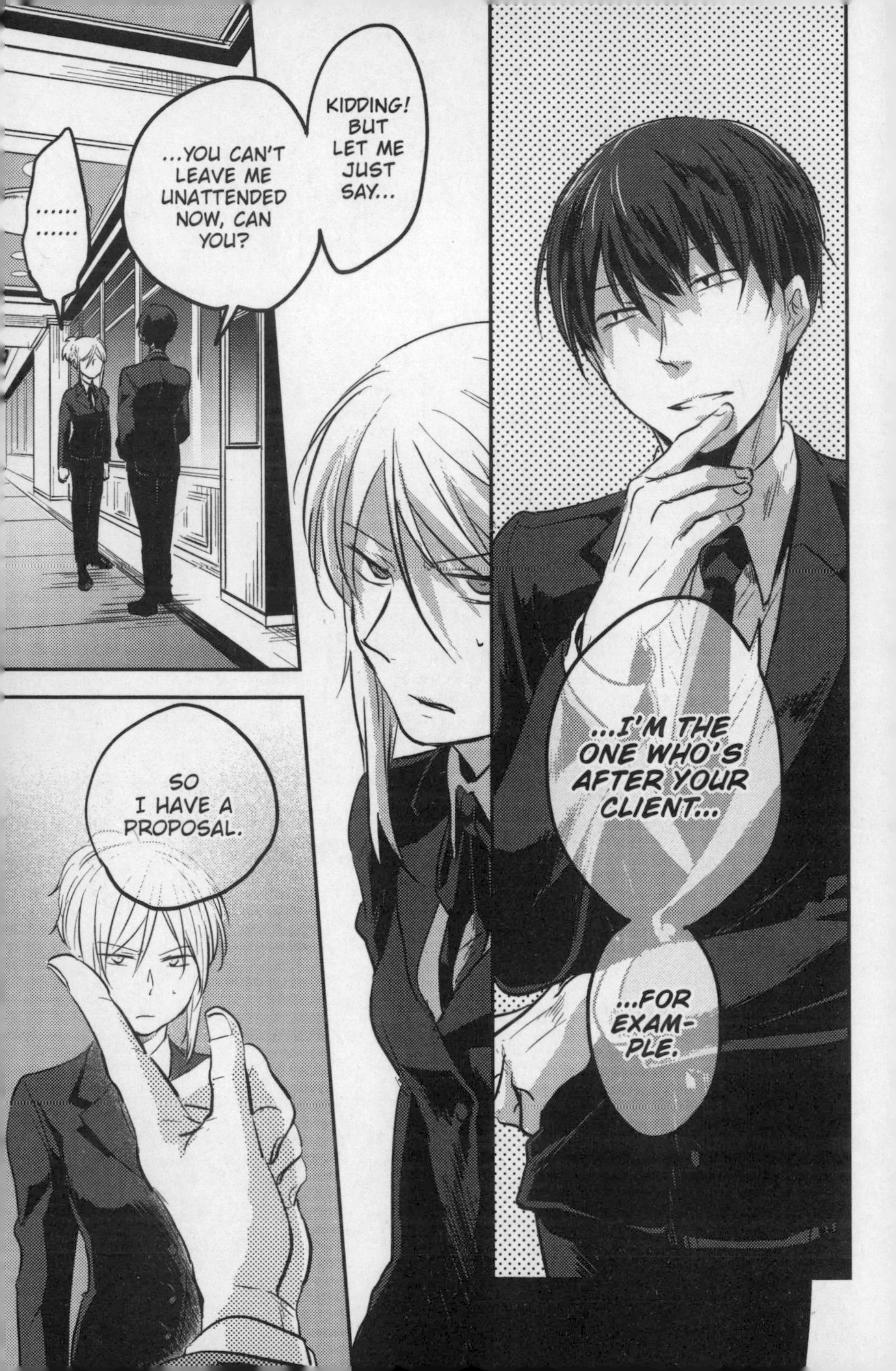
...I'M THE ONE WHO'S AFTER YOUR CLIENT...
...FOR EXAMPLE.
KIDDING! BUT LET ME JUST SAY...
...YOU CAN'T LEAVE ME UNATTENDED NOW, CAN YOU?
......
......
SO I HAVE A PROPOSAL.

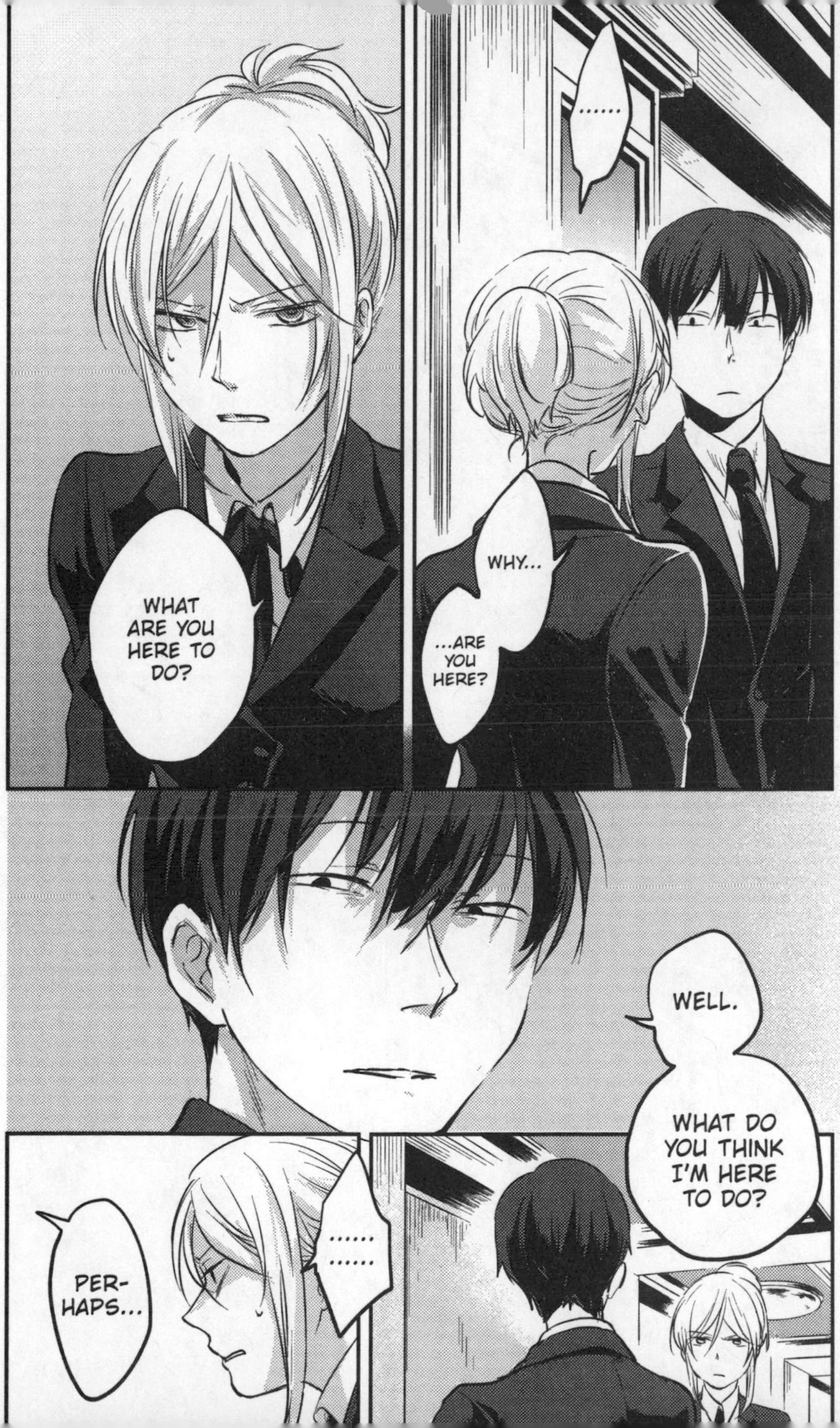
......
WHY...
...ARE YOU HERE?
WHAT ARE YOU HERE TO DO?
WELL.
WHAT DO YOU THINK I'M HERE TO DO?
......
......
PER-HAPS...

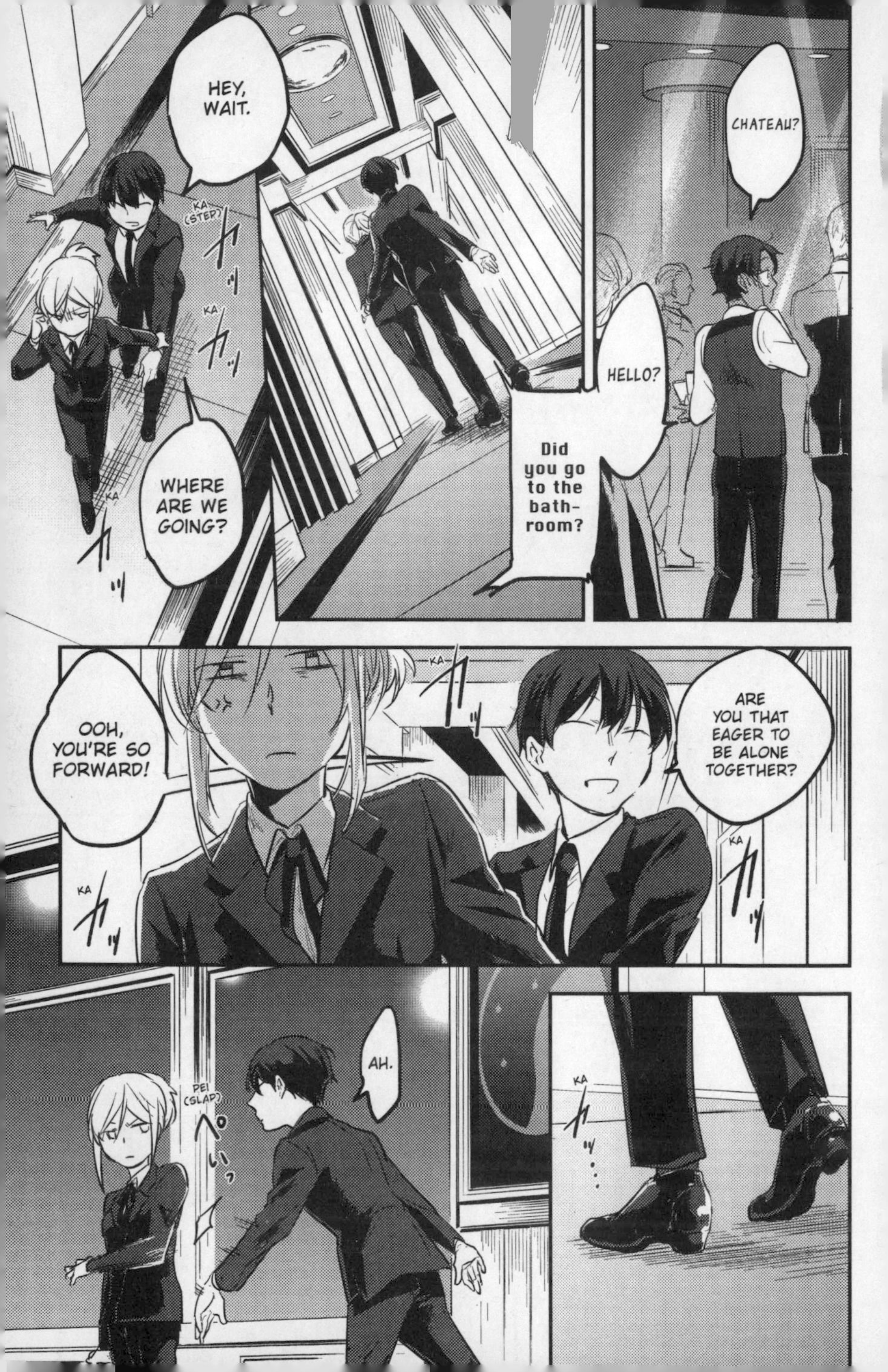

CHATEAU?
HELLO?
Did you go to the bathroom?
HEY, WAIT.
KA (STEP)
KA
WHERE ARE WE GOING?
KA
KA
ARE YOU THAT EAGER TO BE ALONE TOGETHER?
KA
OOH, YOU'RE SO FORWARD!
KA
KA
AH.
PEI (SLAP)

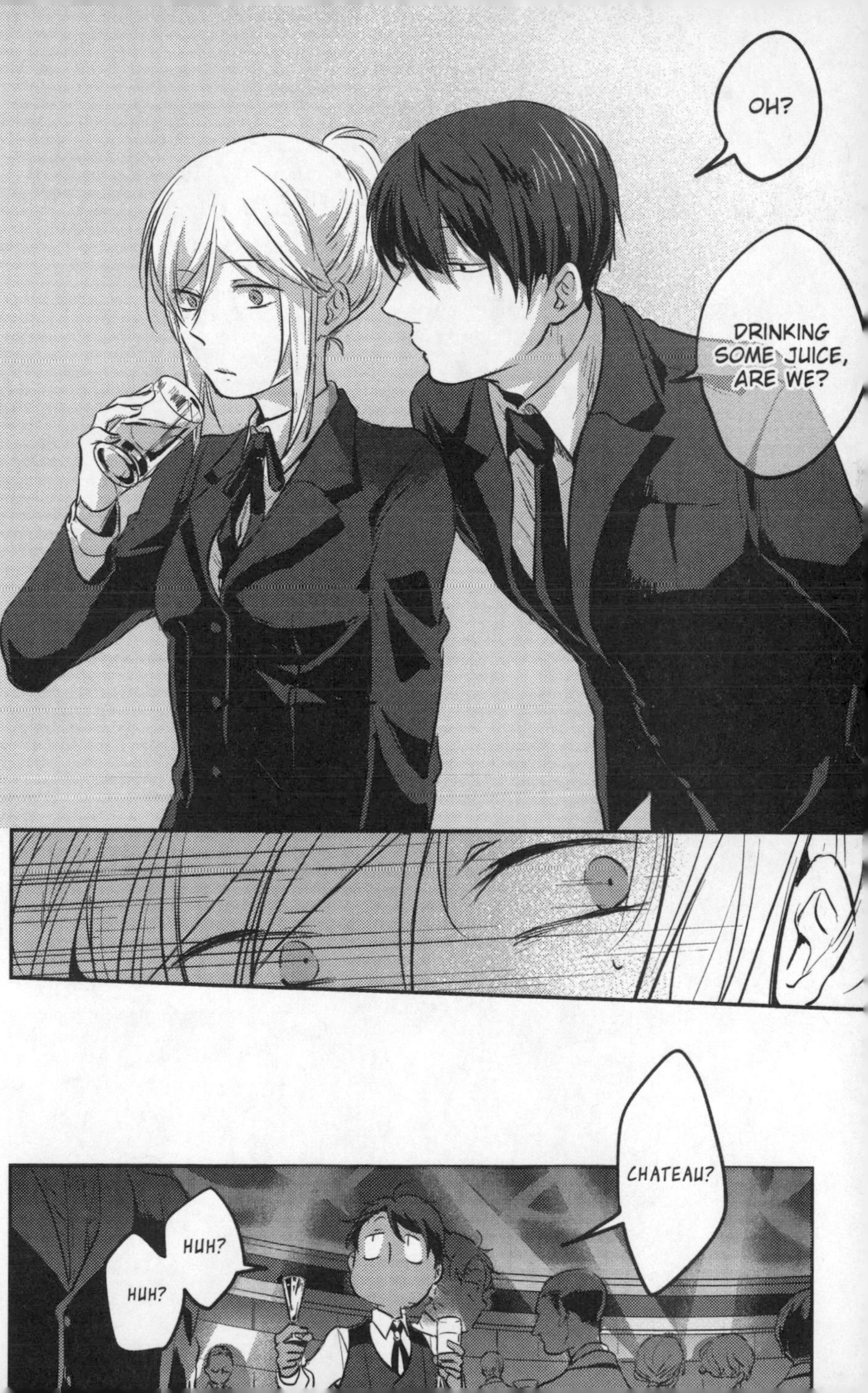
OH?
DRINKING SOME JUICE, ARE WE?
CHATEAU?
HUH?
HUH?

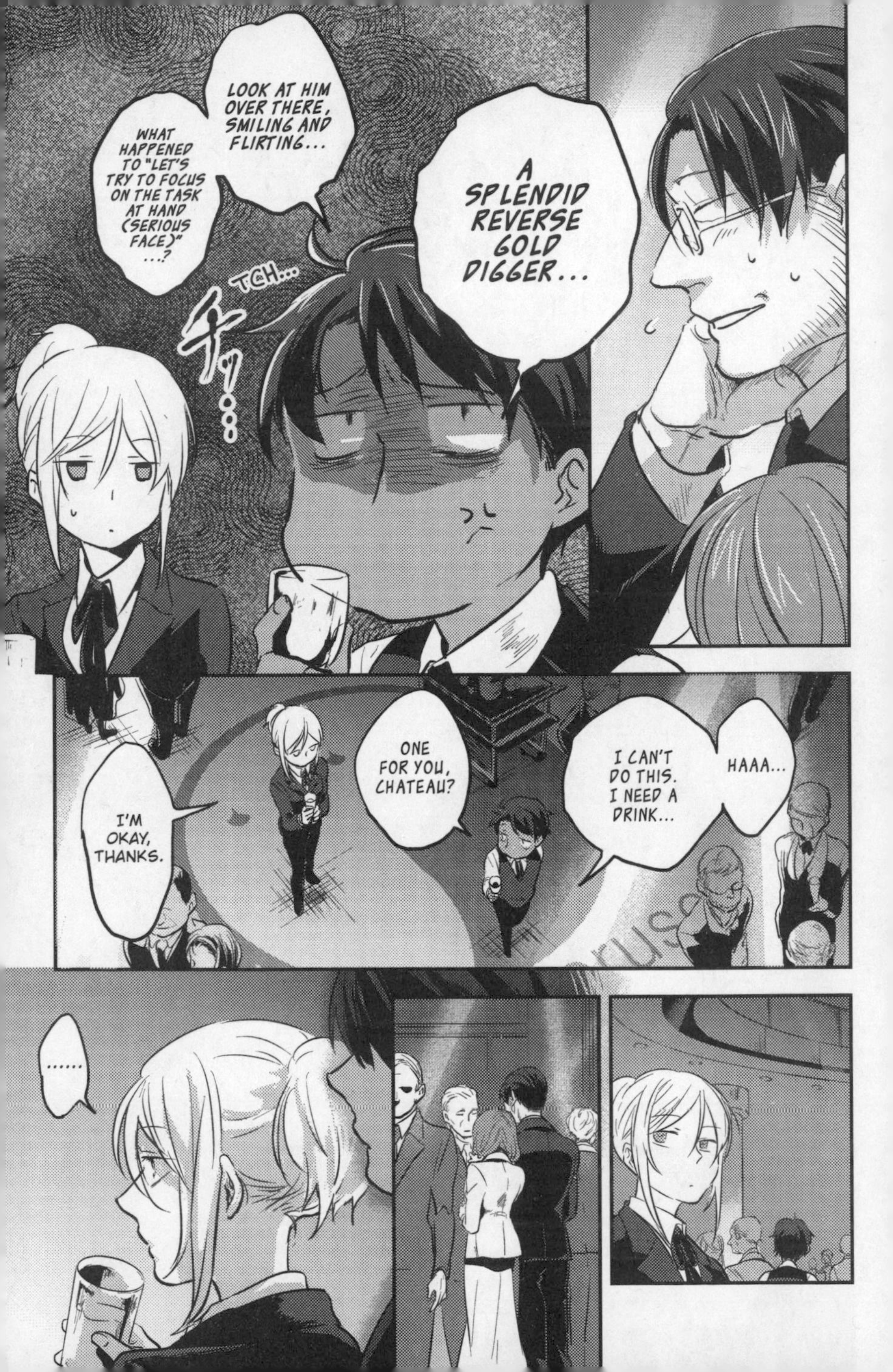
A SPLENDID REVERSE GOLD DIGGER...
LOOK AT HIM OVER THERE, SMILING AND FLIRTING...
WHAT HAPPENED TO "LET'S TRY TO FOCUS ON THE TASK AT HAND (SERIOUS FACE)" ...?
TCH...
チッ
HAAA...
I CAN'T DO THIS. I NEED A DRINK...
ONE FOR YOU, CHATEAU?
I'M OKAY, THANKS.
....

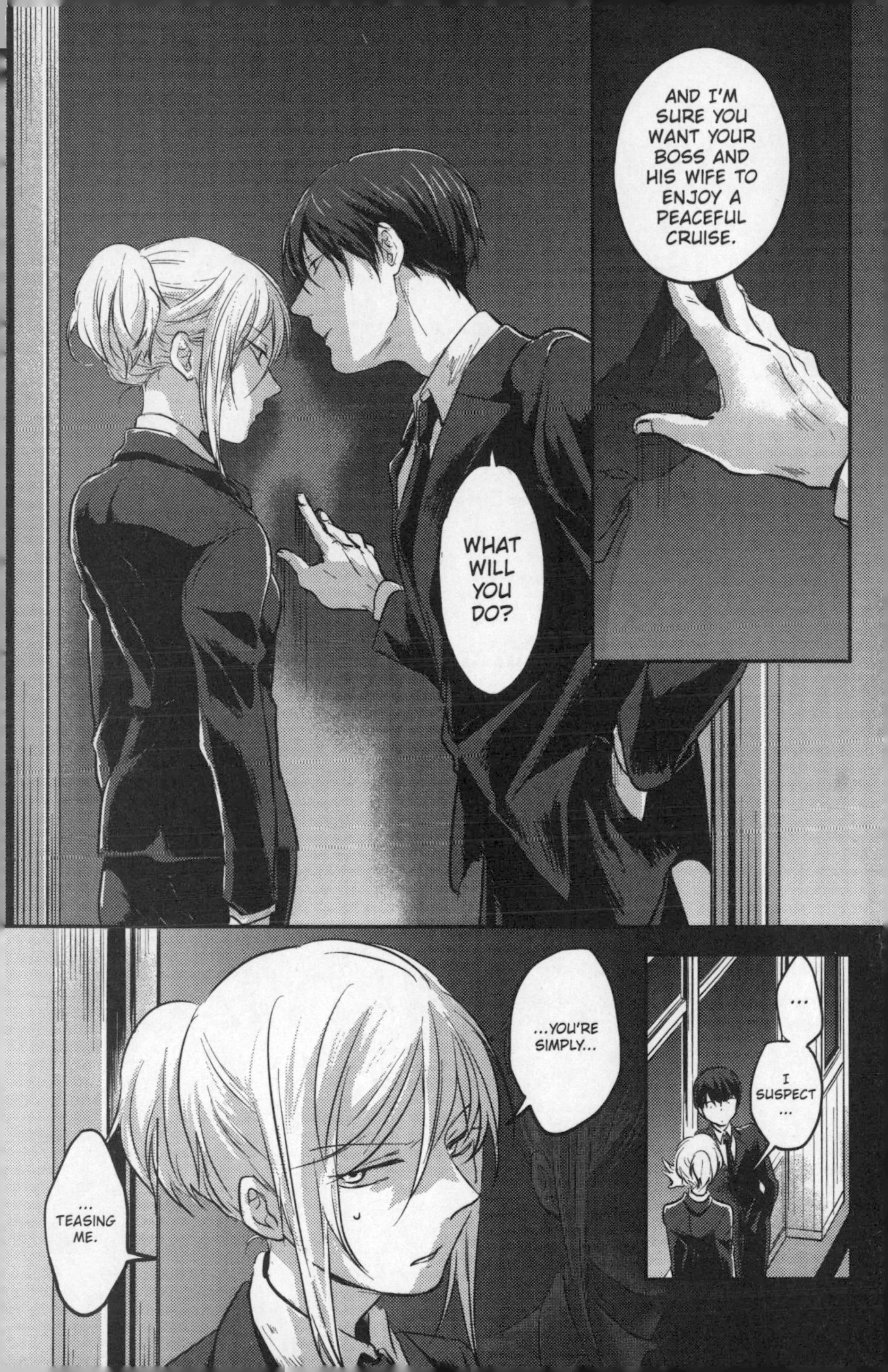
AND I'M SURE YOU WANT YOUR BOSS AND HIS WIFE TO ENJOY A PEACEFUL CRUISE.
WHAT WILL YOU DO?
...
I SUSPECT ...
...YOU'RE SIMPLY...
... TEASING ME.

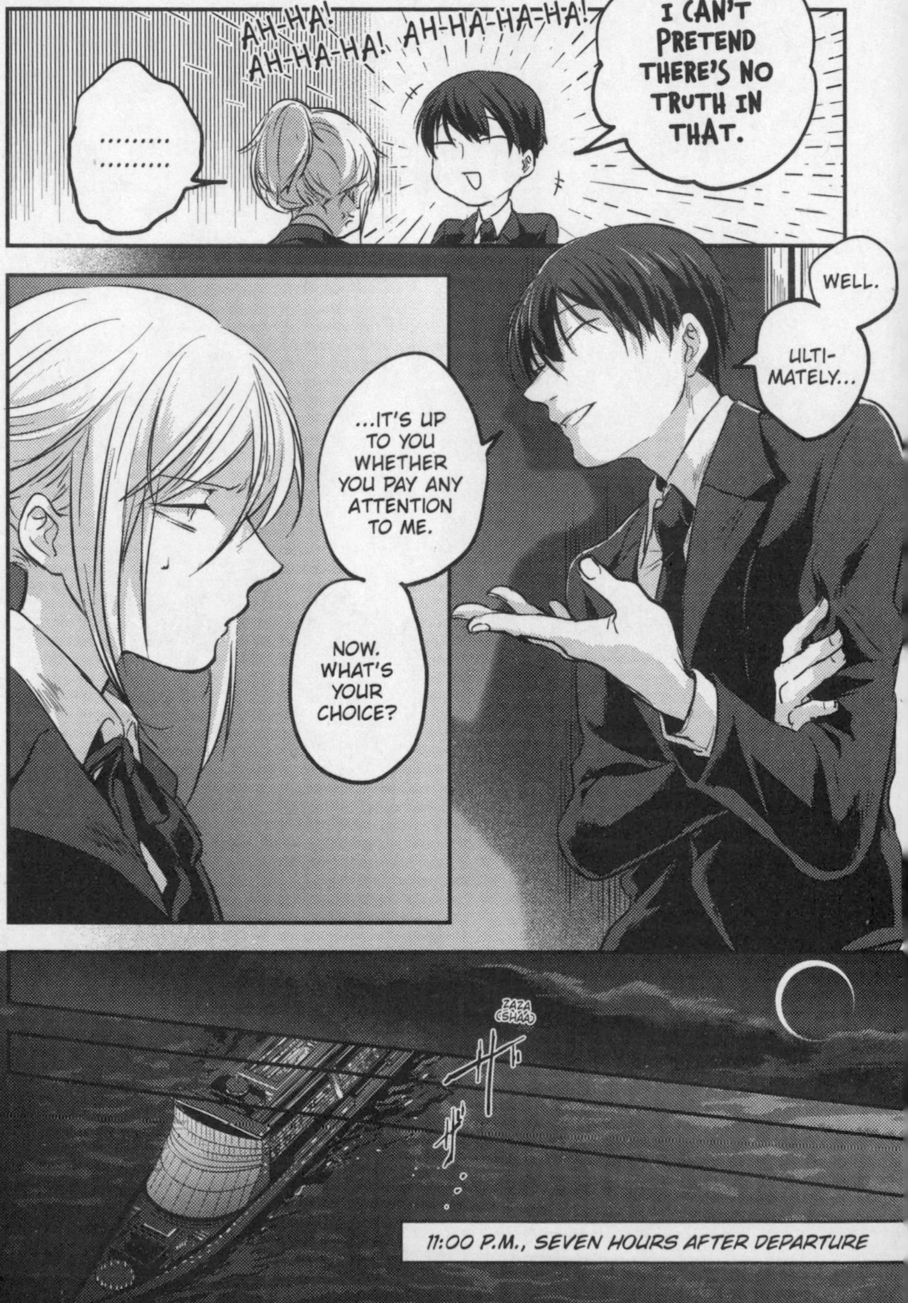
I CAN'T PRETEND THERE'S NO TRUTH IN THAT.
AH-HA! AH-HA-HA! AH-HA-HA-HA!
....
WELL.
ULTI-MATELY...
...IT'S UP TO YOU WHETHER YOU PAY ANY ATTENTION TO ME.
NOW. WHAT'S YOUR CHOICE?
ZAZA (SHAA)
11:00 P.M., SEVEN HOURS AFTER DEPARTURE

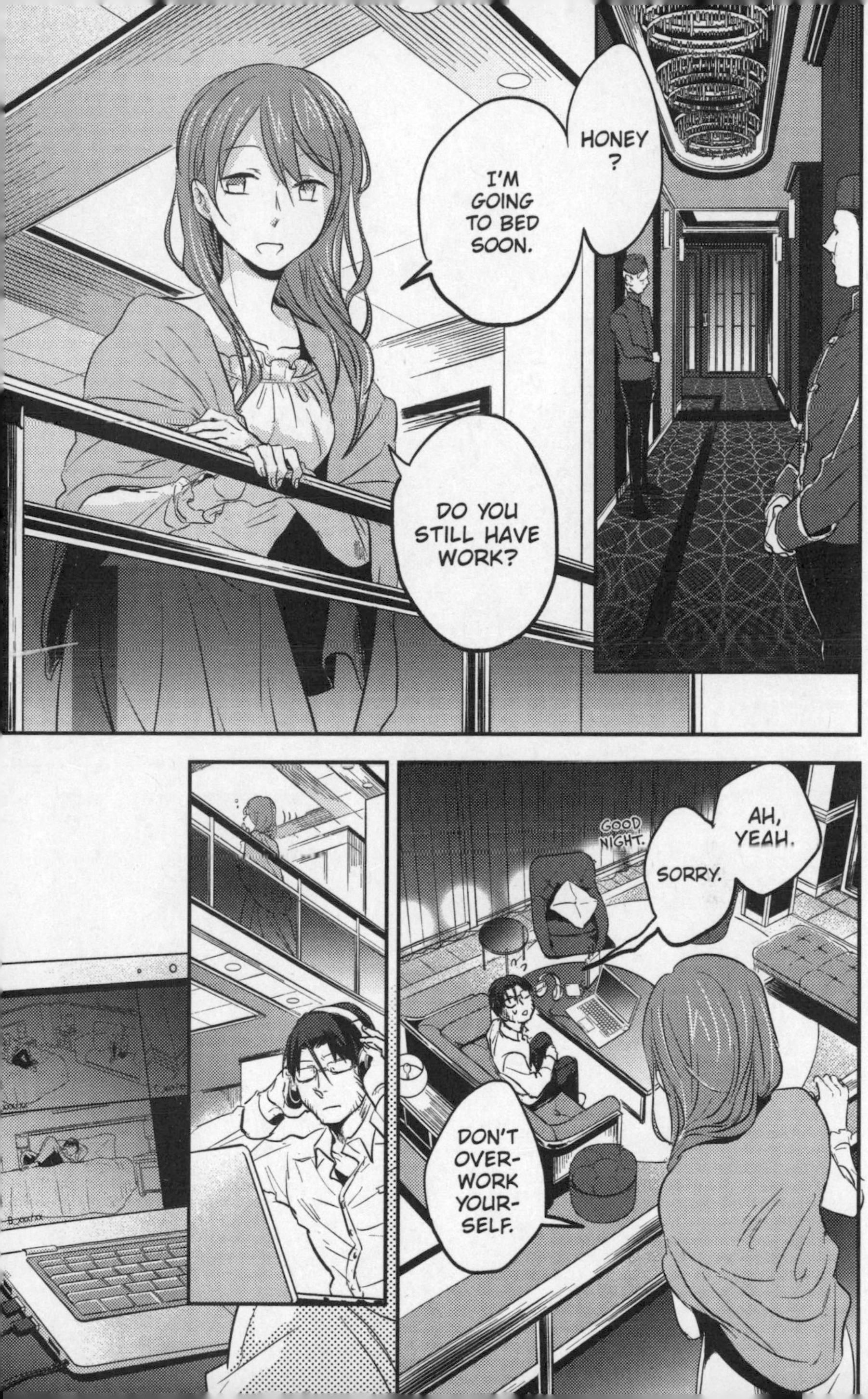
HONEY ?
I'M GOING TO BED SOON.
DO YOU STILL HAVE WORK?
AH, YEAH.
SORRY.
GOOD NIGHT.
DON'T OVER-WORK YOUR-SELF.

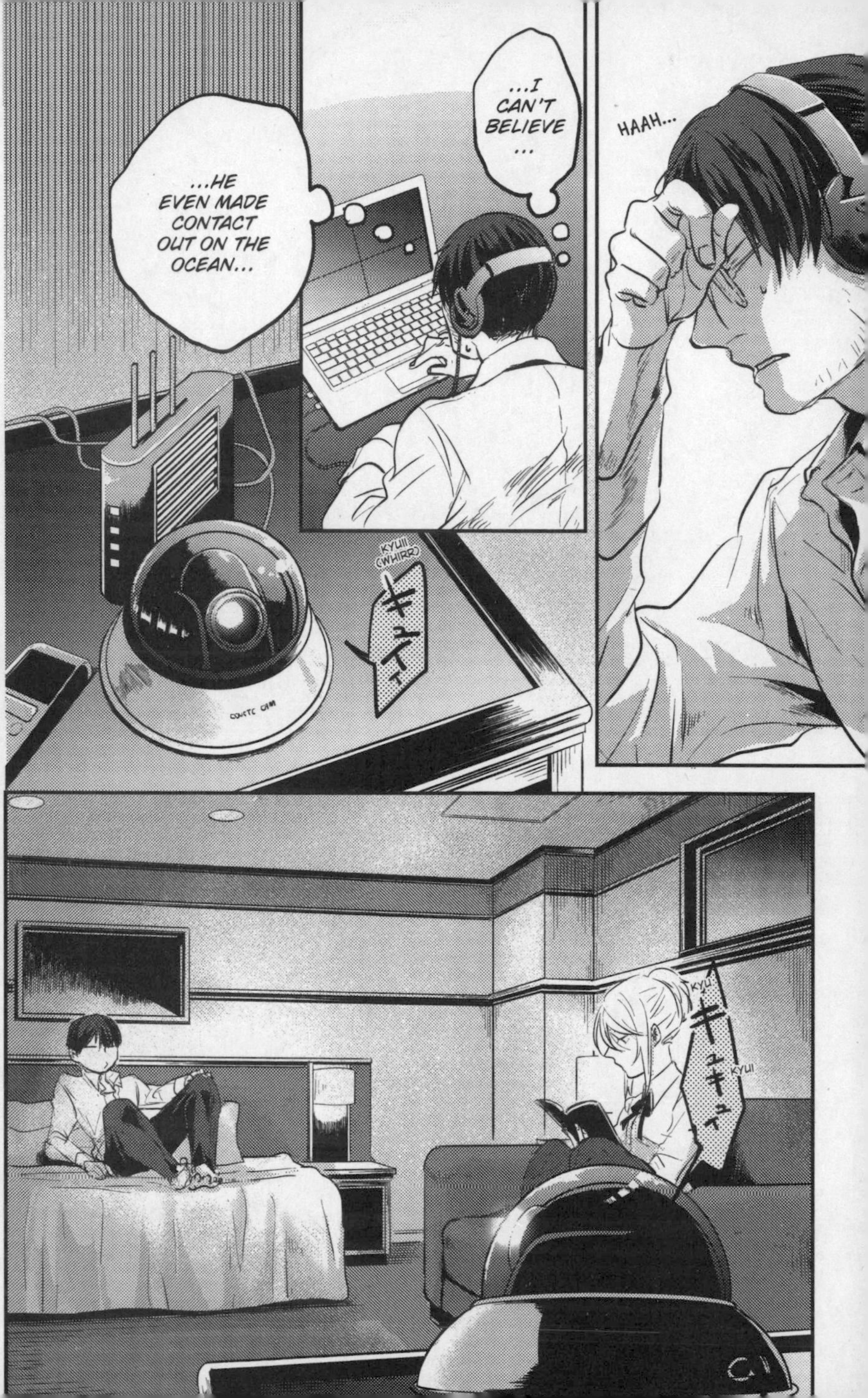

HAAH...
...I CAN'T BELIEVE...
...HE EVEN MADE CONTACT OUT ON THE OCEAN...
KYUII (WHIRR)
KYU
KYUI

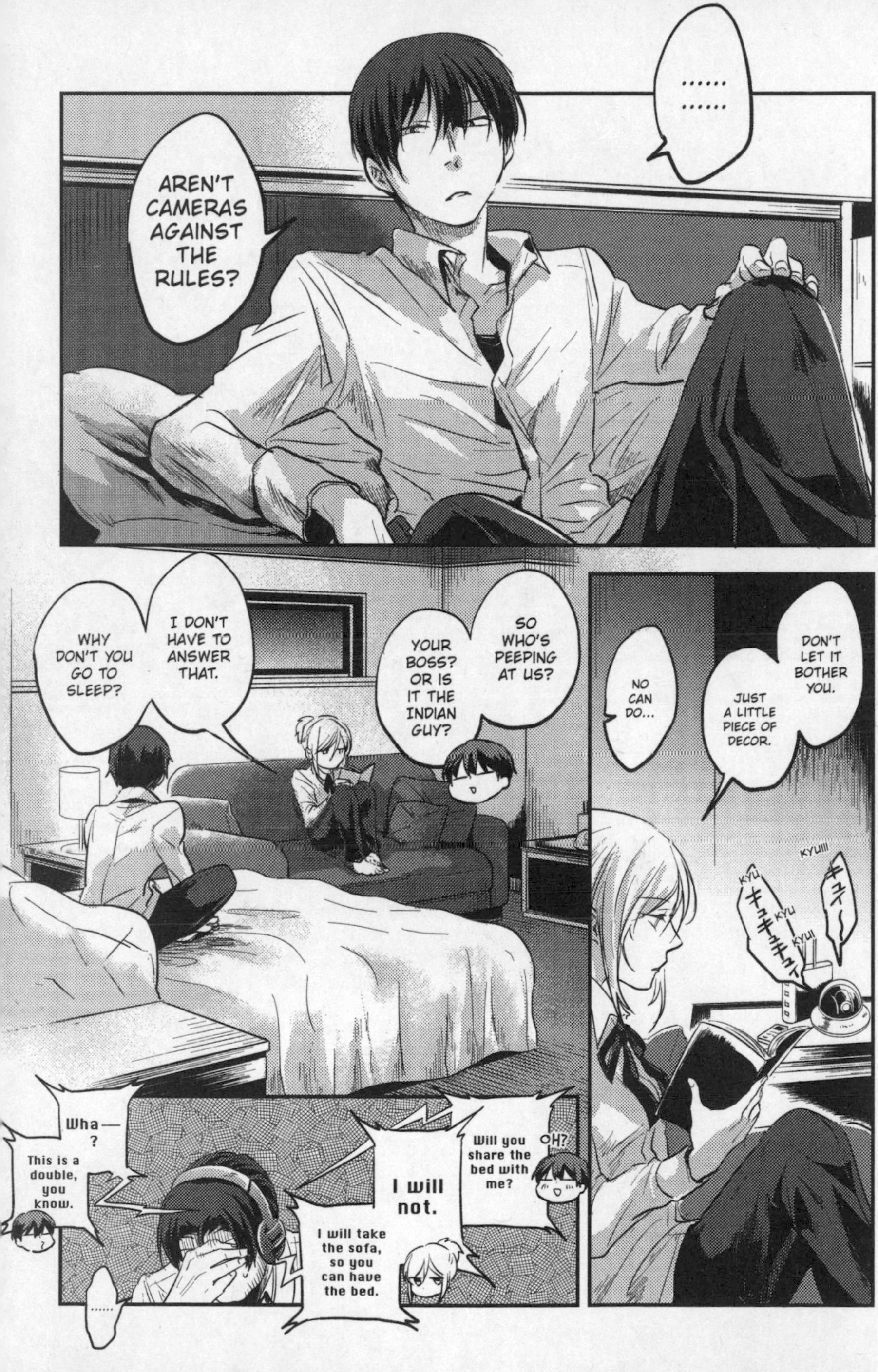

......
......
AREN'T CAMERAS AGAINST THE RULES?
DON'T LET IT BOTHER YOU.
JUST A LITTLE PIECE OF DECOR.
NO CAN DO...
KYUIII
キュイー
KYU KYU KYUI
キュキュキュイ
SO WHO'S PEEPING AT US?
YOUR BOSS? OR IS IT THE INDIAN GUY?
I DON'T HAVE TO ANSWER THAT.
WHY DON'T YOU GO TO SLEEP?
OH?
Will you share the bed with me?
I will not.
I will take the sofa, so you can have the bed.
Wha— ?
This is a double, you know.
......

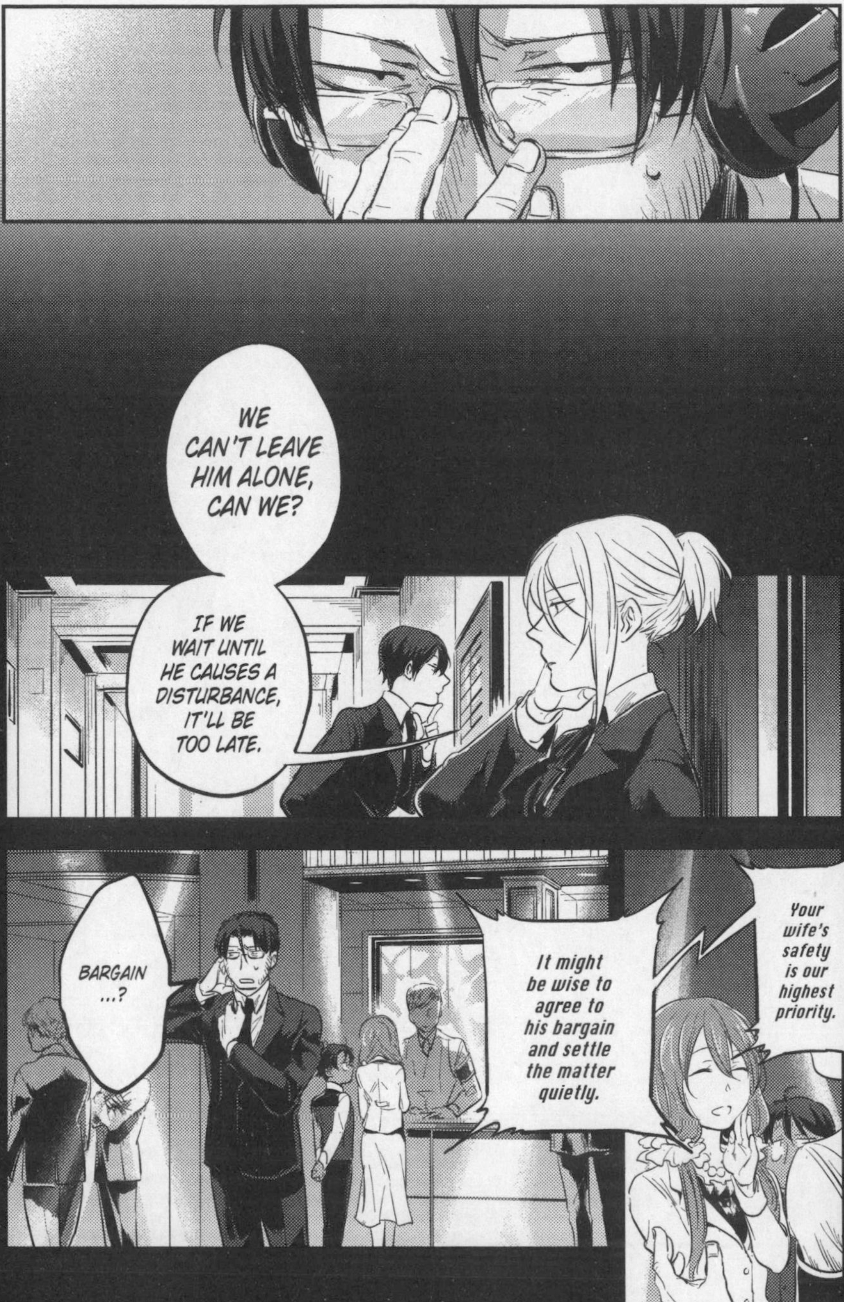
WE CAN'T LEAVE HIM ALONE, CAN WE?
IF WE WAIT UNTIL HE CAUSES A DISTURBANCE, IT'LL BE TOO LATE.
Your wife's safety is our highest priority.
It might be wise to agree to his bargain and settle the matter quietly.
BARGAIN ...?

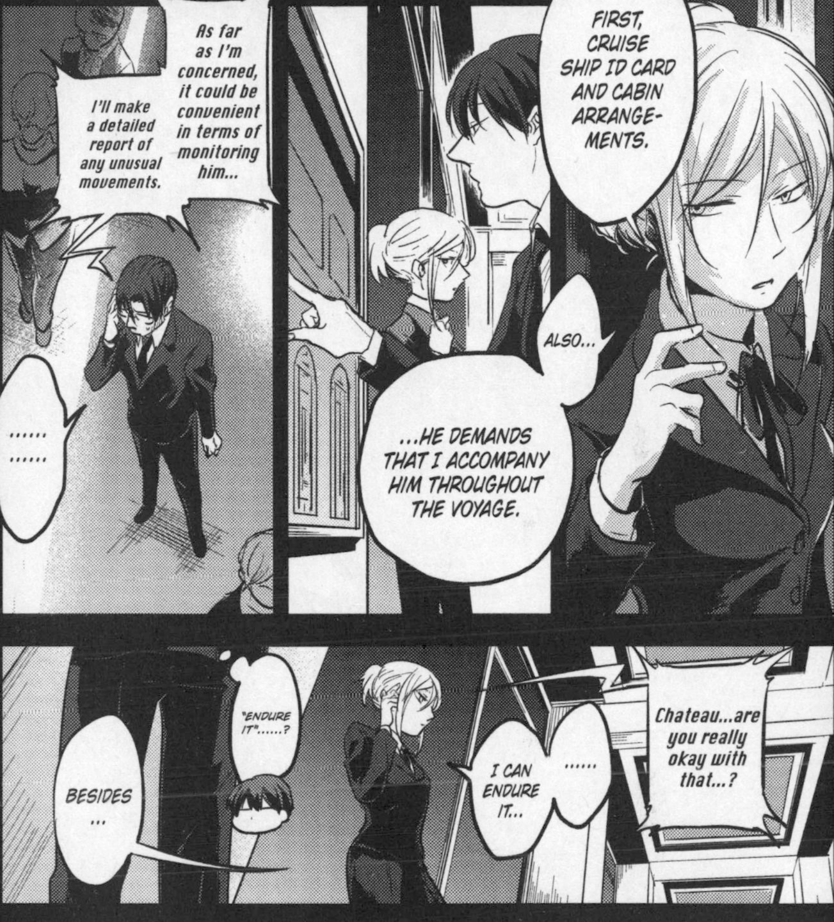
FIRST, CRUISE SHIP ID CARD AND CABIN ARRANGE-MENTS.
ALSO...
...HE DEMANDS THAT I ACCOMPANY HIM THROUGHOUT THE VOYAGE.
As far as I'm concerned, it could be convenient in terms of monitoring him...
I'll make a detailed report of any unusual movements.
....
Chateau...are you really okay with that...?
......
I CAN ENDURE IT...
"ENDURE IT"......?
BESIDES...

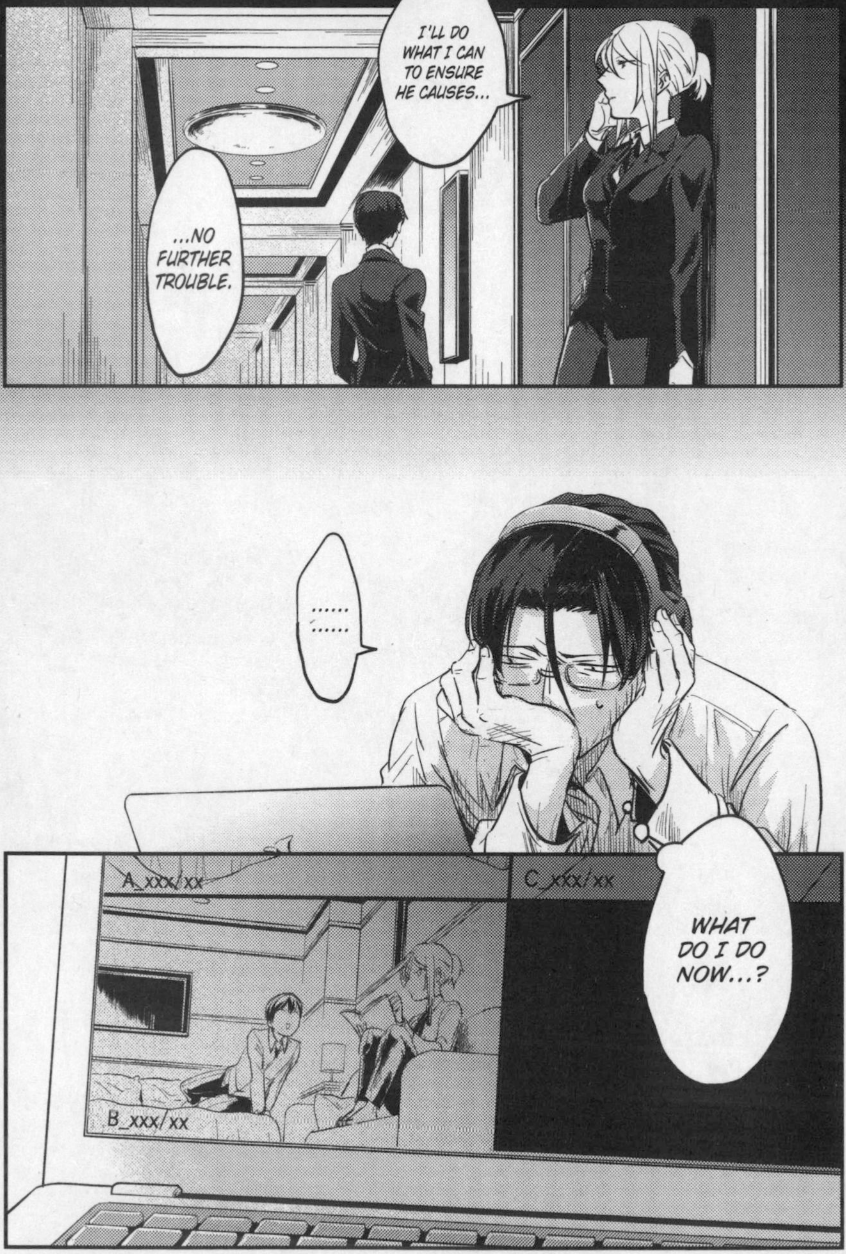
I'LL DO WHAT I CAN TO ENSURE HE CAUSES...
...NO FURTHER TROUBLE.
......
......
C_xxx/xx
A_xxx/xx
WHAT DO I DO NOW...?
B_xxx/xx

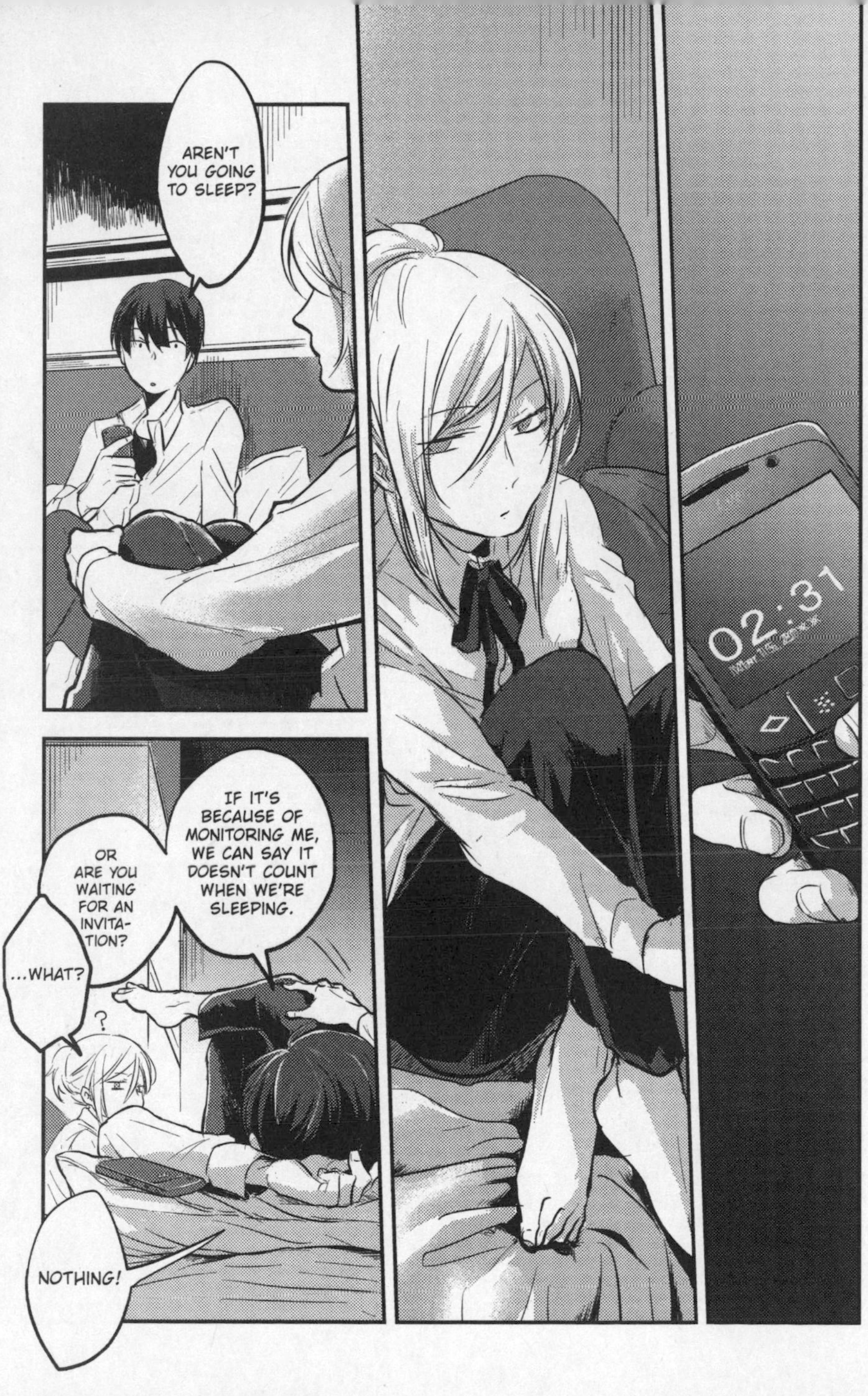
02:31
AREN'T YOU GOING TO SLEEP?
IF IT'S BECAUSE OF MONITORING ME, WE CAN SAY IT DOESN'T COUNT WHEN WE'RE SLEEPING.
OR ARE YOU WAITING FOR AN INVITA-TION?
...WHAT?
?
NOTHING!

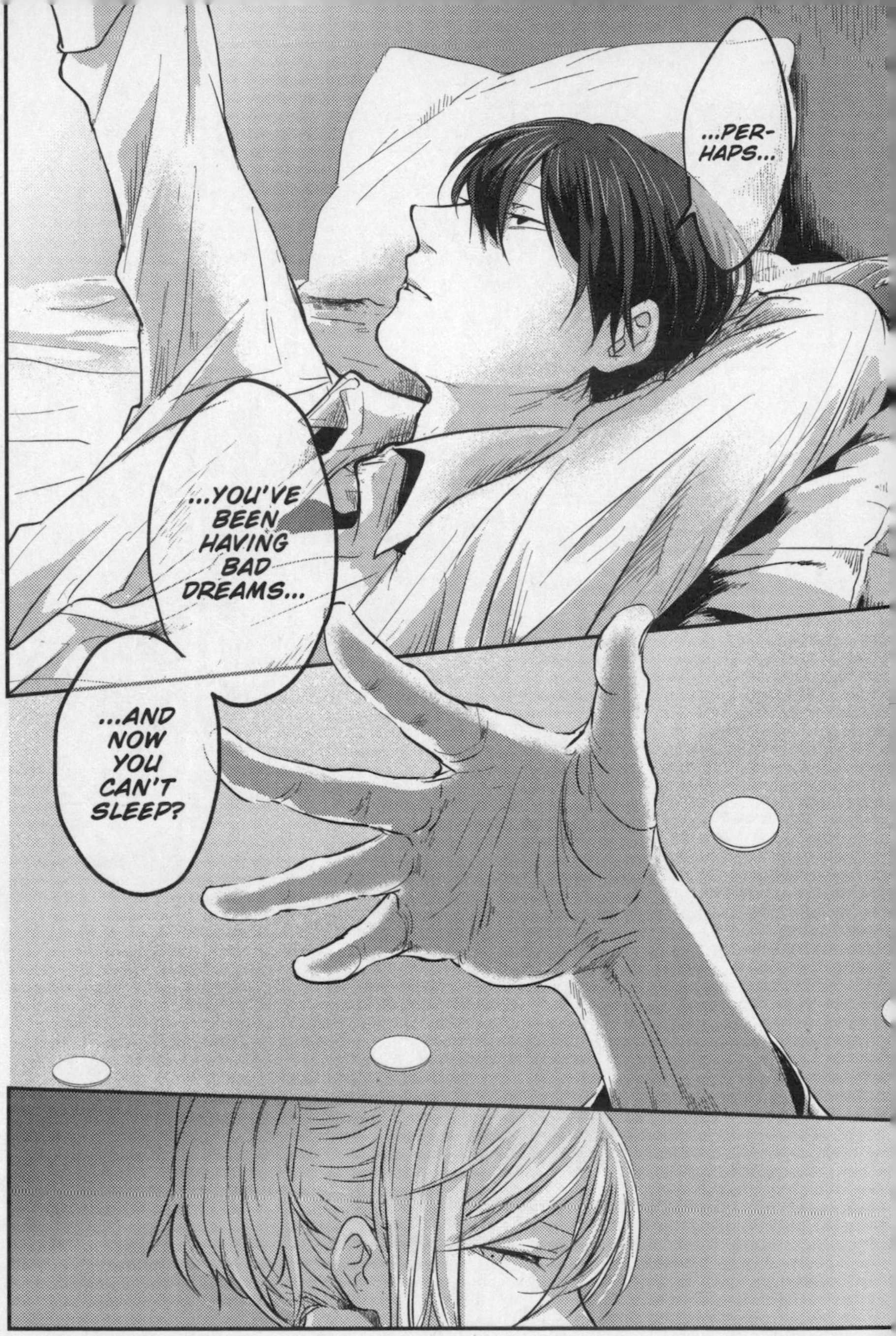
...PER-HAPS...
...YOU'VE BEEN HAVING BAD DREAMS...
...AND NOW YOU CAN'T SLEEP?

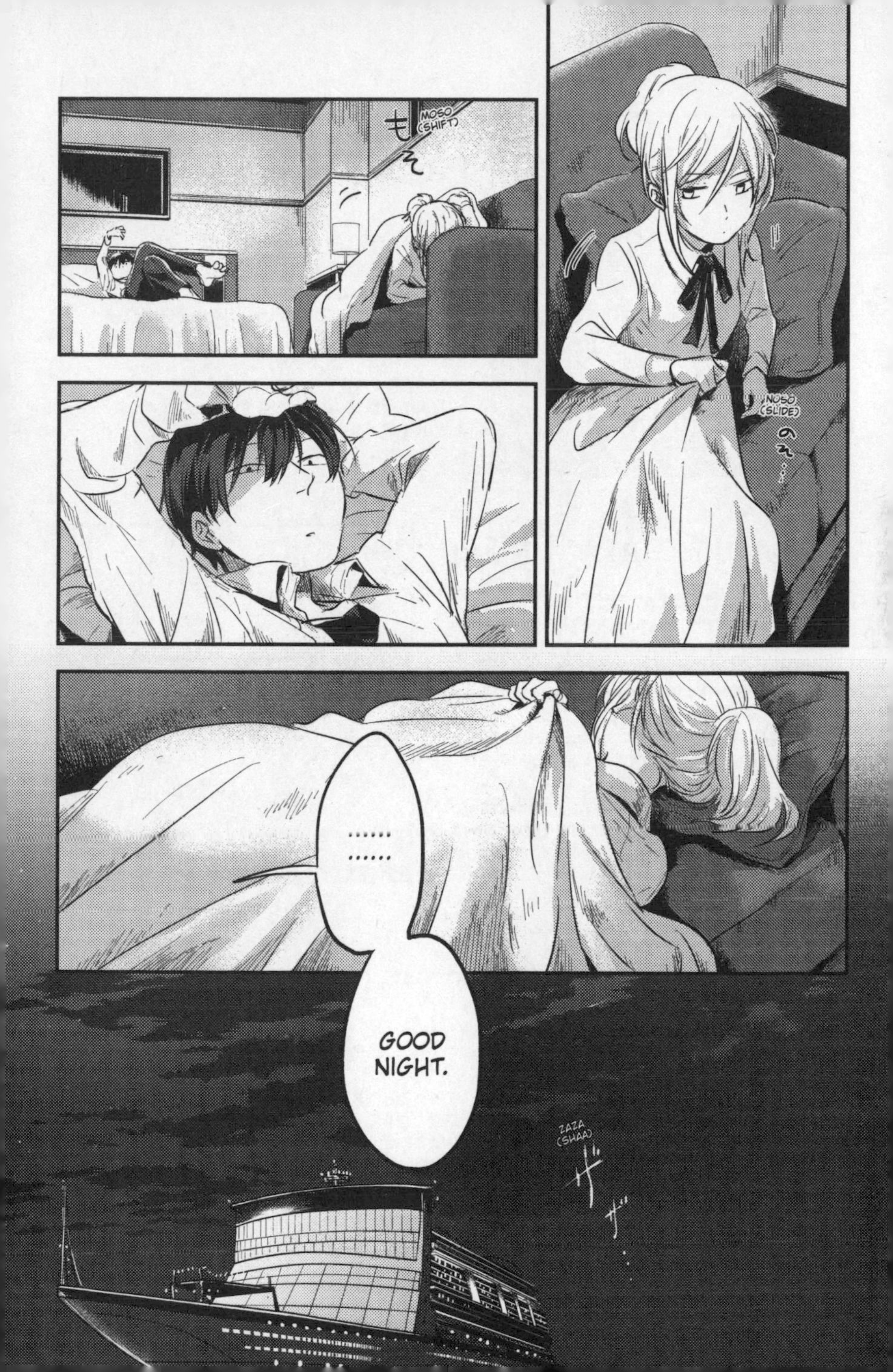
NOSO (SLIDE)
のそ…
MOSO (SHIFT)
もそ
……
……
GOOD NIGHT.
ZAZA (SHAA)
ザザ

FILE 16: WHO ARE YOU?

A NEW DEVELOPMENT.
I HAD THE OPPORTUNITY TO SPEAK TO SOMEONE WHO TRAVELED ON THE *QUEEN ELIZABETH*, A CLASSIC EXAMPLE OF A LUXURY CRUISE SHIP, AND WHILE I WAS DRAWING, I FELT MORE AND MORE AS THOUGH I WAS ON A JOURNEY MYSELF...
I WANT TO SAVE MONEY TO GO ON A CRUISE ONE DAY...

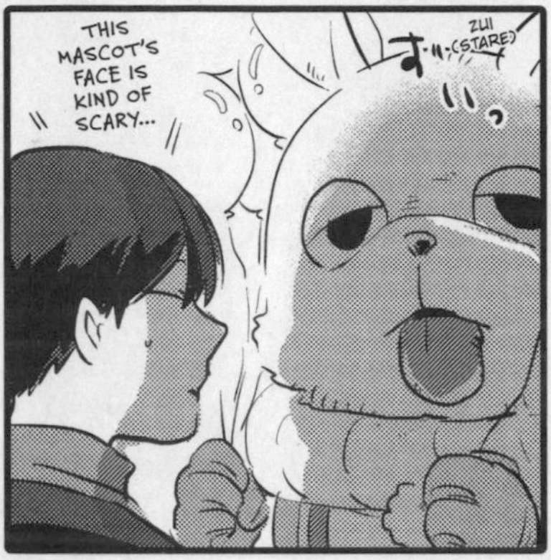
ZUI (STARE)
THIS MASCOT'S FACE IS KIND OF SCARY...

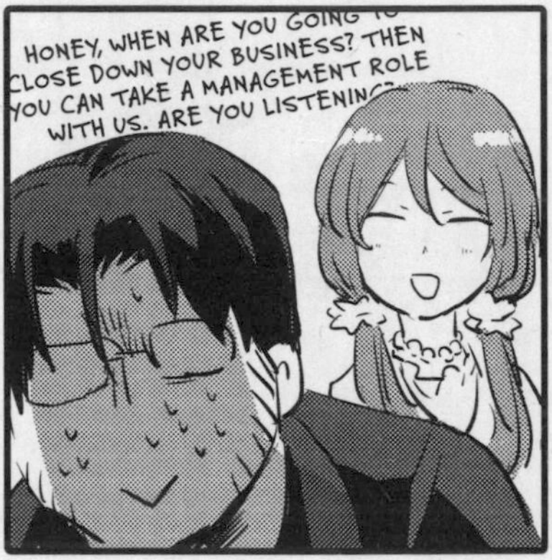
HONEY, WHEN ARE YOU GOING TO CLOSE DOWN YOUR BUSINESS? THEN YOU CAN TAKE A MANAGEMENT ROLE WITH US. ARE YOU LISTENING?

FILE 17: DARK DREAM

THE FIRST APPEARANCE OF THE BOSS'S WIFE. I HAVE A FEELING SHE SHOWED UP MUCH EARLIER IN THE WEB VERSION, BUT SOMEHOW THE TIMING WAS NEVER RIGHT IN THE OFFICIAL SERIALIZATION...
I FINALLY MANAGED TO INCLUDE HER. SHE IS MARRIED TO RITZLAND, BUT THEY LIVE SEPARATELY; SHE SEEMS TO BE THE TYPE OF BUSINESSWOMAN WHO GIVES HER WORK TOP PRIORITY. INCIDENTALLY, SHE IS OLDER THAN HIM.

FILE 18: MAIN ISSUE

I THINK THIS MIGHT BE THE MOST DATE-LIKE CHAPTER SO FAR.
IT'S CLICHÉD, BUT COSTUME CHANGES LIKE THIS ARE FUN TO DRAW, LOL. CHATEAU'S DRESS IS MOST LIKELY BLUE...MAYBE...?
I THINK SHE WAS PROBABLY FORCED TO TRY ON SEVERAL OTHER DRESSES TOO.

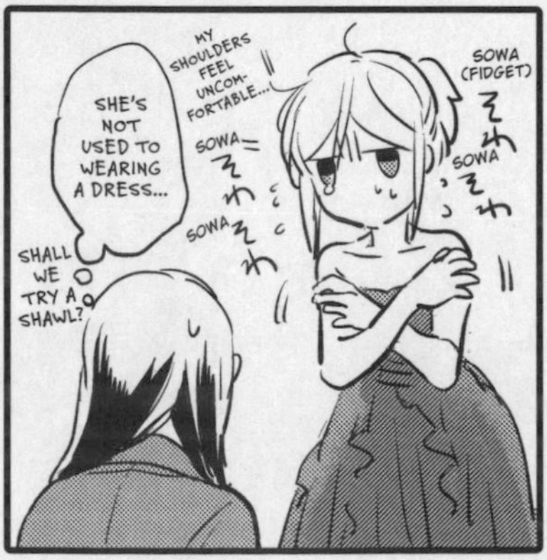
SOWA (FIDGET)
MY SHOULDERS FEEL UNCOMFORTABLE...
SOWA
SOWA
SOWA
SHE'S NOT USED TO WEARING A DRESS...
SHALL WE TRY A SHAWL?

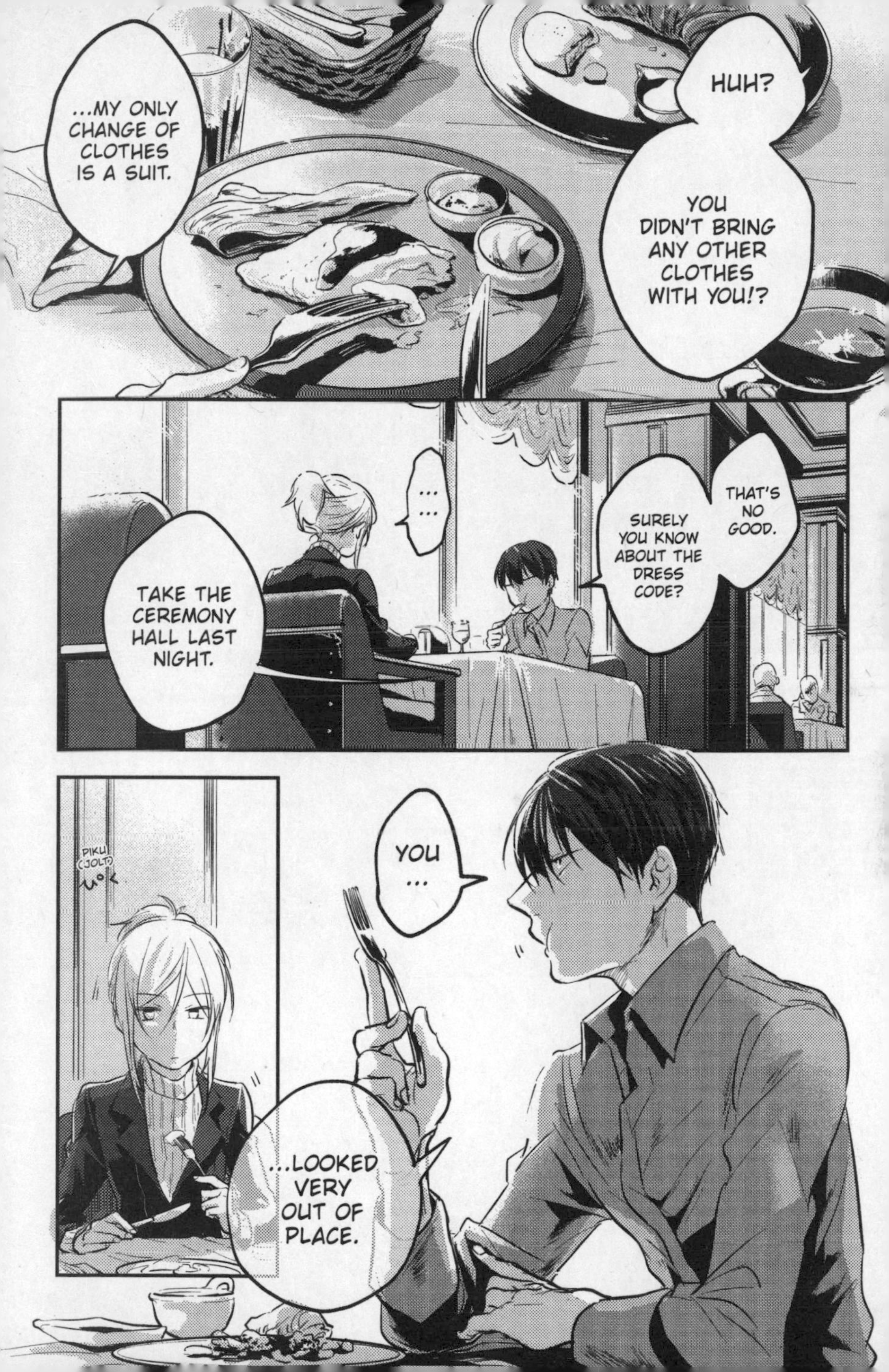
HUH?
YOU DIDN'T BRING ANY OTHER CLOTHES WITH YOU!?
...MY ONLY CHANGE OF CLOTHES IS A SUIT.
THAT'S NO GOOD.
SURELY YOU KNOW ABOUT THE DRESS CODE?
......
TAKE THE CEREMONY HALL LAST NIGHT.
YOU ...
...LOOKED VERY OUT OF PLACE.
PIKU (JOLT)

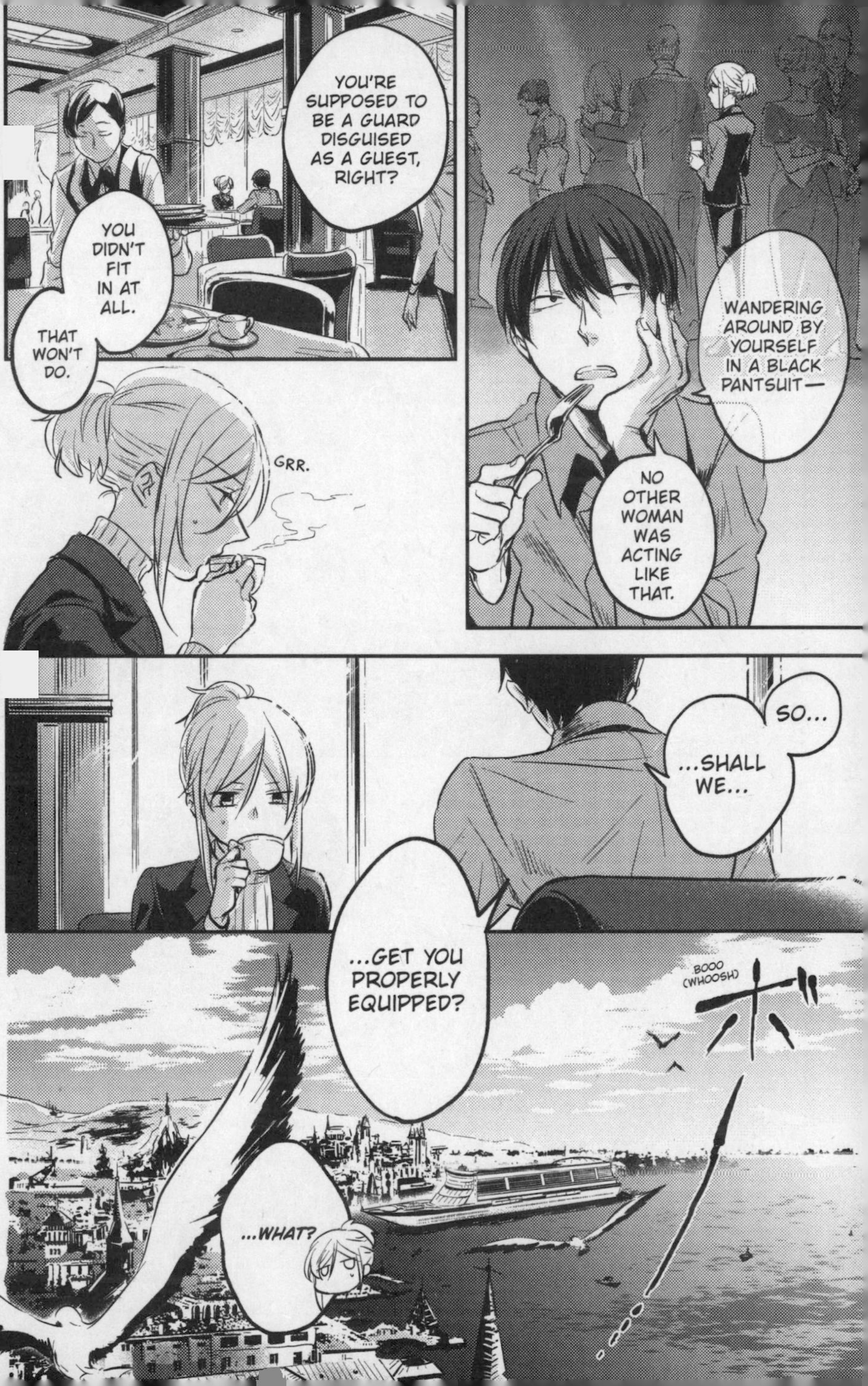
WANDERING AROUND BY YOURSELF IN A BLACK PANTSUIT—
NO OTHER WOMAN WAS ACTING LIKE THAT.
YOU'RE SUPPOSED TO BE A GUARD DISGUISED AS A GUEST, RIGHT?
YOU DIDN'T FIT IN AT ALL.
THAT WON'T DO.
GRR.
SO...
...SHALL WE...
...GET YOU PROPERLY EQUIPPED?
BOOO (WHOOSH)
...WHAT?

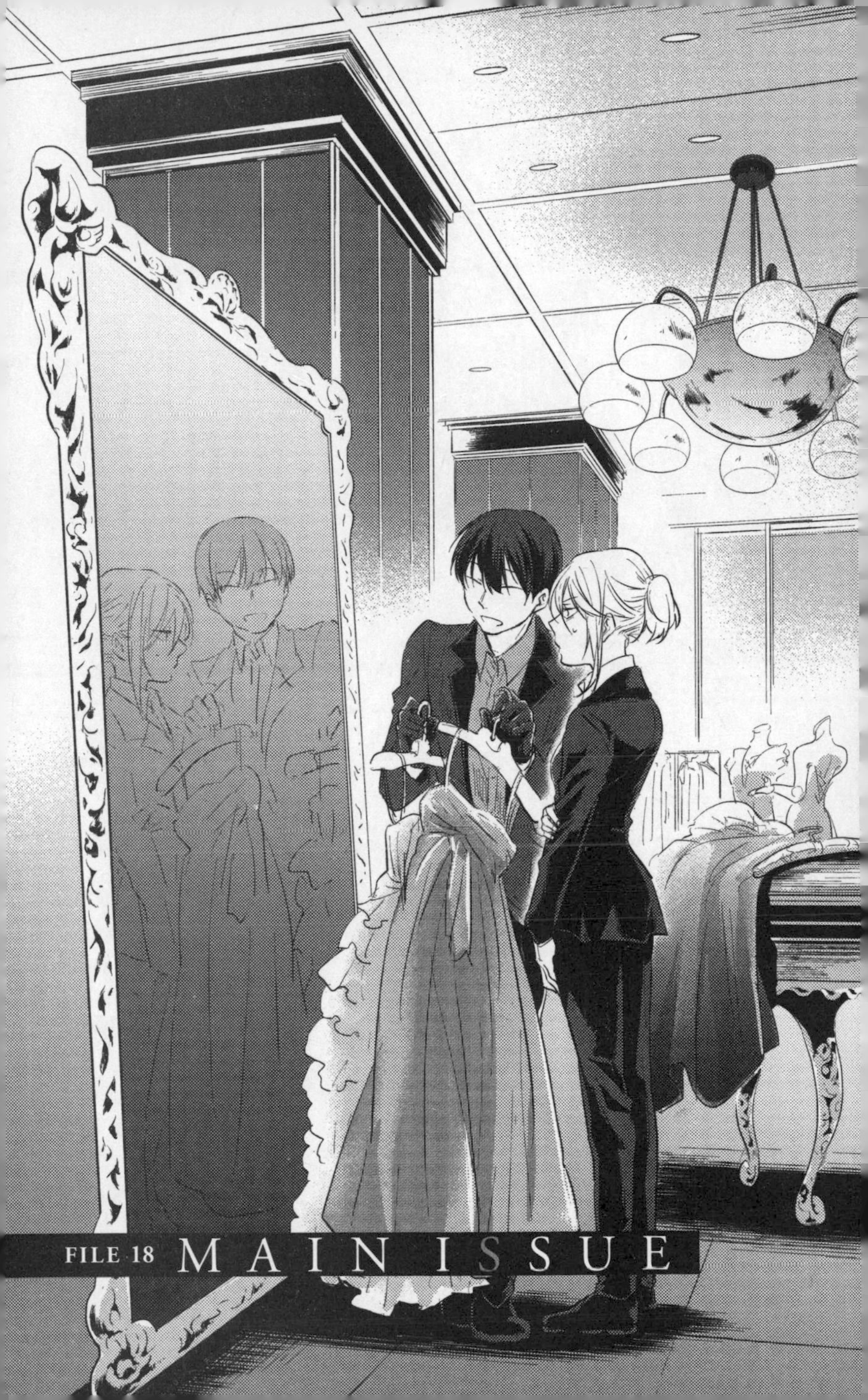
FILE 18 MAIN ISSUE

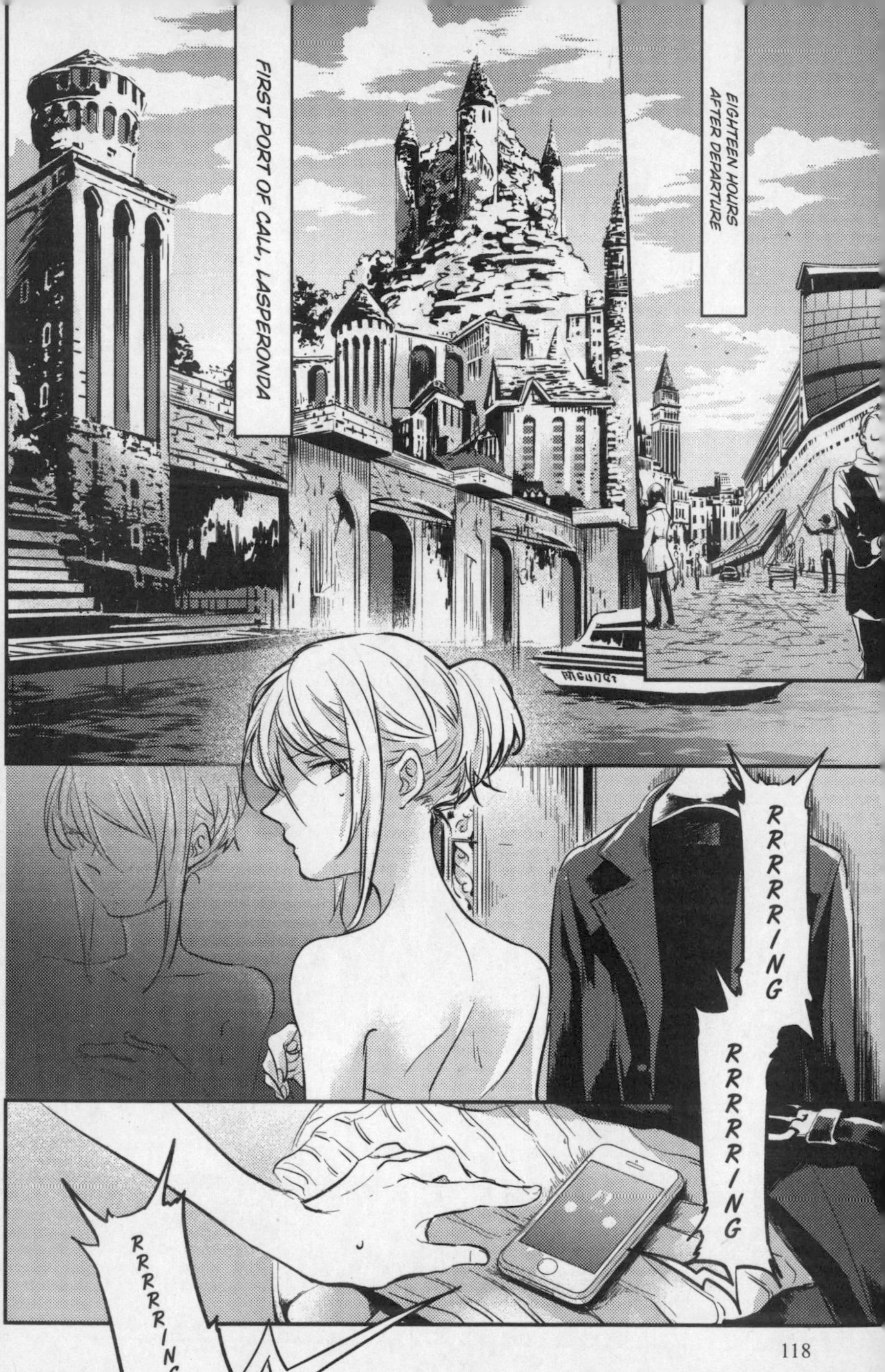
EIGHTEEN HOURS AFTER DEPARTURE
FIRST PORT OF CALL, LASPERONDA
RRRRRING
RRRRRRING
RRRRRING

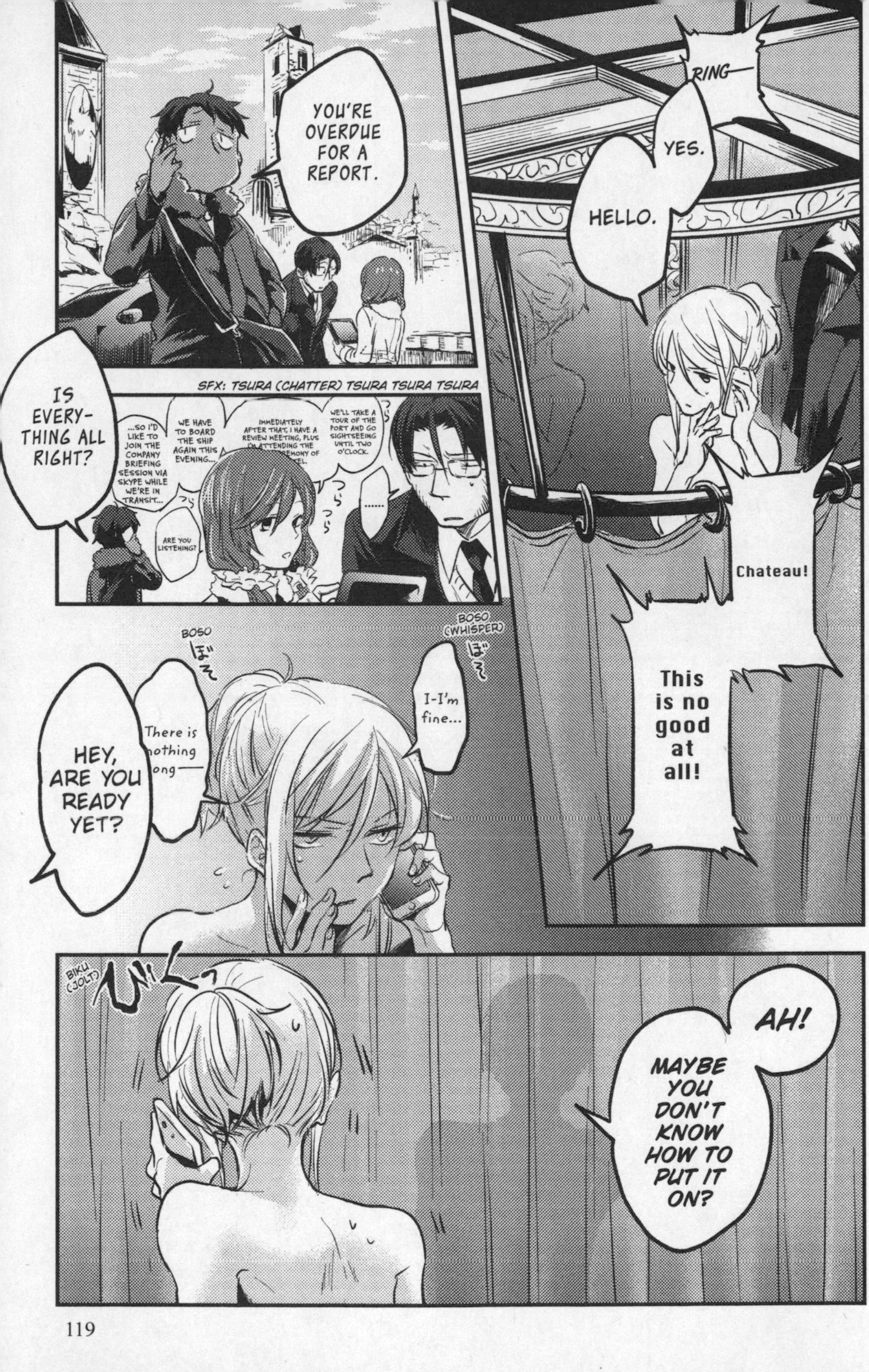
RING—
YES.
HELLO.
Chateau!
This is no good at all!
YOU'RE OVERDUE FOR A REPORT.
SFX: TSURA (CHATTER) TSURA TSURA TSURA
WE'LL TAKE A TOUR OF THE PORT AND GO SIGHTSEEING UNTIL TWO O'CLOCK.
IMMEDIATELY AFTER THAT, I HAVE A REVIEW MEETING, PLUS I'M ATTENDING THE
WE HAVE TO BOARD THE SHIP AGAIN THIS EVENING...
...SO I'D LIKE TO JOIN THE COMPANY BRIEFING SESSION VIA SKYPE WHILE WE'RE IN TRANSIT...
......
ARE YOU LISTENING?
IS EVERY-THING ALL RIGHT?
BOSO (WHISPER)
I-I'm fine...
BOSO
HEY, ARE YOU READY YET?
AH! MAYBE YOU DON'T KNOW HOW TO PUT IT ON?
BIKU (JOLT)

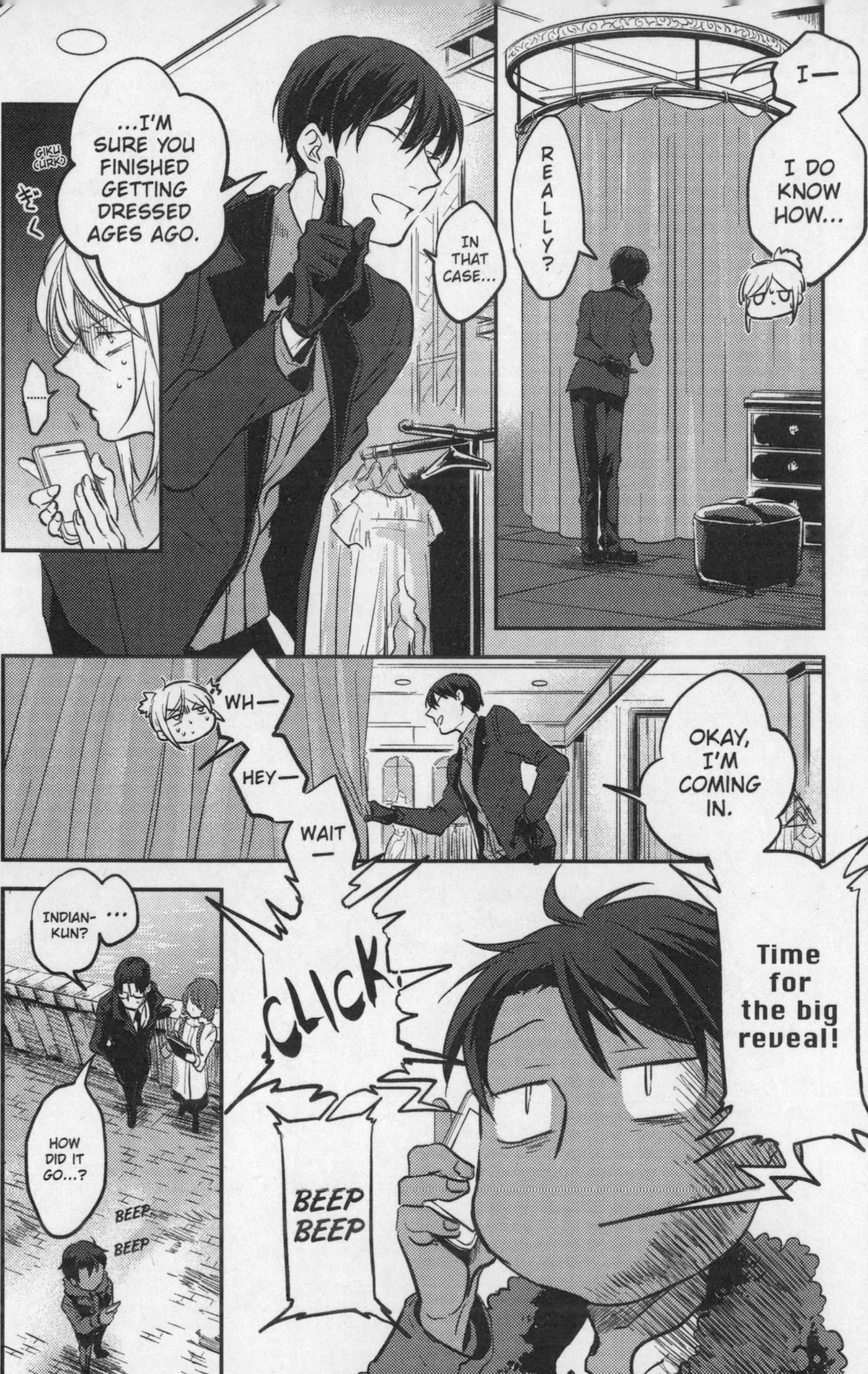

I—
I DO KNOW HOW...
REALLY?
IN THAT CASE...
...I'M SURE YOU FINISHED GETTING DRESSED AGES AGO.
GIKU (URK)
ぎく
......
OKAY, I'M COMING IN.
WH—
HEY—
WAIT—
CLICK
Time for the big reveal!
BEEP BEEP
...
INDIAN-KUN?
HOW DID IT GO...?
BEEP
BEEP

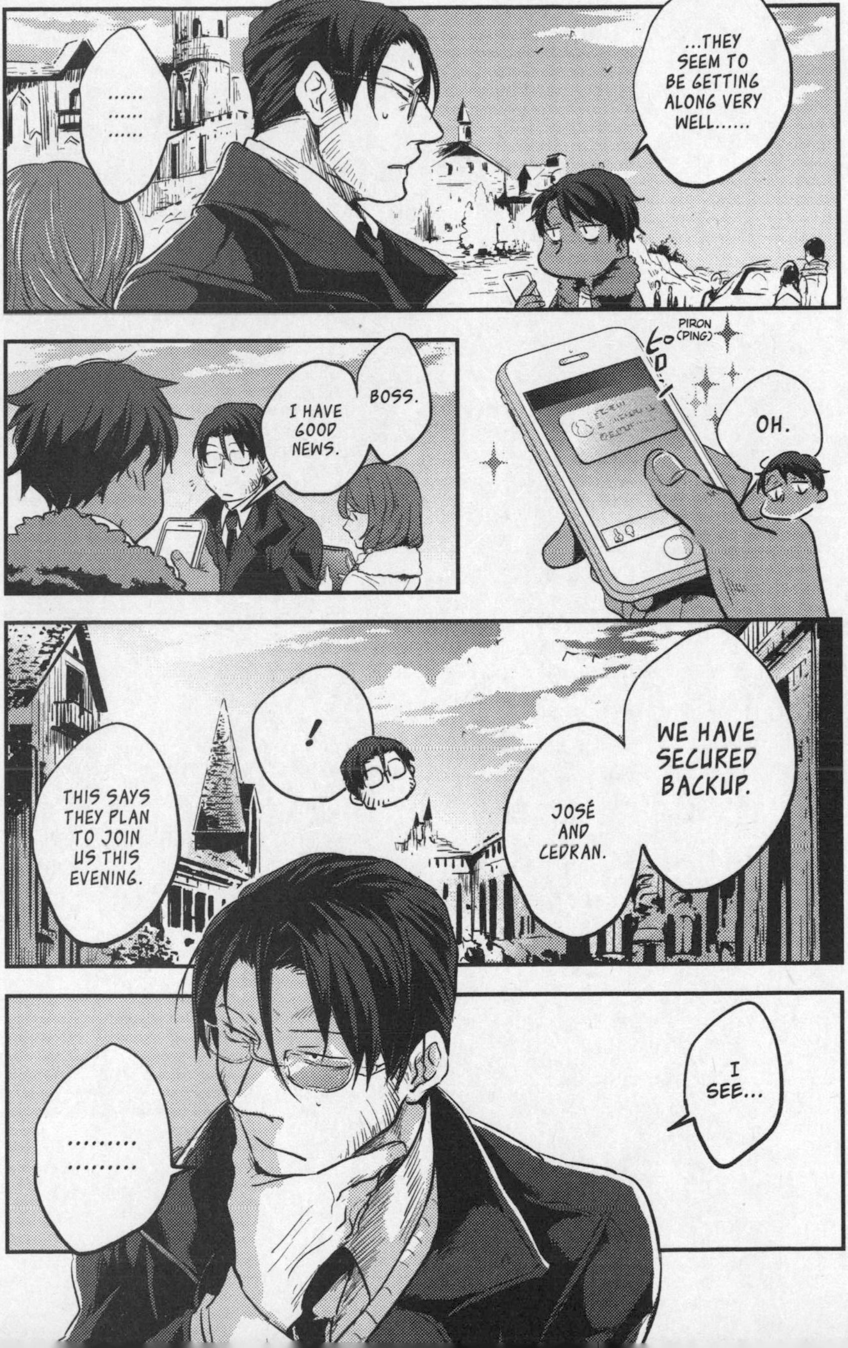
...THEY SEEM TO BE GETTING ALONG VERY WELL......
....
PIRON (PING)
OH.
BOSS.
I HAVE GOOD NEWS.
WE HAVE SECURED BACKUP.
JOSÉ AND CEDRAN.
!
THIS SAYS THEY PLAN TO JOIN US THIS EVENING.
I SEE...
....

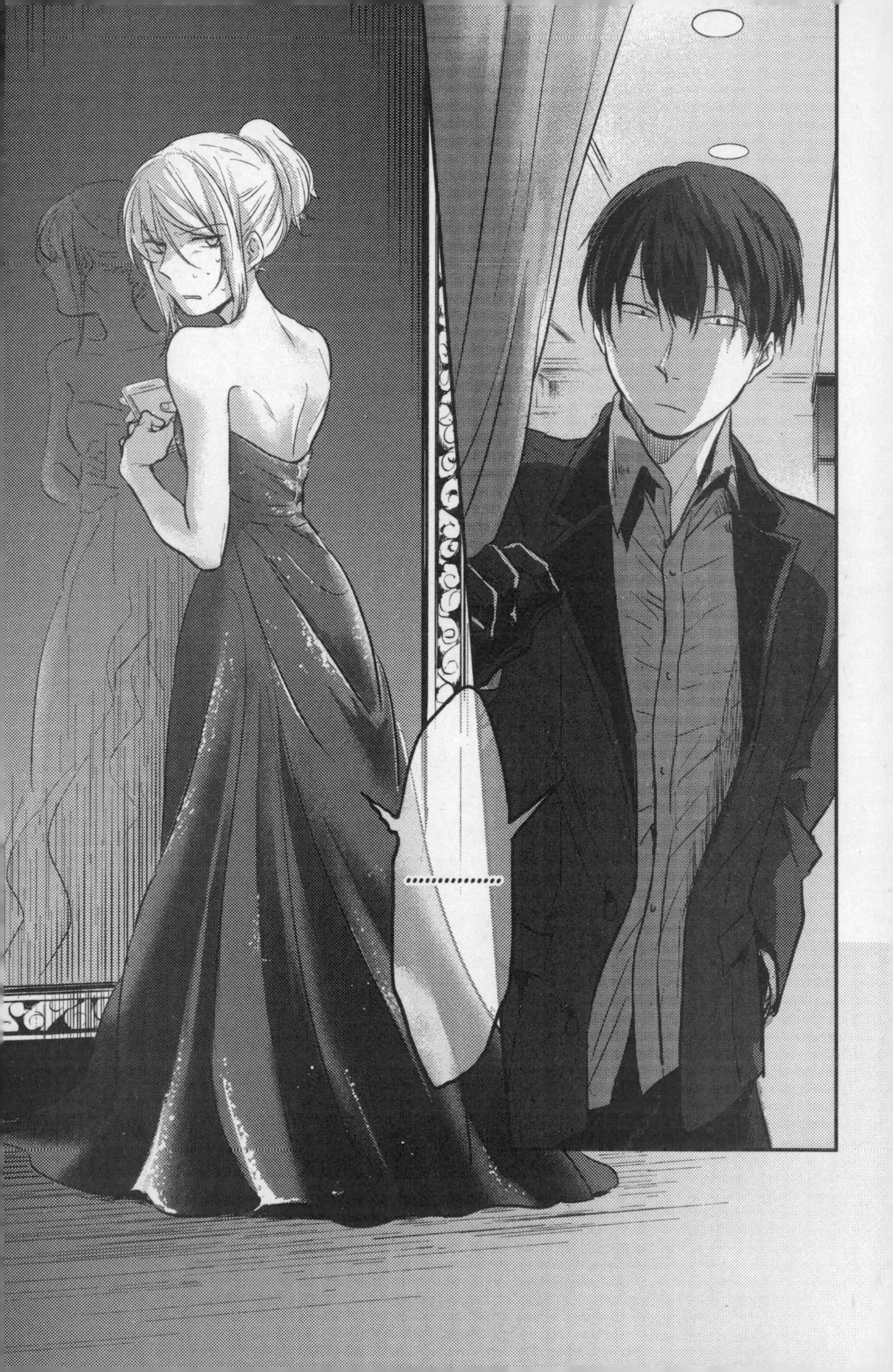
....

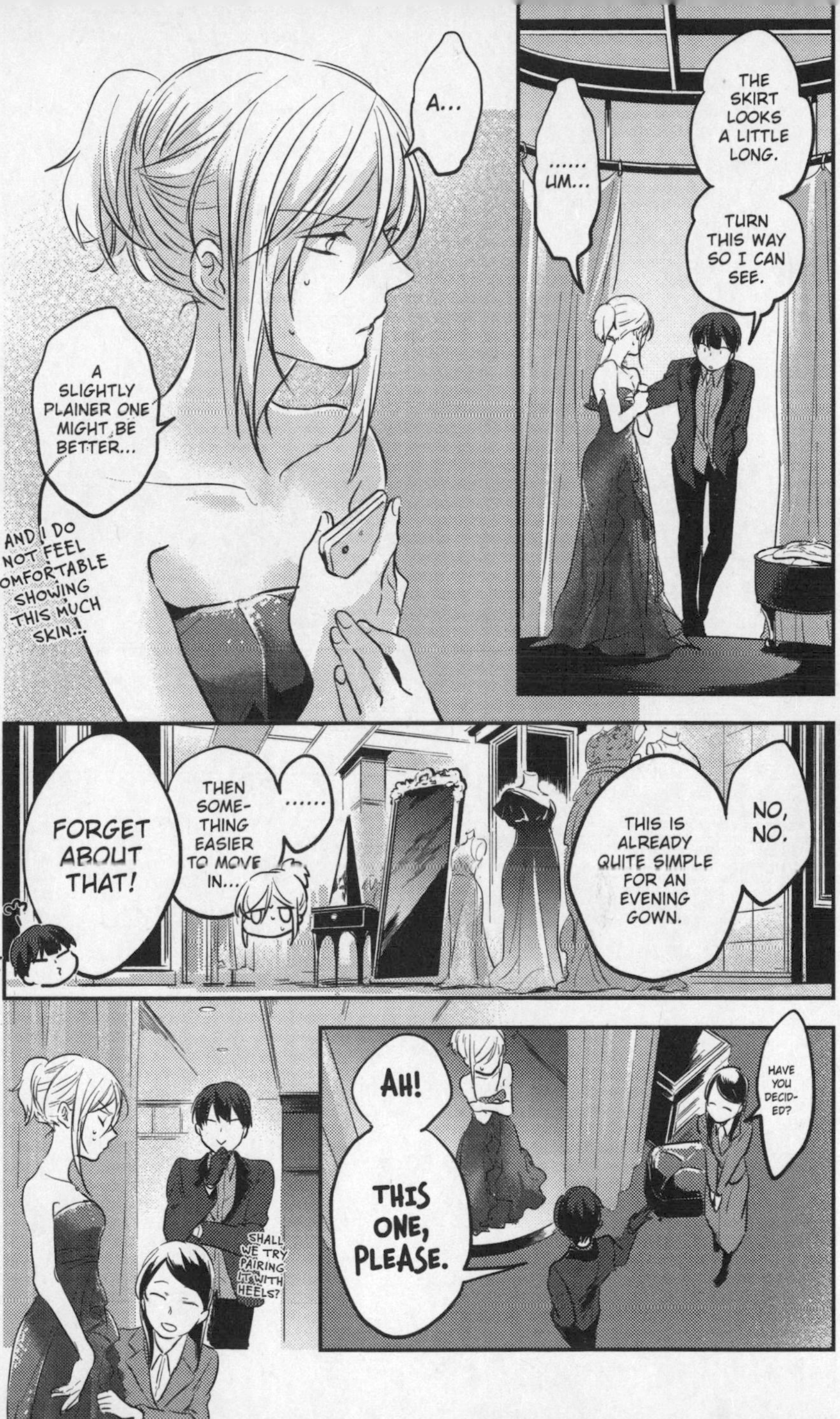
THE SKIRT LOOKS A LITTLE LONG.
TURN THIS WAY SO I CAN SEE.
...... UM...
A...
A SLIGHTLY PLAINER ONE MIGHT BE BETTER...
AND I DO NOT FEEL COMFORTABLE SHOWING THIS MUCH SKIN...
NO, NO.
THIS IS ALREADY QUITE SIMPLE FOR AN EVENING GOWN.
......
THEN SOME-THING EASIER TO MOVE IN...
FORGET ABOUT THAT!
HAVE YOU DECID-ED?
AH!
THIS ONE, PLEASE.
SHALL WE TRY PAIRING IT WITH HEELS?

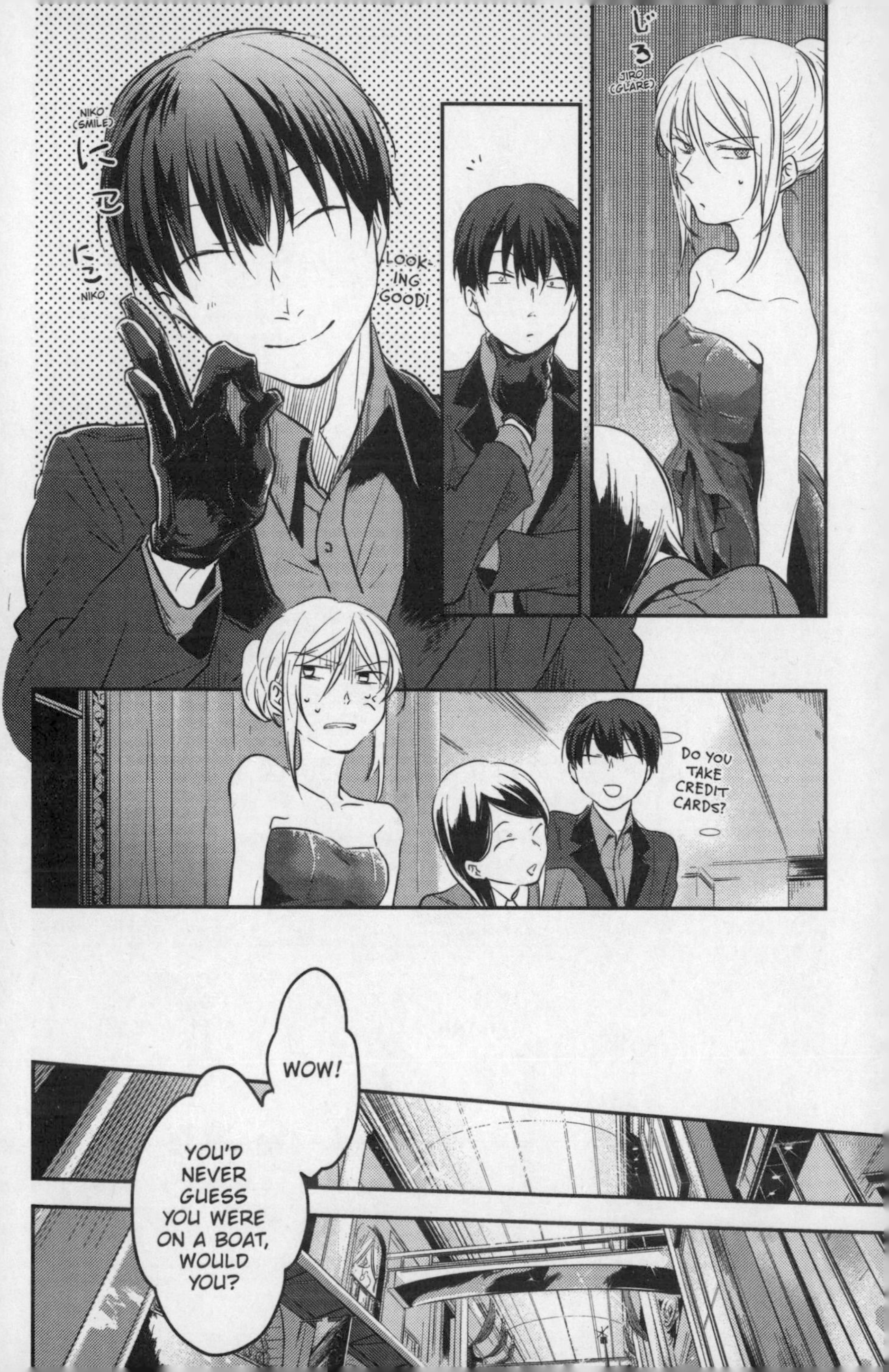
じろ
JIRO (GLARE)
にこ
NIKO (SMILE)
LOOKING GOOD!
にこ
NIKO
DO YOU TAKE CREDIT CARDS?
WOW!
YOU'D NEVER GUESS YOU WERE ON A BOAT, WOULD YOU?

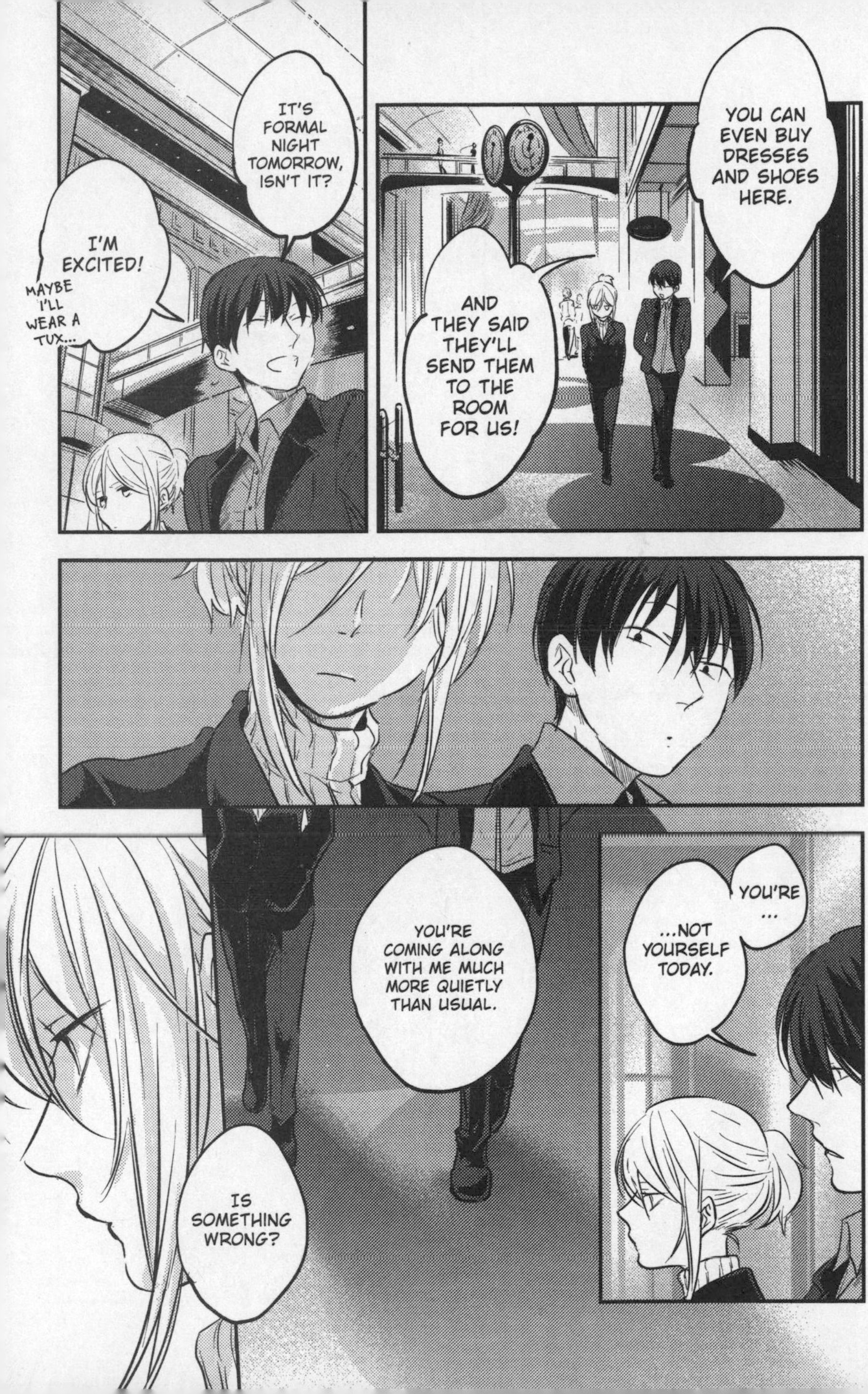

YOU CAN EVEN BUY DRESSES AND SHOES HERE.
AND THEY SAID THEY'LL SEND THEM TO THE ROOM FOR US!
IT'S FORMAL NIGHT TOMORROW, ISN'T IT?
I'M EXCITED!
MAYBE I'LL WEAR A TUX...
YOU'RE ...
...NOT YOURSELF TODAY.
YOU'RE COMING ALONG WITH ME MUCH MORE QUIETLY THAN USUAL.
IS SOMETHING WRONG?

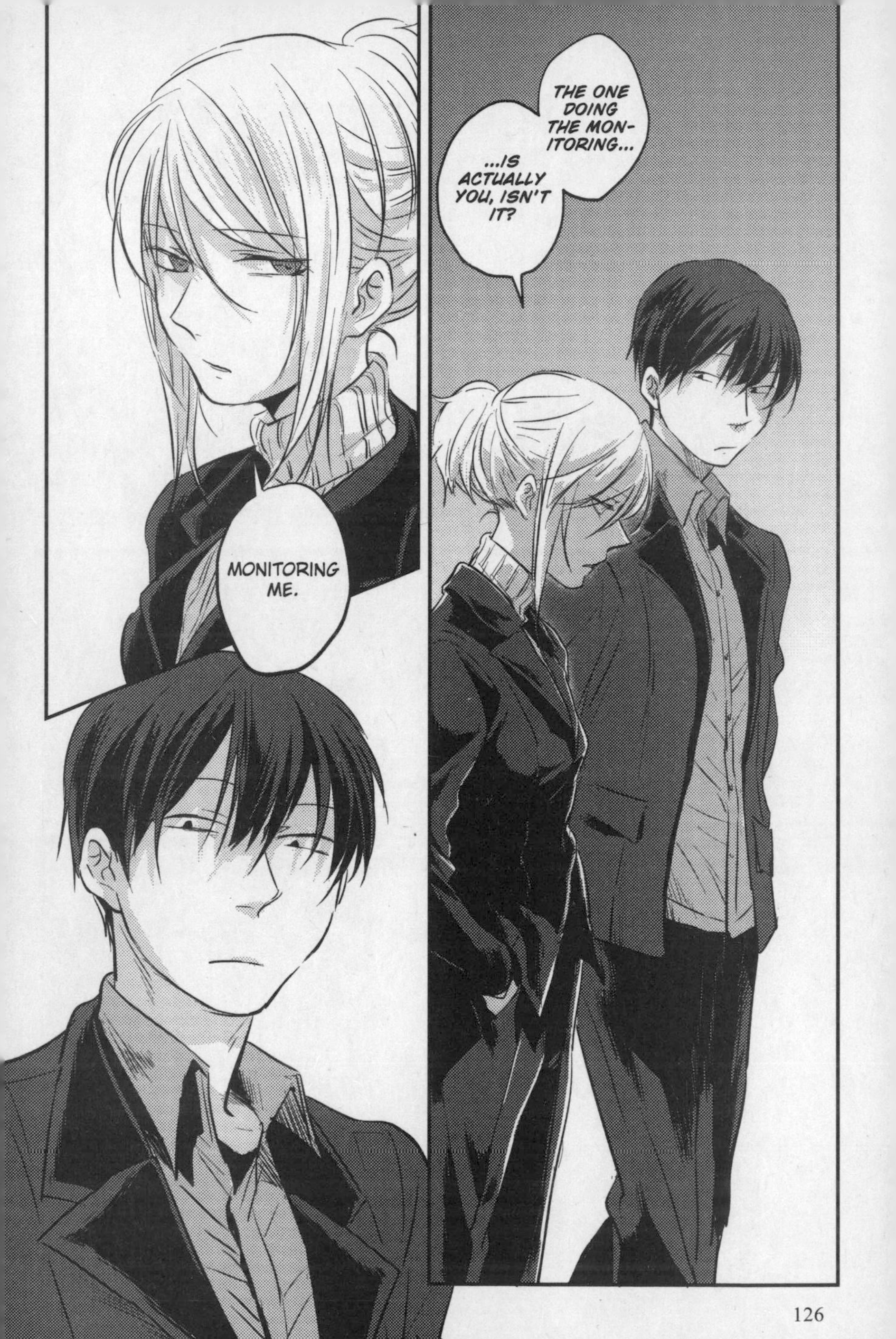
THE ONE DOING THE MON-ITORING...
...IS ACTUALLY YOU, ISN'T IT?
MONITORING ME.

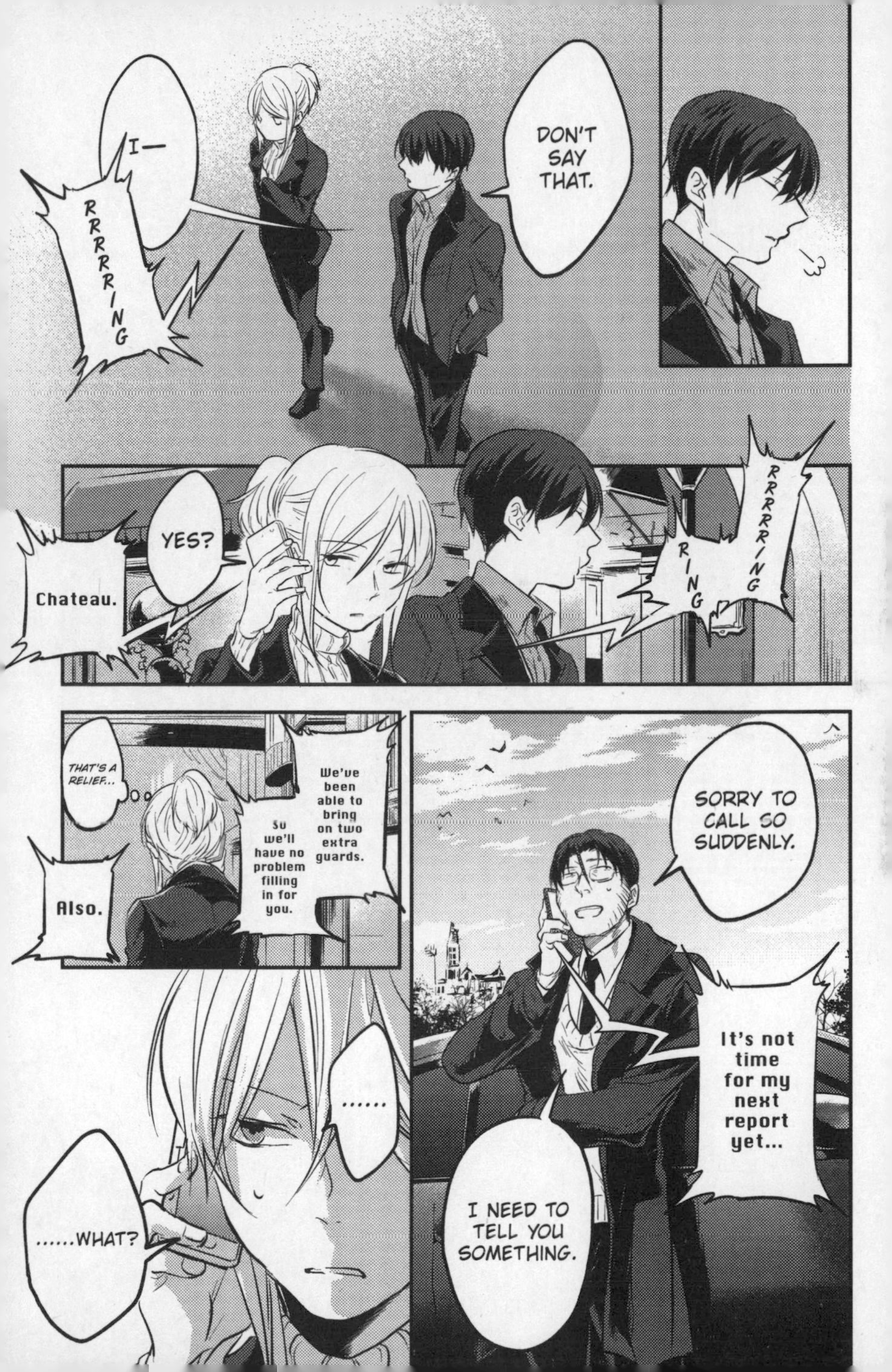
DON'T SAY THAT.
I—
RRRRRING
RRRRRING RING
YES?
Chateau.
SORRY TO CALL SO SUDDENLY.
It's not time for my next report yet...
I NEED TO TELL YOU SOMETHING.
We've been able to bring on two extra guards.
So we'll have no problem filling in for you.
THAT'S A RELIEF...
Also.
......
......WHAT?

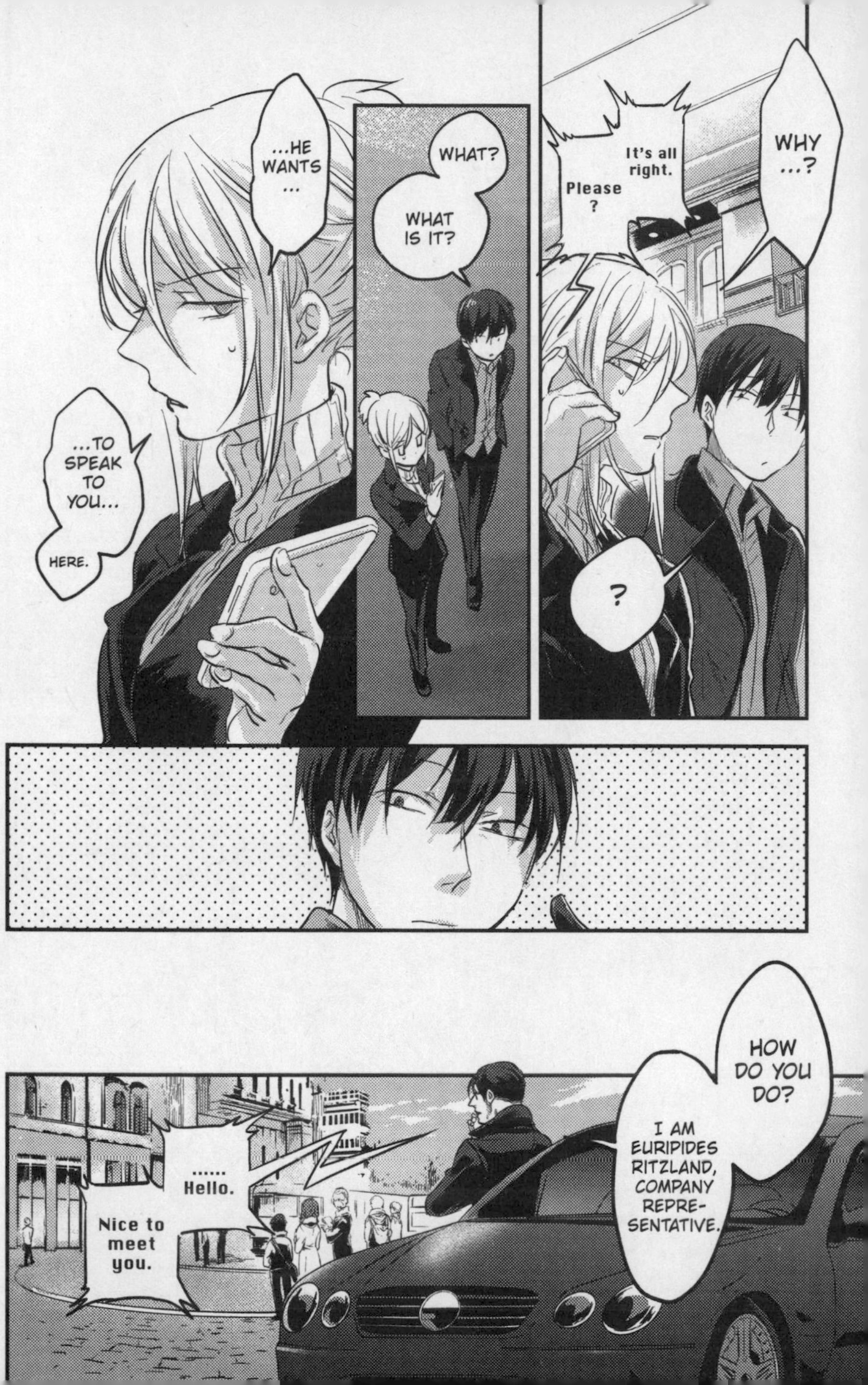
WHY ...?
It's all right.
Please ?
?
WHAT?
WHAT IS IT?
...HE WANTS ...
...TO SPEAK TO YOU...
HERE.
HOW DO YOU DO?
I AM EURIPIDES RITZLAND, COMPANY REPRESENTATIVE.
...... Hello.
Nice to meet you.

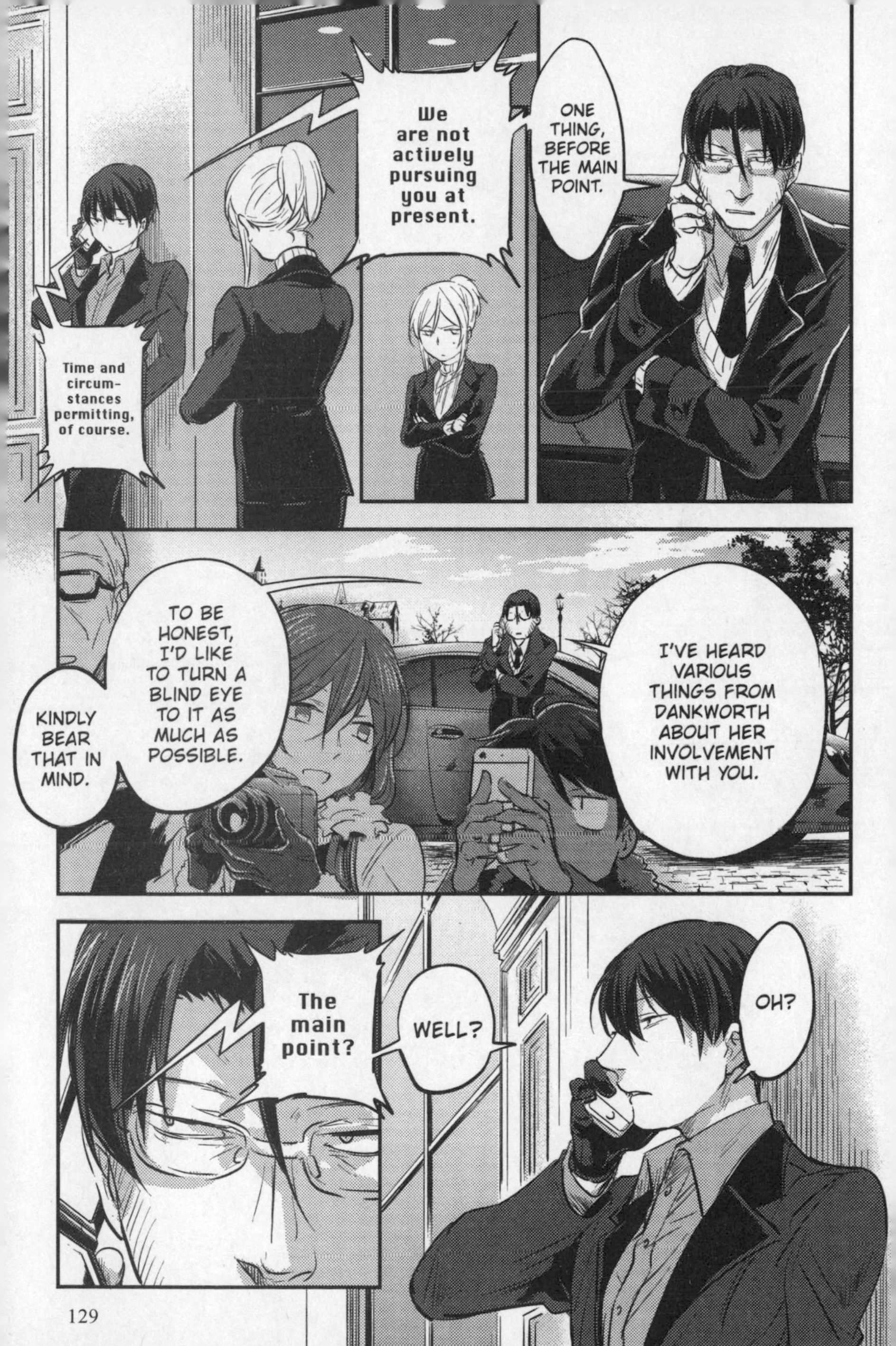
ONE THING, BEFORE THE MAIN POINT.
We are not actively pursuing you at present.
Time and circumstances permitting, of course.
I'VE HEARD VARIOUS THINGS FROM DANKWORTH ABOUT HER INVOLVEMENT WITH YOU.
TO BE HONEST, I'D LIKE TO TURN A BLIND EYE TO IT AS MUCH AS POSSIBLE.
KINDLY BEAR THAT IN MIND.
OH?
WELL?
The main point?

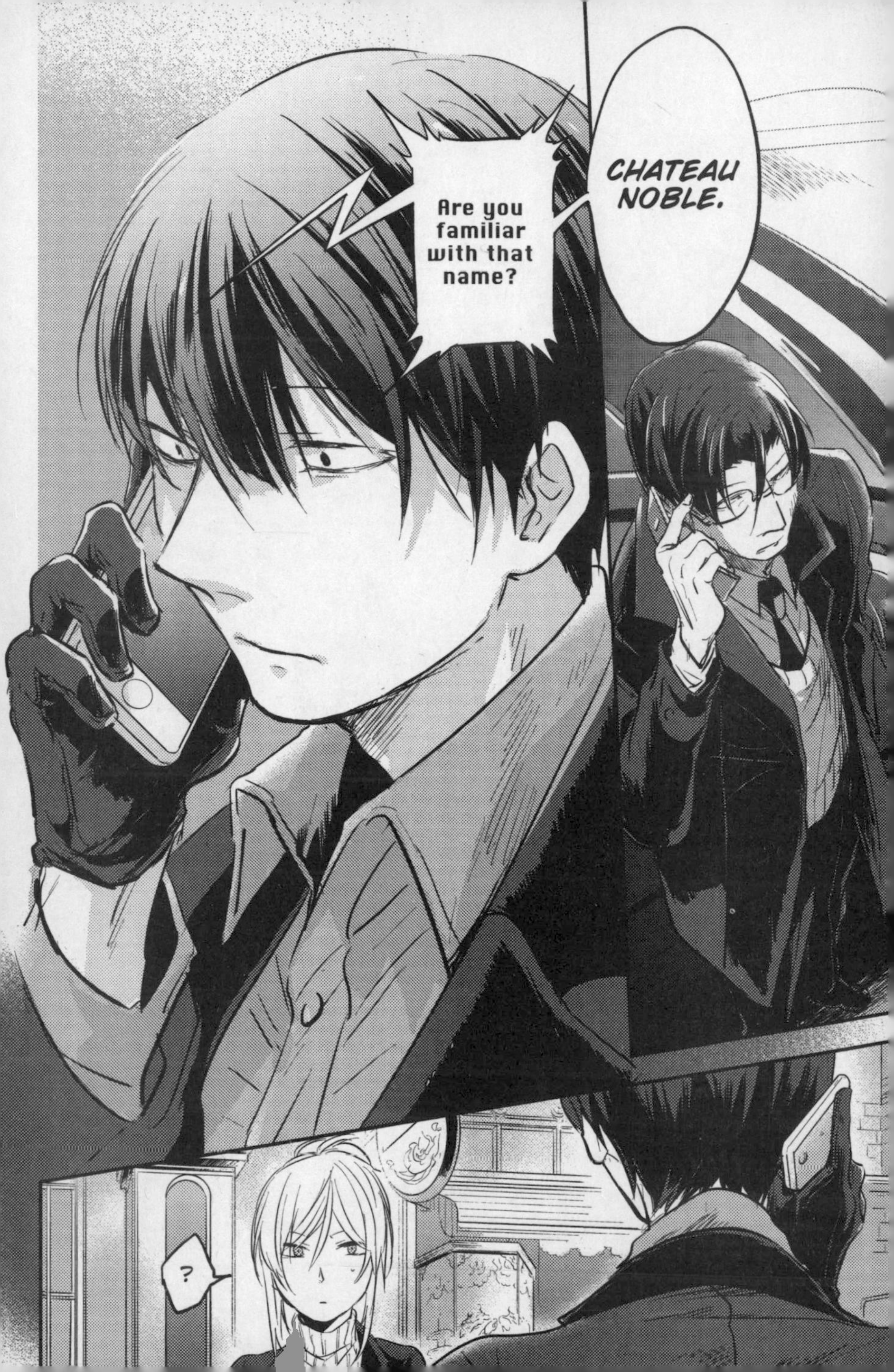
CHATEAU NOBLE.
Are you familiar with that name?
?

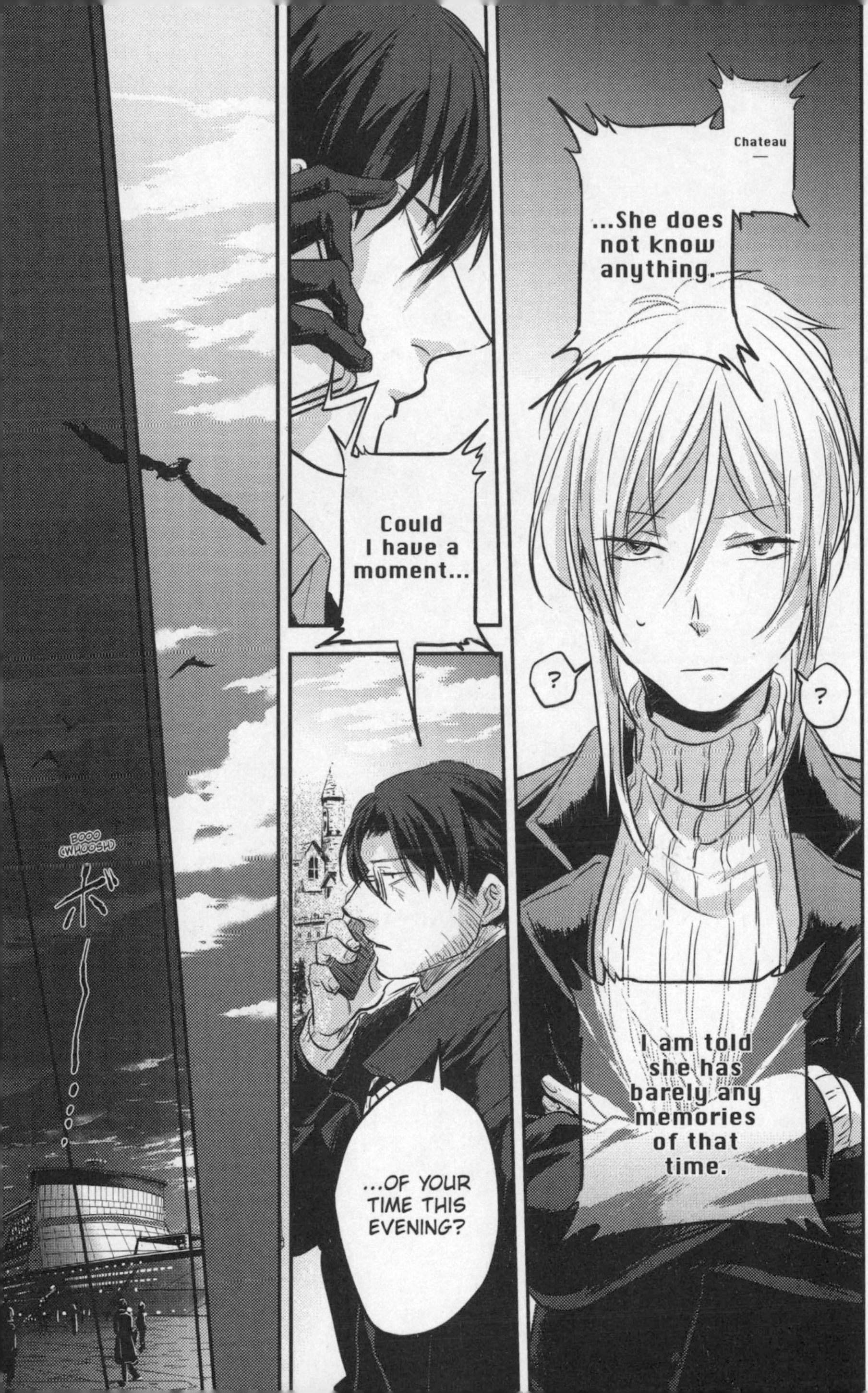
Chateau
...She does not know anything.
?
?
I am told she has barely any memories of that time.
Could I have a moment...
...OF YOUR TIME THIS EVENING?
ボー
BOOO (WHOOSH)

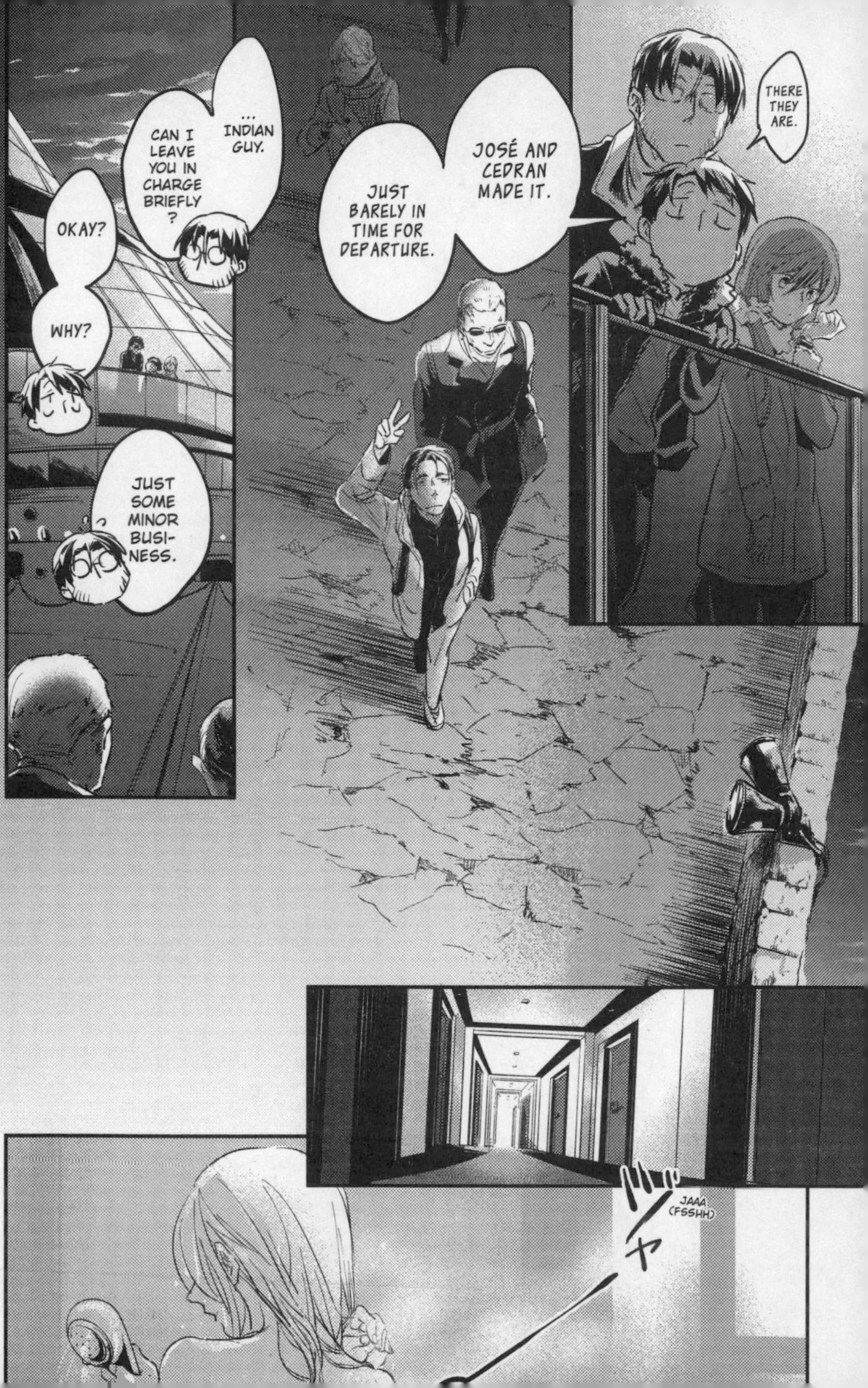
THERE THEY ARE.
JOSÉ AND CEDRAN MADE IT.
JUST BARELY IN TIME FOR DEPARTURE.
... INDIAN GUY.
CAN I LEAVE YOU IN CHARGE BRIEFLY?
OKAY?
WHY?
JUST SOME MINOR BUSINESS.
JAAA (FSSHH)

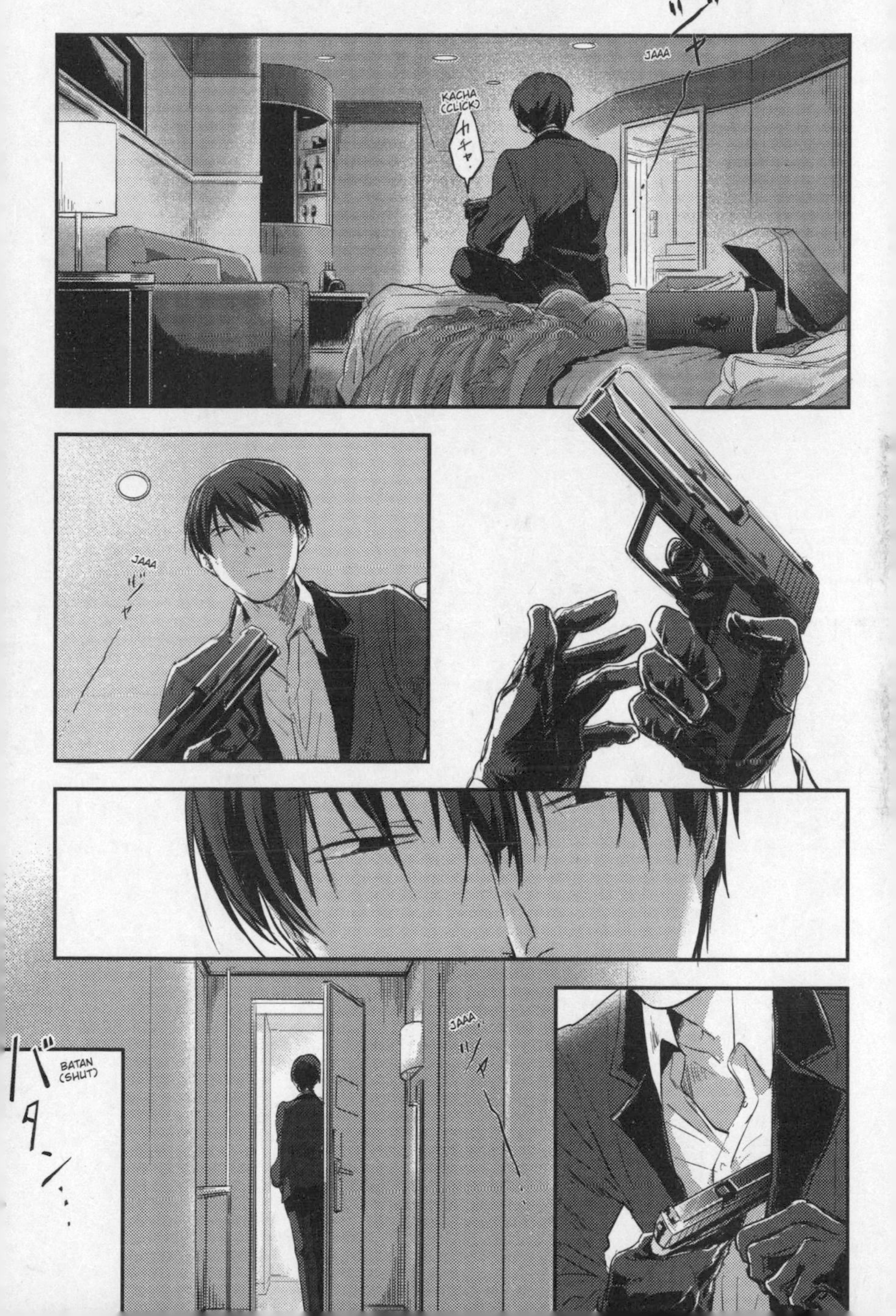
JAAA
ジャ
KACHA (CLICK)
カチャ
JAAA
ジャ
JAAA
ジャ
BATAN (SHUT)
バタン

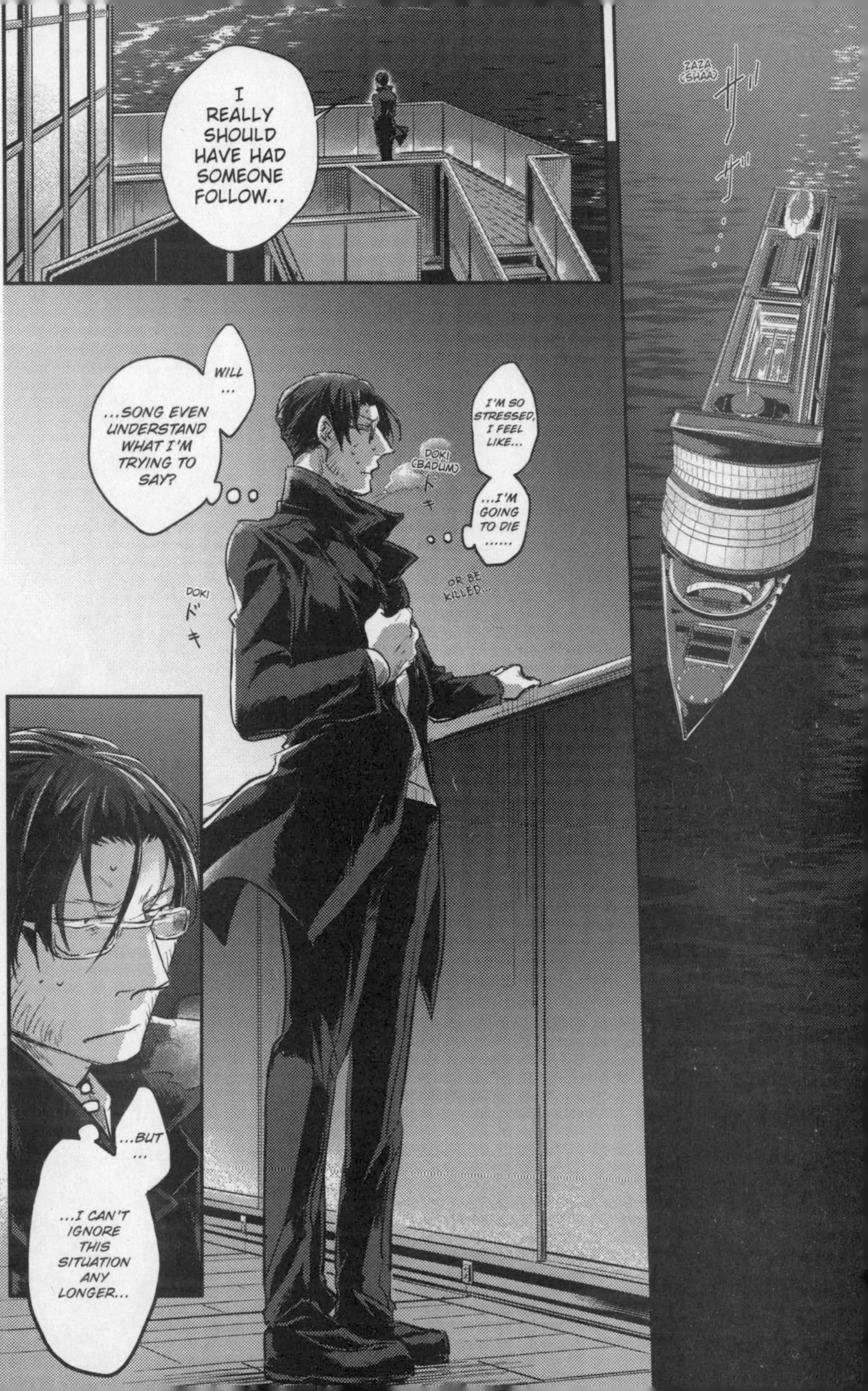
ZAZA (SHAA)
I REALLY SHOULD HAVE HAD SOMEONE FOLLOW...
I'M SO STRESSED, I FEEL LIKE...
...I'M GOING TO DIE ......
DOKI (BADUMP)
OR BE KILLED...
WILL ...
...SONG EVEN UNDERSTAND WHAT I'M TRYING TO SAY?
DOKI
...BUT ...
...I CAN'T IGNORE THIS SITUATION ANY LONGER...

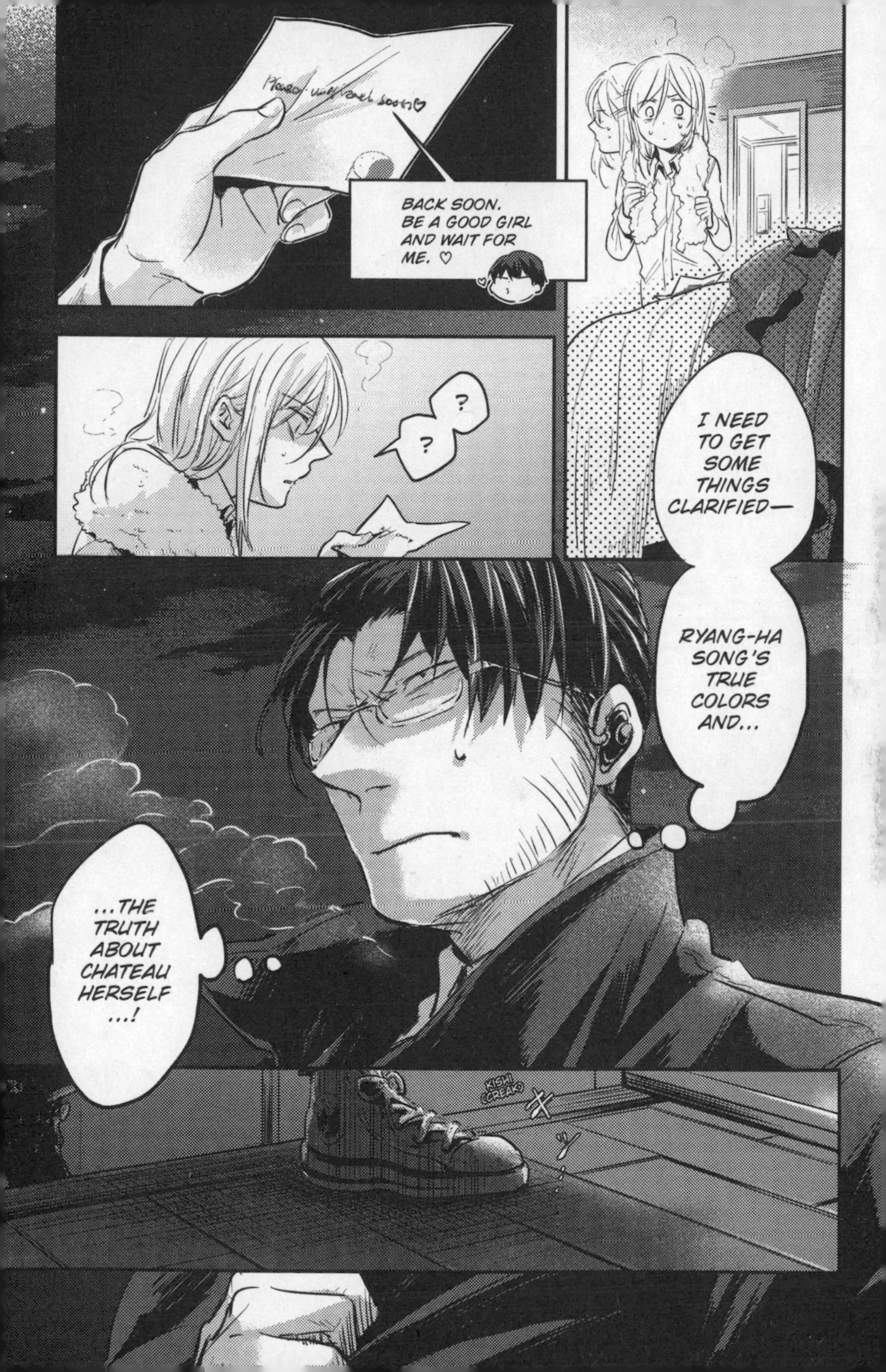
BACK SOON. BE A GOOD GIRL AND WAIT FOR ME. ♡
? ?
I NEED TO GET SOME THINGS CLARIFIED—
RYANG-HA SONG'S TRUE COLORS AND...
...THE TRUTH ABOUT CHATEAU HERSELF ...!
KISHI (CREAK)

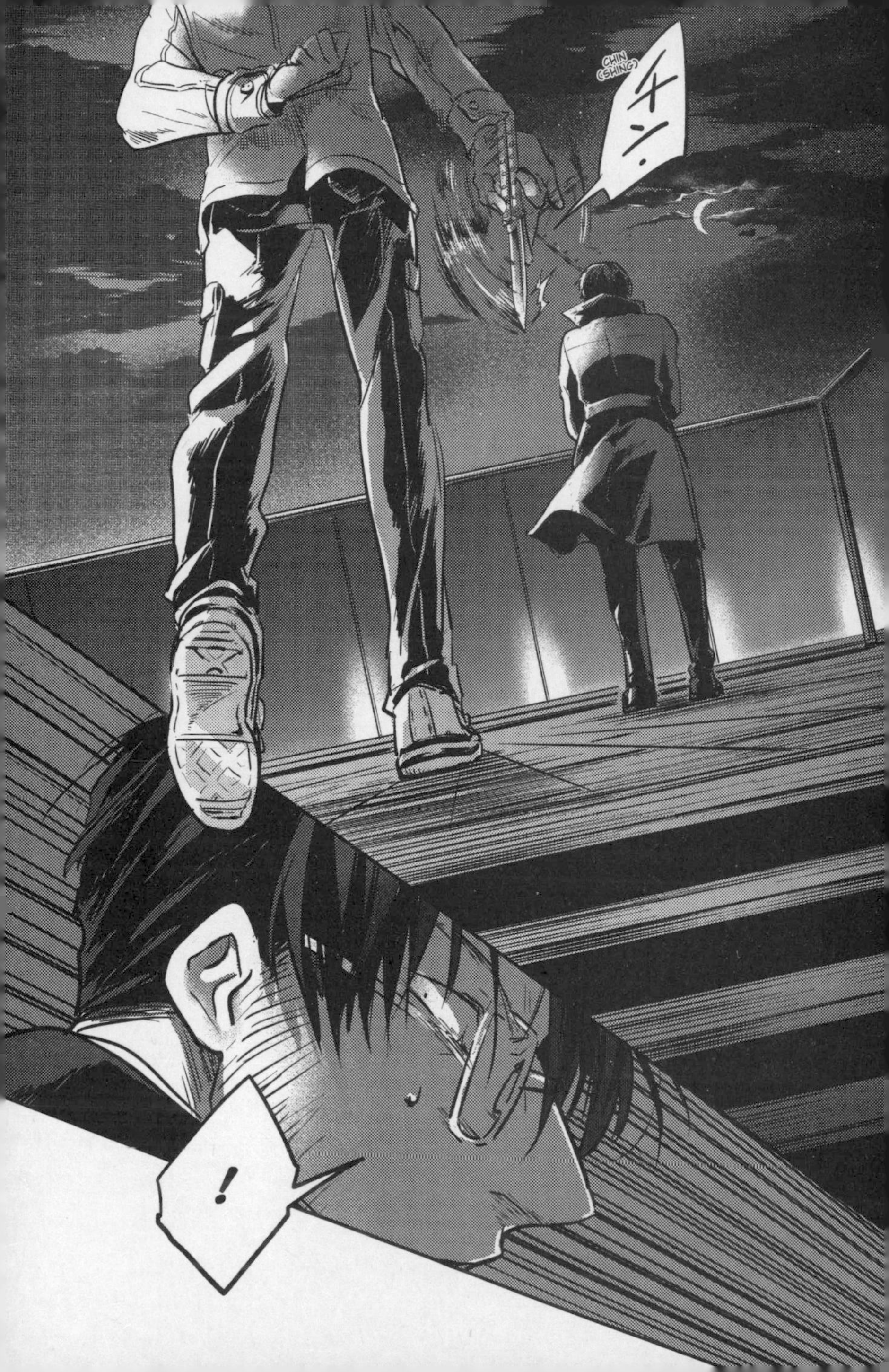
CHIN (SHING)
!

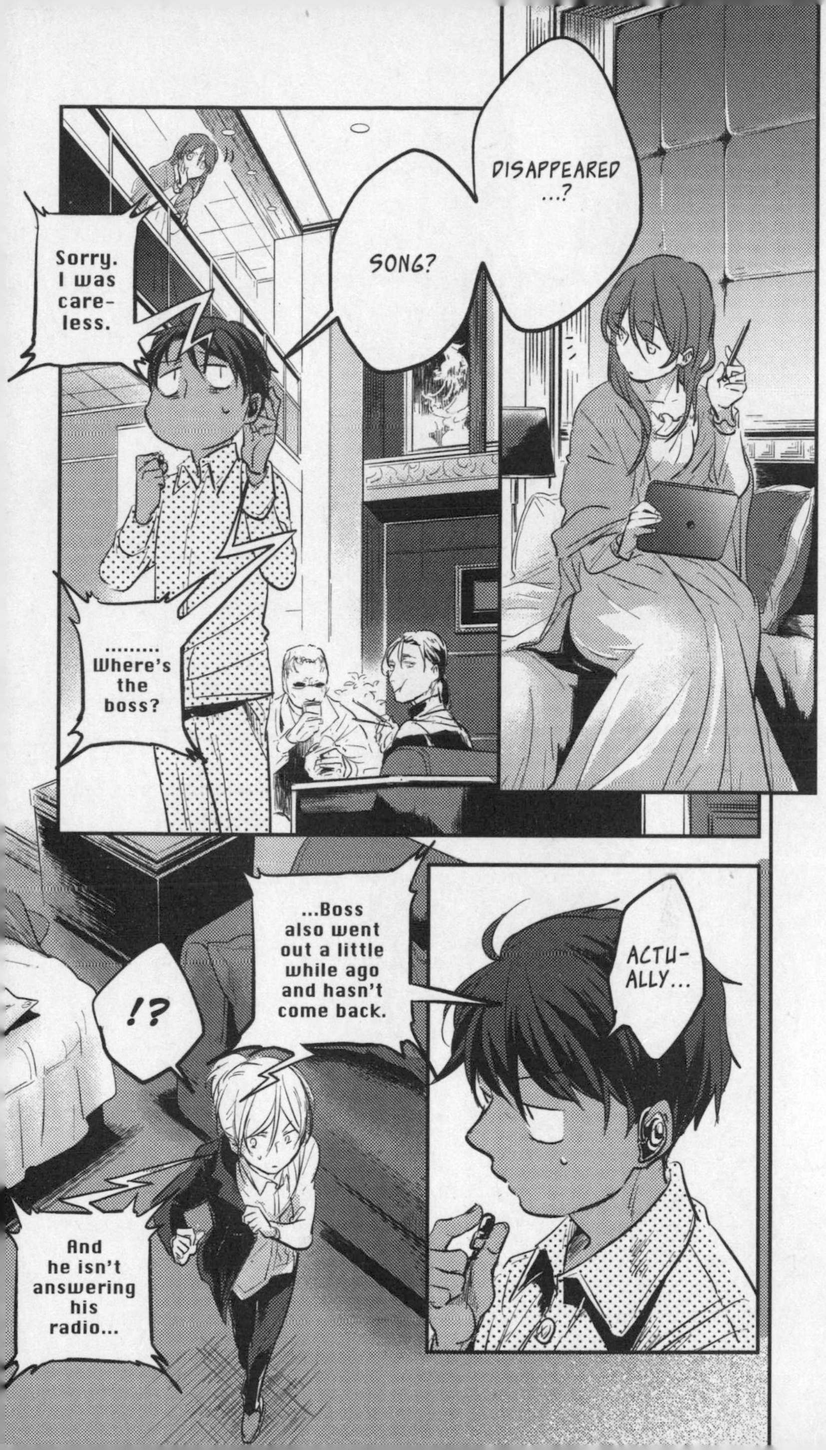
DISAPPEARED ...?
SONG?
Sorry. I was care-less.
.... Where's the boss?
ACTU-ALLY...
...Boss also went out a little while ago and hasn't come back.
!?
And he isn't answering his radio...

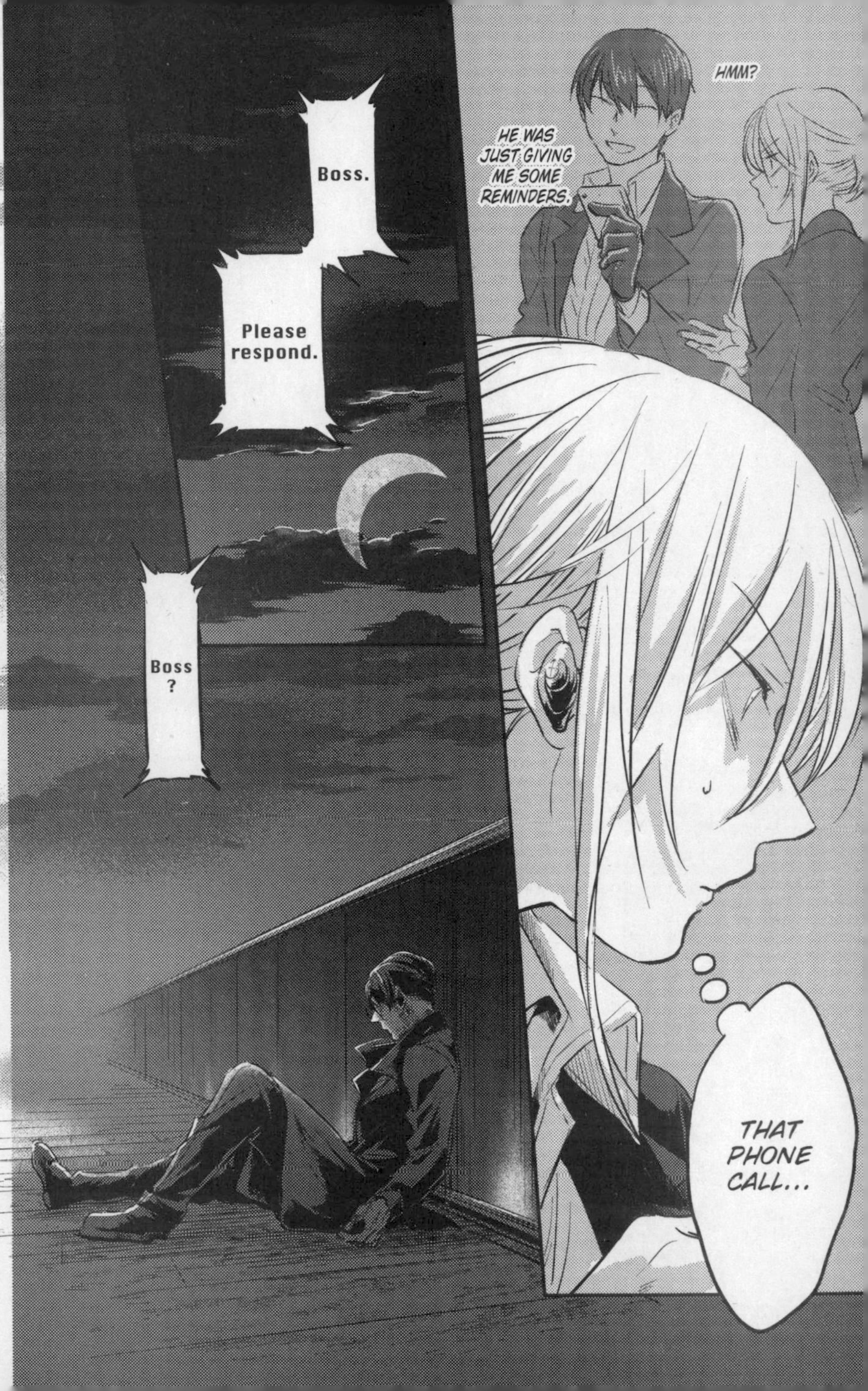
HMM?
HE WAS JUST GIVING ME SOME REMINDERS.
THAT PHONE CALL...
Boss.
Please respond.
Boss?

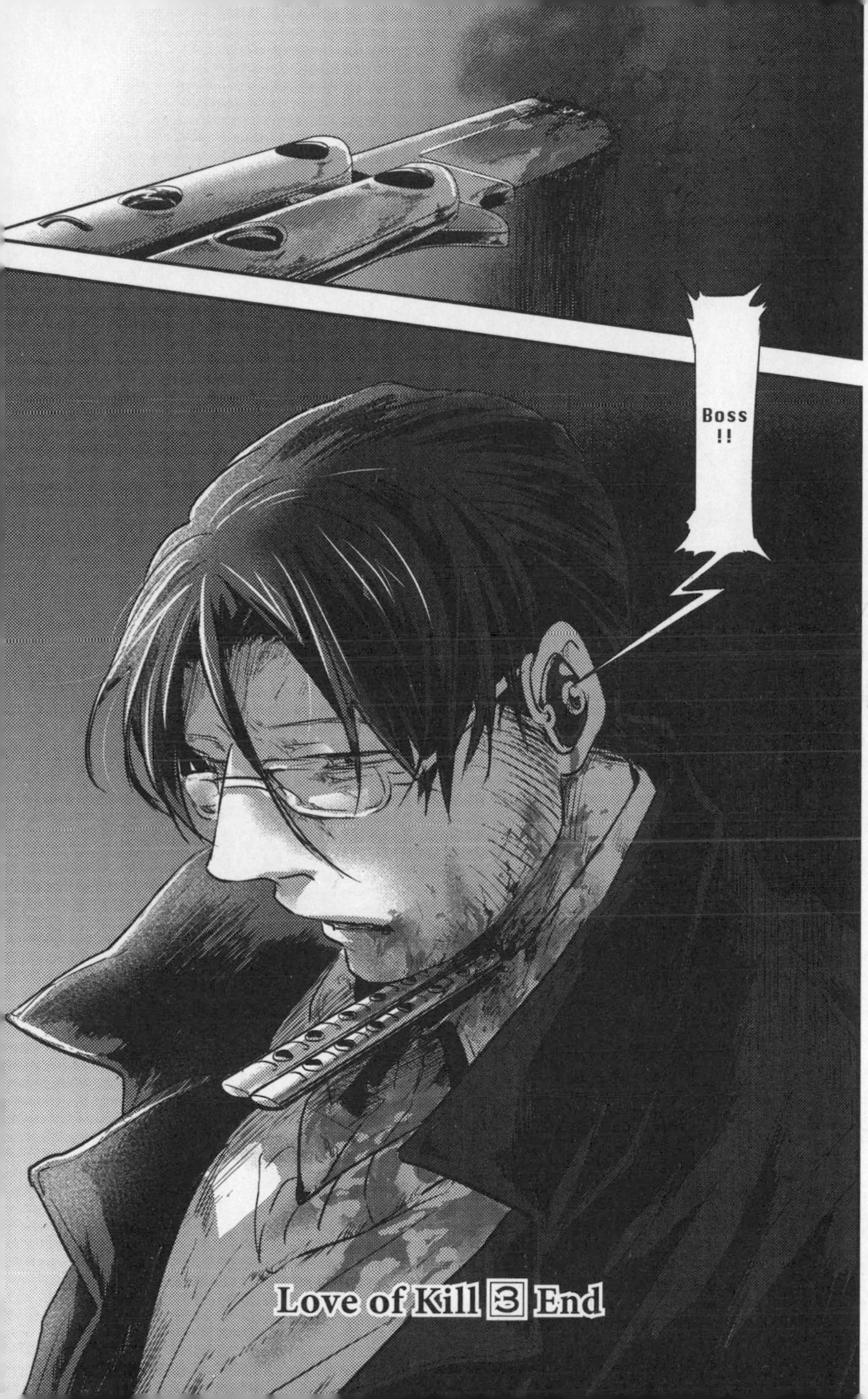
Boss !!
Love of Kill 3 End

THE
FOLLOWING
IS A SPECIAL
COMIC
FOR THE
COLLECTED
VOLUME.

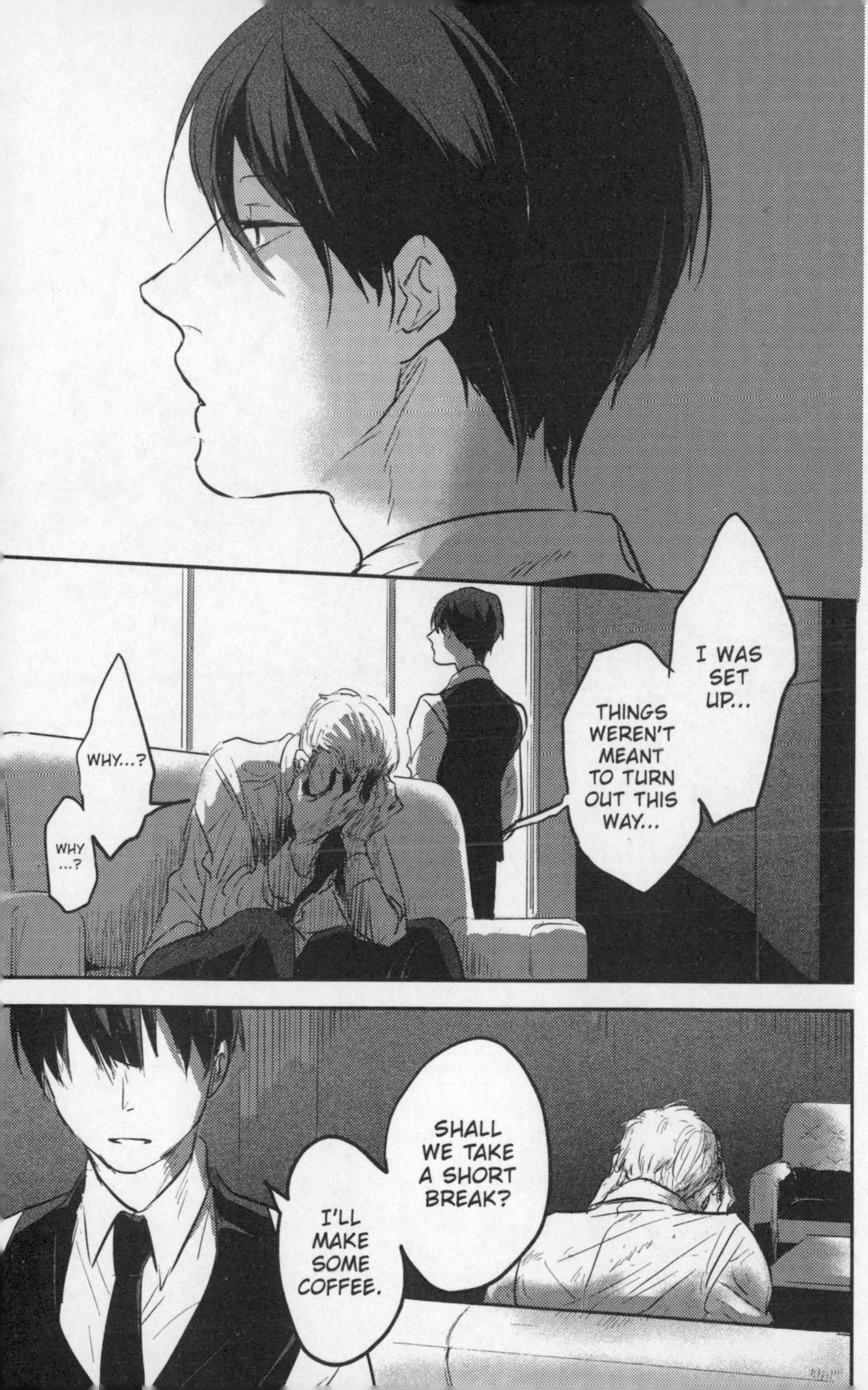
I WAS SET UP...
THINGS WEREN'T MEANT TO TURN OUT THIS WAY...
WHY...?
WHY...?
SHALL WE TAKE A SHORT BREAK?
I'LL MAKE SOME COFFEE.

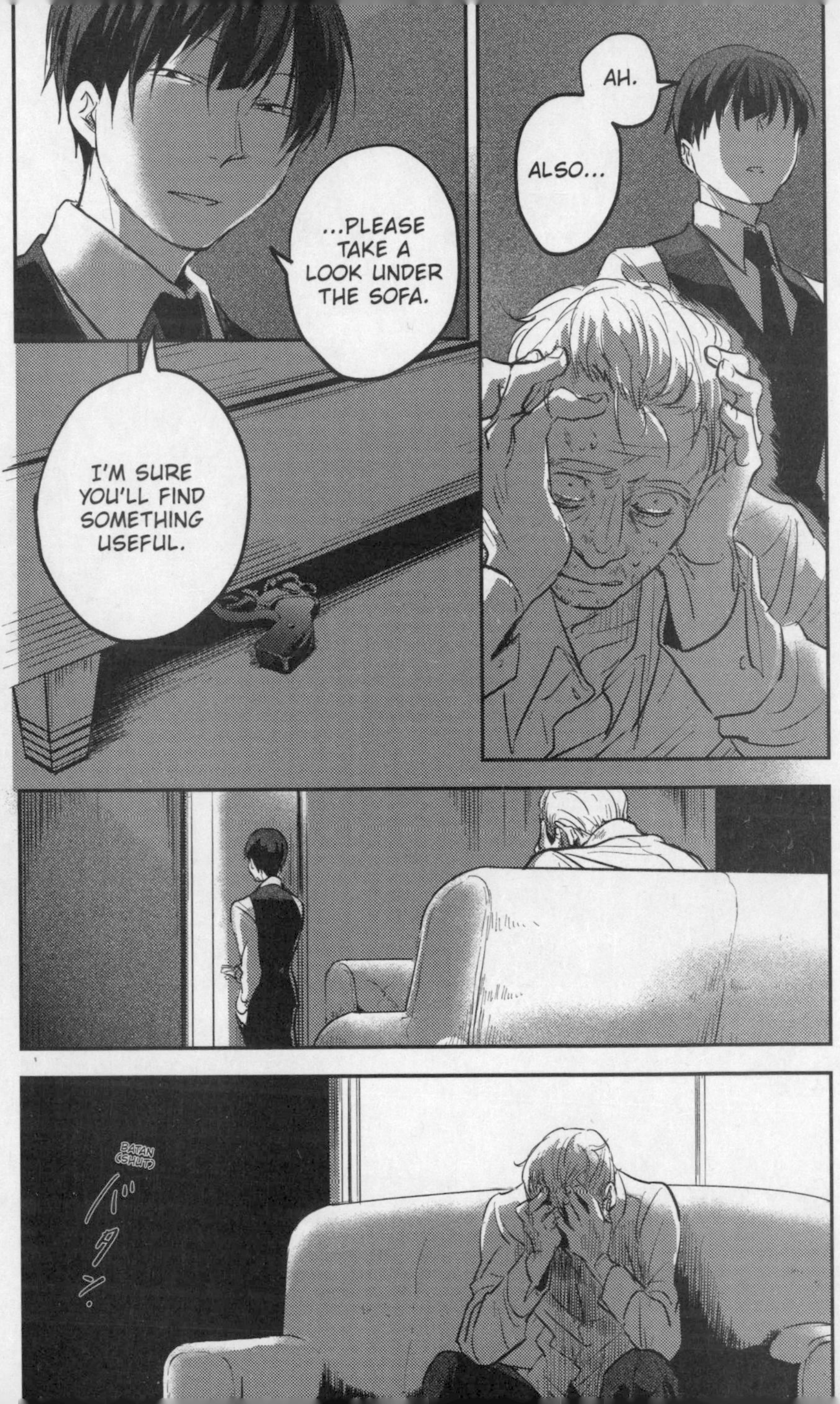
AH.
ALSO...
...PLEASE TAKE A LOOK UNDER THE SOFA.
I'M SURE YOU'LL FIND SOMETHING USEFUL.
BATAN (SHUT)

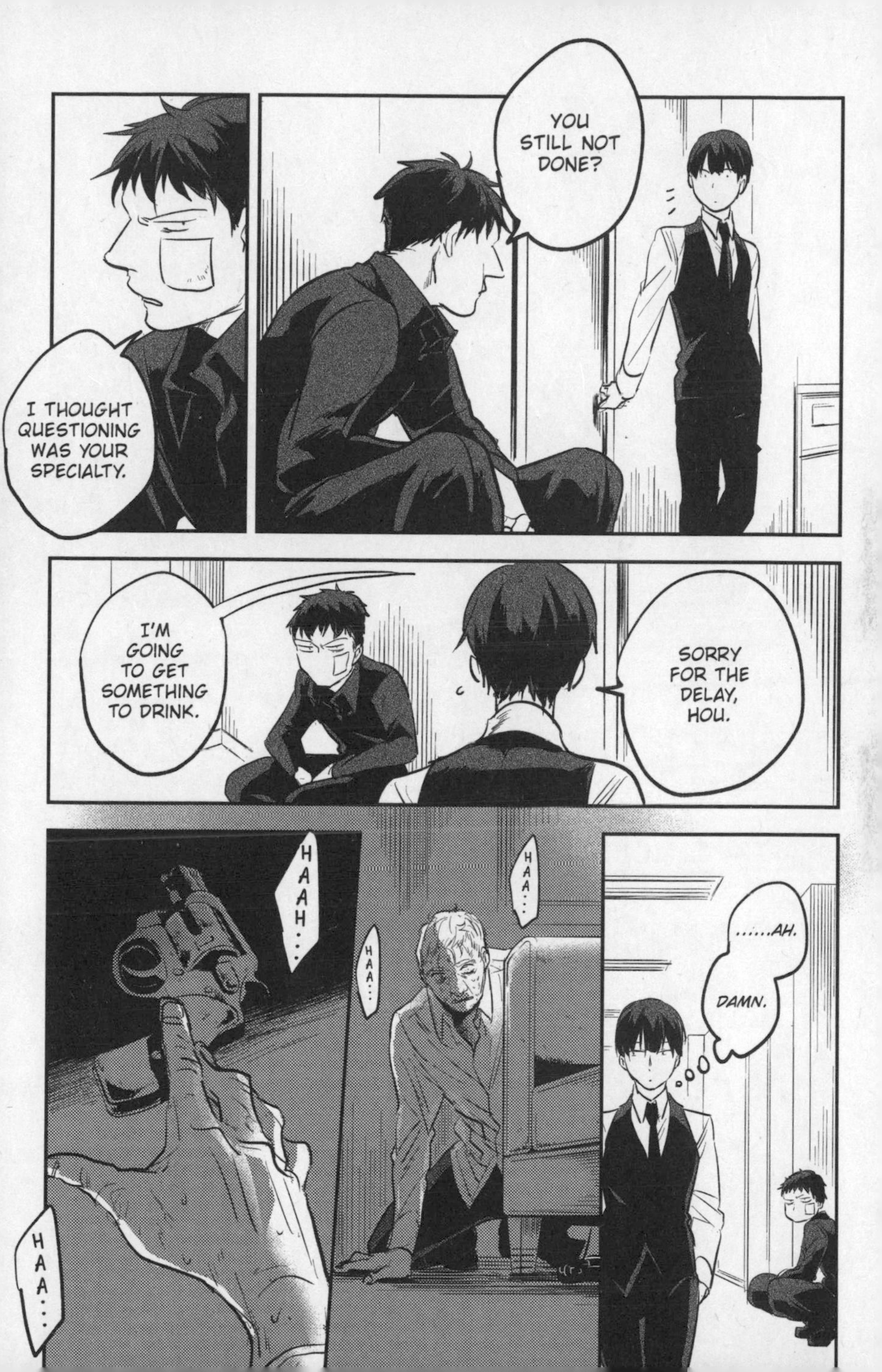
YOU STILL NOT DONE?
I THOUGHT QUESTIONING WAS YOUR SPECIALTY.
SORRY FOR THE DELAY, HOU.
I'M GOING TO GET SOMETHING TO DRINK.
......AH.
DAMN.
HAA...
HAA...
HAAAH...
HAA...

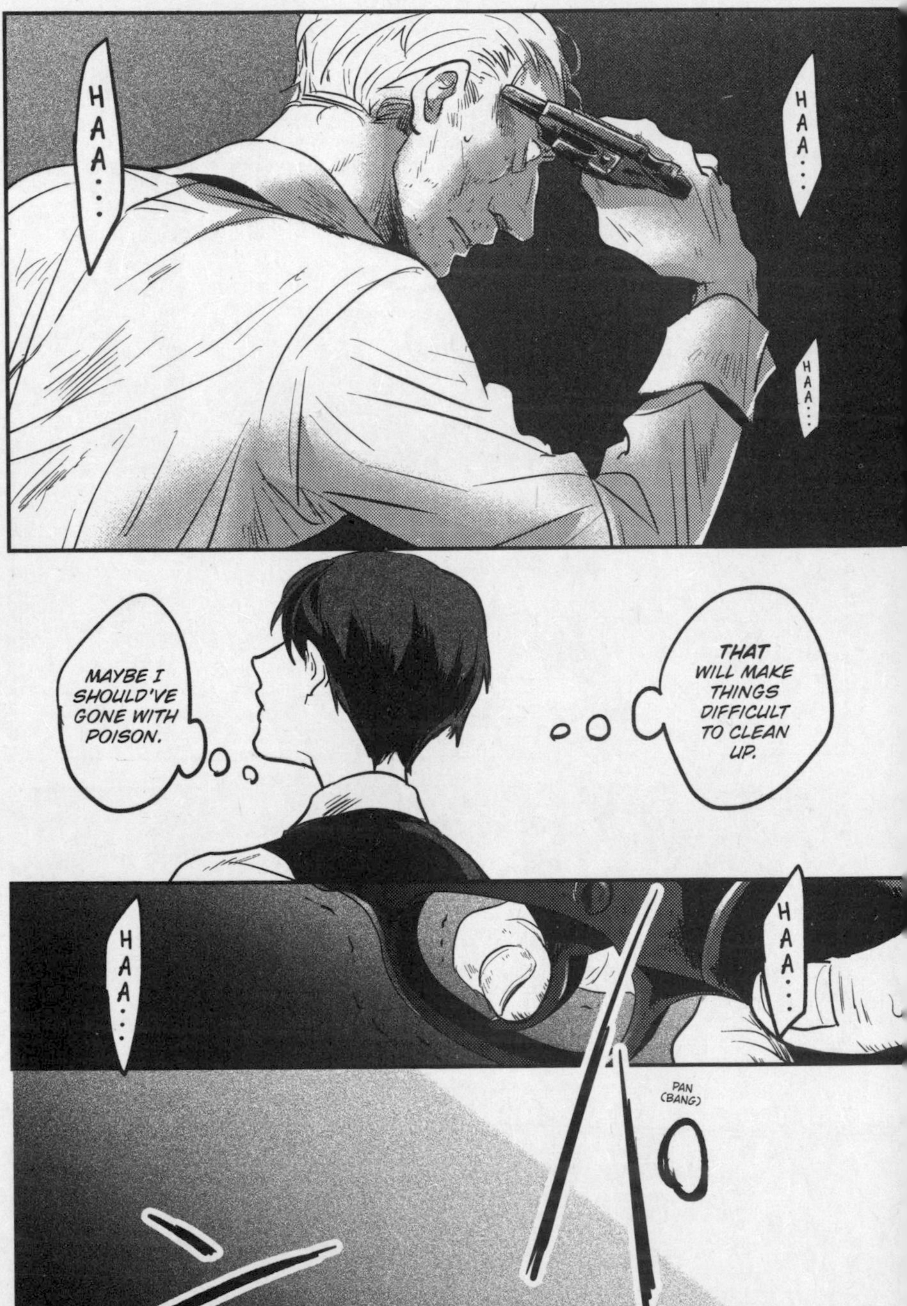
HAA...
HAA...
HAA...
THAT WILL MAKE THINGS DIFFICULT TO CLEAN UP.
MAYBE I SHOULD'VE GONE WITH POISON.
HAA...
HAA...
PAN (BANG)

Special File

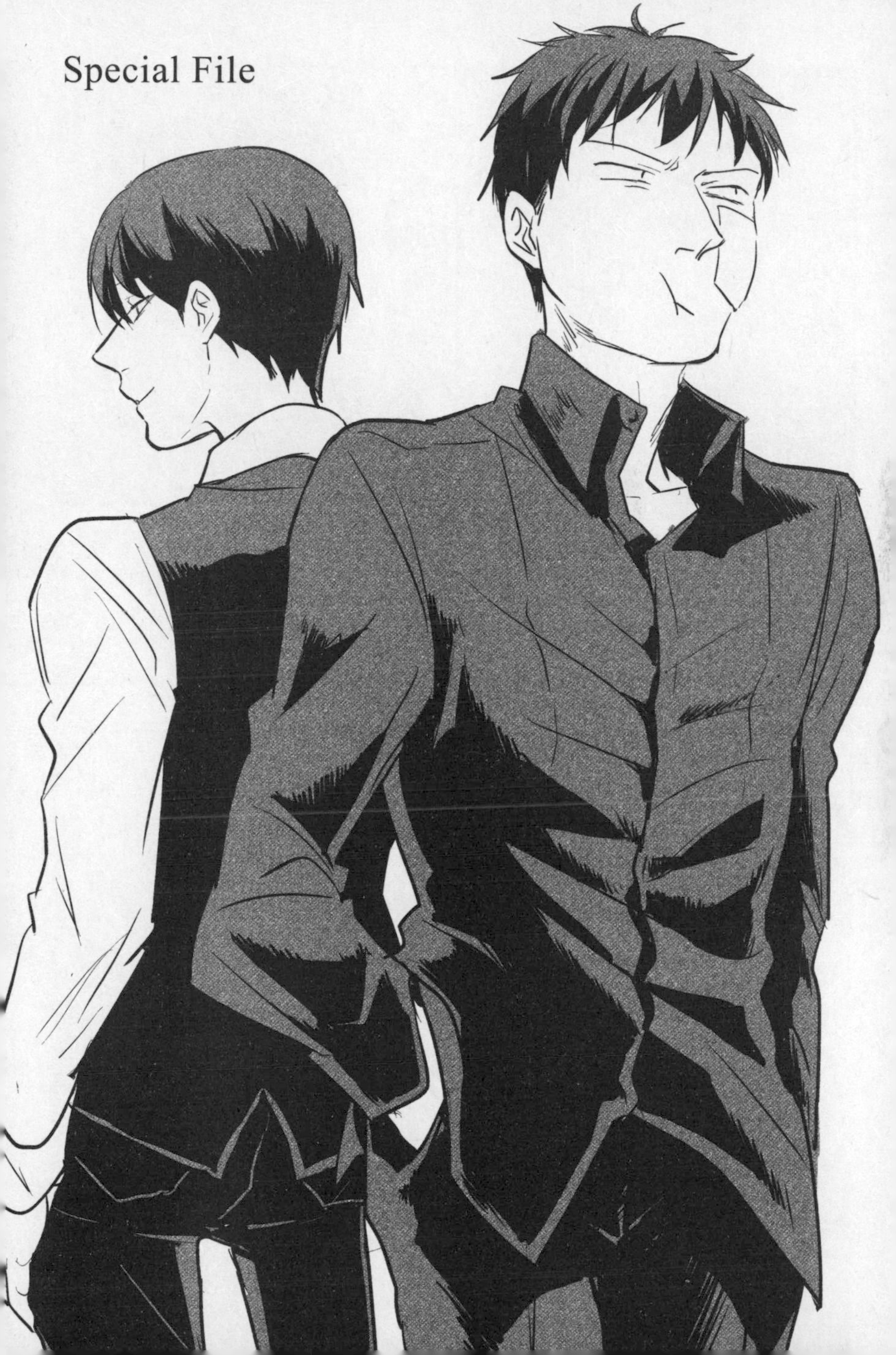

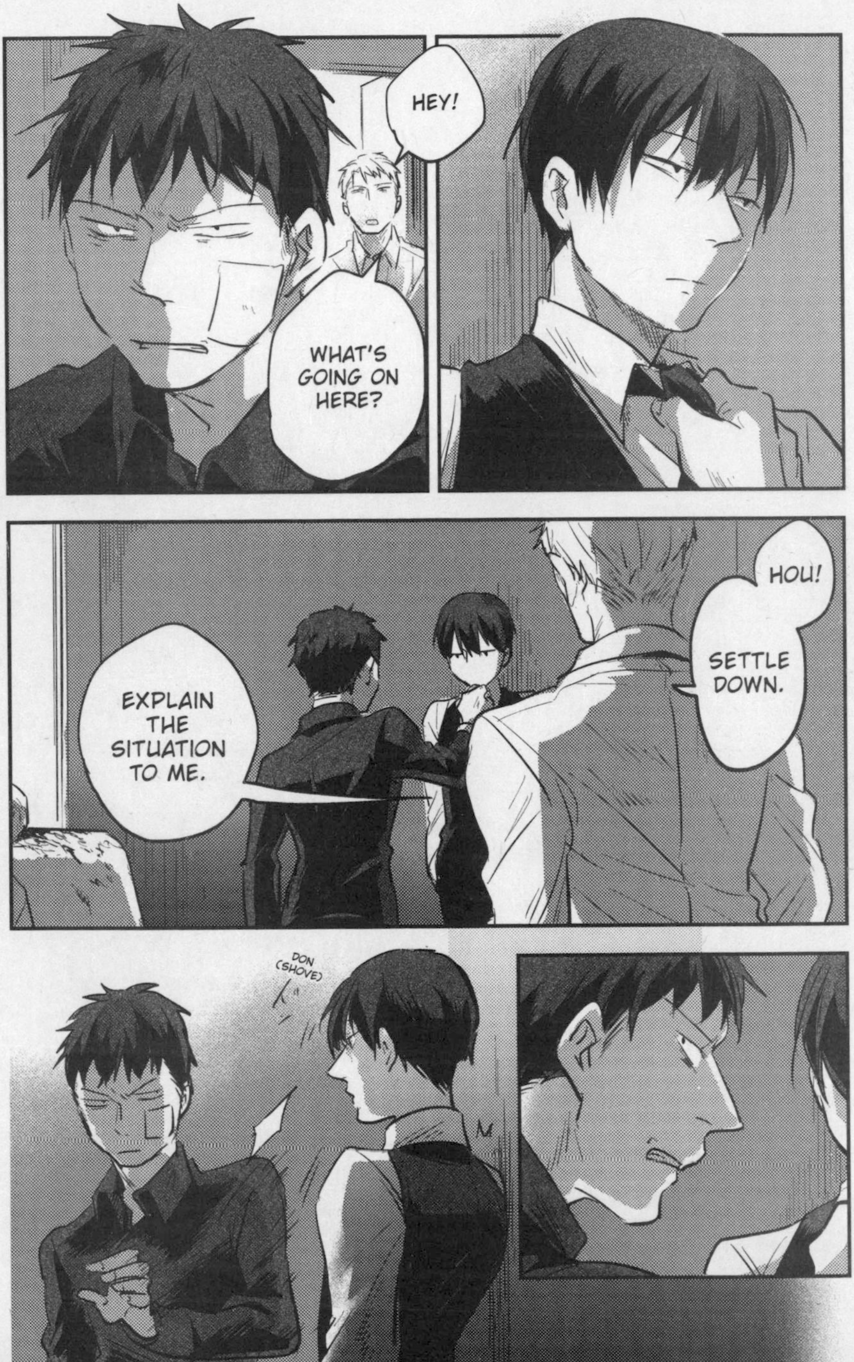
HEY!
WHAT'S GOING ON HERE?
HOU!
SETTLE DOWN.
EXPLAIN THE SITUATION TO ME.
DON (SHOVE)

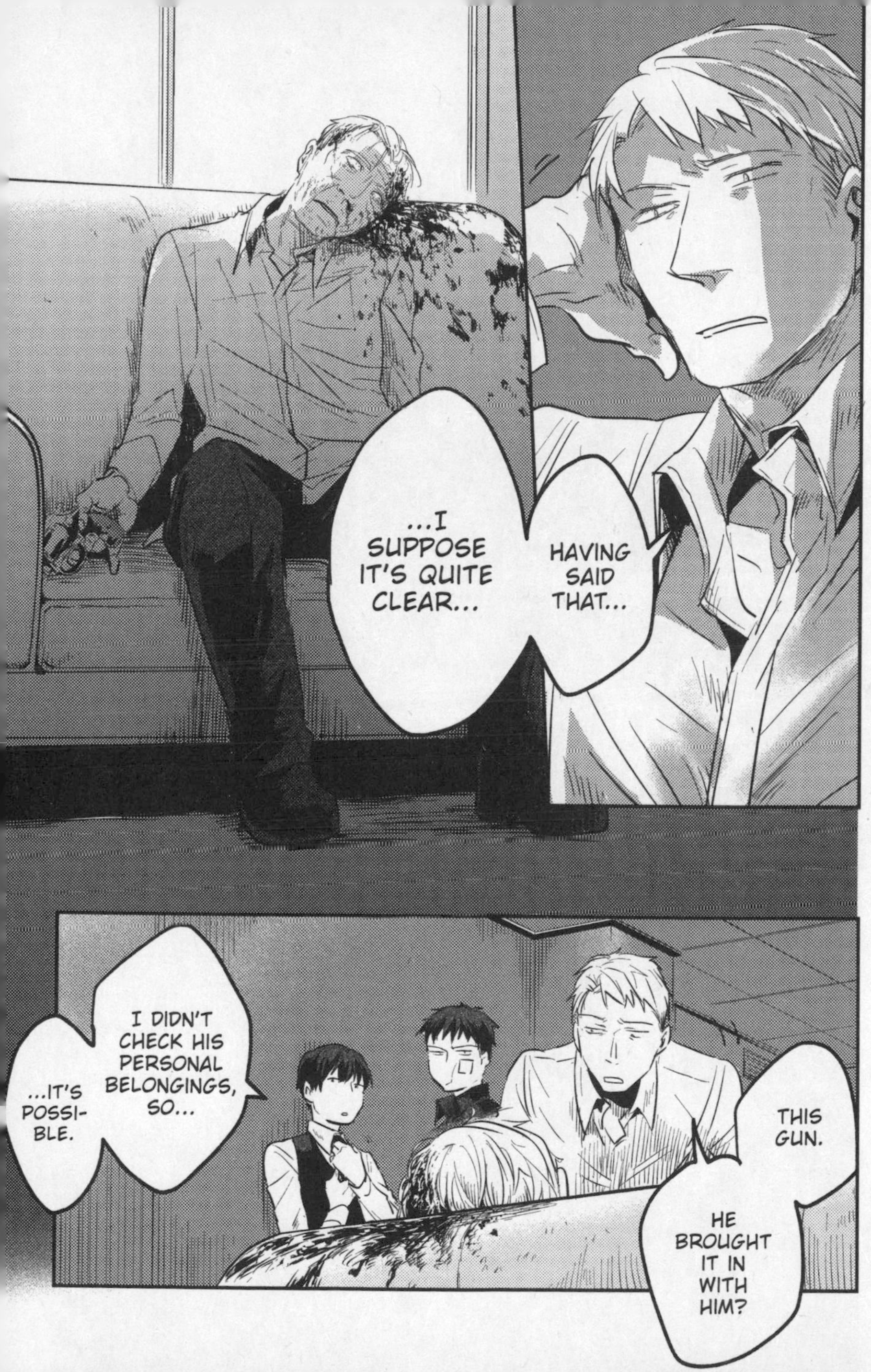
HAVING SAID THAT...
...I SUPPOSE IT'S QUITE CLEAR...
THIS GUN.
HE BROUGHT IT IN WITH HIM?
I DIDN'T CHECK HIS PERSONAL BELONGINGS, SO...
...IT'S POSSI-BLE.

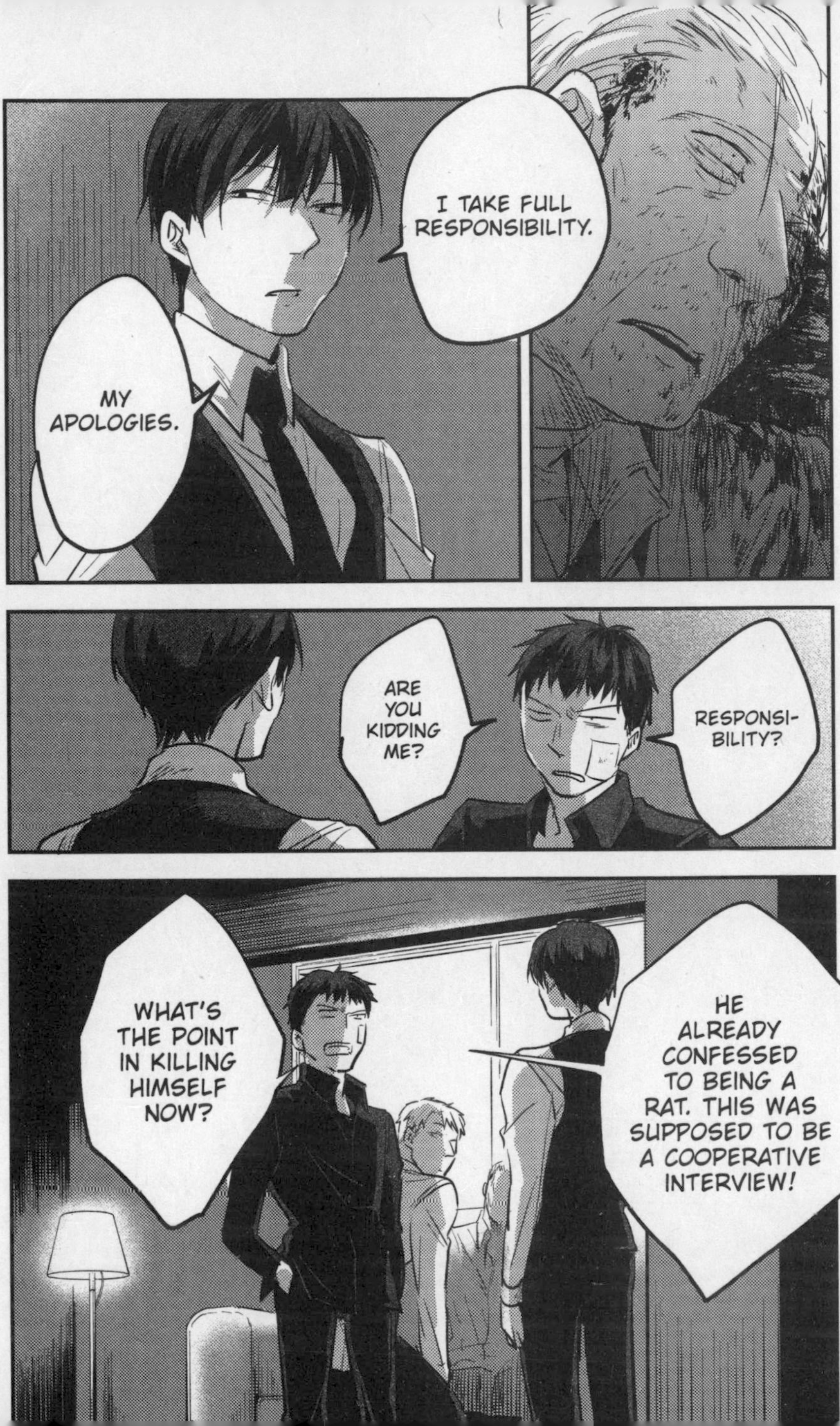
I TAKE FULL RESPONSIBILITY.
MY APOLOGIES.
RESPONSI-BILITY?
ARE YOU KIDDING ME?
HE ALREADY CONFESSED TO BEING A RAT. THIS WAS SUPPOSED TO BE A COOPERATIVE INTERVIEW!
WHAT'S THE POINT IN KILLING HIMSELF NOW?

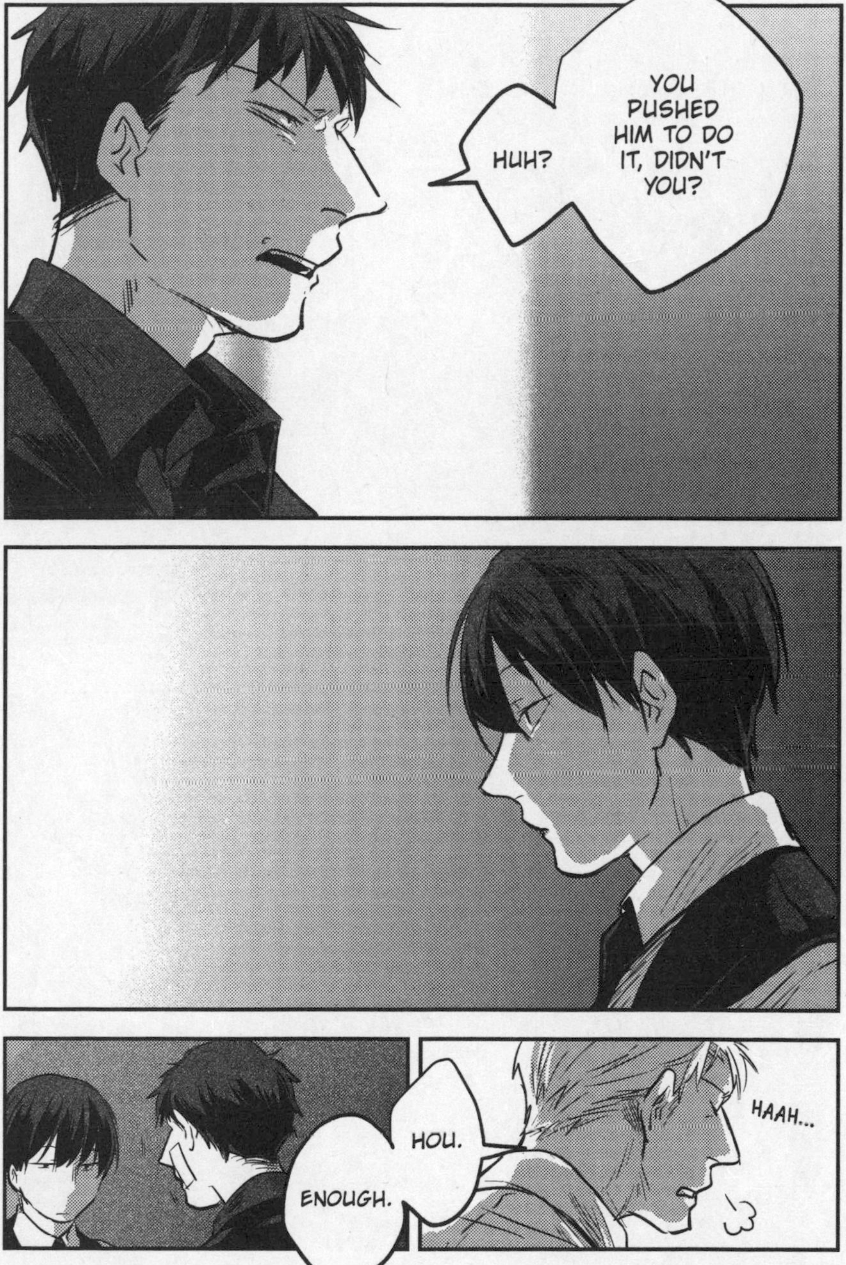
YOU PUSHED HIM TO DO IT, DIDN'T YOU?
HUH?
HAAH...
HOU.
ENOUGH.

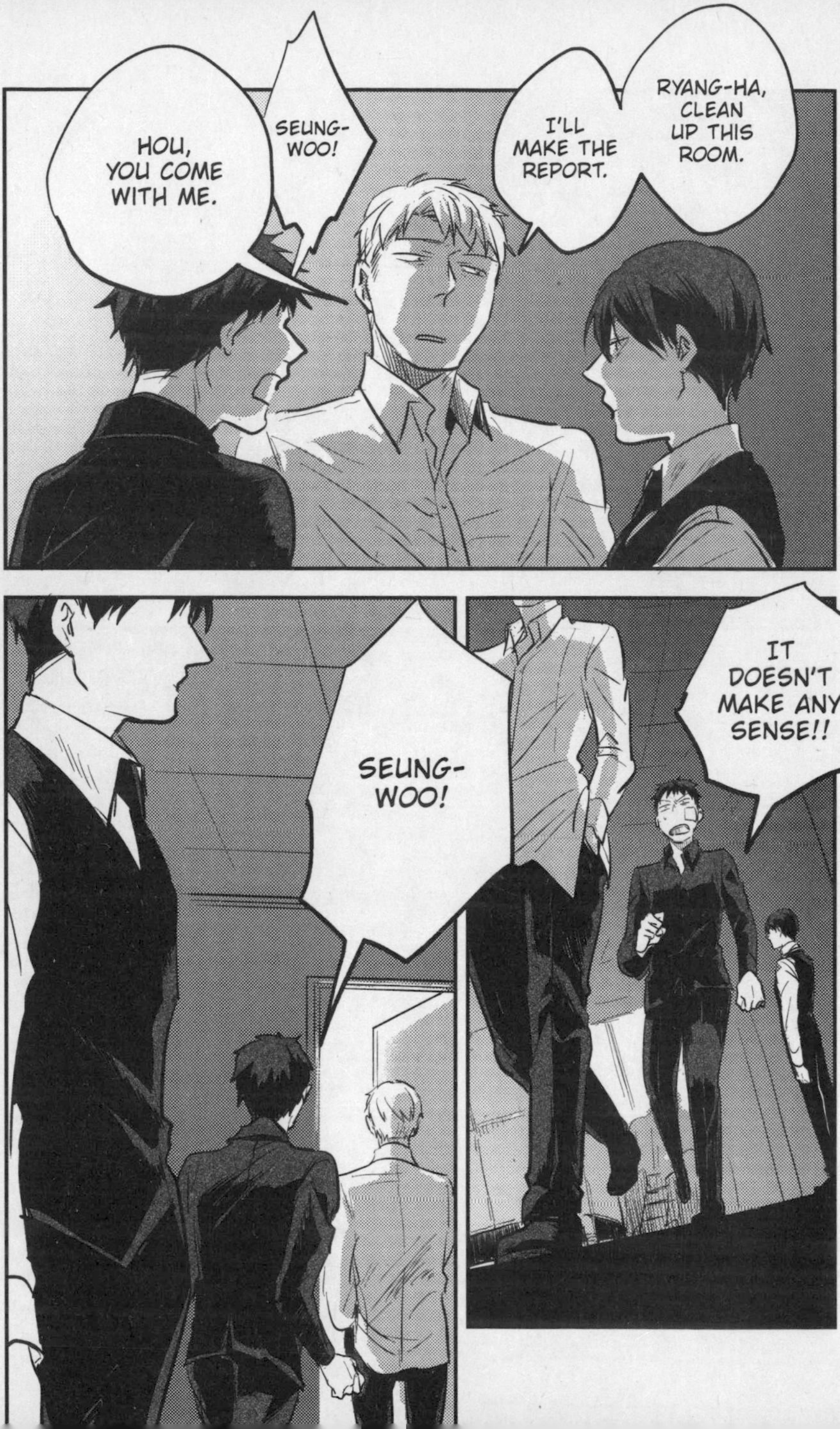
RYANG-HA, CLEAN UP THIS ROOM.
I'LL MAKE THE REPORT.
SEUNG-WOO!
HOU, YOU COME WITH ME.
IT DOESN'T MAKE ANY SENSE!!
SEUNG-WOO!

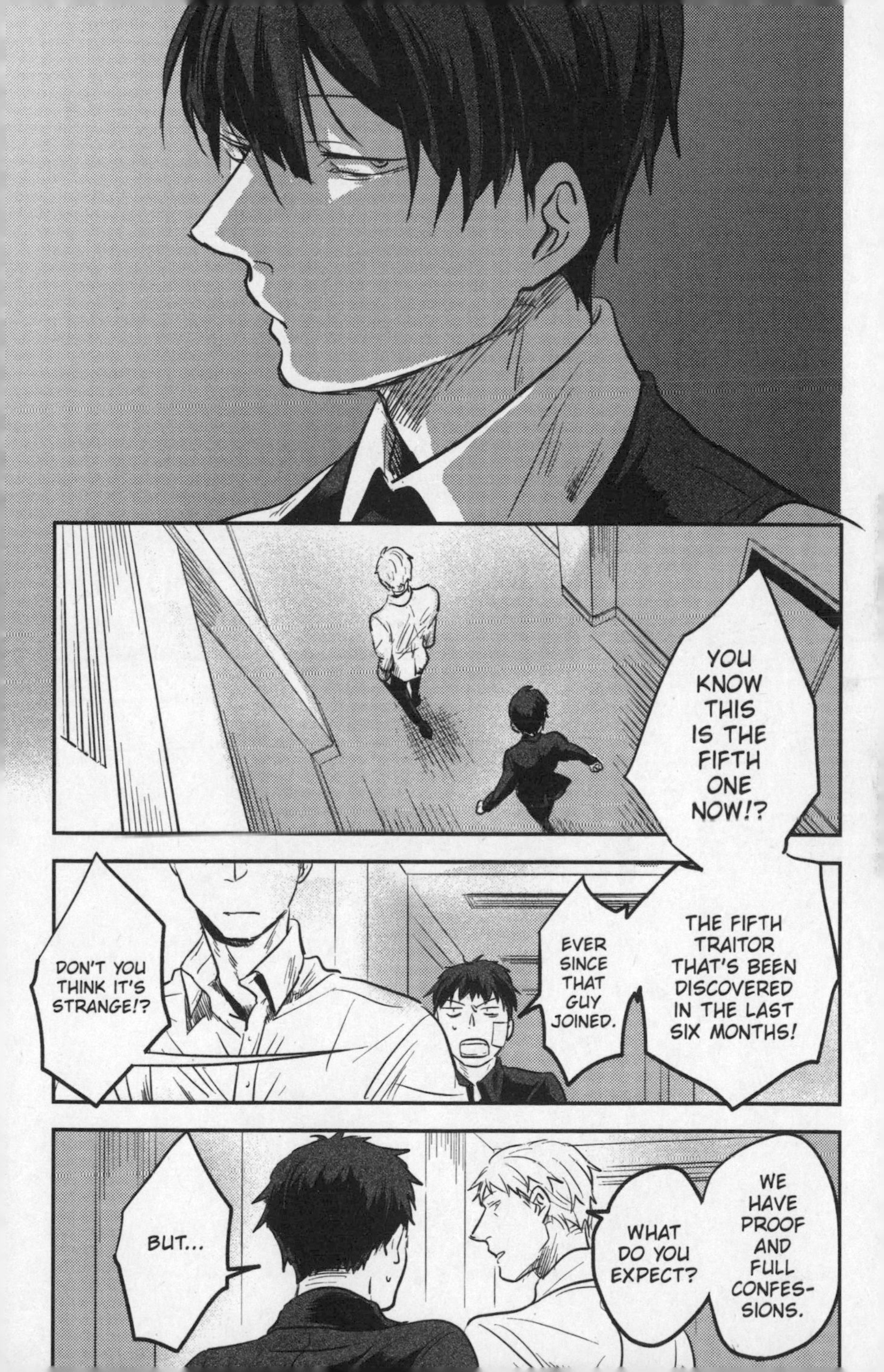
YOU KNOW THIS IS THE FIFTH ONE NOW!?
THE FIFTH TRAITOR THAT'S BEEN DISCOVERED IN THE LAST SIX MONTHS!
EVER SINCE THAT GUY JOINED.
DON'T YOU THINK IT'S STRANGE!?
WE HAVE PROOF AND FULL CONFES-SIONS.
WHAT DO YOU EXPECT?
BUT...

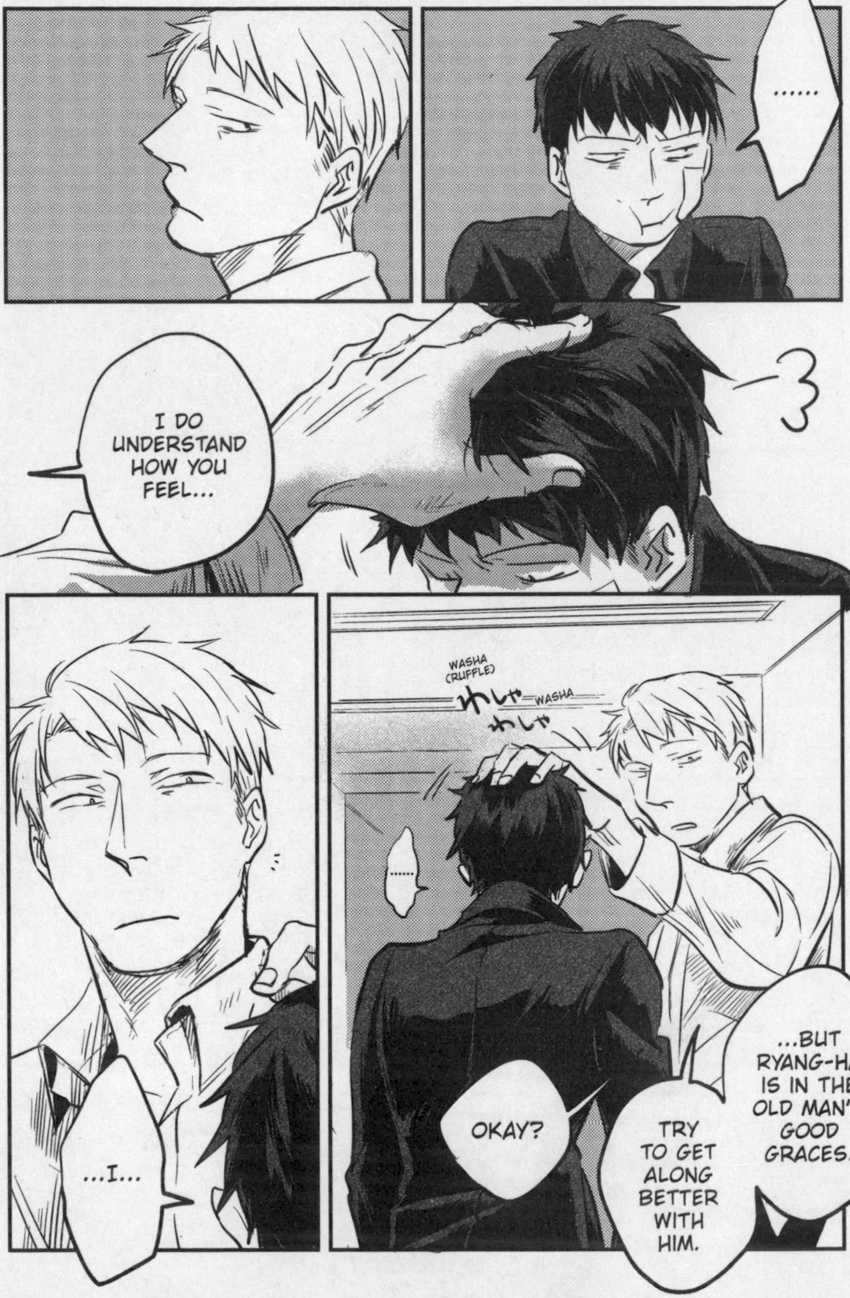
......
I DO UNDERSTAND HOW YOU FEEL...
WASHA (RUFFLE)
わしゃ
WASHA
わしゃ
......
...BUT RYANG-HA IS IN THE OLD MAN'S GOOD GRACES.
TRY TO GET ALONG BETTER WITH HIM.
OKAY?
...I...

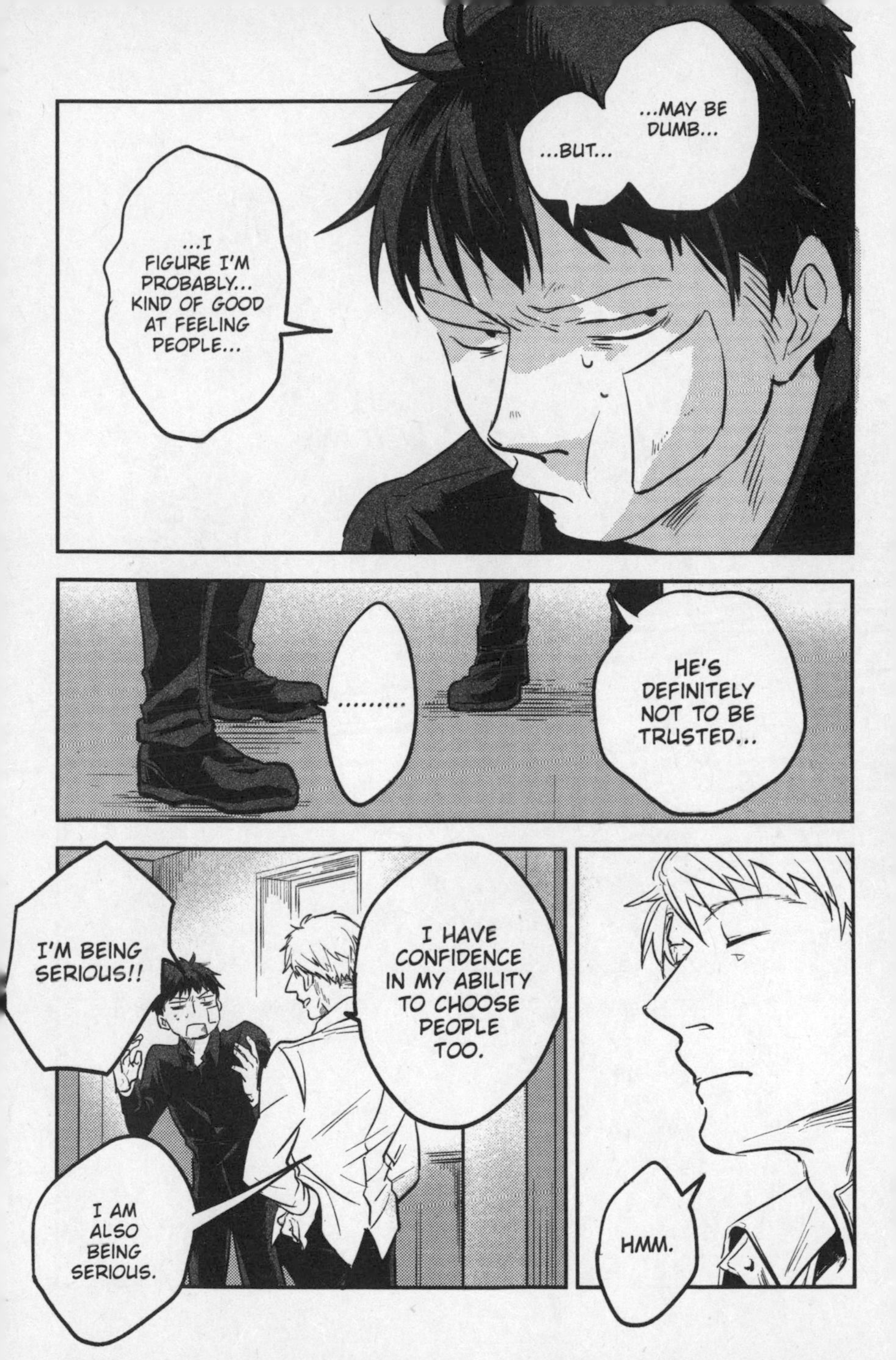
...MAY BE DUMB...
...BUT...
...I FIGURE I'M PROBABLY... KIND OF GOOD AT FEELING PEOPLE...
HE'S DEFINITELY NOT TO BE TRUSTED...
....
HMM.
I HAVE CONFIDENCE IN MY ABILITY TO CHOOSE PEOPLE TOO.
I'M BEING SERIOUS!!
I AM ALSO BEING SERIOUS.

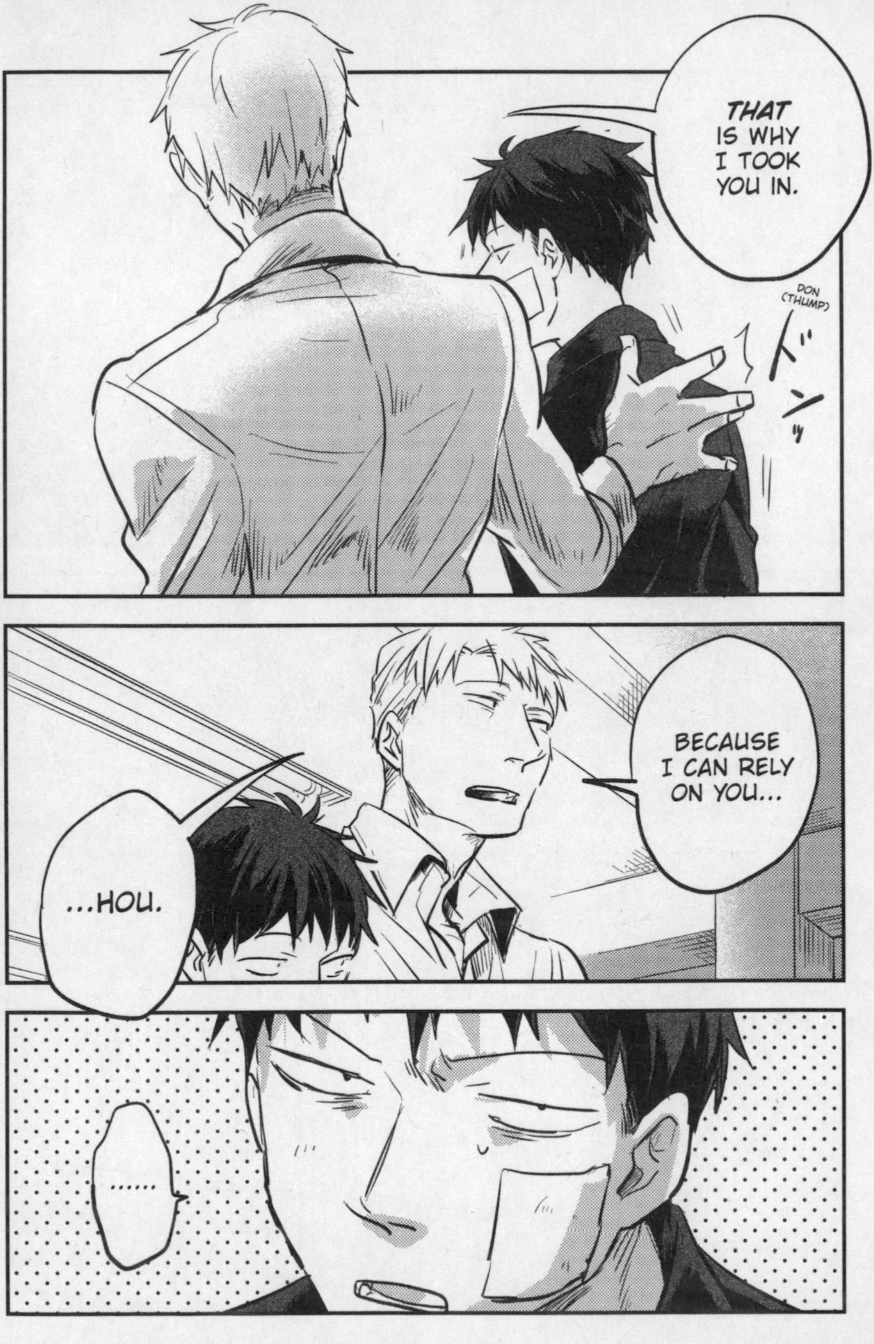
THAT IS WHY I TOOK YOU IN.
DON (THUMP)
ドンッ
BECAUSE I CAN RELY ON YOU...
...HOU.
......

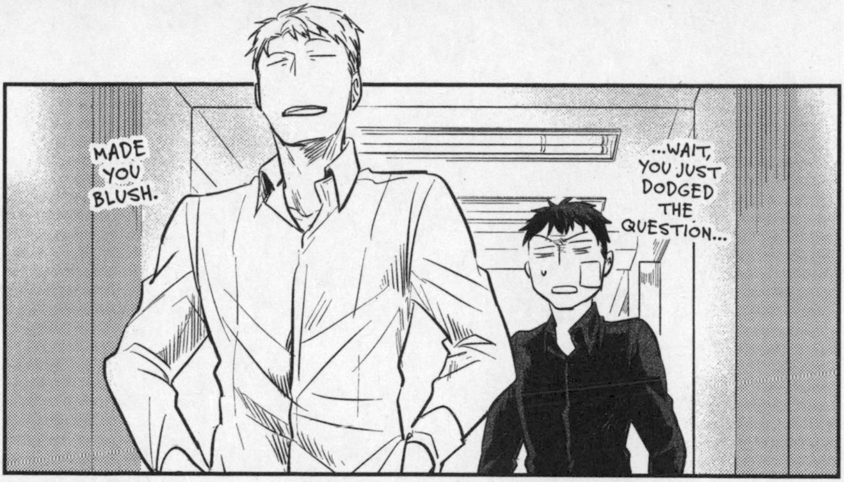
...WAIT, YOU JUST DODGED THE QUESTION...
MADE YOU BLUSH.

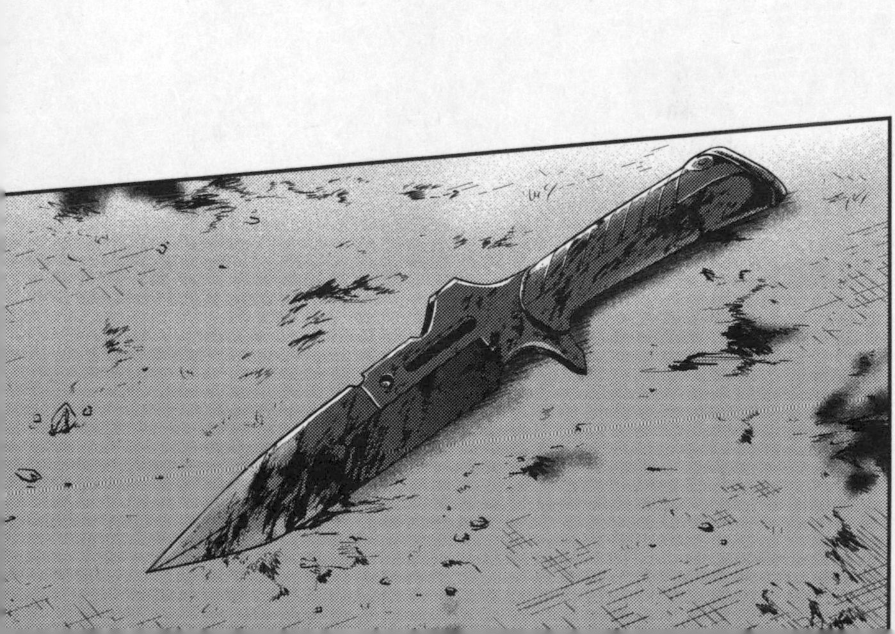

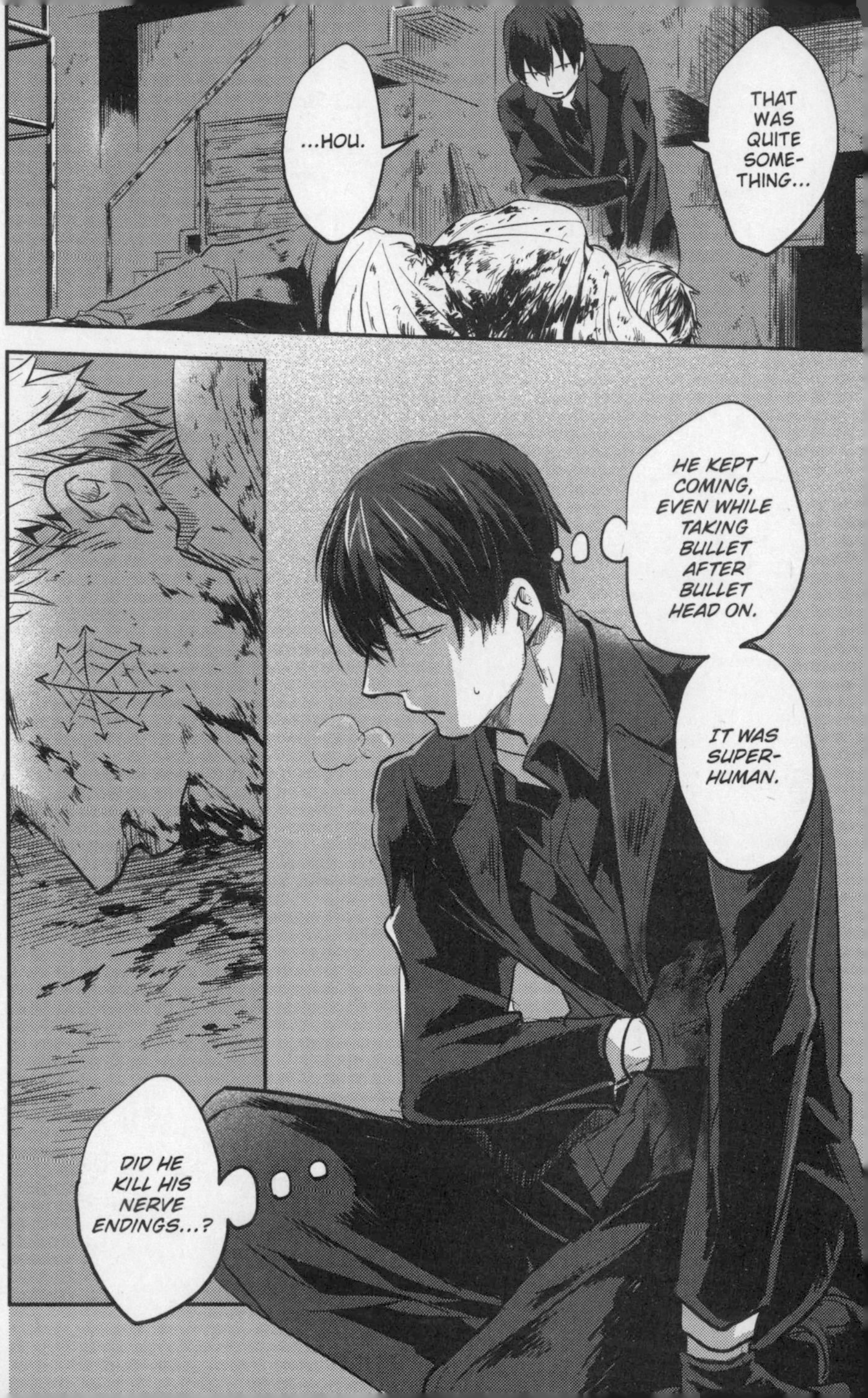
THAT WAS QUITE SOME-THING...
...HOU.
HE KEPT COMING, EVEN WHILE TAKING BULLET AFTER BULLET HEAD ON.
IT WAS SUPER-HUMAN.
DID HE KILL HIS NERVE ENDINGS...?

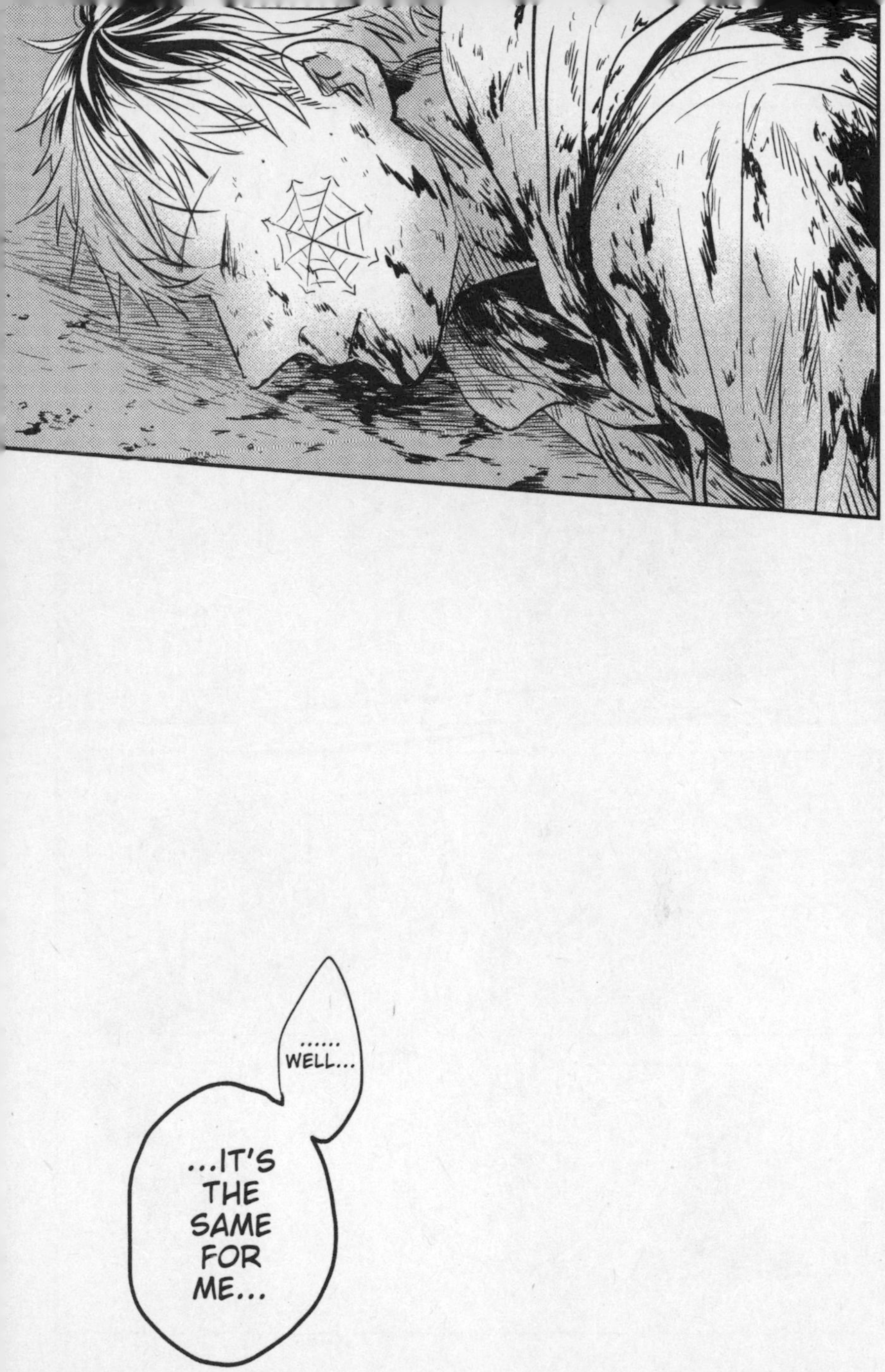

......WELL...
...IT'S THE SAME FOR ME...

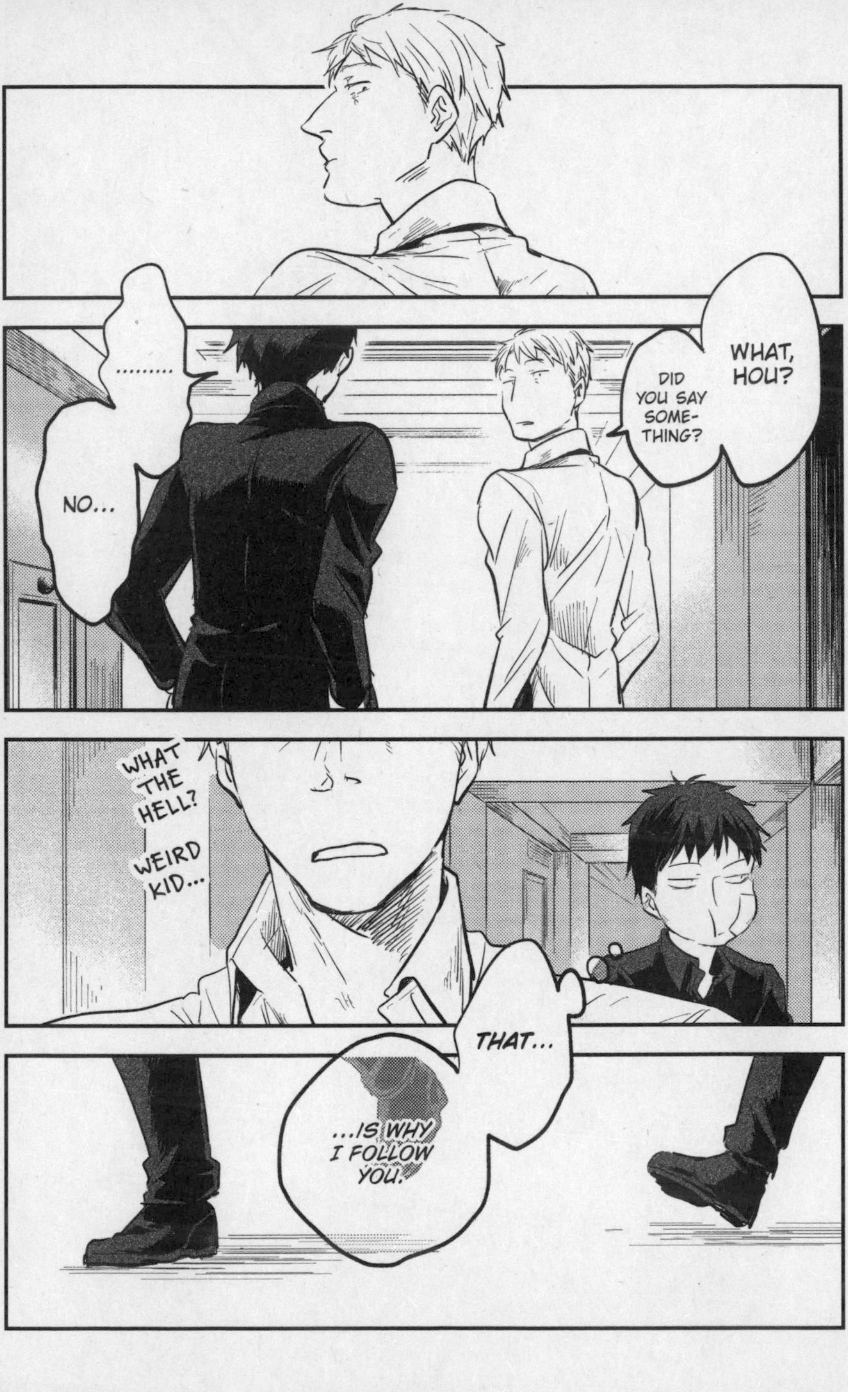
WHAT, HOU?
DID YOU SAY SOME-THING?
....
NO...
WHAT THE HELL?
WEIRD KID...
THAT...
...IS WHY I FOLLOW YOU.

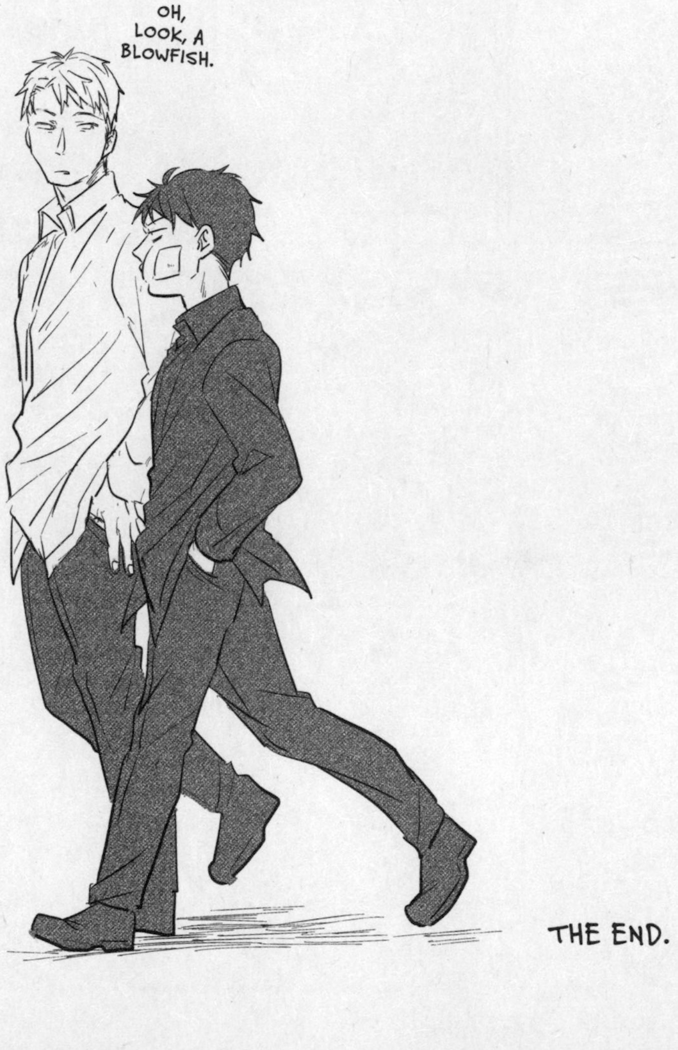
OH, LOOK, A BLOWFISH.
THE END.

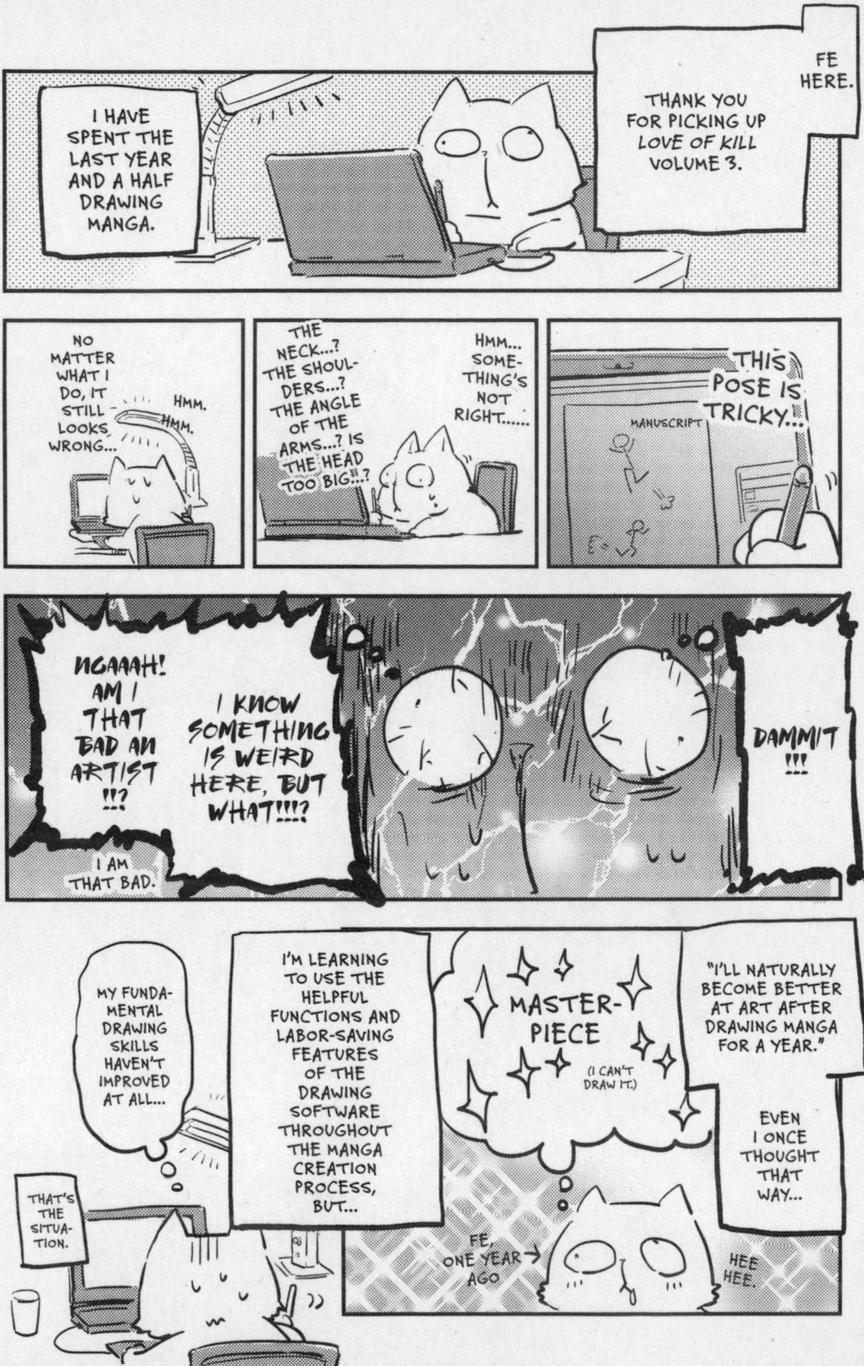
FE HERE.
THANK YOU FOR PICKING UP LOVE OF KILL VOLUME 3.
I HAVE SPENT THE LAST YEAR AND A HALF DRAWING MANGA.
THIS POSE IS TRICKY...
MANUSCRIPT
HMM... SOMETHING'S NOT RIGHT......
THE NECK...? THE SHOULDERS...? THE ANGLE OF THE ARMS...? IS THE HEAD TOO BIG...?
HMM. HMM.
NO MATTER WHAT I DO, IT STILL LOOKS WRONG...
DAMMIT!!!
I KNOW SOMETHING IS WEIRD HERE, BUT WHAT!!!?
NGAAAH! AM I THAT BAD AN ARTIST!!?
I AM THAT BAD.
"I'LL NATURALLY BECOME BETTER AT ART AFTER DRAWING MANGA FOR A YEAR."
EVEN I ONCE THOUGHT THAT WAY...
MASTERPIECE
(I CAN'T DRAW IT.)
HEE HEE.
FE, ONE YEAR AGO
I'M LEARNING TO USE THE HELPFUL FUNCTIONS AND LABOR-SAVING FEATURES OF THE DRAWING SOFTWARE THROUGHOUT THE MANGA CREATION PROCESS, BUT...
MY FUNDAMENTAL DRAWING SKILLS HAVEN'T IMPROVED AT ALL...
THAT'S THE SITUATION.

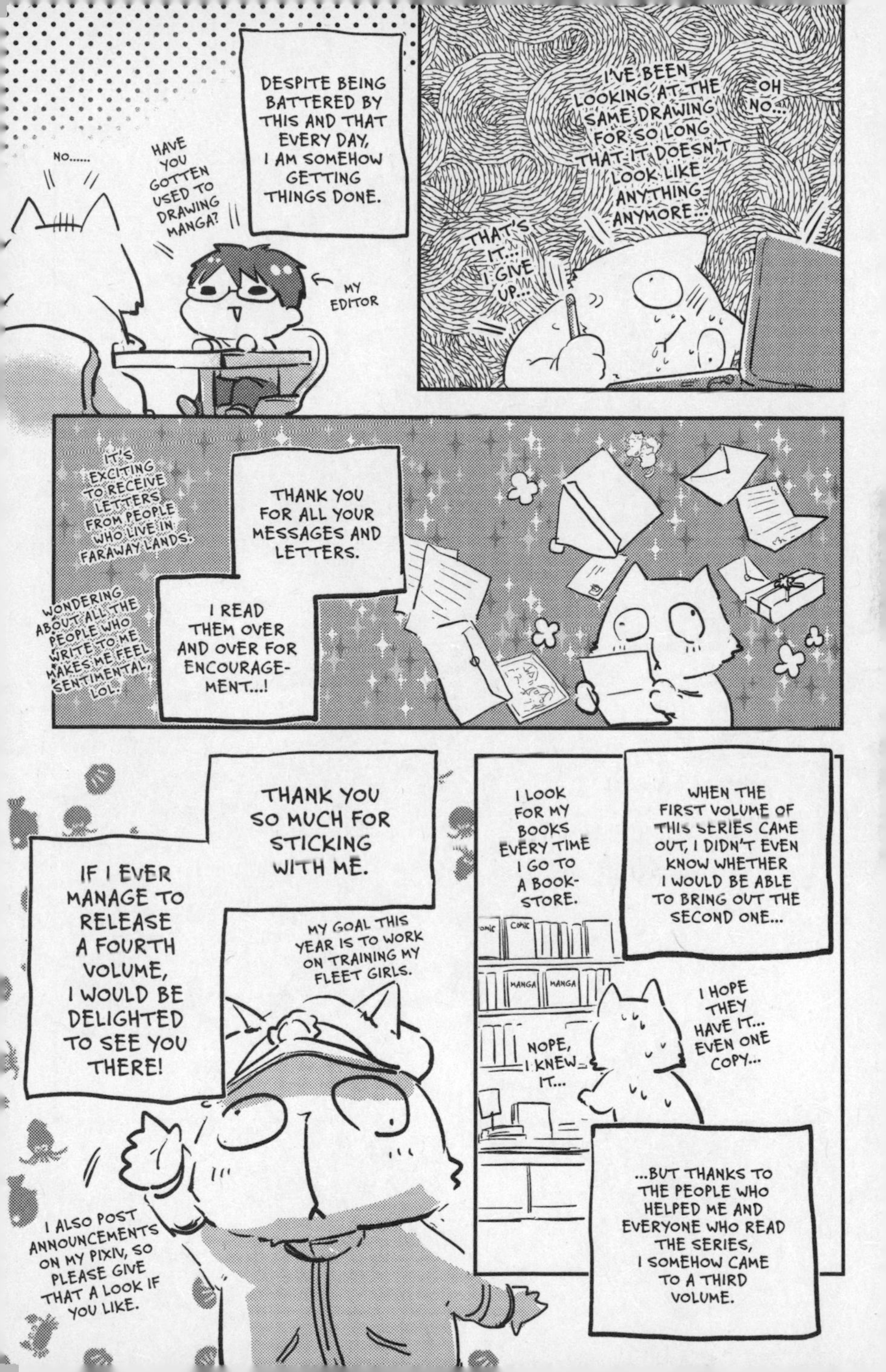

OH NO...
I'VE BEEN LOOKING AT THE SAME DRAWING FOR SO LONG THAT IT DOESN'T LOOK LIKE ANYTHING ANYMORE...
THAT'S IT... I GIVE UP...
DESPITE BEING BATTERED BY THIS AND THAT EVERY DAY, I AM SOMEHOW GETTING THINGS DONE.
HAVE YOU GOTTEN USED TO DRAWING MANGA?
NO......
MY EDITOR
THANK YOU FOR ALL YOUR MESSAGES AND LETTERS.
I READ THEM OVER AND OVER FOR ENCOURAGE-MENT...!
IT'S EXCITING TO RECEIVE LETTERS FROM PEOPLE WHO LIVE IN FARAWAY LANDS.
WONDERING ABOUT ALL THE PEOPLE WHO WRITE TO ME MAKES ME FEEL SENTIMENTAL, LOL.
WHEN THE FIRST VOLUME OF THIS SERIES CAME OUT, I DIDN'T EVEN KNOW WHETHER I WOULD BE ABLE TO BRING OUT THE SECOND ONE...
I LOOK FOR MY BOOKS EVERY TIME I GO TO A BOOK-STORE.
COMIC
COMIC
MANGA
MANGA
I HOPE THEY HAVE IT... EVEN ONE COPY...
NOPE, I KNEW IT...
...BUT THANKS TO THE PEOPLE WHO HELPED ME AND EVERYONE WHO READ THE SERIES, I SOMEHOW CAME TO A THIRD VOLUME.
THANK YOU SO MUCH FOR STICKING WITH ME.
MY GOAL THIS YEAR IS TO WORK ON TRAINING MY FLEET GIRLS.
IF I EVER MANAGE TO RELEASE A FOURTH VOLUME, I WOULD BE DELIGHTED TO SEE YOU THERE!
I ALSO POST ANNOUNCEMENTS ON MY PIXIV, SO PLEASE GIVE THAT A LOOK IF YOU LIKE.

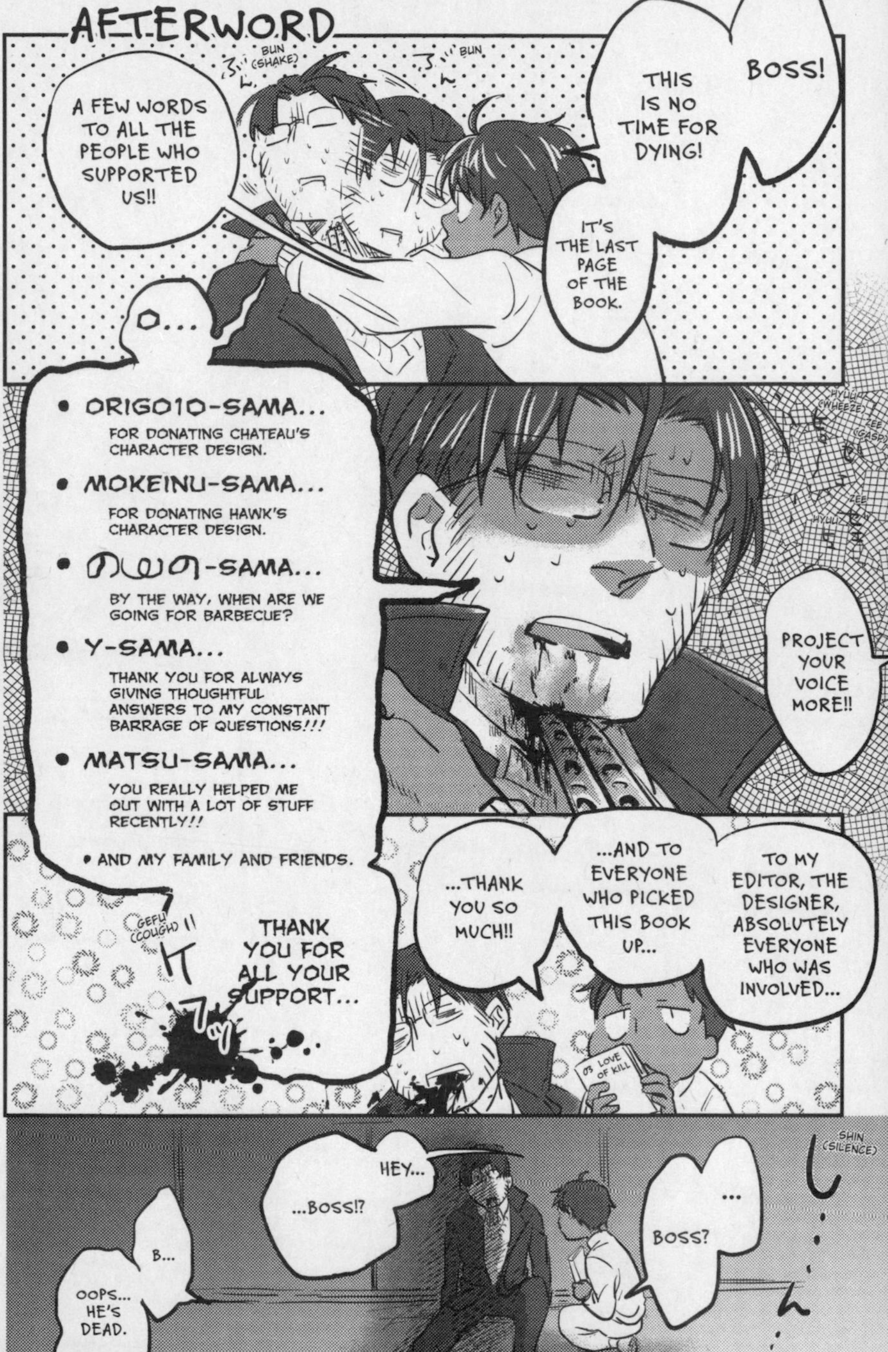
AFTERWORD
BOSS!
THIS IS NO TIME FOR DYING!
IT'S THE LAST PAGE OF THE BOOK.
BUN
BUN (SHAKE)
A FEW WORDS TO ALL THE PEOPLE WHO SUPPORTED US!!
O...
HYUU (WHEEZE)
ZEE (GASP)
ZEE
HYUU
PROJECT YOUR VOICE MORE!!
• ORIGO10-SAMA... FOR DONATING CHATEAU'S CHARACTER DESIGN.
• MOKEINU-SAMA... FOR DONATING HAWK'S CHARACTER DESIGN.
• のゆの-SAMA... BY THE WAY, WHEN ARE WE GOING FOR BARBECUE?
• Y-SAMA... THANK YOU FOR ALWAYS GIVING THOUGHTFUL ANSWERS TO MY CONSTANT BARRAGE OF QUESTIONS!!!
• MATSU-SAMA... YOU REALLY HELPED ME OUT WITH A LOT OF STUFF RECENTLY!!
• AND MY FAMILY AND FRIENDS.
TO MY EDITOR, THE DESIGNER, ABSOLUTELY EVERYONE WHO WAS INVOLVED...
...AND TO EVERYONE WHO PICKED THIS BOOK UP...
...THANK YOU SO MUCH!!
THANK YOU FOR ALL YOUR SUPPORT...
GEFU (COUGH)
03 LOVE OF KILL
SHIN (SILENCE)
...
BOSS?
HEY...
...BOSS!?
B...
OOPS... HE'S DEAD.

NEXT IN LOVE OF KILL

WHO STABBED RITZLAND? WAS IT RYANG-HA...OR...!? ON THE SHIP, WHERE THERE IS NOWHERE TO RUN, AN UNFORESEEN DANGER STRIKES.

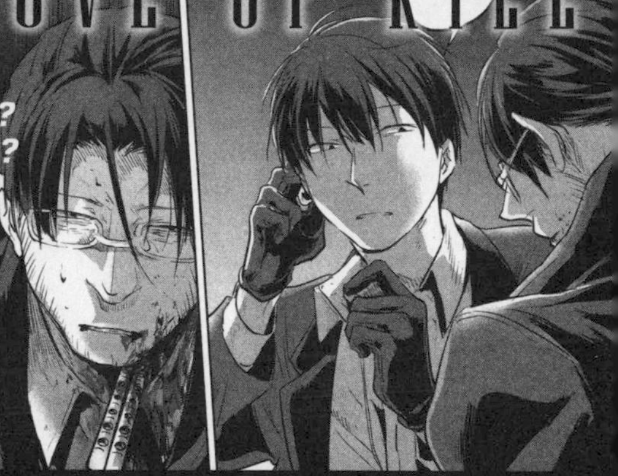

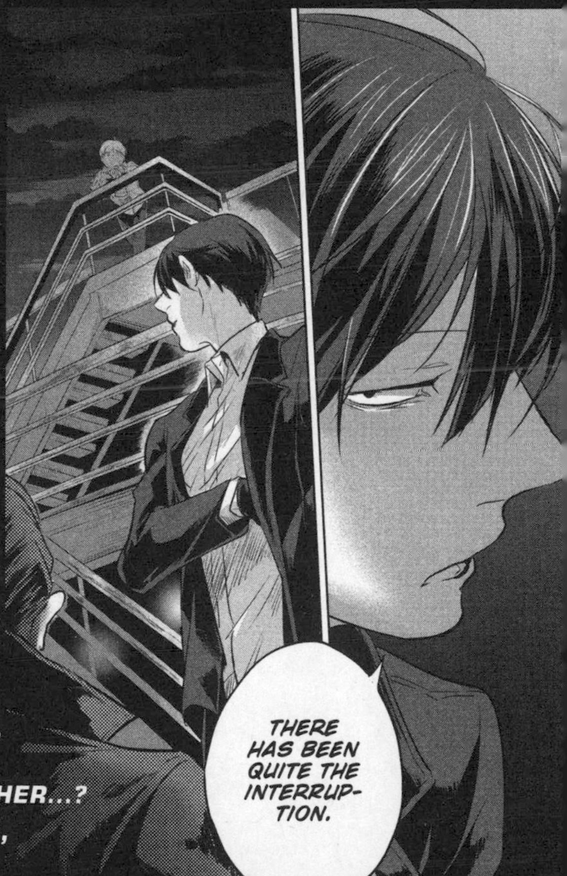
THERE HAS BEEN QUITE THE INTERRUP-TION.

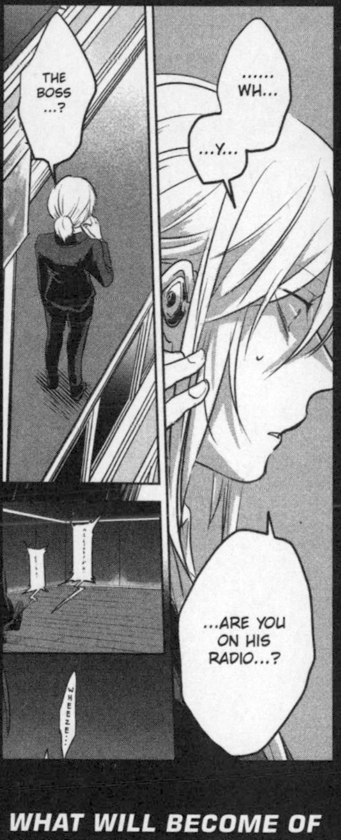
......WH...
...Y...
THE BOSS...?
...ARE YOU ON HIS RADIO...?
WHEEZE...

WHAT WILL BECOME OF CHATEAU AND RYANG-HA? AND WHAT IS THEIR TRUE CONNECTION TO EACH OTHER...?

LOVE OF KILL VOLUME 4, COMING THIS FALL!!

LOVE -OF- KILL 03

Fe

Translation: Eleanor Ruth Summers Lettering: Chiho Christie

KOROSHIAI Vol. 3
© Fe 2017
First published in Japan in 2017 by KADOKAWA CORPORATION, Tokyo. English translation rights arranged with KADOKAWA CORPORATION, Tokyo, through Tuttle-Mori Agency, Inc., Tokyo.

English translation © 2021 by Yen Press, LLC

Yen Press
150 West 30th Street, 19th Floor
New York, NY 10001

Visit us at yenpress.com
facebook.com/yenpress
twitter.com/yenpress
yenpress.tumblr.com
instagram.com/yenpress

First Yen Press Edition: July 2021

Yen Press is an imprint of Yen Press, LLC.
The Yen Press name and logo are trademarks of Yen Press, LLC.

The publisher is not responsible for websites (or their content) that are not owned by the publisher.

Library of Congress Control Number: 2020951788

ISBNs: 978-1-9753-2543-5 (paperback)
       978-1-9753-2544-2 (ebook)

10 9 8 7 6 5 4 3 2 1

WOR

Printed in the United States of America